THE

ENGLISH ROMANTIC

POETS & ESSAYISTS

A Review of Research

and Criticism

REVISED EDITION

Contributors

NORTHROP FRYE   KENNETH CURRY

MARTIN K. NURMI   HOOVER H. JORDAN

GEORGE L. BARNETT   R. H. SUPER

STUART M. TAVE   CAROLYN W. HOUTCHENS

ELISABETH W. SCHNEIDER   LAWRENCE H. HOUTCHENS

JAMES T. HILLHOUSE   JOHN E. JORDAN

ALEXANDER WELSH   CARLISLE MOORE

THE

ENGLISH ROMANTIC

POETS & ESSAYISTS

A Review of Research

and Criticism

REVISED EDITION
EDITED BY

Carolyn Washburn Houtchens

Lawrence Huston Houtchens

Published for

THE MODERN LANGUAGE ASSOCIATION OF AMERICA
by New York University Press, 1966

London · University of London Press Limited

LIBRARY OF CONGRESS CATALOG CARD NUMBER: 66–12599
MANUFACTURED IN THE UNITED STATES OF AMERICA
DESIGN BY ANDOR BRAUN

TO

Clarence De Witt Thorpe

WHOM WE DELIGHT

TO HONOR

PREFACE

THIS BOOK is a companion volume to *The English Romantic Poets: A Review of Research* (Revised), edited by Professor Thomas M. Raysor and published by the Modern Language Association, 1956. It is part of a long-range plan by the Committee on Research Projects of Group IX, which included the preparation of a second volume to supplement the first one in re-evaluating the research in the romantic period. At the time the work was initiated the committee consisted of Professors Josephine Miles, A. D. McKillop, Bennett Weaver, Earl Leslie Griggs, Thomas M. Raysor, and Clarence D. Thorpe, chairman. In general we have consistently followed the pattern of organization employed in the first volume because those who have had occasion to use it have found the plan convenient and time-saving.

The aim of the present volume remains substantially the same as that given by Professor Raysor for the first one: "Its prime purpose is to furnish help to the graduate student as he begins the specialized study of the field. Such a student may be nearly overwhelmed by the great mass of research listed in the bibliographies, and often needs a guide to interpret values. A director of a seminar is such a guide, but since he cannot always be accessible for consultation, he may welcome a large general review of research like this to supplement his own teaching."

Though the book is compiled mainly with the graduate student in mind, it should be useful to both the general reader and the advanced undergraduate as well, particularly as a supplement to standard bibliographies.

L. H. H.

C. W. H.

PREFACE

REVISED EDITION

THE COLLABORATORS in this second edition of *The English Romantic Poets* have faced one problem in common, namely, the unusually large number of scholarly studies that have been produced in the comparatively short period of eight years since the appearance of the first edition. Most of the original contributors have assumed the responsibility for bringing their respective chapters up to date, and in some instances have amplified their previous critical comments. Alexander Welsh of Yale University has revised the chapter on Scott by the late James T. Hillhouse, and Dean Martin K. Nurmi of Kent State University has revised the chapter on Blake by Northrop Frye. All concerned with the preparation of the first edition felt the need for a concluding chapter on Carlyle to provide a transition between the Romantic and Victorian periods, though at the time it was not possible to include one. Carlisle Moore of the University of Oregon has prepared such a transitional chapter, pointing out that Carlyle was "first of all a Romantic" and that he "wrote some of his most original and durable works before 1832."

L. H. H.

C. W. H.

November 1964

CONTENTS

ABBREVIATIONS IN REFERENCES

ABC	American Book Collector
ABR	American Benedictine Review
AF	Anglistische Forschungen
AL	American Literature
Archiv	Archiv für das Studium der neueren Sprachen und Literaturen
AS	American Speech
A Sch	American Scholar
AUMLA	Journal of the Australasian Universities Language and Literature Association
BB	Bulletin of Bibliography
BC	Book Collector
BJRL	Bulletin of the John Rylands Library
BMQ	British Museum Quarterly
BNYPL	Bulletin of the New York Public Library
Bu R	Bucknell Review
BYUS	Brigham Young University Studies
Cai SE	Cairo Studies in English
Cath W	Catholic World
CBEL	Cambridge Bibliography of English Literature
CE	College English
CEA	CEA Critic
CJ	Classical Journal
CL	Comparative Literature
CLSB	Charles Lamb Society Bulletin
Crit Q	Critical Quarterly
Cweal	Commonweal
DUJ	Durham University Journal
DVLG	Deutsche Vierteljahrsschrift für Literaturwissenschaft und Geistesgeschichte
EA	Études anglaises
E&S	Essays and Studies by Members of the English Association

EC	Études celtiques
EDH	Essays by Divers Hands
ELH	English Literary History
ELL	The English Language and Literature (Eng. Lit. Soc. of Korea)
ELN	English Language Notes
ES	English Studies
ESQ	Emerson Society Quarterly
EUQ	Emory University Quarterly
Expl	Explicator
FL	Figaro littéraire
FSUS	Florida State University Studies
GRM	Germanisch-romanische Monatsschrift, Neue Folge
HJ	Hibbert Journal
HLB	Harvard Library Bulletin
HLQ	Huntington Library Quarterly
HR	Hispanic Review
HZM	Handelingen van de Zuidnederlandse Maatschappij voor Taal- en Letterkunde en Geschiedenis
JAAC	Journal of Aesthetics and Art Criticism
JAF	Journal of American Folklore
JEGP	Journal of English and Germanic Philology
JHI	Journal of the History of Ideas
JJR	James Joyce Review
JRUL	Journal of the Rutgers University Library
JWCI	Journal of the Warburg and Courtauld Institutes
KM	Kansas Magazine
KSJ	Keats-Shelley Journal
KSMB	Keats-Shelley Memorial Bulletin (Rome)
Let N	Lettres nouvelles
MCR	Melbourne Critical Review (Univ. of Melbourne)
MdF	Mercure de France
MFS	Modern Fiction Studies
MHRA	Modern Humanities Research Association Bibliography
Miss Q	Mississippi Quarterly
MLN	Modern Language Notes
MLQ	Modern Language Quarterly
MLR	Modern Language Review
MP	Modern Philology
NA	Nuova antologia

N&Q	Notes and Queries
NCF	Nineteenth-Century Fiction
ND	La Nueva democracia (New York)
NRF	Nouvelle revue française
NS	Die neueren Sprachen
PBA	Proceedings of the British Academy
PBSA	Papers of the Bibliographical Society of America
PEGS	Publications of the English Goethe Society
PMHB	Pennsylvania Magazine of History and Biography
PMLA	Publications of the Modern Language Association
PQ	Philological Quarterly
PR	Partisan Review
PULC	Princeton University Library Chronicle
QQ	Queen's Quarterly
QR	Quarterly Review
RDM	Revue des deux mondes
REL	Review of English Literature (Leeds)
RES	Review of English Studies
RLC	Revue de littérature comparée
RLMC	Rivista di letterature moderne e comparate (Firenze)
Rom N	Romance Notes (Univ. of North Carolina)
RR	Romanic Review
SAQ	South Atlantic Quarterly
Sat R	Saturday Review
SB	Studies in Bibliography: Papers of the Bibliographical Society of the University of Virginia
SEL	Studies in English Literature, 1500–1900 (Rice Univ.)
SE Lit	Studies in English Literature (Eng. Literary Soc. of Japan, Univ. of Tokyo)
SIR	Studies in Romanticism (Boston Univ.)
SN	Studia neophilologica
SoQ	Southern Quarterly
SP	Studies in Philology
SR	Sewanee Review
SRL	Saturday Review of Literature
SS	Scandinavian Studies
TLS	Times Literary Supplement (London)
TRSC	Transactions of the Royal Society of Canada
TSL	Tennessee Studies in Literature

TSLL   Texas Studies in Literature and Language
TWA   Transactions of the Wisconsin Academy of Sciences, Arts, and
          Letters
UEJ   University of Edinburgh Journal
UKPHS   University of Kansas Publications, Humanistic Studies
UTQ   University of Toronto Quarterly
UTSE   University of Texas Studies in English
VN   Victorian Newsletter
VP   Victorian Poetry (W. Va. Univ.)
VS   Victorian Studies (Indiana Univ.)
WHR   Western Humanities Review
YR   Yale Review
YWES   Year's Work in English Studies

1

William Blake

By Northrop Frye
UNIVERSITY OF TORONTO

Revised by
Martin K. Nurmi
KENT STATE UNIVERSITY

I. BIBLIOGRAPHIES

T HE LITERARY WORKS of William Blake consist, with unimportant exceptions, of: (a) the juvenile *Poetical Sketches,* published in 1783, (b) *The French Revolution,* one of seven announced books, of which the only surviving copy is a proof, (c) the "Descriptive Catalogue" printed to accompany the 1809 exhibition, (d) marginalia to a number of books, (e) the engraved (or more strictly, etched) works, (f) manuscript material. The engraved works, or illuminated books, form the central canon of Blake's literary production. When the textual unit is an aphorism or a lyric poem, it normally goes on a single plate, with an accompanying design; when it is a longer work, or "Prophecy," it forms part of a series of plates, in which a plate may be all text, all design, or any proportion of the two. An important bibliographical aid of a type peculiar to Blake study is supplied by Geoffrey Keynes and E. Wolf, *William Blake's Illuminated Books: A Census* (1953). It is obvious that each original copy of the engraved works is a separate bibliographical item. The manuscript material includes letters, a few unpublished works in foul draft (*Tiriel, An Island in the Moon, The Four Zoas*), a set of lyrics in a fair draft known as the Pickering MS, and the notebook that Blake kept by him for a great part of his life, now known as The Notebook or the Rossetti MS, into which he huddled an extraordinary amount of both literary and pictorial material.

The most recent bibliography with any pretensions to completeness is that by G. E. Bentley, Jr., and Martin K. Nurmi, *A Blake Bibliography* (1964). In addition to listing critical studies and other materials, this book includes, as a result of the labors of Bentley, many previously unknown contemporary references and very full accounts of books with illustrations engraved by Blake. It does not, however, supersede Sir Geoffrey Keynes's *A Bibliography of William Blake* (1921), which is still indispensable, especially for its careful descriptions of primary works, but which is hard to come by, having been published in a very limited edition. Bunsho Jugaku's *William Blake shoshi* (1929), in Japanese, is partly based on Keynes's bibliography but extends it. A great deal of important bibliographical information is included in the notes of Keynes's

3

The Complete Writings (1957) and in *The Poetry and Prose of William Blake* (1965) by David Erdman. Current Blake studies are regularly reviewed in "The Romantic Movement: A Selective and Critical Bibliography," (*ELN*). The excellent unpublished bibliography, *La Poésie de William Blake en France* . . . , by Mr. Charles Moore, of London, Ontario, has been of great assistance in the preparation of this essay.

II. EDITIONS

EDITIONS which are reproductions of the engraved plates will be considered below in a separate section. The first major editors of Blake's text were the Rossetti brothers, Dante Gabriel and William, who owned The Notebook which has been called the Rossetti MS after them. (One may speak of them both as owning it, as the ten shillings that Dante Gabriel paid for it was borrowed from William.) Dante Gabriel edited a selection of Blake's poems for the second volume of Gilchrist's life (1863), and William produced *The Poetical Works of William Blake*, with an appreciative essay, in 1874. Dante Gabriel especially followed the bad tradition of trying to improve Blake's text. *The Works of William Blake, Poetic, Symbolic and Critical*, by Edwin J. Ellis and William Butler Yeats, appeared in three volumes in 1893. This edition has its importance, as we shall see, but from the point of view of textual criticism the less said about it the better. The first genuinely critical edition of large scope was the Oxford edition of the lyrical poems, by John Sampson, which later included excerpts from the Prophecies (1905; rev., 1913). It was supplemented by the edition of *Jerusalem* by E.R.D. Maclagan and A.G.B. Russell in 1904, and of *Milton* in 1907.

In 1925 Keynes published the three-volume edition of *The Writings of William Blake*, which provided a clean, complete, and reliable text, well illustrated and chronologically arranged, of the whole of Blake's literary output then known. This was for many years the standard edition, though the practical edition used by most critics was the condensed version of this text, without variant readings and with very few notes, published as *The Poetry and Prose of William Blake* (1927) and slightly revised through different printings until 1939, when, unfortunately, it was reset with different pagination. A little, but not much, has turned up since then, chiefly a few letters (the gaps in Blake's letters between 1815 and 1818 and between 1819 and 1825 remain), a copy of Dante's *Inferno* (see Keynes in *TLS*, 3 May 1957, p. 277), and Blake's copy of Bacon's *Essays* with his annotations (see *TLS*, 8 March 1957, p. 152), which are fuller than the Gilchrist transcription on which the 1925 edition had to depend. These new items are included in Keynes's 1957 edition of *The Complete Writings of William Blake, with All Variant Readings,* which provides in one slim volume all the materials and more of the 1925 edition and has been the standard text.

The Oxford edition by Sampson, still being reprinted, though scrupulously edited had not included the complete Prophetic Books, which were edited by D. J. Sloss and J. P. R. Wallis in two volumes in 1926—though for some curious reason they did not consider *The French Revolution* a Prophetic Book. The textual editing of this edition was very painstaking and thorough and included good bibliographic descriptions, but the extensive commentary on Blake's meaning is practically a total loss.

All these editions are punctuated ones, at times rather over-punctuated. Important texts of *Vala or The Four Zoas* which give transcriptions of the manuscript "not only . . . *literatim* but also *punctuatim*" were published by the late H. M. Margoliouth in 1956 and by G. E. Bentley, Jr., in 1963. Margoliouth's edition, *William Blake's Vala: Blake's Numbered Text* (1956), as the title implies, attempts to get at the poem that Blake started with, by stripping off layers of revisions and additions. Bentley's *William Blake. Vala or The Four Zoas* (1963) gives a transcription of the whole manuscript with elaborate typographical devices and copious notes to show deletions, revisions, and additions, and with it a full-size facsimile, all bound in a beautiful large folio, necessarily too large for any shelf. Both of these editions are indispensable to any serious study of Blake because an edited text cannot help but give the impression that the poem was much more nearly finished than it actually was. As Bentley especially shows, it was not abandoned for use as a quarry for *Milton* and *Jerusalem,* for, though passages from it get into these works, the reverse is also true. The sketches in the facsimile show that Blake thought from the beginning in terms of a series of designed plates, not of writing a poem and then illustrating it. Bentley's transcription should be compared with that of Erdman in *Poetry and Prose,* prepared with the aid of infrared photography and strong magnification. Neither Bentley's nor Erdman's texts of this poem can be used in the way that De Selincourt's text of *The Prelude* can because the problems involved in deciphering the MS are simply impossible to solve completely, especially as concerns the sequence of revisions.

Keynes's edition of *The Letters of William Blake* (1956) includes not only all the letters known (with one exception, a recent discovery by George M. Harper reported in *SP*, 1964) and published in *The Complete Writings* but letters to Blake, as well as accounts, receipts, documents relating to his trial for sedition, memoranda, and a letter from Richmond to Palmer about Blake's death.

Unpunctuated texts of some early works, including a fresh transcription of the manuscript of *Tiriel*, are included in Robert Gleckner's *Piper and the Bard* (1959), and David Erdman has published transcriptions of the prose fragments "Woe cried the muse" and "then she bore pale desire" in *BNYPL* (1958), which should be consulted. An unpublished but nevertheless widely used transcription of *The Island in the Moon* has been made by Palmer Brown.

For Blake's engraved poems the engraving process itself helps to establish a definitive text—though not quite: variants do occur from copy to copy. The differences that exist among various copies are usually not strictly textual differences: a passage may appear in one copy and be missing or deleted from another, but some variants also occur that are important. In *Jerusalem* Blake suppressed and altered some passages on the plates themselves, which Erdman has been able to restore by painstaking detective work (see "The Suppressed and Altered Passages in Blake's *Jerusalem*," *SB*, 1964).

Some of Keynes's readings were disputed by a team of Blake scholars headed by David Erdman in the process of freshly collating the works for a forthcoming concordance, and David Erdman has now prepared a new edition of Blake, *The Poetry and Prose of William Blake* (1965), incorporating the textual work of these scholars and a great deal more of his own. This edition, which gives variant readings and discusses textual problems much more fully than Keynes did and includes some critical notes prepared by Harold Bloom, will supersede Keynes's text, except for the letters, which are given in it only in selections. The text that is given is as complete as can be recovered at the present time and includes many readings hitherto unavailable. Punctuation follows Blake's punctuation (or the lack of it in the longer works) as closely as the limitations of print will allow, his characteristic dots being printed as periods, for instance; but the whole matter of his pointing is discussed succinctly in the notes.

Important for the study of Blake's drafts of many of the Songs as well as other works is The Notebook, or the Rossetti MS, which was published in facsimile by Keynes in 1935 as *The Note Book of*

William Blake Called the Rossetti Manuscript, with a transcription that is not to be trusted (Sir Geoffrey was unable to see this volume through the press himself). Bunsho Jugaku's *A Bibliographical Study of William Blake's Note-Book* (1953), based not on the manuscript itself but on the facsimile, leaves many problems still unsolved, editorial and otherwise, most of which should be solved by Erdman, who has carefully examined the manuscript with the aid of infrared photography and who is preparing a study of it.

Of current popular editions, the text in Everyman's Library is well edited by Max Plowman, and what it has is complete, though it omits some important things, including *The Four Zoas*. The Viking Portable and Modern Library editions, with introductions by Alfred Kazin and Northrop Frye, respectively, use the Keynes text, and have only selections from the longer Prophecies. A Modern Library Giant contains the complete poetical works of Blake and Donne, and will be useful to anyone who wants to have Blake and Donne bound together.

III. BIOGRAPHIES

THE MORE IMPORTANT biographical primary sources are available in two volumes. *The Letters of William Blake Together with a Life by Frederick Tatham*, edited by Archibald G. B. Russell (1906), contains what the title says it contains, and the remainder are assembled in the back of Arthur Symons' *William Blake* (1907), which also contains Benjamin Heath Malkin's contemporary account (1806). The most important for the development of the Blake legend are the diary and reminiscences of Crabb Robinson, the sketch by J. T. Smith in the second volume of *Nollekens and His Times* (1828), and the account in Alan Cunningham, *Lives of the Most Eminent British Painters, Sculptors, and Architects* (1830), which was widely reprinted in magazines in England and America. The memoirs of the younger painters who came into contact with Blake in his later years are also of importance, especially A. H. Palmer, *The Life and Letters of Samuel Palmer* (1892), Alfred T. Story, *The Life of John Linnell* (1892), and *A Memoir of Edward Calvert*, "by his third son," Samuel Calvert (1893).

Blake's letters practically begin with his removal to Felpham at the age of forty-three, and the above memoirs come almost entirely from the last period of his life. In this last period Blake had, in the Linnell circle, a few friends he trusted, but for those outside this circle, half a century of derision and neglect had developed in him a kind of intellectual deafness, not unlike the physical deafness of Beethoven in some of its social results. The main interest of these memoirs is anecdotal, and the impression they give of Blake is in the strictest sense of the word a caricature: the features are striking, the points they make may be accurate, but our impression of Blake's personality is gained from their treatment of him and not from Blake himself. It is clear too that, though among his real friends Blake may have been "a man without a mask," elsewhere he was always ready to caricature himself, to assume whatever mask seemed to be called for; and he has confused biographers in consequence more than so intensely personal a writer would normally be expected to do. The cranky but shrewd Tatham observes that "many of his eccentric speeches were thrown forth more as a piece of sarcasm upon the inquirer than from his real opinion." The early attaching of the word "mystic" to Blake helped to suggest an earnestly oracular temperament, an innocent who could write songs of innocence, but one to be smiled at sympathetically, like a solemn child. A glance at a picture of Blake's life mask should be enough to disturb this conception of him. A highly unofficial but attractive little sketch of Blake's personality may be found in a poem in Jacques Prévert's *Paroles* (1943).

The Life of William Blake, Pictor Ignotus, by Alexander Gilchrist, appeared in 1863, two years after its author's death: his wife and the Rossettis were responsible for finishing it and for issuing the revised and enlarged edition of 1880. The second volume of the 1880 edition is an extraordinary (and still very useful) grab bag containing D. G. Rossetti's edition, lists of engravings and drawings, reproductions, and a fine "Essay on Blake," a review of the first edition, by James Smetham. The reprint of the first volume in Everyman's Library, with an introduction, notes, and bibliography by Ruthven Todd, makes a handbook practically indispensable for the Blake student. Gilchrist's is technically a most superior biography, which makes a real effort to arrange both the poetic and pictorial works in chronological order—if Blake ever has a definitive biographer, he will follow Gilchrist's method. Further, his life is a sprightly and charming narrative: it is permeated with a deep sympathy for Blake, and it could never have clouded up Blake in the way that, for instance, Dowden clouded up Shelley. But of course it transmitted and expanded the anecdotal interest of Gilchrist's predecessors, and hence unconsciously helped to popularize Blake as a kind of Theophrastan character type: a lovable, absent-minded, enthusiastic artist, heroic in the sense of doing his work cheerfully and obstinately in the face of neglect, and preserving the peculiarly Victorian and English sense of the right of genius to harmless eccentricities.

The biographical part of almost every general book on Blake since then has been mainly potted Gilchrist, and the biographical interest in Blake has been oppressively anecdotal. The consequences for Blake criticism have been disastrous, for the biographical picture thus dubiously highlighted becomes the basis for criticism. That is, the critic makes his value judgments on Blake's poetry in terms of what his biographical stereotype might have been expected to produce. Even as late a study as Bernard Blackstone's *English Blake* (1949) follows the same procedure, if with more sympathy than usual. Gilchrist's own conception of the relation of biographical to critical study is, in contrast to most of his successors, very well balanced, which is one reason why his biography is so good as a biography.

The Ellis and Yeats edition of 1893, already mentioned, included a memoir, the only new feature of which was Yeats's attempt to provide Blake with an Irish ancestry. Hazard Adams' *Blake and Yeats: The Contrary Vision* (1955) disposes briefly of what was left of the evidence for this, which was never impressive. Ellis carried on by himself in *The Real Blake* (1907), a biography whose chief resemblance to the real Blake is in a certain facility for drawing without the model.

Harold Bruce's *William Blake in This World* (1925) was the first real attempt since Gilchrist to sift fact from legend, and provide a solid chronological framework. It was followed in 1927 by Mona Wilson, *The Life of William Blake* (reissued with additions, 1948). This is a clearly written presentation of the biographical knowledge of Blake up to 1927, which means that it is still essentially a revision of Gilchrist. Its chief disadvantage is its highly selective treatment of Blake's total output: there are, for example, many useful clues to Blake's life and thought in his work as illustrator and engraver that still await investigation. Thomas Wright's *The Life of William Blake* (2 vols., 1929) has more data on this point. The tone of Wright's book is that of the enthusiastic antiquarian, and there are a few lapses in judgment (such as his sponsoring of the notion of a romantic attachment between Blake and Mary Wollstonecraft, a legend which may have been transferred to Blake from Fuseli), but he writes with much pungency and firsthand insight. Wright was the chief promoter of the Blake Society, whose papers also contain some scattered biographical information; he had previously written a life of Cowper and used the special knowledge of the Hayley circle gained from it to good advantage. On this last the student may also consult Morchard Bishop, *Blake's Hayley* (1951).

More recent biographical scholarship has been fragmentary. Geoffrey Keynes's *Blake Studies* (1949) is a series of essays, mainly biographical, dealing with such topics as the Rossetti MS, the corrections in the *Poetical Sketches*, some of the lesser-known engraving commissions in Blake's later life, and the disentangling of its subject from another contemporary engraver with the same name. The material in these studies will be indispensable to the next biographer, and so will the new material being brought forward in a number of biographical research articles, including several by D. V. Erdman: one may note especially his "William Blake's Exactness in Dates" (*PQ*, 1949) and "Blake's Early Swedenborgianism" (*CL*, 1953), which gets rid of one of Ellis' red herrings. Among other recent biographical articles may be mentioned G. E. Bentley's "William Blake and 'Johnny of Norfolk'" (*SP*, 1956); "Blake, Hayley, and Lady Hesketh" (*RES*, 1956); "Blake's Engravings and His Friendship with Flaxman" (*SB*, 1959); "A Footnote to Blake's Treason Trial" (*N&Q*, 1955); "The Promotion of Blake's *Grave* Designs" (*UTQ*, 1962, showing more reason for anger with Cromek); "William Blake as a Private Publisher" (*BNYPL*, 1957). Paul Miner traces Blake's residences in an article (*BNYPL*, 1958), and Keynes gives detailed connections between the Blakes and John Linnell in two notes (*TLS*, 13 and 15 June 1958), and between Blake and Hayley in "Blake's Miniatures" (*TLS*, Jan. 29, 1960). William Gaunt's *Arrows of Desire: A Study of William Blake* (1956) fills the need for a "background" biographical narrative which deals less with Blake than with figures who came in contact, personal or intellectual, with him, ranging from Ossian and Chatterton to Linnell and Gilchrist. It is a useful supplement to such an introduction to Blake as that of H. M. Margoliouth, mentioned above, which effectively uses biographical facts. The books of Schorer and Erdman, mentioned below under "Criticism," provide a great deal of historical and potentially biographical information about Blake's surprisingly numerous social contacts.

But Erdman was able to remark in 1953 that "Blake biography is still in a pre-scientific state." The first step, for any approach to definitiveness in biography, is a *catalogue raisonné* of all Blake's work in both literature and the graphic arts, dated as carefully as possible, and including of course the complex problems of dating raised by the manuscripts. The most competent person to undertake such a work, Sir Geoffrey Keynes, has listed it in *Blake Studies* as in progress, and thus far *Engravings by William Blake: The Separate Plates: A Catalogue Raisonné* (1958) and *William Blake's Illustrations to the Bible* (1957), both by Keynes and with reproductions in color, have appeared. Blake's life was quiet, verging on humdrum, for all his reputation for eccentricity, and the rewards of biographical research are unlikely to be picturesque: the Annette Vallons and Harriet Westbrooks of Blake's life appear to have been confined to his imagination. It is probable, for instance, that we know so little of the period between the failure of his exhibition in 1809 and his meeting with Linnell in 1818 because there is really not much to be known. But for so remarkable a personality facts are surely better than anecdote or impressionism. The question of Blake's "madness," of course, is now recognized to be not a question of fact at all, but a pseudoproblem.

IV. CRITICISM

THE REPUTATION of Blake as a poet has followed much the same curve as the reputation of Shelley. He is presented at first as a natural genius in exquisite and spontaneous lyric, a naïve intelligence who could react only emotionally, his more didactic Prophecies illustrating a tendency to squirt ink like a cuttlefish at anything that annoyed him. Gradually, the inconsistency of this with the real character of the poet who defined poetry as "allegory addressed to the intellectual powers" forces critics to approach, however gingerly, the more intricate involutions of the longer poems containing the substance of Blake's thought. At first, of course, the tendency is not to read them but to write them off or argue about them, on the ground that they are schizophrenic, heretical, not "real poetry," too private in symbolism to be understood, and so on and so on. Such judgments are contemporary with the biographical pictures of Blake as deficient in a sense of reality. But, as Blake has slowly established his authority in one field after another, it becomes clear that his critic, like the critic of Shelley, must simply stop arguing and come to grips with the real strength, complexity, and normality of his subject's mind.

In engraving his poetry, one of Blake's aims was undoubtedly to make himself independent of publishers, but by a curious irony he produced the exact opposite of what his own conception of art was. That is, what he produced were *objets d'art* for well-to-do connoisseurs. This fact has both delayed and isolated Blake's reputation. He was a professional engraver, but more of an amateur poet than any other poet of his rank; consequently he was known for many years after his death chiefly as a pictorial artist. Even now, the variety of his appeal makes it peculiarly difficult to assess his creative personality, so to speak, as a unit. The advance of Blake scholarship, even the scholarship of interpretation, has been substantial enough to discourage some of those who, to paraphrase Thomas Wright, rush into print to announce that the Prophetic Books are unintelligible; yet it has had its own disadvantages. The responsible student of English literature, even the eighteenth-century or romantic specialist, confronted with the weighty commentaries that are still essential, is likely to feel that Blake is a special interest, to be taken up like chess by those who fancy it. Hence a good deal of Blake criticism falls into the hands of the irresponsible student, who contributes nothing to Blake scholarship but simply makes value judgments on the poetry, the basis of the judgments being usually the fact that he does not know what five sixths of the poetry means. Some simplification of genuine Blake scholarship is in order, now that there is less risk of distorting its subject, and what follows will be an attempt to indicate the direction that such a simplification might take.

Swinburne's brilliant and generous essay, *William Blake*, appeared in 1868 as a critical pendant to the Gilchrist life, and established Blake once for all as an important poet. The virtues of this essay speak eloquently for themselves; its limitations are unfortunately the main concern of the historian of Blake scholarship, however ungrateful the task. In the first place, Swinburne, on the authority less of Gilchrist than of his own temperament, strongly emphasized the social isolation of Blake, and passed over Blake's radical, even revolutionary, political views, dismissing *The French Revolution*, for instance, as "mere wind and splutter." The stereotype that he took from Gilchrist was rather that of the rebellion of the artist against society, and it was this aspect of Blake that was stressed in later Victorian criticism of him. Blake thus became a prophet of the aesthetic radicals, whose enemies were the Philistine and the Puritan rather than the tyrant and the usurer. Yeats, for instance, speaks of Blake as having begun the practice of "preaching against the Philistine."

In the second place, Blake became, for Swinburne, an exponent of the "romantic agony," maintaining that conventional or moral good was evil and that the salvation and freedom of man lay in the recrudescence of long-suppressed instincts. The chief document used in this presentation of Blake was *The Marriage of Heaven and Hell*, apparently the most explicit of the Prophecies, but actually, because of its highly ambiguous irony, one of the most elusive. (It is in fact Blake's second prose satire, and it is significant that his first, *An Island in the Moon*, was unknown to Swinburne and despised by Symons.) Swinburne interprets this work as a document falling within his own conception of the sadist tradition—Swinburne refers to Sade, though not by name, in a long footnote. The influence of this sadist or diabolist Blake is visible in Bernard Shaw, who seems to have made some use of Blake for *The Devil's Disciple*, and in André Gide, who translated *The Marriage of Heaven and Hell* (1922). The same view of Blake was evidently accepted by Mario Praz in his influential *Romantic Agony* (1933), and it is still doing duty, though largely for schematic reasons, in D. G. James's *The Romantic Comedy* (1948). It would be convenient enough to have a genuine example of what Swinburne calls a "dysangel," if only as a clay pigeon, in the ultrarespectable English tradition, but criticism is reluctantly forced to say that this conception of Blake could hardly be more mistaken.

Blake's lyrical gifts, his anticonventional views, and his unification of poetry and painting made him a considerable influence on the late pre-Raphaelite developments around the turn of the century. The two fine essays of Yeats in *Ideas of Good and Evil* (1903) did much to establish Blake as a prophet of English *symbolisme*. The second volume of the Ellis and Yeats edition is an exposition of Blake's symbolism, which assimilates Blake to occult, Gnostic, and theosophical writers. Some genuine interpretation is present and some interesting parallels, especially with Boehme, are established, but the charts and diagrams rely heavily on forced symmetries and manipulated evidence (such as the identification of two quite different characters, Tiriel and Thiriel). It is curious that a critic who was also a very great poet should have treated Blake's Prophetic Books not as poems to be read but as code messages to be deciphered, especially when he also shows such incisive understanding of Blake's theory of imagination. This commentary must, if anything, have increased the prevalence of the notion that any interpretation of Blake is as good as any other.

Arthur Symons' *William Blake* (1907) gives us a less sadistic but even more aesthetic Blake than Swinburne's, a Blake whose defense of the more energetic virtues was now seen to have affinities with the *Herrenmoral* of Nietzsche. In the same year Pierre Berger produced *William Blake, mysticisme et poésie,* translated by D. H. Conner as *William Blake: Poet and Mystic* (1914). Berger's book was, among other things, the first really thoughtful and systematic study yet made of the Prophetic Books. It demonstrated a coherent and controlling mind at work in them; the commentary provides much new and specific information about Blake's meaning—something that Swinburne and Symons hardly provide at all outside *The Marriage of Heaven and Hell*—and it marks the beginning of the critical effort to clear up these poems for the common reader. Also, as one might have expected from his nationality, Berger's view of *The French Revolution,* and of the political and social reference of Blake's outlook generally, was better balanced than Swinburne's.

Of minor critics in this early period, a place of honor should be reserved for Garth Wilkinson, a Swedenborgian who referred to Blake several times in his works and produced an indifferent edition of the *Songs of Innocence and Experience* in 1839. It was Wilkinson who first attracted James Thomson ("B. V.") to Blake; Thomson appended an essay on Blake to his poem *Shelley* in 1884. Other early studies of Blake, stimulated by Swinburne and Yeats, include those of Alfred T. Story (1893), Richard Garnett (1895), Irene Langridge (1904), François Benoît (1906), and Elizabeth Cary (1907). All of these had their insights; some, especially Garnett, helped to develop Blake scholarship, and they were as well illustrated as the methods of reproduction of sixty years ago allowed. But with the passing of time they take on an increasingly historical importance. To these we may add Paul Elmer More, *Shelburne Essays,* Fourth Series (1906), a review of the Sampson edition.

After 1907 there follows something of an interregnum in Blake scholarship, in which the information and apparatus provided by the earlier critics was absorbed into the academic tradition by a steady though often reluctant osmosis. Basil de Selincourt's *William Blake* (1909) follows the older tradition in maintaining a balance between the literary and pictorial aspects of Blake criticism, which now tended increasingly to concentrate on purely literary aspects. G. K. Chesterton's *William Blake* (1910) is a breezy little book, doubtless of interest to admirers of Chesterton. Charles Gardner's *Vision and Vesture: Blake and Modern Thought* (1916) makes, as its subtitle indicates, an interesting attempt to align Blake with other nineteenth-century currents of thought. His second book, *William Blake the Man* (1919), is less distinctive, but has some good passages on the relation of Blake to Swedenborg. Perhaps the chapter on Blake in Oliver Elton's *A Survey of English Literature, 1780–1830* (1920) may be taken as summing up this transitional period.

The decade of the 1920's, with the centenary year falling in 1927, was the time when the study of Blake came to full maturity, what with the appearance of the Keynes bibliography and standard edition, already mentioned. In interpretation the great landmark is S. Foster Damon's *William Blake: His Philosophy and Symbols* (1924). This was the first, and in many respects still the best, effort to attempt commentary as well as comment, to pursue Blake's meaning into the texture of his poetry and the details of his symbolism. For the special student of Blake it is the commentary, the second half of the book, which is of greatest value, although there is much in the first half too that is unique. Not only was Damon's sheer erudition of formidable range, but his general literary culture was broader and richer than that of any previous critic of Blake since Swinburne. His commentary is based largely on a translation of Blake's characters into personifications, and the result, if not exhaustive of Blake's meaning, at any rate does give a meaning, and a coherent and consistent one. In his commentary on the designs he is unsurpassed, and there are several smaller areas of Blake criticism, such as the question of the purely poetic merits of the Prophecies, upon which he is still the only critic to have made much headway.

Of minor studies during this decade, Max Plowman's *An Introduction to the Study of Blake* (1927) is just that, a lucid and unpretentious book. Osbert Burdett's *William Blake* (1926) is the volume in the English Men of Letters series, and a good, if now somewhat dated, general study. Jack Lindsay's *William Blake, Creative Will and the Poetic Image* (1927) is a lively appreciative essay, and Philippe Soupault's *William Blake* (1928), translated by Lewis May in the same year, is more sophisticated, almost a minor classic of Blake criticism, with some illuminating suggestions about Blake's pictorial affinities. The studies by Allardyce Nicoll (1922), Herbert Jenkins (1925), Ernest Short (1925), C. H. Herford (1928), and Alan Clutton-Brock (1933) are expendable. With the growing specialization of Blake scholarship, the general essay has become a somewhat obsolete genre: a belated example is Stanley Gardner's *Infinity on the Anvil* (1954). For the contemporary student looking for a handbook to serve as a general introduction to Blake, H. M. Margoliouth's *William Blake* (1950), a volume in the Home University Library, is up to date and admirably concise.

But while Blake scholarship and criticism advanced immeasurably in the twenties, Blake himself lost the place of honor with the avant-garde that he had held ever since his original discovery. In the shifting and regrouping of critical values which took place around Eliot and Pound, Blake was one of the poets, along with Milton and Shelley, who fell under the disapproval of the romantic in literature, the radical in politics, and the Protestant in religion. The remarks about Blake in Irving Babbitt's *Rousseau and Romanticism* (1919), ill-informed as they are, may have helped to popularize the conception of Blake as an apocryphal writer in a new canon of orthodoxy. Eliot's influential essay on Blake in *The Sacred Wood* (1920) identified him as an intellectual Robinson Crusoe, weakening his poetic energies in an effort to construct a philosophy out of the bits and pieces of his self-educated reading, instead of working within a more central cultural tradition, deriving his thought from professional thinkers, in the manner of Dante. Blake accordingly became a major interest chiefly among poets and critics holding to the more old-fashioned romantic and liberal sympathies, and to the unification of art and thought within the creative personality.

Among these was Middleton Murry, whose *William Blake* (1933) is best classified, on the whole, as a general introduction to Blake, though more elaborate than Plowman's. It presents Blake in the light of its author's preoccupation with a personal version of the Christian tradition liberalized by some insights of Marx in economics and of D. H. Lawrence in psychology—that is, it is to some extent a self-projecting study. But it does not really distort Blake or manipulate his thought in some other interest. It seldom comes to grips with the details of the symbolism, but in the area of general comment, and particularly in dealing with such critical issues as the revisions of *The Four Zoas*, it remains one of the best and closest studies of Blake's poetry and thought. An essay in the same author's *Mystery of Keats* (1949) compares Keats with Blake.

The study of Blake since 1933 may be divided into two main parts, dealing respectively with what in the criticism of Spenser would be called the moral and the historical allegory. We begin with the former, the books dealing primarily with Blake's "thought" as a system of ideas and its relation to certain intellectual traditions in religion and philosophy.

It has been increasingly recognized that the kind of scholarly problem represented by such words as "mysticism" and "occultism" is of less importance in the study of Blake than used to be assumed. Damon's book, it is true, did accept Blake as a mystic, and interpreted much of his symbolism in mystical terms. Some errors of interpretation resulted—*The Mental Traveller*, for example, was interpreted as a poem of a "mystic way," although its imagery is obviously closer to Freud's *Interpretation of Dreams* than to *The Cloud of Unknowing*. (On this poem see also John H. Sutherland, "Blake's 'Mental Traveller'," *ELH*, 1955, and other articles listed below.) This was the only point on which Damon's conception of Blake was seriously questioned. Helen White's *The Mysticism of William Blake* (1927) comes to the conclusion that Blake does not fit very well into the tradition ordinarily called "mystical," the tradition in which, say, the Spanish saints of the Counter Reformation would have a central place; and on the whole she must be regarded as having made her point. The result has been a tendency to deprecate or ignore the term "mystic" in connection with Blake, a tendency marked in Schorer, in Frye's attempts to distinguish a "mystic" from a "visionary," in Erdman, and others.

Yet it is still possible to rehabilitate the term for Blake if some other conception of it, less ethical and more speculative and aesthetic, is taken as a norm. For instance, if one begins by reading the *Bhagavadgita*, preferably in the Wilkins translation that Blake used, then learns from such traditions as those of Zen Buddhism how mysticism and art may be associated, then cautiously makes his way to the Western world by way of the Christianized Platonism of the Renaissance, he will come much closer to the kind of associations with the term which fit Blake. Suggestions about the affinities between Blake and Oriental thought are made from time to time: the affinities are remarkable, but probably few would care to follow them up in a field where almost nothing but pure analogy can be established. A more solid link is afforded by Blake's very probable knowledge of some of Thomas Taylor's translations from Plato and the Neoplatonists. This study is still fragmentary, and perhaps Blake's rare and crotchety references to Plato indicate the limitations of its value. The interested reader may consult, with caution, articles by F. E. Pierce, especially "Blake and Thomas Taylor" (*PMLA*, 1928), several recent articles by George M. Harper (e.g., "The Neo-Platonic Concept of Time in Blake's Prophetic Books," also in *PMLA*, 1954), and John E. Brown, "Neo-Platonism in the Poetry of William Blake" (*JAAC*, 1951). The value of all such work depends on the accuracy of its reading of Blake, and there is certainly room for a good analogical study of Blake's relation to Oriental and Platonic traditions. One by P. F. Fisher of the Royal Military College (Canada) has appeared (see below).

Other studies of Blake's mysticism, which do not upset the views advanced above, are Adeline Butterworth's *William Blake, Mystic* (1911), a somewhat rhapsodic essay notable for bringing some of the designs to Young's *Night Thoughts* to attention; Maung Ba-Han's *William Blake: His Mysticism* (1924); Jacomina Korteling's *Mysticism in Blake and Wordsworth* (1928); Waldemar Bagdasarianz' *William Blake: Versuch einer Entwicklungsgeschichte des Mystikers* (1935). A readable popular account of Blake as a mystic is in Sheldon Cheney's *Men Who Have Walked with God* (1946).

The linking of Blake with various occult traditions stems from the conviction that a "dysangel" who talks so much and so fervently about Jesus must be some kind of Christian heretic. It goes without saying that Blake's religious views have been persistently misinterpreted, usually through a desire to make him bizarre in some way or other, the resulting muddle of inconsistencies being promptly attached to Blake's mind instead of the critic's. Actually (for the fact is as well established as any other in Blake scholarship) Blake is a Bible-soaked middle-class English Protestant: all his theological conceptions are quite consistent with this position, most of his symbolism, especially in *Milton* and *Jerusalem*, is elementary Biblical typology, and the bulk of his mysterious and esoteric doctrines come straight out of the New Testament. It is clear that he was interested in Boehme and Swedenborg, for example, not as occultists but as Christian visionaries. Any attempt to locate a major source for Blake's *beliefs* (as distinct from whatever symbols or concepts he might have absorbed into his iconography) outside the general Christian tradition as it came to him is sure to result in, at best, a negative thesis, in which his divergences will be of far greater significance than his resemblances.

The word "pantheist" was attached to Blake by Swinburne, but is a most unlucky guess for the author of the *Songs of Experience*. Attempts to connect Blake with the Gnostic tradition have always had a curious fascination for his critics, but have not yet been established on any basis that does not do violence to Blake's meaning. Some of the Gnostics interpreted the Bible as a straightforward antithesis of law and gospel, with everything in the New Testament contradicting and canceling out everything in the Old, but it is quite wrong to ascribe such views to Blake, as is done in John Henry Clarke's *William Blake on the Lord's Prayer* (1927). A persistent exaggeration of the esoteric elements in Blake's thought vitiates much of the work of Denis Saurat on Blake, not least his *William Blake* (Paris, 1954), and has apparently extended elsewhere. (Cf. Kathleen Raine, "Who Made the Tyger?" *Encounter*,

1954.) Blake's relation to Boehme and Swedenborg is a subject for careful investigation, because Blake may have got some of his Biblical typology from Swedenborg's doctrine of correspondence (instead of getting it, as a modern poet would do, from Dante or some other sacramental symbolist). However, the usual tendency is to compare Swedenborg's visions with Blake's legendary powers of visualization and second sight, a tendency marked in Jacques Roos's *Aspects littéraires du mysticisme philosophique* . . . (1951). The conception of Blake as an intellectual Robinson Crusoe might not have arisen if studies of his thought had not been so peripheral in their emphasis.

Some attempt at clearing up the doctrinal confusion is made in J. G. Davies' *The Theology of William Blake* (1948), which, besides having a good chapter on Swedenborg, quotes Blake accurately and brings out certain points, such as his belief in original sin, that are central to any serious study of his religious thought. Its standard, however, is a somewhat pedestrian conception of orthodoxy which leaves little room for paradox in statement, and some curious misconceptions greatly weaken it, such as its view of the status of the doctrine of the resurrection of the body in the Prophecies, a doctrine as central to them as the Incarnation is to the Quartets. The chapter on Blake in H. N. Fairchild's *Religious Trends in English Poetry* (1949) is a competent piece of scholarly writing, but very far from being a systematic presentation of Blake's religious position. M. Bottrall's *The Divine Image: A Study of Blake's Interpretation of Christianity* (1950) is on the whole the most satisfactory treatment to date of its theme, and suggests some interesting parallels with William Law.

The student interested in Blake's religious views should first get what few contemporary critics have, a coherent idea of Protestantism, and then investigate the doctrine technically known as pre-existence: the doctrine that Christ's humanity is coeternal with his divinity. This doctrine is not strictly a heresy, in the sense of being a doctrine inconsistent with the Christian tradition (in Blake's day it was held by Isaac Watts), but it is the only unusual feature of Blake's religious beliefs, granted his Protestant premises.

As for Blake's philosophical views, it is becoming more obvious that he got them chiefly from a negative reaction to the English philosophers of the Enlightenment: he not only refers frequently to Bacon, Newton, and Locke, but says explicitly that he had read at least Bacon and Locke with some care. Some parallelism between his thought and that of other critics of Locke, especially Berkeley, would be expected, though Blake's reading of Berkeley cannot be definitely proved except for *Siris*, which proves very little. The eighteenth-century context of Blake's epistemology is dealt with by Frye, and, independently and with more documentation, by Bernard Blackstone in *English Blake* (1949). The study of Blake's antagonism to Locke and similarity to Berkeley is the most distinctive contribution made by Blackstone's book to Blake scholarship, the rest of it being for the most part repetitive of biographical and historical data available elsewhere. It is especially Blake's knowledge and conception of Newton that needs further clarification at present.

At the same time, Blake's use of certain occult sources is undeniable: Damon has shown how he used Agrippa for *Tiriel* and Porphyry's allegory of Homer's cave of the nymphs for *The Book of Thel*. Some explicit statements, too, such as his identification of Arthur with the constellation Boötes in the *Descriptive Catalogue*, show his interest in the contemporary astrologizing of myth. M. O. Percival's *William Blake's Circle of Destiny* (1938) is a remarkable essay in this field, the main achievement of which is to establish a number of analogous patterns between Blake's symbolism and the symbols of astrology, alchemy, and cabbalism. The disadvantage of the book for the Blake student is that in establishing analogues to such symbols as the "Seven Eyes" the author frequently fails to lay the primary emphasis on the (usually Biblical) source. But, with this reservation, Percival's book is a study that will become steadily more useful and enlightening as Blake's own argument becomes more clearly understood, and as the morphology of occult systems of thought becomes better established.

This last has already been investigated, on a psychological basis, by Jung and his school. In Blake criticism there are at least two "Jungian" approaches to Blake: L. A. D. Johnstone's *A Psychological Study of William Blake* (1945) and W. P. Witcutt's *Blake: A Psychological Study* (1946). The former is brief and the latter is not very reliable in its interpretation of Blake, besides leaving out some aspects which should be central to any psychological study, such as the Oedipus situation in the Preludium to *America*. However, its identification of Jung's four faculties with the four Zoas seems sound enough.

It has long been the dream of students of occultism, mythology, and comparative religion that some day a key to a universal language of symbolism will be discovered. Works which seem to move in the direction of establishing a theory or grammar of symbolism have also always attracted poets; there were many such works in Blake's day, and Blake used them just as Spenser used Natalis Comes and as modern poets use Frazer and Frobenius. The study of Blake's handling of such material is obviously indispensable. Denis Saurat's *Blake and Modern Thought* (1929) is the pioneer study in this field: the second chapter, much the most valuable part of the book, stresses the importance of Davies' *Celtic Researches,* which Blake certainly read, of Bryant's *Ancient Mythology,* which he certainly illustrated, and of contemporary theories about the antiquity and survival of the "Druids." Further information on this subject may be found in the essays on Blake in E. B. Hungerford's *Shores of Darkness* (1941) and in Ruthven Todd's *Tracks in the Snow* (1946). The latter stresses also the influence of Stukeley and Owen Pughe. More work in this direction, especially on the Welsh sources, needs to be done, although it should be done without value judgments. The poetic merits of Blake's Prophecies, whatever they may be, no more depend on the scholarly merits of Davies or Bryant than the poetic merits of *The Waste Land* depend on the view that Arthurian scholars take of *From Ritual to Romance.*

The same hope of finding some sort of grammar of symbolism has led a few of Blake's critics to look for it in Blake. The Ellis-Yeats commentary, which shows the influence of Blavatskian theosophy, belongs to this tradition to some extent, and so perhaps does Emily Hamblen's *On the Minor Prophecies of William Blake* (1930), where we return to etymological speculation, of the kind that so attracted Bryant. Northrop Frye's study, *Fearful Symmetry* (1947), the most sustained attempt at a critical translation of Blake's moral allegory, locates this grammar of symbolism within literature itself: in other words, as a result of trying to solve a specific problem in literary criticism, the argument of Blake's Prophecies, this book became unconsciously an example of contemporary mythical or archetypal criticism. Thus Orc is Blake's example of the literary and mythical dying god, Urizen, Blake's example of the literary and mythical father-god, and so on. There are mistakes in the book, but it seems to have been useful to those who have used it, and the author has not changed his mind about any of his renderings of Blake's meaning.

If this literature-based approach to Blake's symbolism is sound, more investigation is clearly needed of Blake's relations, conscious and unconscious, with literature in general and English literature in particular. The studies of Platonic influence have no counterpart in any study of Blake's surprisingly extensive knowledge of classical literature, which included much of Ovid, Virgil, Homer, Hesiod, and Apuleius, besides lesser authors. Blake's view of classical imagination as comparatively debased did not prevent him from using a good deal of it. In English literature the chief influence on Blake was Milton, an influence not satisfactorily studied in Denis Saurat's *Blake and Milton* (1920; rev. ed., 1935), or in Raymond D. Havens' *The Influence of Milton on English Poetry* (1922). The latter is obsolete and the former, even in the revised edition, makes some reckless statements (e.g., "Blake never calls the Redeemer to help him in his struggles") which are not simply slips but indicate a wrong conception of Blake—and, one may parenthetically add, of Milton. Blake's literary relation to his own time is a still more important subject, yet a sadly neglected one. Margaret Ruth Lowery's *Windows of the Morning* (1940) is a study of Blake's early *Poetical Sketches*, which makes a real effort to relate Blake to the other poets of the later eighteenth century. In spite of some controversial points, such as her view of the influence of Chatterton on Blake, the study is of considerable importance. Northrop Frye has frequently expressed the view that a more coherent conception of Blake's cultural period, avoiding the false teleologies of "post-Augustan" and "preromantic," would do much to make sense of the problem of Blake's place in English literature.

The rhetorical or "new" critics have not been much attracted by Blake, though a steady series of notes on the lyrics has appeared in the *Explicator*. The best essay on Blake's poetic vocabulary is Josephine Miles's "The Language of William Blake," published in the volume *English Institute Essays 1950* (1951), a volume which also contains essays on the archetypal and historical approaches to Blake by Frye and by Erdman, respectively. There are brief but perceptive comments about Blake's versification in Lytton Strachey's *Books and Characters* (1922), in Edith Sitwell's *The Pleasures of Poetry*, Second Series (1931), and some close explication of the lyrics in Stanley Gardner's *Infinity on the Anvil*, mentioned above.

Turning now to the "historical allegory," there are three books that lay particular stress on the social context of Blake's work. Jacob Bronowski's *A Man Without a Mask* (1943; 2d ed., 1954, published under the title *William Blake* as a Pelican Book), the title of which is a phrase used about Blake by Samuel Palmer, is a crisp and incisive study which sketches in the historical background of Blake's time and sets Blake against it. It had always been obvious that Blake's poetry was in part a poetry of social protest, but Bronowski's study was the first to show in detail how wide open

Blake's eyes were and how much of the life around him he absorbed and recorded.

Mark Schorer's *William Blake: The Politics of Vision* (1946) is a longer study with the same general emphasis, though independent of Bronowski and more varied in range. It has more allusions to twentieth-century poetry and criticism than any other book on Blake, and hence is one in which the modern reader may feel particularly at home, Blake's affinities with the modern world being more frequently asserted than documented. It lays stress on Blake as an intellectual revolutionary, as one who was in contact, through the publisher Johnson, with a good deal of English radical sentiment. The book has a clear grasp of the central problem of all historical study of Blake, the peculiarly English combination of the political radical and the religious evangelical, a combination which made the intellectual basis of the French Revolution as intolerable to him as the misery of the London poor. Schorer sees in the impossible demands which this attitude made on life the key to what for him is the essential characteristic of the Prophecies: a powerful energy of expression which never finds its appropriate form.

David V. Erdman's *Blake; Prophet Against Empire* (1954) does for the two previous studies more or less what Damon did for the criticism before his time: that is, it pursues the social reference of Blake's poetry into its texture and details. The book is based on a clear and accurate reading of the whole of Blake's poetry, including the Prophecies, besides keeping in view the total range of his work as illustrator and engraver, which often throws unexpected light on the symbolism. Many traditional errors and vague notions, parroted from one writer to another, are corrected or cleared up, and an exhaustive program of research not only explains an extraordinary number of obscure points and problems, but builds up a logical biographical narrative as it goes on. For it is obvious that the historical study of Blake is, in contrast to the philosophical approach, much more closely involved with questions of biography, and anyone who wishes to follow this line of scholarship must become something of a biographer. The historical background too has been studied in its primary sources: instead of generalizations about the dark Satanic mills, we are told just what social phenomena, from exploitation to the new machinery, did catch Blake's eye and got recorded in the poems and designs.

Studies of Blake's influence on later poets will not detain us long. The influence of Blake on Yeats is dealt with in Margaret Rudd's *Divided Image* (1953), in Virginia Moore's *The Unicorn* (1954), and in Hazard Adams' *Blake and Yeats: The Contrary*

Vision (1955). The last-named is the only satisfactory study of the Blake side. There are also several studies of Blake and Dante Gabriel Rossetti, the fullest being Kerrison Preston's *Blake and Rossetti* (1944). Irving Fiske's *Bernard Shaw's Debt to William Blake* (1951) is a Shaw Society pamphlet enthusiastically endorsed by Shaw himself. In the *James Joyce Review* (1957) Northrop Frye has set out the chief parallels between the myths of the Prophecies and of *Finnegans Wake*, without committing himself on the question of how far Joyce was aware of them. The influence of Blake on Dylan Thomas still awaits study.

V. BLAKE AS A GRAPHIC ARTIST

OF BLAKE'S WORK as painter, engraver, and illustrator, there has been little criticism of much freshness or distinctiveness. Blake, as D. H. Lawrence said, "dares handle the human body," but he was far more daring than that, and his dizzy foreshortenings and swirling calligraphic rhythms still await competent exposition. There is a good historical account of Blake in R. H. Wilenski's *English Painting* (1933); there is an essay in Sturge Moore's *Art and Life* (1910), and a more important one in Roger Fry's *Vision and Design* (1920). The relation of Blake's theories of painting to eighteenth-century aesthetic theory and taste has been little explored, beyond some incidental information in Erdman's book and a useful chapter on Blake in Stephen A. Larrabee's *English Bards and Grecian Marbles* (1943), which, as its title indicates, deals with what for Blake was the negative side of it.

On Blake's iconography the pioneer work, one of the major efforts of Blake scholarship, is Joseph H. Wicksteed's *Blake's Vision of the Book of Job*, a brilliant commentary on the Job engravings which was first published in 1910, but did not make its full impact on Blake criticism until the revised edition of 1924. It established once for all the existence of a coherent iconography in one of Blake's greatest works of art, especially in the significance given to right and left hands, to Gothic and "Druid" buildings, and the like. Albert

S. Roe's *Blake's Illustrations to the Divine Comedy* (1953) does for the Dante drawings and engravings what Wicksteed did for the Job series. The book, beautifully produced by the Princeton University Press, contains the hundred Dante drawings and an able commentary, which shows very deftly how Blake managed to illustrate Dante's poem and his own reading of that poem at the same time.

Some of Blake's pictures are complicated enough to require separate iconographical treatment. Unfortunately the commentaries on "The River of Life" by Joseph Wicksteed, and on "The Spiritual Condition of Man" and "The Sea of Time and Space" by Kerrison Preston are not readily available; one would like to see such commentaries gathered together in book form. More accessible, and equally useful, is Piloo Nanavutty's "A Title-Page in Blake's Genesis Manuscript" (*JWCI*, 1947). The study of the sources of Blake's iconography begins, and so far practically ends, with two important articles—Collins Baker's "The Sources of Blake's Pictorial Expression" (*HLQ*, 1940–41) and Anthony Blunt's "Blake's Pictorial Imagination" (*JWCI*, 1943)—and a few other articles of more restricted interest in the latter journal. A rare example of Blake's pictorial relation to a contemporary is studied in D. V. Erdman's "William Blake's Debt to James Gillray" (*Art Quart.*, 1949). Finally, the only really serious study to date of the mystery of Blake's engraving process has been made by Ruthven Todd in "The Techniques of William Blake's Illuminated Printing" (*Print Collectors' Quarterly* and *Print*, both 1948). The defunct Canadian magazine *Here and Now* carried in its first issue (1948) reproductions of poems of Todd illustrated by Joan Miro, his collaborator in working out the process, exemplifying it in practice.

Two well-produced collections of Blake's graphic work appeared in the twenties. Darrell Figgis' *The Paintings of William Blake* (1925) is a fine anthology of Blake's most famous paintings, mostly in black and white, with a few in color. The companion volume is Laurence Binyon's *The Engraved Designs of William Blake* (1926). These two books are essential to any serious study of this side of Blake. Geoffrey Keynes's *The Pencil Drawings of William Blake* (1927) contains the Visionary Heads and some wonderful sketches. *Blake's Pencil Drawings, Second Series*, appeared in 1956. The finest set of Blake's woodcuts, the illustrations made to Thornton's edition of Virgil's *Georgics*, was issued by Geoffrey Keynes, also in 1927. No attempt can be made here to list everything that comes into the general category of miscellaneous "picture books," catalogues of exhibitions, and the like, which may be found in the bibliography by Bentley and Nurmi. Adrian van Sinderen's *Blake: The Mystic Genius* (1949), Geoffrey Keynes's *William Blake's Engravings* (1950), and the descriptive catalogue of an exhibition assembled from American collections by the Philadelphia Museum of Art in 1939 may be mentioned, more or less at random, for their general variety of interest. Also of interest are the catalogues of exhibitions in the bicentenary year, 1957. The van Sinderen book contains color reproductions of the twelve illustrations to Milton's "L'Allegro" and "Il Penseroso."

A complete set of the paintings, drawings, and engravings of the Job series was issued by Laurence Binyon and Geoffrey Keynes in 1935, except for the more recently discovered "New Zealand" set, which appeared with a note by Philip Hofer in 1937. *William Blake's Designs for Gray's Poems* (1922), with a note by H. J. C. Grierson, is a fine example of one of Blake's most interesting series. There is as yet, not unnaturally, no complete edition of the five-hundred-odd illustrations to Young's *Night Thoughts*, but a selection, with some of the most gorgeous designs Blake ever made reproduced in color, was issued by Geoffrey Keynes in 1927. (A study of these by H. M. Margoliouth is included in *The Divine Vision*, mentioned below.) It was also Geoffrey Keynes who was responsible for reproducing the illustrations to *The Pilgrim's Progress* in 1941 and for most of the editions of Blake's illustrations to Milton's poems, nearly all of which have now been reproduced. Another edition of a *Paradise Lost* set was published by the Heritage Press in 1941.

It is hardly necessary to labor the point that Blake's engraved poems cannot be safely studied from the text alone. Many misled and misleading interpretations of Blake might never have been proposed if this had been kept in mind. Further, text and designs in a long poem form different aspects of it. The design may sometimes illustrate the text on the same plate, but it by no means invariably does so. It is curious how little literary criticism of Blake appears to have been based on the designs equally with the text. Damon's book, which covers more of Blake's output in both arts than any other single commentary, is a mine of information about the designs accompanying the engraved poems, where the characters and themes are identified with great skill and accuracy. Joseph Wicksteed, *Blake's Innocence and Experience* (1928), also pays close attention to the iconography of the designs, as one would expect from the author of the Job commentary. Erdman's commentary and Frye's make a consistent use of the designs, though the latter gives little direct evidence of the fact: Frye's article "Poetry and Design in William Blake" (*JAAC*, 1951) is intended to be a general introduction to this aspect of Blake criticism. Blake's *Gates of Paradise*, the only one of the engraved poems which is completely unintelligible without the designs, has been studied by Chauncey B. Tinker in *Painter and Poet* (1938).

All the engraved poems have been reproduced in some form or other. The third volume of the Ellis and Yeats edition contains a practically complete set of reproductions of the Prophetic Books, in black and white lithograph. The unique *Book of Ahania* does not seem to have been reproduced (a facsimile of it had been made in 1892, probably by William Griggs). One's admiration for this heroic early effort should not interfere with one's opinion of the quality of the reproductions, which look rather as though the originals had been stamped on highly absorbent blotting paper. Since then, a number of reproductions of the engraved poems, of varying merit, in both color and black and white, have appeared from time to time. Nearly all of them have been reproduced by the Blake Press (William Muir, Edmonton, Eng.) at various dates from 1884 on; the edition of *Europe* is particularly successful. Finally, the Blake Trust in England has begun to issue a series of color reproductions in expensive and limited editions, using the whole resources of modern methods of reproduction, printed by the Trianon Press. A superb *Jerusalem* appeared in 1952, along with a black-and-white reproduction of the Rinder copy of the same poem in a second volume, and a commentary by Joseph Wicksteed in a third. *Songs of Innocence and Experience* followed in 1955. *The Book of Urizen*, pictorially one of the most splendid of them all, appeared in 1958, and one hopes that the series will eventually embrace the whole canon.

The present essay, though it has tried to record everything of permanent value for the contemporary student of English literature interested in Blake, has still given only a selection from the vast spate of comment which, in less than a century, has followed Gilchrist's discovery of his "pictor ignotus." Two things should be said in conclusion. First, Blake scholarship today moves ahead fairly fast. This essay will be out of date in some respects before it appears: new studies are springing up on all sides. Ignoring this scholarship will assuredly result in ignoring many essential facts. Second, the days of looking into one's heart to write about Blake are over. It is now possible to say with some authority that some approaches to Blake are fruitful and that others are blind alleys; that some readings of Blake are right and others wrong; and that the right reading is increasingly a matter of fact, not of guesswork. The permanently valuable critics of Blake are those who have realized that Blake will repay any amount of time and patience expended on

him, and that nothing in him is to be glibly dismissed or rejected.
The permanently valuable critics of the future will be those who
follow in this tradition.

ADDENDA. CRITICAL WORKS SINCE 1956

T HE PREVIOUS EDITION of this book was published just before the
     bicentenary year in 1957, and the profusion of publications on
Blake appearing that year and since has been too great to insert into
Northrop Frye's essay, the latter half of which in any case is
organized chronologically and is as much a guide to the kinds of
studies needed as it is a bibliographical essay on what has been done.
In bringing his essay up to date, therefore, the reviser has made some
revisions in the bibliographical and textual sections and has added
only a few titles to the later part, preferring instead to mention most
studies appearing since in this addendum.

    In addition to the expected commemorative essays, the best of
which is Frye's "Blake After Two Centuries" (*UTQ*), the bicentenary year produced the revised text, by Keynes, already mentioned;
William Blake's Illustrations to the Bible, also by Keynes; George
Wingfield Digby's rather Jungian little book on Blake's art, *Symbol
and Image in William Blake;* F. W. Bateson's edition of *Selected
Poems of William Blake,* worthy of being singled out from among
similar collections because of its fresh critical notes; a commemorative volume, *The Divine Vision,* edited by V. de S. Pinto; and many
shorter studies. Though the years following have not been this
productive, Blake studies continue to appear in considerable number,
most of them, even explications of the lyrics, displaying a responsibility that was hard to find before the publication of Frye's *Fearful
Symmetry* (1947), which gave students of Blake a fruitful critical
methodology, and Erdman's *Blake: Prophet Against Empire*
(1954), which restored Blake firmly to the world of living men.

    With Frye, Erdman, and earlier Damon, Percival, as well as the
indispensable Gilchrist, as guides, critics of Blake have increasingly
turned to specialized studies of various kinds and to close studies of
particular works.

    Most active in gathering detailed biographical information

have been Keynes and G. E. Bentley, Jr., in various articles. Bentley has collected a great many previously unknown contemporary references to Blake, soon to be published as a book. Still urgently needed is a modern critical biography incorporating what has been learned biographically, bibliographically, and critically since the publication of *The Life of William Blake* (1927; rev. ed., 1948) by Mona Wilson, whose facts supplement Gilchrist but who lacks his zest and is an unsure critical guide to the works.

Margaret Rudd's *Organiz'd Innocence: The Story of Blake's Prophetic Books* (1956), a commentary on the major prophecies, is actually more a biographical than a critical work, taking off from the postulate that a feeling of doubt and ambivalence on Blake's part toward his work and his marriage "is certainly what the prophetic books are *about*" (Rudd's italics) and written without help from any critic but Middleton Murry.

Recent studies of Blake's sources, a problem which continues to have some of the fascination that the identity of Shakespeare has, have in general taken two forms: studies of the traditions in which Blake participated and studies of particular writers he may have drawn on. Unfortunately, some writers of both kinds of studies have tried to advance one claim or another too hard and have on occasion come dangerously close to explaining him away altogether. This is a latter-day instance of the common earlier tendency to find "keys" to Blake. A. L. Morton, in *The Everlasting Gospel* (1958), a slight little volume, would unlock him by means of English Antinomianism. And George M. Harper, in *The Neoplatonism of William Blake* (1961), though he makes a more modest claim for Blake's dependence on Thomas Taylor than in his earlier articles, still finds hard to resist the idea that Blake could not have written as he did without Taylor; and in order to make this case, Harper is compelled to do a good deal of translation of Blake piecemeal into "conceptions" which have parallels in Taylor. Apparently independently of Harper, Kathleen Raine has also advanced strong claims for Taylor as a particular source in which the Neoplatonic form of the "perennial philosophy" came to a focus for Blake. She argues for Neoplatonic influences in such studies as her article in *The Divine Vision* (1957), mentioned earlier, and in "The Sea of Time and Space," a study of the Arlington Court Picture (*JWCI*, 1957). Her most extended discussion of Blake's connection with the general tradition of which Neoplatonism is a part is to be found in "Blake's Debt to Antiquity," a book-length article in the *Sewanee Review* (1963), printing the Mellon Lectures for 1963. A fuller version of this is scheduled for publication.

The attempts to explain Blake specifically through Neoplatonism or particular Neoplatonists have not proved enlightening enough to demonstrate convincingly that his debt to Neoplatonism is as great as has been claimed, but there is no doubt that Plato and Neoplatonism were influences on him. More satisfactory studies of Platonic and other related influences have been those such as the late Peter Fisher's very fine *The Valley of Vision* (1961), which considers Plato, among others, as part of the intellectual context in which Blake wrote, and Desirée Hirst's *Hidden Riches: Traditional Symbolism from the Renaissance to Blake* (1964), which traces the Platonic tradition through iconography and symbolism. Miss Hirst does not doubt that Blake knew Thomas Taylor, but she believes that Taylor, far from being a powerfully formative influence on him, was quite quickly rejected, like Swedenborg, as being inadequate. An excellent short study of Blake's occultism is included in John Senior's *The Way Down and Out: The Occult in Symbolist Literature* (1959).

A necessary preliminary step to any study of particular sources must be a reading of Keynes's "Blake's Library" (*TLS*, 6 Nov. 1959) and Bentley's "Additions to Blake's Library" (*BNYPL*, 1960)—though of course Blake read, and heard discussed, more books than he owned.

The wildest source studies of Blake by far are those of Elizabeth O'Higgins in the *Dublin Magazine* appearing between 1950 and 1956. Miss O'Higgins simply assumes Blake's Irish origin as her starting point and translates him back into Irish, arguing that not only is Blake illuminated thereby but so is Irish literature.

Relatively little has been done on Blake's influence on other writers, and most of that has been on James Joyce, by Frye in "Quest and Cycle in *Finnegans Wake*" (*JJR*, 1957), and Karl Kiralis in "Joyce and Blake: A Basic Source for 'Finnegans Wake'" (*MFS*, 1959). Articles by Robert F. Gleckner and Morton Paley on Joyce and Blake appear in *The James Joyce Miscellany* (1962). Joyce's lecture on Blake, in Italian, was edited by Ellsworth Mason and Richard Ellmann and appears in *Criticism* (1959), as well as in *The Critical Writings of James Joyce* (1959). Scattered studies of other authors may be located through the index in Bentley's and Nurmi's bibliography.

Some indication of the fact that Blake studies have now come of age may be seen in the numerous "readings" and other close studies of particular works appearing since the last edition of this book. Before the publication of Frye's *Fearful Symmetry* especially, it was difficult to talk in detail about a particular work without having to undertake a discussion of Blake's work as a whole. Critics of Blake still feel obliged to explain briefly that part of his "system" which is relevant to the matter at hand, but they can do so with the assurance that a fairly good general understanding of his work can be assumed. Prior to about 1955 there were relatively few published essays— other than biographical and bibliographical studies—which a student of Blake need consult. But of the essays and studies which John E. Grant thought should be included in his collection *Discussions of William Blake* in 1961, all but three were published after 1950, and those three were letters by Lamb, Coleridge, and Frederick Tatham. A specialized study of a particular mythological personage such as Henri Petter's *Enitharmon: Stellung und Aufgabe eines Symbols in dichterischen Gesamtswerk William Blakes* (1957), which, as the title implies, traces the figure of Enitharmon through his works, would have been all but impossible much more than a decade ago. And it is possible for Alicia Ostriker, in *Vision and Verse in William Blake* (1965), to study Blake's prosody in a visionary context, assuming a good deal of familiarity with even the later prophecies on the part of the reader.

Even in the study of the lyrics, critical amateurism of the kind seen in *Infinity on the Anvil* (1954) by Stanley Gardner, who had not penetrated to the later works, has given way to the learned criticism of such works as Robert F. Gleckner's *Piper and the Bard* (1959) and Hazard Adams' *William Blake: A Reading of the Shorter Poems* (1963), both of which bring to bear on the lyrics some of the perspectives gained from study of Blake's Prophetic Books—indeed, they may overdo it a bit at times, putting more emphasis on "system" than is appropriate for some of the lyrics. Gleckner concentrates on the early works after *Poetical Sketches* and reads them in terms of a cumulative symbolic context. Adams, who conceives of the lyrics and the prophecies as being different kinds of attempts to express a system that was already in Blake's mind when he wrote *Songs of Innocence* and *Songs of Experience*, begins with the later lyrics of the Pickering MS and returns to read the Songs from a prophetic or "visionary" perspective.

A sustained reading of all of Blake's works in which his system —to continue using this term as convenient shorthand for the coherent body of ideas and images that gives form to Blake's thought—is firmly connected with explication of the text is *Blake's Apocalypse: A Study in Poetic Argument* (1963) by Harold Bloom, carrying further the sort of reading Bloom had given Blake in *The Visionary Company* (1961). Bloom's emphasis is on the poetry, in the Prophecies as well as in the shorter works, though, as the subtitle suggests, he expounds Blake's argument as well. Acknowledging an over-all indebtedness to Frye (relatively few other critics of Blake are mentioned in the text or in the notes), Bloom provides a personal yet sound and often brilliantly illuminating introduction to Blake's poetry—the engraved designs are not considered. He minimizes Blake's historical allegory and has little patience with attempts to find esoteric sources.

Among recent short general studies, Karl Kiralis' "A Guide to the Intellectual Symbolism of William Blake's Prophetic Writings" (*Criticism*, 1959), Paul Miner's "The Polyp as a Symbol in the Poetry of William Blake" (*TSLL*, 1960), and Peter Fisher's "Blake and the Druids" (*JEGP*, 1959) might be singled out as being valuable. Benjamin Sankey's "A Preface to Blake" (*Spectrum*, 1960) would steer readers away from Blake on the ground that most of his poetry is not poetry at all, and E. D. Hirsch, Jr., in "The Two Blakes" (*RES*, 1961), attempts unsuccessfully to show Blake as oscillating between worldliness and otherworldliness. Hirsch has since expanded the argument of his article into a book, *Innocence and Experience: An Introduction to Blake* (1964), which is no more convincing than the article.

Except for Kiralis' article on the intellectual symbolism of Blake's later works, and "The Theme and Structure of *Jerusalem*" (*ELH*, 1956; reprinted in *The Divine Vision*), W. H. Stevenson's "Blake's Jerusalem," *Essays in Criticism* (1959), and Edward J. Rose's "The Structure of Blake's *Jerusalem*" (*Bu R*, 1963), by far most of the shorter studies have been concerned with the earlier and smaller works, especially the lyrics. Some of these, by Gleckner, Harper, and Adams, have been incorporated in books, mentioned previously. Martin Nurmi's monograph, *Blake's* MARRIAGE OF HEAVEN AND HELL: *A Critical Study* (1957), examines the structure of that work in some detail, and Harold Bloom's "Dialectic in *The Marriage of Heaven and Hell*" (*PMLA*, 1958) analyzes the dialectical interplay of its themes. Frye sets a model for explicators of Blake in "Blake's Introduction to Experience" (*HLQ*, 1957), but unfortunately explications still occasionally appear which read certain lyrics out of context and therefore misread them. Jacob Adler's "Symbol and Meaning in The Little Black Boy" (*MLN*, 1957) grasps the complexities of the poem, and A. E. Dyson's "The Little Black Boy: Blake's Song of Innocence" (*Crit Q*, 1959), though it offers little that is new, is sound enough.

As might be expected, some of the weightier articles have been on "The Tyger," and, while they arrive at no clear consensus as to the meaning of the poem—if that were possible—they have at least shown that the poem cannot be approached as a baffled musing on conventional Good and Evil, as it has been taught in countless classrooms. All critics stress the poem's great complexity and its apocalyptic aspect, but divide into those who emphasize the positive side of the tiger's symmetry (Schorer, Erdman, Nurmi, and Adams) and those who emphasize the uncertainty, the question, posed by the fact that the tiger *is* symmetrical (Frye, in *UTQ*, 1957, John E. Grant, Paul Miner, and Harold Bloom). Since the particular critical positions of these writers would be meaningless out of context, there is no point in attempting to state them. Anyway, the studies are of value more for the way in which they bring the crucial problems to a focus than for their answers. Many of the studies call attention to a particular aspect of the poem: Blake's revisions (Nurmi in *PMLA*, 1956), the engraved design (Grant in *TSLL*, 1960), the visionary perspective as seen in the poem (Adams in *TSLL*, 1960, and in *William Blake*, 1964), and the genesis of the symbol (Miner in *Criticism*, 1962). "The Tyger" is that kind of difficult poem whose meaning no amount of erudite criticism will settle for most readers, but critical study of it has at least made vague, isosyncratic, and silly readings harder to sustain.

After "The Tyger," among the most intriguing poems are "The Fly," though little has been written on it, and "The Mental Traveller." Gleckner passed over "The Fly" in *The Piper and the Bard*, frankly confessing that he did not know how to read it. Leo Kirschbaum's reading of it (*EC*, 1961), with a comment by F. W. Bateson, drew a reply from John E. Grant (also *EC*, 1961), who published the most extensive study of it that we have (*BNYPL*, 1964). Criticism of "The Mental Traveller" has been more extensive. Studies of this poem typically attempt to get at its meaning by emphasizing one "key" or aspect of it, and there is nothing wrong with this if not carried too far. John Sutherland, whose article was noted earlier, emphasizes Blake's vortexes and is solid on the parts of the poem dealing with them; and Frye in *Anatomy of Criticism* (1957) stresses pithily and suggestively the lunar cycle. Kathleen Raine's emphasis in "A Traditional Language of Symbols" (*Listener*, 1958) is suggested by her title, as are those of Irene Chayes in "Plato's *Statesman* Myth in Shelley and Blake" (*CL*, 1961), Morton D. Paley in "The Female Babe and 'The Mental Traveller' " (*SIR*, 1962), and Martin Nurmi in "Joy, Love, and Innocence in Blake's 'The Mental Traveller' " (*SIR*, 1964). Very good readings indeed, which have the advantage of a larger critical context, are those of Bloom and Adams, whose books were mentioned earlier.

A few other short studies of particular works that might be

mentioned briefly are Kathleen Raine's "Some Sources of *Tiriel*"
(*HLQ*, 1957; Sophocles, Cornelius Agrippa, Shakespeare, and
others); Gleckner's "Blake's *Thel* and the Bible" (*BNYPL*, 1960)
and "William Blake and the Human Abstract" (*PMLA*, 1961);
Hilton Landry's "The Symbolism of Blake's Sunflower" (*BNYPL*,
1962); Martin Nurmi's "Fact and Symbol in 'The Chimney
Sweeper' of Blake's *Songs of Innocence*" (*BNYPL*, 1964); and
John E. Grant's "Apocalypse in Blake's 'Auguries of Innocence'"
(*TSLL*, 1964).

Much remains to be done with Blake's art. Some of the studies
of his art, such as Kathleen Raine's article on "The Sea of Time and
Space" and Digby's book have been more concerned with his
symbolism than with his painting. The fullest recent study is Sir
Anthony Blunt's *The Art of William Blake* (1959). Sir Anthony,
who seems quite impatient with the present emphases of Blake
studies, applies to him the "ordinary methods of art history" and
shows that as an artist he is not as unusual as he has been generally
thought. The book is a worth-while corrective and helps us see
Blake's art in a new, because more conventional, light. Still, the
ordinary methods of art history are not quite enough for an artist
who thinks as much as Blake does simultaneously in graphic and
verbal images and who writes lengthy literary exegeses of his
pictures, as he does in "The Last Judgment" and *The Descriptive
Catalogue*. And a method that avoids wherever possible involvement
with his "mystical symbolism" is simply unable to deal with the
engraved designs in the illuminated books, which are studied by Jean
H. Hagstrum in *William Blake, Poet and Painter: An Introduction
to the Illuminated Verse* (1964). Hagstrum's book is what its
subtitle says it is, an introduction, but it is a surprisingly detailed
one despite its brevity, and well worth consulting even for specialists.
Some critics of Blake's text are not sure the engraved designs really
add anything (A. M. Wilkinson, *MLR*, 1962), and many are not
attracted to them. Yet Blake himself published almost all of his
poems with engraved designs — and even had designs in mind for some
while he wrote, as the *Four Zoas* manuscript shows. Part of the
reason for the lack of interest in the designs is that until the Blake
Trust, through the Trianon Press, began publishing their superb
facsimiles, hand-colored (with stencils), readily available reproductions were so wretched as to give little impression of the originals.
Blake was reproduced in exquisite hand-colored facsimiles by the
Griggses in Edmonton in the 1880's and 1890's, but these facsimiles
are now almost as hard to come by as the originals. Recent Blake
Trust facsimiles are *Songs of Innocence and Experience* (1956), the

beautiful *Book of Urizen* (1958), *The Visions of the Daughters of Albion* (1959), and *The Marriage of Heaven and Hell* (1960). A facsimile of the Blair's *Grave* illustrations, with an introductory essay on the plates and a brief commentary on each of them by S. Foster Damon was published in 1963.

A few shorter studies of Blake's art are Albert S. Roe, "A Drawing of the Last Judgment" (*HLQ*, 1957) ; H. M. Margoliouth, "William Blake, Historical Painter" (*Studio*, 1957), and "Blake's Drawings for Young's *Night Thoughts*," in *The Divine Vision;* Charles Ryskamp, "Blake's Cowperian Sketches" (*RES*, 1958) and "Blake's Drawing of Cowper's Monument" (*PULC*, 1963) ; and Sir Geoffrey Keynes's "Blake's Visionary Heads and The Ghost of a Flea" (*BNYPL*, 1960).

When S. Foster Damon published his pioneering work in 1924, Blake was hardly a subject for respectable academic scholarship. The important development in Blake scholarship since that time, however, has not been the improvement in his scholarly public image but the improvement in general understanding of what he attempted to do. If the Blakean view of things, especially as embodied in the gigantic imaginative forms of his later works, is not yet as familiar to students of literature as are Milton's doctrine of the fortunate fall or his attitude toward divorce, it is familiar enough and respected enough so that few critics can now praise the lyrics and dismiss the prophecies as incomprehensible. Indeed, two recent books are able to assume enough familiarity on the part of readers to approach other Romantic poets from the Blakean point of view, Harold Bloom in *The Visionary Company* (1961) and Bernard Blackstone in *The Consecrated Urn* (1959) – though this approach has been criticized by many (see, for instance, René Wellek in *Romanticism Reconsidered*, ed. Northrop Frye, 1963). Four decades after publishing the book that began modern Blake studies, Damon completed *A Blake Dictionary* (1964), a compendium of a lifetime of imaginative scholarship. The *Dictionary* is a personal book rather than an objective compilation of scholarly opinion – and Damon retains his earlier opinion of Blake's mysticism, notably in the article on "Mysticism" – but this book will take its place as one of the essential works that any student of Blake must consult.

2

Charles Lamb

By *George L. Barnett*
INDIANA UNIVERSITY

AND

Stuart M. Tave
UNIVERSITY OF CHICAGO

I. BIBLIOGRAPHIES*

T HE SIX-PAGE Lamb bibliography provided by Edmund Blunden for *The Cambridge Bibliography of English Literature* (1940) indicates the large amount of writing that has been done on Lamb. The items are conveniently grouped according to subject, but much that bears only indirectly on Lamb could have been omitted. More selective, thorough, and up to date—partly, no doubt, because of its indebtedness to the first edition of the present volume, to which it makes reference—is the bibliography compiled by Ian Jack for Volume X of the *Oxford History of English Literature* (1963). In addition to these, one should also consult the annual bibliographies in *PMLA*, *English Literary History* (1937–49), *Philological Quarterly* (1950–64), and *English Language Notes* (1965–). Since the founding in February 1935 of the Charles Lamb Society (London), the successive editors of the *C. L. S. Bulletin* have added from time to time a "Current Bibliography," which includes notes and criticism submitted to provincial papers.

Described as a "Collectors' Bibliography," cataloguing only first editions of Lamb's books and those containing contributions by him and his sister, *A Bibliography of the First Editions in Book Form of the Writings of Charles and Mary Lamb published prior to Charles Lamb's Death in 1834* was compiled by Luther S. Livingston for J. A. Spoor in 1903. The facsimiles of title pages and the descriptions of the various items, taken in part from Lamb's correspondence, make the book readable. Also fully annotated is the *Bibliography of the Writings of Charles and Mary Lamb, A Literary History*, compiled by J. C. Thomson (1908). It is complete and accurate to the date of Lamb's death and includes a few items after that date which possess unusual interest. It improves on Livingston's work in its inclusion of Lamb's contributions to periodicals.

Printed as a part of Benjamin E. Martin's topographical biography, *In the Footprints of Charles Lamb* (1890), is a classified bibliography by Ernest D. North. The addition of prices brought by

* Bibliography, Editions, and Biography Sections by George L. Barnett; Criticism Section by Stuart M. Tave.

the various first editions just prior to 1890 reveals the great increase in value attached to Lamb books over the past half century. North included editions, biographies, criticisms, and magazine articles published up to the date of compilation.

The convenient "Bibliographical List (1794–1834)," compiled by Thomas Hutchinson for his Oxford Standard Authors edition of *The Works of Charles and Mary Lamb* (1908), while not so completely annotated as Thomson's and Livingston's works, contains the essential information about first editions and periodical contributions. Of great interest to anyone concerned with the development of Lamb scholarship is a commentary called "Growth of the Body of Collected Works." Of course, this survey ends at 1908, and much has since been done.

Selective bibliographies of editions, biographies, and criticisms —both books and articles—may be found in many recent works, such as A. C. Ward's *The Frolic and the Gentle* (1934), E. C. Johnson's *Lamb Always Elia* (1935), W. D. Howe's *Charles Lamb and His Friends* (1944), R. L. Hine's *Charles Lamb and His Hertfordshire* (1949), and Ernest Bernbaum's *Guide through the Romantic Movement* (2d ed., 1949). "A Charles Lamb Library" (*CLSB*, 1962), containing first editions, association items, and books about Lamb is lovingly described by C. A. Prance.

There are also descriptions of special collections, such as *Charles Lamb: An Exhibition of Books and MSS in the Library of the University of Texas Commemorative of the Centenary of His Death* (1935), by R. H. Griffith, which discusses first editions and manuscript letters. J. S. Finch has described the Lamb manuscripts in the collection given to Princeton University by Charles A. Scribner in "Charles Lamb's 'Companionship . . . in Almost Solitude'" (*PULC*, 1945). He has also provided in the same periodical (1946) an elaborately annotated list of the printed works in this collection: "The Scribner Lamb Collection." Carl Woodring's scholarly survey, "Charles Lamb in the Harvard Library" (*HLB*, 1956) is the most extensive of this useful type of bibliographical work. Lamb items owned by the Carl H. Pforzheimer Library are noted among the several references to the Lambs in *Shelley and His Circle, 1773–1822* (1961), superbly edited in two volumes by Kenneth Cameron. Lamb's "Autobiography" is accurately transcribed for the first time from Upcott's autograph album, for which it was written, by David Erdman, who describes the manuscript now owned by the New York Public Library in "Reliques of the Contemporaries of William Upcott, 'Emperor of Autographs'" (*BNYPL*, 1960).

Manuscript essays and letters sold at Sotheby's in 1959 are described and purchasers and prices given in an unsigned article, "Charles Lamb in the Sales Rooms" (*CLSB*, 1960).

Many of John M. Turnbull's numerous articles and notes indicate that there is still bibliographical work to be done on Lamb: he points out an early appearance of "Charles Lamb's Lines 'In the Album of Catherine Orkney'" (*TLS*, 25 Dec. 1924); he notes "An Unrecorded Issue of Lamb's 'Album Verses'" (*TLS*, 20 March 1930; cf. DeV. Payen-Payne, *TLS*, 27 March 1930); he raises a textual question in "Cancels in 'Last Essays of Elia'" (*TLS*, 23 June 1932); from a study of the manuscript fragment of "A Quaker's Meeting," he deduces that part of the original was deleted and that "The Confessions of H. F. V. H. Delamore, Esq." was a filler ("An Elian Make-Weight," *N&Q*, 22 Jan. 1949); he determines that the *Reflector* was "The Originally Intended Destination of Lamb's 'Confessions of a Drunkard'" (*N&Q*, 6 Aug. 1949); and he cites the inclusion of a portion of Lamb's poem "Living Without God in the World" in a periodical, *Recreations in Agriculture*, as the "Earliest Disinterested Recognition of Charles Lamb as Poet" (*N&Q*, 18 Feb. 1950).

J. S. Finch notes marginalia in "Charles Lamb's Copy of the History of Philip de Commines with Autograph Notes by Lamb and Coleridge" (*PULC*, 1947). The exact publication dates of the "Garrick Extracts" and of eight other contributions to Hone's *Table Book* of 1827 have been determined for the first time in my article, "Dating Lamb's Contributions to the *Table Book*" (*PMLA*, 1945). Using a previously unpublished Lamb letter, together with bibliographical evidence, I show that "Charles Lamb's Part in an Edition of Hogarth" (*MLQ*, 1959) was responsible for the inclusion of one of Hazlitt's essays in the 1833 volume, as well as of his own well-known criticism. A valuable contribution to our knowledge of *Charles Lamb in America to 1848* (1963) is made by Wallace Nethery, who has revised for this volume material previously printed in booklets on his private press (1956, 1957, 1959, 1960) and in the *American Book Collector* (1960, 1961). Writing wittily, succinctly, and informatively, Nethery traces Lamb's literary associations with America, the sale in 1848 of the sixty books from Lamb's library, stage productions of *Mr. H.*, and his reputation as indicated by editions of his works and by reviews and commentary. A continuation of this excellent survey to the date of Barry Cornwall's *Memoir* may be found in the same bibliographer's "Charles Lamb in America 1849–1866" (*American Book Collector*, 1962).

II. EDITIONS

THE FIRST FIVE volumes of *The Works of Charles and Mary Lamb* (1903–05), edited by Edward Verrall Lucas, remain the standard edition. The last two, containing the letters, have been superseded by the separate edition of the correspondence (1935) noted below. The two volumes containing the letters were first revised for the 1912 edition, which, in its new format of six volumes, omitted the "Dramatic Specimens." In 1912 also, Volume I, "Miscellaneous Prose," and Volume II, "Elia and Last Essays," were reprinted separately with condensed notes. This standard edition included many additions to the canon of Lamb's prose and verse—some previously made by Lucas in article form—but it is difficult to fix the credit for some additions between him and William Macdonald, whose twelve-volume edition appeared at the same time, *The Works of Charles Lamb* (1903–04). Like Lucas, and working independently of him, he ascribed several short pieces of prose and verse on the evidence of style and manner. Most of the ascriptions of both editors have been treated with caution by later editors. One, a short piece of prose entitled "London Fogs," was subsequently found printed over Lamb's signature in the *Examiner* by John M. Turnbull (*N&Q*, 23 Aug. 1947), but no such definite disposition has been made of the other ascriptions, for the most part brief and unimportant.

Lucas' edition was the culmination of a long process of successive editions with a gradual accumulation of uncollected and unidentified items. Lamb's friend Thomas Noon Talfourd edited *The Works of Charles Lamb* (1840), which included his earlier *Letters of Charles Lamb with a Sketch of His Life* (1837). Aside from letters, he merely collected the contents of Lamb's *Works* (1818), *Elia* (1823), *Last Essays of Elia* (1833), and *Album Verses* (1830), plus the ten poems added by Moxon in his *Poetical Works of Charles Lamb* (1836). Moxon had previously published Lamb's *Prose Works* in three volumes (1835). In 1850 Talfourd published his *Works* in four volumes, of which the first two were new editions of the *Letters* and his *Final Memorials of Charles Lamb: Consisting Chiefly of Letters Not Before Published* (1848).

J. E. Babson reawakened interest in Lamb's works by reprinting for the first time from periodicals a large number of poems, prose pieces, and fourteen letters: *Eliana: Being the Hitherto Uncollected Writings of Charles Lamb* (1864). Including Babson's additions, as well as some other new material, *The Complete Correspondence and Works of Charles Lamb* (1870) was edited by Thomas Purnell, aided by W. C. Hazlitt, who concentrated on the restoration of many suppressed passages to the letters, although he is not named on the title page because he resigned before publication. This is a reissue of the only volume published of George A. Sala's edition by the same name (1868), with the addition of three volumes and the substitution of a thirty-page introduction by Purnell for Sala's essay, "On the Genius of Charles Lamb." Another miscellany, like that of Babson, is W. C. Hazlitt's *Mary and Charles Lamb: Poems, Letters, and Remains* (1874), which includes the list of books sold from Lamb's library. In the same year, another of the great recoverers of uncollected poems and prose pieces, R. H. Shepherd, published his edition of *The Complete Works in Prose and Verse of Charles Lamb* (1874), one feature of which was the reproduction of the original text, utilizing, for example, the *London Magazine* text for the Elia essays. Shepherd, a noted bibliographer, had edited in 1872 *Poetry for Children* by Charles and Mary Lamb, a collection of previously printed poems. His 1878 edition reprinted the complete contents of the original volume, a copy of which had just been discovered in Australia, together with several other poems collected here for the first time. Also gathering various prose pieces and verses, as well as adding forty new letters, Percy Fitzgerald edited *The Life, Letters and Writings of Charles Lamb* (1875). But the greatest and most highly respected of the Victorian editors of Lamb was Alfred Ainger, whose collected *Works of Charles Lamb* (1883–88) was the standard edition until superseded by those of Lucas and Macdonald. Ainger judiciously rejected many of the pieces, both prose and verse, conjecturally attributed to Lamb by previous editors, adding only a few items himself. He was the first editor to collect Mary's share in *Mrs. Leicester's School* and *Tales from Shakespear*.

The ascription of new items to the canon of Lamb's work has continued in the twentieth century, after the Lucas edition of the *Works* appeared. Eleven poems and short critical papers were reprinted from the *London Magazine* and assigned to Lamb by Bertram Dobell in his *Sidelights on Charles Lamb* (1903); some have not been generally accepted. The usual inability to agree on the ascription of new items is pointed up by William Macdonald's discussion in "Lamb Trouvailles" (*Athenaeum*, 8 Aug. 1903). Lane Cooper suggested the inclusion in the canon of an anonymous passage in the *Indicator* of 1821 in "Lamb on Wordsworth's 'To

Joanna' " (*N&Q*, 22 March 1913). Walter Jerrold likewise adduced no proof but simply Elian characteristics for his opinion that several anonymous prose essays in the *Laughing Philosopher* of 1835 might be Lamb's ("Charles Lamb and the Laughing Philosopher," *Cornhill Mag.*, 1924). More reliable evidence is presented succinctly by John M. Turnbull for the ascription to Lamb of a letter to the *Champion* signed "J. D." in reply to Lamb's essay "On the Melancholy of Tailors," published therein one week previously ("A Retort to Elia," *RES*, 1927). On the sole basis of style and general likeness, Edmund Blunden reprinted in his *Leigh Hunt's 'Examiner' Examined* (1928) four essays of minor interest which one is tempted to accept even on this tenuous reasoning. Another discovery by E. V. Lucas was that of the album verse to Frances Barrow referred to in Letter No. 981 of his 1935 edition ("Charles Lamb Again," *TLS*, 8 May 1937). "An Unprinted Poem by Charles Lamb" (*HLQ*, 1943) presented the text of "The Boy, the Mother, and the Butterfly," which I discovered. A previously unpublished acrostic to Harriet Isola is given in my *Charles Lamb: The Evolution of Elia* (1964). Another short poem is given by Turnbull in "Two Lamb Poems" (*TLS*, 5 Feb. 1949), where he also adds to his earlier note on "Charles Lamb's Lines 'In the Album of Catherine Orkney' " (*TLS*, 25 Dec. 1924). "A Forgotten Skit by Lamb" (*TLS*, 9 Feb. 1951) reprints from the *London Magazine* of November 1823 a letter to the editor entitled "Cockney Latin" and signed "Philopatris Londiniensis," with convincing evidence by C. A. Prance that Lamb was the author. Pointing out the existence in manuscript of "An Unpublished Review by Charles Lamb" (*MLQ*, 1956), I have recently added to the Lamb canon a lengthy criticism of Hazlitt's *Table Talk*, together with a discussion of the reason it was never printed. In "A Disquisition on Punch and Judy Attributed to Charles Lamb" (*HLQ*, 1962) I recovered the text of another major essay from the *Monthly Repository* (1837) and adduced evidence in favor of accepting its attribution therein to Lamb.

Numerous brief notes include annotations that must be considered by editors of Lamb's essays and letters. Among these writers, and serving here to exemplify the best, is Turnbull, who, besides his bibliographical work and discovery of additions to the Lamb canon, has made identifications and critical annotations that supplement the notes in Lucas' edition. In the former category is "Lamb's 'Mr. Sea-gull' " (*TLS*, 6 Sept. 1928), identified as Scargill (further described by Blunden, *TLS*, 20 Sept. 1928). Lamb's "pastoral M . . ." of his "South-Sea House" is asserted to be Thomas Maynard in "An Elian Annotation" (*N&Q*, 14 Dec. 1946);

prompted by this solution, W. H. Phillips borrowed Turnbull's title the following year to present possible identifications for "old surly M . . .," the father of "pastoral M . . ." (*N&Q*, 15 Feb. 1947). "An Elian Annotation" is also the title for an earlier note by Turnbull, showing the source of the story near the conclusion of "A Complaint of the Decay of Beggars . . ." to be the "Miscellanea" column of the *Champion* for 4 June 1815 (*N&Q*, 27 Sept. 1924). Two less important notes by Turnbull are "Wordsworth's Part in the Production of Lamb's 'Specimens'" (*N&Q*, 18 Feb. 1928) and "Wordsworth's 'Flying Tailor'" (*TLS*, 24 Oct. 1929). Procter's debt to Lamb for his method of interpreting portraits of authors by their written works is pointed out by Turnbull in "Charles Lamb— Some Sidelights from Barry Cornwall" (*Bookman* [London], 1930). Lamb's method of personalizing the experiences of others is detailed and exemplified in "A Matter-of-lie Man" (*N&Q*, 26 May 1928). Replying to a query by D. S. Adams ("Lamb's Multiple Portrait," *N&Q*, 28 Dec. 1946) regarding Lamb's sitting for a "whole series of British admirals," Turnbull adduces facts to prove that Lamb was simply substituting himself in his characteristic manner of exaggeration (*N&Q*, 6 March 1948).

The best inexpensive and reliable edition of the essays and poems is *The Works of Charles Lamb*, edited by Thomas Hutchinson in two volumes in 1908 and in one volume in 1924. A well-edited selection of essays and letters is J. Milton French's edition of *Charles Lamb: Essays and Letters* (1937); this has a good introduction, classified according to "life," "friends," and so on. An attractive two-volume edition of the essays is Robert Lynd's *Collected Essays of Charles Lamb* (1929), with an introduction by Lynd, notes by Macdonald, and drawings by Brock.

Separate editions of *Elia* and of *Last Essays of Elia* are rightly said to be "innumerable." Although *Elia* (1823), the first collected edition, was not immediately successful, from the time of the publication of *Last Essays* (1833) to the end of the century the essays were reprinted in some fifty editions. Similarly innumerable are the *Tales from Shakespear*, of which one notable edition was that by F. J. Furnivall in 1901. Eight *Tales* were published separately, according to David Foxon's "The Chapbook Editions of the Lambs' *Tales from Shakespear*" (*BC*, 1957). His scholarly examination of extant copies includes the observations that "these single tales are probably the greatest rarities of more recent English literature" and "the trend of evidence is that the collected *Tales* preceded the chapbooks." Separate essays have also been issued, particularly "A Dissertation upon Roast Pig," "Detached Thoughts on Books and

Reading," and "Old China." One such edition of a single essay, completely annotated although without any mention of the manuscript or revisions therein, is F. D. Mackinnon's edition of *The Old Benchers of the Inner Temple* (1927). Lamb's longer works have likewise been separately edited: *The Adventures of Ulysses* by A. Lang in 1890 and by E. A. Gardner in 1921; *Specimens of the English Dramatic Poets Who Lived About the Time of Shakespeare* with the *Extracts from the Garrick Plays* by I. Gollancz in 1893 and by J. D. Campbell in 1907. Lamb's essays on the drama have been edited by Percy Fitzgerald, *The Art of the Stage as Set Out in Lamb's Dramatic Essays* (1885); by Brander Matthews, *The Dramatic Essays of Charles Lamb* (1892); and by Rudolf Dircks, *Plays and Dramatic Essays by Charles Lamb* (1893). Selections of Lamb's criticism, taken from his essays and letters, were edited by E. M. W. Tillyard under the title *Lamb's Criticism* (1923), with an introduction praising "Lamb as a Literary Critic."

The latest separate and most nearly complete edition of Lamb's extensive correspondence is *The Letters of Charles Lamb, to which are added those of his sister, Mary Lamb*, edited by E. V. Lucas in three volumes (1935). Lucas has been justly praised for his extensive annotation in addition to his notable accomplishment of bringing together for the first time the texts of over one thousand letters, and this is still the standard edition of the correspondence. However, it is unfortunate that for more than half of the letters he failed to note the source of his text. Moreover, this edition must be used with extreme caution, for it is full of errors of every conceivable —and inconceivable—type. For a complete discussion with numerous examples of these errors, see my article, "A Critical Analysis of the Lucas Edition of Lamb's Letters" (*MLQ*, 1948) which concludes that "we do not yet possess a definitive edition of the letters of Charles Lamb." Included in this article is a summary of the history of the publication of Lamb's correspondence, a more extensive discussion of which may be found in Richard Garnett's introduction to the beautiful Boston Bibliophile Society edition of the *Letters of Charles Lamb*, edited by Henry H. Harper (1905) in five volumes, Volume I containing numerous facsimiles of letters. This edition was motivated by the fact that no complete and unexpurgated edition of the letters had been given to the public. My "Corrections in the Text of Lamb's Letters" (*HLQ*, 1955) supplies all the significant corrections and omissions for the texts of the extensive collection of Lamb's letters now at the Henry E. Huntington Library. Similarly, P. F. Morgan made some corrections and additions to Lucas' text of ten letters in the John Forster Collection at the Victoria and Albert Museum in his note "On Some Letters of Charles Lamb" (*N&Q*, Dec. 1956). The same investigator printed a selection of notes, largely on the letters, made by "Alexander Dyce on Charles Lamb" (*N&Q*, March 1957) in his copies of Lamb's works (now also at the same museum).

Because Mary Lamb was still alive in 1837 when Talfourd published the first edition of the correspondence, *The Letters of Charles Lamb with a Sketch of His Life*, he felt obliged to omit such portions as referred to the tragedy of 1796 or alluded to mental afflictions, as well as references to still-living members of the Lamb circle who might have taken offense. Although credited with being the first to introduce the general public to the charm of Lamb's letters and personality, Talfourd has been criticized for a scrupulousness that to some seems mistaken, for example, the omission of strong expletives. After Mary's death in 1847 he compensated somewhat by printing some previously omitted passages in his *Final Memorials of Charles Lamb; Consisting Chiefly of Letters Not Before Published* (1848), later incorporated into *Memoirs of Charles Lamb*, edited and annotated by Percy Fitzgerald (1868). However, Talfourd failed to indicate where the restored passages should be inserted! Although W. C. Hazlitt recognized the shortcomings of Talfourd's edition in his *Mary and Charles Lamb: Poems, Letters, and Remains* (1874) and complained in his *The Lambs: Their Lives, Their Friends, and Their Correspondence* (1897) that no edition to date was satisfactory when compared with the original manuscripts, neither his first texts nor those in his revision of Talfourd's work for the Bohn Library (*Letters of Charles Lamb*, 1886) avoided the chief fault of all editions of Lamb's letters: reliance on an earlier transcription instead of on the original manuscripts. Hazlitt added twenty-two letters in *The Lambs* and another twelve in *Lamb and Hazlitt—Further Letters and Records* (1900). The contribution of the successive editors lay mainly in adding to the corpus, but they all took liberties with the text. Ainger published a large number of letters for the first time in 1888 and more still in his de luxe edition of 1900, but the original manuscripts of some of these letters still show light, vertical pencil lines drawn through the center of passages that he omitted—for reasons of delicacy or on grounds of insignificance—but without indicating the omission. Macdonald continued many of the faulty and incomplete texts in his *Works* (1903–04). The attempt of the Bibliophile Society, therefore, to base a new edition on the original manuscripts was fully justifiable, and it is unfortunate that Lucas failed to follow the example and perpetuated errors of transcription and omission, in many instances when the original was available to him.

In preparing his 1935 edition of Lamb's correspondence, Lucas took into account most of the articles and notes that had previously given the texts of uncollected or unprinted letters. He recognized particularly the work of Gertrude A. Anderson, whose research had produced texts, as in "Some Unpublished Letters of Lamb" (*London Mercury*, 1922), and corrections, as in "On the Dating of Lamb's Letters" (*London Mercury*, 1928). Her edition of *The Letters of Thomas Manning* was published (1925) by P. P. Howe, who later, in reviewing Lucas' edition, praised her while regretting Lucas' failure to give the source of his text for every letter ("Lamb's Letters Complete," *London Mercury*, 1935); on another occasion Howe corrected one of Lucas' notes ("Lamb and Hazlitt," *TLS*, 26 Sept. 1935). Many other scholars have noted errors in Lucas' text as well as the existence of letters not therein included. Lucas himself contributed "An Unpublished Letter of Charles Lamb" (*TLS*, 13 Feb. 1937), the contents of which he says weakens the accuracy of one of the notes in his edition. John H. Birss pointed out a sales catalogue description of "A New Letter of Charles Lamb" (*N&Q*, 16 Oct. 1937); I printed the complete text of this letter with a discussion in "Charles Lamb to John Britton: An Unpublished Letter" (*MLQ*, 1952). A sentence, omitted in Lucas' version of Letter No. 692, is restored from a sales catalogue transcription by "Olybrius" ("Complete Text of a Letter of Charles Lamb," *N&Q*, 8 Jan. 1938). One of the most important additions to the correspondence was made by M. A. DeW. Howe, who published a long, privately owned letter ("Lamb to Hazlitt: A New-Found Letter," *Spectator*, 5 Aug. 1938). "Olybrius & Co." printed from a sales catalogue what was mistakenly called "An Uncollected Letter of Lamb" (*N&Q*, 17 Dec. 1938); V. Rendall pointed out ("An Uncollected Letter of Lamb," *N&Q*, 28 Jan. 1939) that this had been printed—although only in part—as No. 914 in the Lucas edition. Several errors in the Lucas edition were detected by E. G. B. in "Notes on 'The Letters of Charles and Mary Lamb'" (*N&Q*, 5 Oct. 1941). John H. Birss reprinted an uncollected letter from Curtis Guild's *A Chat About Celebrities* (1897) in his article "Lamb on Revisions: An Uncollected Letter" (*N&Q*, 7 Nov. 1942). "B" commented on ten letters in the Lucas edition in "Letters of Charles Lamb" (*N&Q*, 24 April 1943). Discussing "Charles Lamb's 'Companionship . . . in Almost Solitude'" (*PULC*, 1945), J. S. Finch included no less than eight previously unpublished letters to Maria Fryer. Thomas O. Mabbott noted discrepancies between the Lucas texts and a sales catalogue description in the dating of two letters ("Notes on Two Letters of Charles Lamb," *N&Q*, 28 July 1945). In collaboration with Birss, the same commentator had printed five letters ("Some Uncollected Letters of Charles Lamb," *N&Q*, 1933); one of these was apparently not included by Lucas in his edition two years later, and another is printed under a different date, 16 May 1827, which I prove to be "The Correct Date for a Lamb Letter" (*N&Q*, May 1962). L. E. Holman included in his *Lamb's Barbara S*—— (1935) the complete text of a letter to Miss Kelly, only a small part of which was printed by Lucas under the label "Fragment" (No. 572); Holman's transcription, however, differs slightly in wording from the original manuscript. Lucas' designation of Procter as the addressee of No. 386 is proved erroneous by Wallace Nethery in "Charles Lamb to Janus Weathercock" (*N&Q*, May 1962).

Since the first edition of this book appeared, many new letters by Charles and Mary Lamb, mostly recent acquisitions by major libraries but occasionally holdings of long standing or in private collections, have been published for the first time. A letter to Dodwell and Chambers, East India House colleagues, of 26 August 1819, is utilized by Carl Woodring in "Lamb Takes a Holiday" (*HLB*, 1960). In *Charles Lamb: The Evolution of Elia*, I give the texts of several previously unpublished letters, and another letter is printed for the first time in connection with my discussion of "Charles Lamb's Part in an Edition of Hogarth" (*MLQ*, 1959). John Barker prints three new letters from the Lambs in discussing "Some Early Correspondence of Sarah Stoddart and the Lambs" (*HLQ*, 1960). T. C. Skeat prints Lamb's part of a joint letter with Mary to Mrs. Morgan (21 August 1815) and the extant portion of a letter from Lamb to Morgan (9 July 1816) in "Letters of Charles and Mary Lamb and Coleridge" (*BMQ*, 1962), where he elucidates references and presents photographic plates. Some duplication of effort appears in "Two Hitherto Unpublished Letters of Charles and Mary Lamb to the Morgans" (*ES*, 1963), by W. Braekman, who discusses the same two letters without making reference to Skeat's article. However, Braekman transcribes Mary's part of the joint letter as well as the portions Skeat prints; but differences in the wording of Lamb's part make both transcriptions suspect. Braekman's ampler commentary complements that of Skeat. Of less importance to Lamb's biography and literary career than these recently printed letters, but yet contributing to a fuller knowledge, are "Three New

Letters of Charles Lamb" (*HLQ*, 1963), wherein David Green gives texts of letters to Basil Montagu (30 March 1814), Charles C. Clarke (15 April 1828), and T. N. Talfourd (6 June 1831).

III. BIOGRAPHIES

The *Life of Charles Lamb* in two volumes by E. V. Lucas (1905) remains the standard biography but is no longer in print. The revised fifth edition of 1921 corrected some errors and added new passages; on the other hand, it omitted the illustrations and four appendixes. Additional data on Lamb's life were interspersed in the notes to his 1935 edition of the *Letters*. "E. V." is outstanding among those who have written on Lamb. Freed from the restrictions that had hampered Talfourd in utilizing letters and in treating certain biographical aspects, and exceeding Ainger in his concern with annotation, Lucas set out to write as complete a biography as possible, quoting Lamb's reported conversation and written words so extensively that Lamb, to an extent, is his own biographer. He also explored periodicals for uncollected writings by Lamb. In the dual capacity of biographer and editor of the works and letters, Lucas performed an immense service. The passage of time has seen the emergence of new facts which will serve to correct and enlarge his biography when a new one is written. Perhaps a new biographer, trained in scholarship and methods of research, could supplement the assembling and annotating of materials with more critical comment, of which Lucas was sparing.

The accumulation of the facts of Lamb's life has been a process of adding details rather than of momentous reinterpretations, and it is a process that continues. Because of Lamb's self-revelatory tendency both in his essays and in his letters, the general outlines of his life have been known since the publication in the *New Monthly Magazine* (1835) of "An Autobiographical Sketch," written in 1827. Leigh Hunt's *Lord Byron and Some of His Contemporaries* (1828) included a memoir of Lamb that was later published in Hunt's *Autobiography* (1850). Thomas Noon Talfourd's *Letters of Charles Lamb* (1837) contained a "Sketch of Lamb's Life"; as R. S.

Newdick concludes in *The First Life and Letters of Charles Lamb—A Study of Talfourd as Editor and Biographer* (1935), this was an essentially accurate presentation. Talfourd's twenty-year intimacy with Lamb is evident in the sympathetic approach. Reviews of editions of Lamb's works frequently printed some anecdotes and facts for the first time. Thus, an unsigned review of Moxon's one-volume *Works of Charles Lamb, Including His Life and Letters*, attributed to George H. Lewes, gave readers of the *British Quarterly Review* (1848) the first public disclosure of the tragic murder of Lamb's mother. This article was reprinted under its original running title, "Charles Lamb—His Genius and Writing" as a special supplement to the *Charles Lamb Society Bulletin* (1963). A sixty-five-page biography appeared in *Love's Labour Not Lost* (1863), a portion of which was reprinted as *Recollections of Charles Lamb* (1927), by George Daniel.

The next important, and much-quoted, book-length revelation was the pleasantly written *Charles Lamb: A Memoir* (1866), by Bryan Waller Procter ("Barry Cornwall"). Like Talfourd's "Sketch," this memoir was an informal, leisured presentation of Lamb rather than a documented study. Written when Procter was seventy-nine and Lamb's death thirty-odd years in the past, the book calmly recalls the last seventeen or eighteen years of Lamb's life, when Procter was an intimate friend. He, like Lucas, lets Lamb tell his own story in extensive quotation. Carlyle, whose strictures on Lamb are often recalled, wrote words of high praise to Procter for this book. Procter later added to his reminiscences of Lamb in *An Autobiographical Fragment and Biographical Notes, with Personal Sketches of Contemporaries, Unpublished Lyrics, and Letters of Literary Friends* (1877). Another work in the same vein as the *Memoir* is *Charles Lamb—His Friends, His Haunts, and His Books* (1866), by Percy Fitzgerald, who added some new letters and a rather general commentary. The following year saw the appearance of W. C. Hazlitt's "Charles Lamb: Gleanings After His Biographers" (*Macmillan's Mag.*, 1867).

Still a good biography with sound critical commentary is Alfred Ainger's *Charles Lamb*, published in the English Men of Letters series in 1882, as well as in Volume VIII of his edition of Lamb's *Works*. In 1897 W. C. Hazlitt again added some letters and facts in *The Lambs: Their Lives, Their Friends, and Their Correspondence*. Shortly after the turn of the century, the development of a more scholarly approach was manifested by a French biography: *Charles Lamb: sa vie et ses œuvres* (1904), by Jules Derocquigny, a penetrating and thorough interpreter. In the following year Walter

Jerrold published *Charles Lamb* (1905), a good introduction to the subject, to which he added some facts in a later study, *Thomas Hood and Charles Lamb* (1930). A. H. Thompson's essay for *The Cambridge History of English Literature* (1915) is sympathetic, with emphasis on the biographical aspects.

The 1930's, embracing the centenary of Lamb's death, saw the appearance of several articles and books, some of which are discussed below in the section on criticism. For the most part, they add no facts and give no reinterpretation. F. V. Morley's *Lamb Before Elia* (1932) utilizes a multiplicity of quotation to promote the thesis that the circumstances of Lamb's life, rather than his temperament, determined his interests.

Primarily biography, *The Lambs* (1945), by Katherine Anthony, has been severely criticized as inaccurate in its picture of pre-Victorian England, as adding nothing to our knowledge of the Lambs, and as being confusing and repelling in its psychological and pathological hypotheses. Although she focuses her psychoanalysis on Mary, the Freudian author partially justifies her plural title in a factually baseless attempt to find an unrealized romantic attachment between Lamb and his adopted daughter, Emma Isola, an attempt anticipated by Stephen Southwold ("Neil Bell") in his novel *So Perish the Roses* (1940). Here the suggestion is more excusable but still unsupported by the evidence, as demonstrated in a carefully documented refutation by Ernest C. Ross in his *Charles Lamb and Emma Isola* (Elian Booklet No. 1 of the Charles Lamb Society, 1950). Another scholarly account of this friendship is presented by Finch in "Charles Lamb's 'Companionship . . . in Almost Solitude' " (*PULC*, 1945).

In addition to Nethery's book, *Charles Lamb in America to 1848* (1963), discussed under "Bibliography," two other books — partially biographical in nature and noted also under "Criticism" — have appeared in the sixties. The importance of academic exercises, office employment, reading, conversation, and letters is considered in my *Charles Lamb: The Evolution of Elia* (1964), to show the development of the essayist and the essays. In Japan, Tsutomu Fukuda has treated several aspects of Lamb's life and personality in the second half of *A Study of Charles Lamb's Essays of Elia* (1964), much of which is revised from earlier appearances in periodicals. Written in English, this book devotes Part 1 to a meticulous analysis of Lamb's style.

Besides the books and articles listed above which are specifically concerned with Charles and Mary Lamb, there are numerous sources of biographical information in the recollections of their friends and contemporaries. Some were published during the Lambs' lifetime: Thomas Hood's "Literary Reminiscences" in *Hood's Own* (1822) was reprinted by Walter Jerrold in *Thomas Hood and Charles Lamb* (above). A description of Lamb in the spring of 1825 is furnished in "An Evening with Charles Lamb and Coleridge" (*Monthly Repository*, 1835), by Sarah Flower Adams, author of "Nearer, My God, to Thee."

Among the obituaries, some of which are very informative, may be listed W. Maginn's "Charles Lamb, Esq." (*Fraser's Mag.*, 1835); Procter's "Charles Lamb" (*Athenaeum*, 3 Jan. 1835) and "Recollections of Charles Lamb" (*Athenaeum*, 24 Jan. and 7 Feb. 1835); G. Dyer's "Memoir of Lamb" (*Gentleman's Mag.*, 1835); Leigh Hunt's eulogy (*London Jour.*, 7 Jan. 1835); and Barron Field's "Charles Lamb, Esq." (*Annual Biography and Obituary*, 1836).

From the date of his death until the end of the century, references to Lamb were numerous in the published memoirs of his associates. N. P. Willis tells of him in *Pencillings by the Way* (1835) and was perhaps the author of an important review in the *New York Mirror* (1832), which I rediscovered and discussed in "First American Review of Charles Lamb" (*PMLA*, 1946); in this connection, Stephen Larrabee pointed out three, equally favorable though brief, earlier comments in "Some American Notices of Lamb in 1828" (*PMLA*, 1959). Thomas De Quincey reprinted under "Literary Reminiscences" in his *Works* (1851) his "Recollections of Charles Lamb," published earlier in Tait's *Edinburgh Magazine* (1838). *The Memoirs of Charles Mathews, Comedian* (1839) devoted six pages to Lamb. Benjamin Robert Haydon's *Life, from His Autobiography and Journals* (1853–54) recounted, among other things, the immortal dinner party; Haydon's *Correspondence and Table-Talk* (1876) also contains references to the Lambs. P. G. Patmore included "Charles Lamb" in the first volume of *My Friends and Acquaintance* (1854), Charles R. Leslie remembered Lamb in *Autobiographical Recollections* (1860), and Thomas Westwood contributed "Recollections of Charles Lamb" (*N&Q*, 22 Sept. 1866) and "Charles Lamb: Supplementary Reminiscences" (*N&Q*, 20 May 1882).

Of primary importance as a source of information about Lamb and his contemporaries is Henry Crabb Robinson's *Diary*, edited in 1866 by Thomas Sadler. Edith J. Morley's various editions of Robinson's commentaries should also be consulted: *Blake, Coleridge, Wordsworth, Lamb . . . Selections from the Remains of H. C.*

Robinson (1922); *Correspondence of Henry Crabb Robinson with the Wordsworth Circle (1808–1866)* (1927); and *Henry Crabb Robinson on Books and Their Writers* (1938).

The last part of the nineteenth century produced additional reminiscences of the Lambs. *A Book of Memories of Great Men and Women of the Age, from Personal Acquaintance* (1871) was written by Samuel Carter Hall, who also mentioned Lamb in his *Retrospect of a Long Life* (1883). *An Old Man's Diary, Forty Years Ago* (1871–72), by John Payne Collier, recalled the years 1832–33. "About Charles Lamb" appeared anonymously in *Temple Bar* (1872), and an account of a conversation in 1876 with Lamb's fellow clerk was given in "Concerning Charles Lamb" (*Scribner's Monthly*, 1876), by Joseph H. Twichell. Firsthand *Recollections of Writers* (1878), by Charles and Mary Cowden Clarke, and the latter's *My Long Life* (1896) contain numerous references to Lamb. Anecdotes by an East India House colleague were reported in "Charles Lamb" (*Macmillan's Mag.*, 1879), by Algernon Black. Thomas Carlyle's unfavorable opinion of Lamb as a person was publicized in his *Reminiscences*, edited by Charles E. Norton (1881; see also below under "Criticism"). Another report of a visit to Lamb and some of his opinions was given in "Charles Lamb at Home" (*N&Q*, 1 April 1882), by J. F. Russel.

The best collection of contemporary comments, some of which are not easily available in original form, is *Charles Lamb: His Life Recorded by His Contemporaries* (1934), edited by Edmund Blunden. By assembling the observations on Lamb by men of his own time, Blunden has performed a service that complements that of Samuel M. Rich in *The Elian Miscellany* (1931). Rich, the founder-editor of the *Charles Lamb Society Bulletin* from 1935 to 1947, made a useful collection of excerpts of commentary, verse, and anecdote found among the ephemerae of old and modern newspapers, periodicals, and books. Of interest to the casual reader, it preserves much that would otherwise be difficult to find. Blunden, arranging his work chronologically and not according to theme and form as in Rich's compilation, created a biography through the eyes of Lamb's contemporaries, which E. V. Lucas called "one of the most understanding and beautiful books in the language." A similar work is E. H. Lacon Watson's *Contemporary Comments: 19th-Century Writers As They Appeared to Each Other* (1931). An early collection of extracts from Talfourd, Procter, De Quincey, Patmore, and others is Edward T. Mason's *Personal Traits of British Authors* (1885).

One aspect of Lamb's biography that has received considerable attention is his relations with his friends. "Charles Lamb and His Friends" served both De Quincey and G. H. Lewes as a title for their reviews of Talfourd's *Final Memorials* (1848) in the *North British Review* (1848) and the *British Quarterly Review* (1848), respectively. John Dennis used the same title for an essay in *Fraser's Magazine* (1882). J. R. Rees, author of several contributions to *Notes and Queries* concerning various of Lamb's associates, published *With Elia and His Friends* (1903). Alvin Waggoner's "The Lawyer Friends of Charles Lamb" (*American Law Rev.*, 1916), states: "No other figure in English literature is so closely associated with law and lawyers as Charles Lamb." A brief article examining this aspect further is "Charles Lamb and His Lawyer Friends," by J. S. H. (*Law Times*, 1920). *Literary Friendships in the Age of Wordsworth* (1932), an anthology selected and edited by R. C. Bald, assembles material that shows among other things Lamb's strong influence on Hazlitt and the high quality of Lamb's criticism. *Charles Lamb and His Contemporaries* (1933), the publication of a series of lectures delivered at Cambridge in 1932 by Edmund Blunden, reveals Lamb progressively in an enthusiastic manner without presenting any new facts. Similarly, *Charles Lamb and His Friends* (1944), by Will D. Howe, is a readable summary of the various aspects of Lamb's career without offering anything new, although Chapter v, "And Friends," consists of a useful series of thumbnail sketches of some thirty acquaintances.

In addition to these general studies of Lamb's relations with friends, numerous investigations have been made of his association with a particular friend. As early as August 1836, Walter Wilson discussed his own friendship with Lamb, although his essay was not published until Lucas edited it as "Recollections of Charles Lamb (From a Contemporary Manuscript)" (*London Mercury*, 1934). John Forster, a congenial acquaintance of Lamb's later years, wrote on Lamb and Coleridge in "Charles Lamb—His Last Words on Coleridge" (*New Monthly Mag.*, 1835). An excellent account of this friendship from beginning to end was given by Edith C. Johnson in "Lamb and Coleridge" (*A Sch*, 1937). "Lamb and Hood" is the title of a chapter in Mary Balmanno's book, *Pen and Pencil* (1858). Lamb's personal acquaintance with Procter was discussed by James T. Fields in "Barry Cornwall and Some of His Friends," *Yesterdays with Authors* (1871). A detailed study of the relations between *Charles Lamb and the Lloyds* (1898) was made by Lucas. W. C. Hazlitt added to his collections of records *Lamb and Hazlitt— Further Letters and Records* (1900).

The twentieth century has seen continued interest in detailed studies of Lamb and some of his close acquaintances. Occasionally, as in *William Harrison Ainsworth and His Friends* (1911), by S. M. Ellis, the emphasis is not on Lamb. Orlo Williams reflects the importance of friendship with Lamb in *Lamb's Friend the Census Taker: Life and Letters of John Rickman* (1912). R. W. King's article, "Charles Lamb, Cary and the London Magazine" (*Nineteenth Century*, 1923), gives the particulars of Cary's life and aspects of his association with Lamb. The same author makes numerous references to Lamb in *The Translator of Dante* (1925), discussing the association particularly in his chapter "The British Museum: Cary and Lamb (1825–1834)."

Dudley Wright's "Charles Lamb and George Dyer" (*English Rev.*, 1924) supplies information and anecdotes about Dyer's friendship with Lamb. George Dyer is also mentioned, along with George Daniel, George Dailey, and George Dawe, in Gertrude A. Anderson's "Lamb and the Two G. D.'s" (*London Mercury*, 1925), where some new letters are printed. Katherine A. Esdaile discusses the identity of Philo-Elia in "Lamb and Geo. Dawe: A Postscript" (*London Mercury*, 1929). Lamb's debt to his friends for ideas is pointed up by Turnbull's methodical and convincing study of "Charles Lamb and Griffiths Wainewright" (*Bookman* [London], 1925). Earlier, Turnbull had focused on the same notorious *London Magazine* staffer, who turned forger and poisoner, as the source of "Lamb's 'Poor Relations'" (*Bookman* [London], 1924), anticipating by several years the same identification by Walter Jerrold in his *Thomas Hood and Charles Lamb* (above). A complete account of the relations between Lamb and Leigh Hunt is given in Nettie S. Tillett's "Elia and *The Indicator* (*SAQ*, 1934). In "Lamb and Manning" (*TLS*, 31 Aug. 1946) Edith C. Johnson summarized the facts about Manning, while noting that no full-length biography of him has been written and that his influence on Lamb was of prime significance. The same author had earlier pointed up this significance by including a chapter on "Thomas Manning: Friend of Elia" in her *Lamb Always Elia* (1935). More recently, Victor Allan has given a detailed account from a historian's point of view of Manning's only claim to fame, "A Journey to Lhasa in 1811" (*History Today*, 1962). Vera Watson's "Thomas Noon Talfourd and His Friends" (*TLS*, 20 and 27 Apr. 1956) contains allusions to Lamb and quotations from copies of two letters probably written by Lamb to Talfourd. In "Charles Lamb and the Button Family: An Unpublished Poem and Letter" (*HLQ*, 1956), I reveal still another friendly association, while identifying two "scrap books" mentioned by Lucas and printing for the first time a newly discovered poem and letter written by Lamb. In "Charles Lamb and Thomas Hood: Records of a Friendship" (*Tennessee Studies in Literature*, 1964), Peter F. Morgan gives a thoroughgoing "unvarnished factual account" of this friendship.

Besides Lamb's multitudinous friendships, various other phases of his life and character have served as subjects for research. Numerous books on his school, Christ's Hospital, include references to his attendance or reprint his "Recollections." "Elia and Christ's Hospital" (*E&S*, 1937), by Edmund Blunden, himself a member of the Amicable Society of Blues, deals with contemporary conditions, the masters, and his schoolmates. Other places that have acquired a charm from Lamb's presence have also attracted writers. A pleasant book, enhanced with illustrations by Railton and Fulleylove, is B. E. Martin's *In the Footprints of Charles Lamb* (1891), a topographical biography mostly in Lamb's own words, reminiscent of places he visited and buildings he called home. The handsomely illustrated *Charles Lamb and His Hertfordshire* (1949), by Reginald L. Hine, is a more thoroughgoing and readable organization and interpretation of his associations with this area than is William Graveson's earlier book on the same subject, *Charles and Mary Lamb in Hertfordshire* (1925). A different scene is explored by H. F. Cox in "Charles Lamb at Edmonton" (*Dublin Univ. Mag.*, 1878). Sydney Turner refers to "Old Benchers" among other literary associations in "Some Lost Literary Landmarks in the Temple" (*QR*, 1960).

Lamb's thirty-three years of service in the East India House have, naturally, interested researchers. In a series of ten articles in *Notes and Queries*, Samuel McKechnie has utilized the official records of the Accountant's Office of the India House, meticulously correcting errors and discovering new facts to a greater extent than anyone else: "Charles Lamb of the India House" (*N&Q*, 2 Nov. 1946 to 8 March 1947; reprinted in the *CLSB*, 1948) enlarges our knowledge of Lamb's working conditions, business associates, prevailing salaries, and personnel management. Written around a new letter and a previously unpublished manuscript of facetious whimsy directed to Lamb's fellow clerks, Carl Woodring's "Lamb Takes a Holiday" (*HLB*, 1960) is a valuable supplement to this knowledge. As an employee of the India House, Lamb was in a position to ascertain the facts about the loss of the East-Indiaman *Earl of Abergavenny*, in which John Wordsworth, her captain, perished; his diligent efforts in questioning survivors and consulting the official reports did much to assuage William Wordsworth's distress, caused in part by hints about his brother's dereliction of duty, and are related in a thoroughgoing account of "Wordsworth's Shipwreck" (*PMLA*, 1962), by E. L. McAdam, Jr.

A few studies have been expressly devoted to Lamb's sister. Perhaps the first of any importance was the *Life of Mary Lamb*, by Anne Gilchrist, edited by John H. Ingram (1883). The most thorough analysis is *The Ordeal of Bridget Elia* (1940), by Ernest C. Ross, who discusses her influence on her brother, her own literary work, and the chronology of her periods of derangement. This last aspect was dealt with in "The Tragedy of Mary Lamb" (*TRSC*, 1928), by W. R. Riddell. Helen Ashton and Katharine Davies find a common denominator in Mary Lamb, Dorothy Wordsworth, Caroline Herschel, and Cassandra Austen in *I Had a Sister* (1937). "Charles Lamb's Best Friend" (*TLS*, 24 May 1947), an unsigned appreciation, is brief but good.

IV. CRITICISM[1]

"HIS OWN BOOKS can be lodged in the corner of a shelf; whereas the books relating to him . . . would fill a library. To write about Elia has become an industry" (W. B. Maxwell, *EDH*, 1934). But criticism, one must add, is not its main product. Lamb's life is dramatic and instructive; it attracts novelists, psychologists, and clergymen; he is a fellow almost damned in a fair character. The feeling that the man was greater than the author was understandable in those who knew him, but its effect on too many of his later admirers has been unfortunate; it has turned them away from an intelligent reading of what the man wrote. These are the devotees who are willing to devaluate his literary work. To Sir Walter Raleigh (*On Writing and Writers*, 1926) "Charles Lamb was not a poet, or essayist, or critic—he was a person. His works are a fortunate accident. They consist of: (1) Sayings. (2) Letters. (3) Poems and Essays—to be valued, I think, in that order." J. B. Priestley would have devoted to Lamb a chapter of his book, *English*

---

1   Many of the items listed were published originally in periodicals and were later reprinted, often several times, in books. With a few exceptions, references here are to first appearance in book form.

Humour (1929), even if Lamb had never written a single essay; the essays are peepholes into Lamb's life: "That is why we come to spend more time at last with the letters than with the essays; it is not a question of literary merit; the letters bring us a step or two closer to the man, and that is sufficient for us." The attitude is essentially antirational. Priestley cannot bring to bear the "solemn hocus-pocus" of the literary historian or critic: he limits his reaction to "smiling and gulping."

The refusal to criticize is a major tradition in the literature about Lamb. The best-known expression of it, the one most often quoted in justification, is Swinburne's (*Miscellanies*, 1886): "No good criticism of Lamb, strictly speaking, can ever be written; because nobody can do justice to his work who does not love it too well to feel himself capable of giving judgment on it." And so love renders impotent. Closely related is the tradition of Lamb as the shade of Creusa, eluding the touch, dainty gossamer defying the analytical grasp; he is absorbed, rather, as an odor or flavor. Scholarship itself is hesitant to identify Lamb's literary allusions, lest "the dissolving process of analysis" destroy the charm of the essays. A large part of what is written about Lamb is thereby circumscribed by an embarrassingly personal intimacy that keeps the critic from intruding on his delicate subject; he intrudes, instead, on the reader. Thus J. Lewis May, for example, in his *Charles Lamb: A Study* (1934), does not mind telling us that he has read Anatole France but almost nothing about Lamb, and that he has written a book about himself apropos of Lamb. He spoils a good deal of sensitive perception by burying it under pages of digression and decoration. A leaf-turning of an anthology of literature about Lamb (S. M. Rich's *The Elian Miscellany*, 1931) reveals little criticism, many personal confessions and reveries, verses and letters to Elia, imaginary dialogues with Elia, playlets about Elia, inept imitations of Elia. The *Charles Lamb Society Bulletin*, with all respect for its good work, fills its pages largely with what is irrelevant or peripheral to Lamb the author.

As might be expected from this preoccupation with Lamb the man, his striking life and character, much of the criticism concerns itself chiefly with his moral effect. He has been praised because he is as uplifting as Bret Harte, denounced because he is not so invigorating as Nietzsche. To a Californian of the Gold Rush days, outside the Four Gospels the world did not afford "a better code of ethics—a more charitable and humanizing system of belief and action than is contained in the Essays of Elia"; to a mid-Victorian Englishman, Lamb was "one of the noblest illustrations of our English sense of duty"; to a present-day citizen of India, quoting Kierkegaard en route, Lamb's spirit reached a state not entirely different from nirvana. To others he brings a message that life is beautiful, teaches us contentment, gratitude, how richly the human spirit may live to itself. The "St. Charles" tradition—the epithet was Thackeray's—is well represented by a poem of Lionel Johnson's ("Lamb," *Ireland and Other Poems*, 1891):

> Gentle *Saint Charles!* I turn to thee,
> Tender and true; thou teachest me
> To take with joy, what joys there be,
> And bear the rest.

Lamb as the bringer of solace, soother of cares, healer of the world's wounds, is perhaps the major theme of the many poetic tributes to him.

Other references to this moral type of criticism, and it is often very good, are given below. But one of its main weaknesses, even where it is not obviously irrelevant, is that its proponents are not always clear whether they are discussing the man's life or his writings; furthermore, it is a confusion they tend to insist upon, denying the distinction. The entire problem of the relationship of Lamb's biography to his writings is, as with few other authors, important and difficult to handle, and it is necessary to be on guard continually against those critics who slide with a too easy grace from one to the other. A useful article by Leo Spitzer, "History of Ideas versus Reading of Poetry" (*Southern Rev.*, 1941), tries to demonstrate how a reading of "The Old Familiar Faces" in the light of the assumed biographical facts behind it leads to a narrowing and misinterpretation of the poem.

NATURALLY enough, then, the predominant criticism of Lamb is the kind that seeks for the personality of the author in his work. It is the kind of criticism he himself wrote, and the kind that he has most clearly invited. Probably the largest group of the critics in this category are those who are most taken by Lamb's qualities of heart. They are, of course, closely related to, or identical with, those who look to him primarily for moral inspiration. The key words here are "gentle," against which Lamb himself reacted so violently, "lovable," "charitable," "humane," "sweet." Among his contemporaries, Talfourd, for example, emphasizes these qualities (*New Monthly Mag.*, 1820; Lamb's *Letters*, 1837; *Final Memorials*, 1848). Like many other critics who do so, Talfourd is a lover of Lamb's early work;

like them, too, he characterizes Lamb's work as curious and gemlike. "Exquisite" is the key word of De Quincey's elaborately exquisite essays on Lamb, in *Tait's Magazine* (1838) and the *North British Review* (1848) : perfect within a narrow range, a creator of finished cabinet specimens of literature, Lamb takes his place in the second rank of classics with Pope, Goldsmith, La Fontaine. His character may be read in anagram in his work : as a moral being he was the best man De Quincey had ever known or read of. His style, discontinuous and abrupt, is the expression of his shy, delicate feelings, his wayward nature. Leigh Hunt also (*Examiner*, 21 March 1819, and *London Jour.*, 7 Jan. 1835), like all those who knew him, writes with warmth of the deep charity and humanity of the man and the author. The "sweet" and "exquisite" Lamb may be traced down the years. Wordsworth's epithets, in the "Extempore Effusion upon the Death of James Hogg," return as the title of A. C. Ward's book, *The Frolic and the Gentle* (1934) ; Ward sees Lamb as the genius of the hearth, the ordinary man *in excelsis*, good and simple.

The danger in this concept of Lamb becomes apparent in those critics who ignore his masculinity and strength. "Sweet" and "gentle" merge too quickly into "weak," "naïve," "childlike." S. L. Bensusan, *Charles Lamb* (1910), Flora Masson, *Charles Lamb* (1913), and C. E. Lawrence (*QR*, 1934; *Cornhill Mag.*, 1934), are representative of this tendency. The Peter Pan comparison is popular here. This Lamb is easily patronized—he is lovable but not very bright. This is clearly Macaulay's attitude ("Leigh Hunt," *Critical and Miscellaneous Essays*, 1841–44) ; and to Frederic Harrison (*Tennyson, Ruskin, Mill*, 1899), Lamb was like Keats, delightful and exquisite but short on brains. As an author, this Lamb is the artless warbler, tricksy and elvish, a butterfly, an ingenuous jester. For those critics, both good and bad, to whom the man is "sweet" the works are likely to be "quaint" and "whimsical."

IT SHOULD be clear by now that it is as easy to despise Lamb as to love him, without dropping an adjective. His depreciators, a small but articulate band, are in substantial agreement with a large number of his appreciators on the qualities of the man: he is childlike, weak, whimsical, without many brains, a personality and not an author. A charming fellow, says Horace Gregory ("Great Man," *New Republic*, 14 Feb. 1934), but whatever weakness of character he had appeared overwhelmingly in his poetry and prose. H. V. D. Dyson and John Butt (*Augustans and Romantics*, 1940) begin by deploring the insistence on his personal character, but in the end find themselves forced back upon it; they have some words of praise, but they feel that "like so many of his contemporaries, there is an eternal immaturity about him."

The last phrase introduces us to a group of critics, some of whom are not anti-Elian, and even deeply affectionate, but who find the interpretive key to Lamb's career in his escape from adulthood and serious moral and literary responsibility. Paul Elmer More (*Shelburne Essays*, 2d Ser., 1905; 4th Ser., 1906) does not think highly of Lamb the writer; after 1800, in a half-conscious pose, Lamb humorously refused to harbor the deeper emotions, allowed his intellect to play over the surface of things, evading the truth. Thus there are times when Carlyle is right: Lamb does not look solemnly in the face of life. (For Carlyle, hierarch of the anti-Elians, as Thackeray of the Elians, see esp. *Reminiscences*, 1881; C. G. Duffy, *Conversations with Carlyle*, 1892; *Two Notebooks of Thomas Carlyle*, ed. C. E. Norton, 1898.) But there is a time for laughter and quaint fancy too, More says, and then Thackeray is right; it is Lamb the man who makes his writings so precious, and More can dwell upon the man and re-create a Wednesday evening as tenderly as any Elian. More's essays are excellent examples of the half-Caledonian, half-sentimental approach to Lamb.

F. V. Morley's *Lamb Before Elia* (1932) is the fullest exposition of the escapist reading of Lamb: Lamb's literary biography is a series of increasing defenses against the world, renunciations of love (*Rosamund Gray*), friendship (*John Woodvil*), and intimacy (the letters), after the early disappointments and catastrophe. Behind the mask was an individual mind, but one more and more concealed by humor. Humor, cards, drink, antiquity were all ways of escape, betrayed by periodic waves of self-disgust. After Fanny Kelly's refusal Elia was complete; but even that final dodge couldn't satisfy Lamb. Morley's book is more subtle than this outline suggests; it is also more soft and affectionate: he closes with the Swinburne quotation on the futility of Elian criticism. B. Ifor Evans (*Nineteenth Century*, 1934), J. W. Beach (*History of English Literature*, ed. Hardin Craig, 1950), and Malcolm Elwin (Introd., *Essays of Elia*, 1952) offer similar interpretations with varying degrees of affection.

The essential argument of those who see Elia as an escape is that Lamb raised deliberate barriers around his mind, hiding and atrophying an originally richer spirit. It is a small step from this to Mario Praz (*ES*, 1936; *The Hero in Eclipse in Victorian Fiction*, 1956), who asks whether the original richness is not a myth and Lamb simply a man of narrow soul from the start. Elia, far from silencing Charles Lamb, brought to brief blossom a limited, middle-class mind. W. J. Courthope (review of Pater's *Appreciations, Nineteenth Century*, 1890) and Denys Thompson of the *Scrutiny* critics ("Our Debt to Lamb," *Determinations*, ed. F. R. Leavis, 1934; "The Essayist at Large," *Reading and Discrimination*, 1934) illustrate Lamb's limitations by comparing him with Addison. Addison was serious and witty, at the center of his society, Thompson says, Lamb droll, sentimental, and remote. Lamb invented the whimsy, near relative of the daydream; he has a regressive mind that shrinks from full consciousness; by making a virtue of his own indolence and ignorance he flatters *l'homme moyen sensuel*, gives him the right to preserve his irrationalities, foibles, and prejudices. As a fake stylist and, above all, as the father of the fake personality, he has been a Very Bad Influence. Our debt to him is evident in the drivel of the worst modern essayists, in the writers of advertisements, in the depreciators of D. H. Lawrence, and so on. Thompson's is the most violent of all attacks on Lamb since Gillray's caricature, and its force is certainly dissipated by the indiscrimination of its violence. The significance of his essay is that it probably sums up intemperately the reasons for the relative critical neglect of Lamb in the past thirty years—the personal, eccentric, nonintellectual quality. A similar, but more temperate, current estimate is in G. D. Klingopulos' "The Spirit of the Age in Prose," *From Blake to Byron* (1957; Vol. v of the Pelican Guide to English Literature, ed. Boris Ford), where Lamb comes out least well among the prose writers.

Perhaps the most skillful of the depreciators is Graham Greene (*Spectator*, 30 March 1934). He is unusual in that he grants Lamb a head but not a heart. Lamb had supreme literary skill to convey his personality, but none of the common adjectives, "frank," "child-like," "innocent," does justice to the cunning of the pathos, the guile of the sentiment, the deception inherent in the whole portrait of Elia; personality is a social mask of character, a self-dramatization that has nothing to do with truth. This is not sympathetic or quite true, but it cuts hard, and friends of Lamb can learn from it.

BUT the bibliography of Lamb includes also a list of distinguished critics who, unlike too many of those noted thus far, are neither his fulsome admirers nor his denigrators. These are critics who take him seriously—sometimes too solemnly—who respect him, and who find in him a masculine figure, a man of some complexity and a good share of wisdom and vision.

It is revealing to see how many of his contemporaries, the most

acute of those who knew him best, and men not always fully
sympathetic to Lamb, say that he is at his best when most serious.
Henry Crabb Robinson was one (see the several references in the
section on biographies above). Coleridge, too, so irksome to Lamb
because of his occasional patronizing language, admired Lamb's
critical faculty and praised his serious conversation. (Edith C.
Johnson has collected the references in "Lamb and Coleridge," *A Sch*,
1937.) Hazlitt is a man to whom Lamb and Lamb's writings are
not an unmitigated pleasure (*Table-Talk*, 1821–22; *Spirit of the
Age*, 1825; *Plain Speaker*, 1826; and many other references in
Hazlitt's works). He can praise Lamb's style, but it is essentially
foreign to him; Lamb's province is too much the out-of-the-way; his
tastes are not catholic, and not always constant; he does not draw
lines of distinction clearly enough. But in none of this, Hazlitt
realizes, is there any hint of affectation; Lamb is genuine, and many
things that would disfigure a lesser man become themselves in Lamb:
there is a rich marrow in him. Hazlitt prefers his serious writing;
Lamb is strong against vulgarity, a masculine opponent of cant, a
man with a mind and critical insight that demand respect.

Lamb's criticism has given him the respect of men who otherwise
are rather disturbed by him. A. R. Orage, "The Danger of the
Whimsical" (in his *Selected Essays and Critical Writings*, ed.
Herbert Read and Denis Saurat, 1935), and Louis Kronenberger
(*SRL*, 5 Aug. 1933) are unhappy about his whimsicality but admire
his criticism. Brander Matthews (*The Dramatic Essays of Charles
Lamb*, 1892), along with excellent criticism of Lamb's virtues and
vices as a dramatist, has given him high praise as a dramatic critic.
E. M. W. Tillyard (Introd., *Lamb's Criticism*, 1923), fully aware of
Lamb's limitations as a critic, has written well of his merits: Lamb's
method is dangerous but the fruit of success is "quintessential
criticism," a work of art itself that permanently increases the value
of the work criticized. More recently, W. E. Houghton (*ELH*,
1943) has taken that critical essay of Lamb's which has exposed him
most to the charge of whimsicality, "Artificial Comedy," and has
shown, again with a recognition of its weakness, the acuteness and
validity of Lamb's treatment. Houghton cites many of the writers on
Restoration comedy who have something to say about Lamb's essay;
almost any book or article on the subject can be assumed to have a
reference to Lamb. A good analysis of a closely related subject,
"Charles Lamb's Contribution to the Theory of Dramatic Illusion,"
by Sylvan Barnet (*PMLA*, 1954), places Lamb in the forefront of
English dramatic criticism. M. P. Tilley offers unusual evidence of
Lamb's sensitive reading of poetry in "Charles Lamb, Marston, and

Du Bartas" (*MLN*, 1938). Charles I. Patterson is perhaps over-enthusiastic about "Charles Lamb's Insight into the Nature of the Novel" (*PMLA*, 1952). And tribute to Lamb's perceptiveness is continually offered by other critics; a late example is Lionel Trilling's citation of "The Sanity of True Genius" in *The Liberal Imagination* (1950).

Lamb's strength of mind is emphasized also by those critics who see in him not a gentle, essentially feminine creature, but a distinctive figure, essentially masculine. Ernest Bernbaum's chapter in his *Guide Through the Romantic Movement* (2d ed., 1949) is an excellent example: Lamb's chief general contribution to romanticism is his opposition to narrow formalization. In books as in men, he detested the pretentious, the conventional, the pharisaical; he loved the strongly individual, the positive, the impassioned, the intense and the outspoken; his playful manner hides a deep seriousness. Bernbaum's is one of the best short accounts of Lamb, and therefore difficult to summarize. Lyn Irvine (*Ten Letter-Writers*, 1932) and, more mildly, R. S. Knox (*UTQ*, 1934) both stress the strongly individual character of Lamb. "The Mind of Elia" offered by Bertram Jessup (*JHI*, 1954) is tough, the mind of an empiricist and particularist, relativist and skeptic. The article is a fine presentation of a basic quality in Lamb and an effective antidote to the "escapist" interpretation. It gives insufficient weight to the validity of imagination, of Elian half intuitions, semiconsciousnesses. Both "planes," reality and imaginative experience, are fully recognized in an article by Daniel J. Mulcahy, "Charles Lamb: The Antithetical Manner and the Two Planes" (*SEL*, 1963). Those who make a cult of Lamb's personality overemphasize the reality, he says, while the "escapist" interpreters overemphasize the element of imagination: "In fact, Lamb seldom loses sight of either, and at his best makes them interact profitably without surrendering their independent existence." In a subtle and convincing way Mulcahy goes on to demonstrate how the interaction proceeds in the essays, establishes the special quality of Lamb's mind and experience, and has excellent things to say about the structure of some of the essays as expressions of the mind of their author.

The complexity of Lamb, a man and author who combined seemingly contradictory qualities, struck his earliest admirers. They found him playful and malicious, prudent and mad, gleeful and desolate, witty and melancholy, humorous and pathetic. "Oh [Lamb], thou art a mystery to me!" Charles Lloyd sang, in *Desultory Thoughts in London* (1821). Leigh Hunt in particular is good on the complex and contradictory qualities of Lamb (*Lord*

Byron and Some of His Contemporaries, 1828; *London Jour.*, above). Hazlitt (above) recognizes some of them when he talks of the "vivid obscurity" of Lamb's style, his jests that "scald like tears" and his "smiling pathos." It was the mixture of the comic and the grave that especially caught the imagination of his contemporaries, and of "smiling pathos" we hear a good deal in subsequent criticism: A. H. Thompson writes well on it in his Introduction to *Essays of Elia* (1913) and in *The Cambridge History of English Literature* (1917). Lamb is compared, time and again, to Shakespeare's fools, to Lear's fool most frequently, Touchstone very often, as a wise man in motley, or a tragic jester. Something of the early history of these characterizations of Lamb, in relation to the more general history of ideas of humor, is in my book *The Amiable Humorist* (1960). The religious and solemn basis from which Lamb's humor developed is solemnly expounded by Wolfgang Schmidt-Hidding, who chooses Lamb as one of *Sieben Meister des Literarischen Humors* (1959); Chaucer and Shakespeare are among the other six. This approach to Lamb can be, at its worst, as exaggerated and simple and sentimental as any; he becomes a kind of Pagliacco, as in Gamaliel Bradford's *Bare Souls* (1924).

A more perceptive understanding of the complexity of Lamb's mind can be found in Arthur Symons' *The Romantic Movement in English Poetry* (1909) and *Figures of Several Centuries* (1916). Symons touches on many points, including, like so many critics, the humanizing moral effect of Lamb's work, and, unlike most, Lamb's poetry. Most important, he deals, more cogently than a few words can indicate, with the quality of Lamb's mind, the "beautiful disorder" of contrasting and converging thoughts and feelings that emerges again into a pattern. Louis Cazamian (*A History of English Literature*, with Emile Legouis, trans. 1927), also very much impressed with the complexity of Lamb's mind, stresses its cooler qualities of detachment and practiced artistry. The criticism of Alfred Ainger, though dated by its gentle, moral Elianism, is still very much worth reading (*Charles Lamb*, 1882; *Lectures and Essays*, 1905; the introductions to his editions, and other scattered essays). He sees the weakness of Lamb's criticism, the tendency to take the work out of the author's hands. But he is deeply aware of Lamb's supple strength, the versatility of sympathy, the varied style; he can see the intellectual flexibility and vision of the author, as well as his pathos and humor. Ainger writes good appreciation. Edmund Blunden is in the same tradition of good, sensitive Elian appreciation and is probably its best exponent (*Votive Tablets*, 1931; *Charles Lamb and His Contemporaries*, 1933; and numerous other books and articles, many of which are noted above in the sections on editions and biographies). He is the nostalgic Elian, an assimilator of the style, who dances gracefully before his subject, fragmentizing in the manner of the master. His is the rather feminine Lamb, sweet, sequestered, tender, ethereal. (See R. C. Bald's review, *MLN*, 1935.) But Blunden's work is rich, a source of information and understanding. He perhaps overestimates Lamb's poetic gift, but no one has written better of the intrinsic and historic value of both the poetry and the criticism. He sees in Lamb a man of various mind and authorship, of a splendid range of mind and experience in both the practical and visionary, a very reasonable romantic.

The wise and philosophic quality of Lamb was vigorously defended by Augustine Birrell, who was among the first to react strongly against the patronizing "poor" and "gentle" epithets (*Obiter Dicta*, 2d Ser., 1887; *Res Judicatae*, 1892). Hugh Walker, in *The English Essay and Essayists* (1915), praises him in the same vein, as do K. F. Plesner (*Elia og Hans Venner*, 1934) and J. W. Dodds (*SR*, 1934), among many others.

The depth and vision of Lamb are the subjects of the best-known essay on him, the one most often quoted and most influential, Walter Pater's in *Appreciations* (1889). The weakness of Pater's essay is the weakness of so much Lamb criticism; he overembroiders his subject with so many golden threads of subtlety and tenderness that one is not always certain of where Lamb ends and Pater begins. The virtues of Pater's method, inseparable from his style, like Lamb's own critical virtues, are not amenable to summary. Seemingly unacquainted with great matters, he says, Lamb is in immediate contact with the real, especially in its caressing littleness, in which resides the woeful heart of things; his laughter and tears lie close together, his humor rooted deep in a primitive large pity. He is the possessor of a refined, purged vision that enables him to see the present as if enchanted by distance, to feel the poetry of things old as an actual part of the present. Such a gift depends on the habitual apprehension of man's life as an organic whole. Lucas, Blunden, and scores of lesser students and critics of Lamb are immediate descendants of Pater. Desmond MacCarthy (English Assoc., *English Essays of Today*, 1936) follows Pater closely. John Mason Brown closes his chatty introductory account to the "Portable" *Charles Lamb* (1949) with a quotation from Pater; Brown has a keen awareness of Lamb's oblique, sensitive mind, but also of the toughness and resilience that accompanied its gentle humanity.

THE ATTRACTION, or repellence, of Lamb's personality, the obvious importance of the man, or the mask, in the work of the author, have thus made the criticism of qualities of head and heart, of literary traits, the largest category in the criticism of Lamb. The accompanying inhibitions against detailed or scholarly criticism have weakened, in quality and quantity, the historical, the formal, and the close textual analysis of his work.

To some of his greatest admirers, those in particular, of course, who make most of his whimsical and uncapturable essence, it is a matter of fact and rejoicing that "the work of Charles Lamb forms no integral part of the history of English literature," that he is an "individual sport," without ancestors or disciples. Close by is the tradition of Elia the anachronism, the odd spirit who jumped his own century and the preceding to find congenial inspiration in the antiquity of the Elizabethans and the seventeenth century; as with so much of the criticism of Lamb, the trouble with this is not that it is false but that it is not the whole truth.

To Ainger (above) Lamb was the last of the Elizabethans. Until quite recently he was the man who, in the *Specimens*, effected a singlehanded revival of the Elizabethans when they had been dead for two centuries. And by William Archer and by T. S. Eliot the *Specimens* were made responsible for an unhappy influence on subsequent thought about the drama. Archer, in the *New Review* (1893) and *The Old Drama and the New* (1923), protested that Lamb and his disciples had turned Elizabethan conventions into lasting canons of the drama; poetry is one and eternal and Lamb will always be right on the pure poetry of the Elizabethan drama, but poetry is subordinate, inessential in the drama. Eliot ("Four Elizabethan Dramatists," *Elizabethan Essays*, 1924) finds the opposite sin in Lamb and Lamb's influence; by selecting poetic fragments, Lamb fixed upon modern opinion the ruinous notion that poetry and drama are separate things. But the growth of scholarly knowledge about the reputation of Elizabethan literature in the eighteenth century, without destroying the importance of Lamb's contribution, has shown that he deserves neither single credit for the revival nor similar discredit for piecemeal anthologizing, and that he is neither the sole true expositor nor perverter. R. D. Williams has collected considerable evidence on "Antiquarian Interest in Elizabethan Drama Before Lamb" (*PMLA*, 1938). The fullest studies of the subject are by Earl R. Wasserman, though his *Elizabethan Poetry in the Eighteenth Century* (1947) and articles in *English Literary History* (1937) and *Studies in Philology* (1939) refer only briefly to Lamb. F. S. Boas has analyzed the *Specimens* to determine where Lamb's originality lay, and where the strength and weakness of his treatment of specific dramatists (*E&S*, 1943, 1944). R. C.

Bald (*Univ. of Missouri Stud.*, 1946) has shown, further, how much the *Specimens* are a product of the bias of their own times.

There are a number of special small studies of Lamb's reading in authors other than the Elizabethan dramatists. H. G. Smith's "Charles Lamb and His Bible" (*John O'London's Weekly*, 8 March 1946) is enthusiastic if not very original. E. E. Burriss has collected some of Lamb's classical references as "The Classical Culture of Charles Lamb" (*Classical Weekly*, 6 Oct. 1924); and an exchange of letters in the *Times Literary Supplement* has produced a useful note on "Lamb's Latinity" by R. G. C. Levens (1 Aug. 1952). His criticism of Spenser is given good marks by Frederick Hard (*SP*, 1931); see also subsequent articles by J. M. French and Hard (*SP*, 1933). His allusions to Milton have been catalogued by French (*SP*, 1934). J. V. Logan compares "Yorick and Elia" (*CLSB*, 1948); this is a subject well worth pursuing. There is a bit on it in my *Amiable Humorist* (above) and Jack's history (below). And among assorted studies of lesser influences on Lamb may be mentioned Maurice Hewlett's "One of Lamb's Creditors [James Howell]" (*Last Essays*, 1924), and, more scholarly, Benjamin Boyce's "Tom Brown and Elia" (*ELH*, 1937). More ambitious studies of important influences are Bernard Lake's *A General Introduction to Charles Lamb: Together with a Special Study of His Relation to Robert Burton* (1903), and J. S. Iseman's *A Perfect Sympathy: Charles Lamb and Sir Thomas Browne* (1937). Iseman is useful, often detailed, perceptive, and enlightening, but also very uneven. There is a dissertation, too, on "The Nineteenth-Century Reputation of Sir Thomas Browne," by Ruth Vande Kieft (Univ. of Michigan, 1958), in which Lamb plays a role. Further studies of this type, of larger scope, will be noted later, but there is still need for investigation of Lamb's reading and its importance. A collection of his marginalia has been long desired; and the materials are mainly in America, as both Lucas and Blunden pointed out some years ago.

The position of Lamb in his own age, as influencer and influenced, has received even less attention and is in greater need of it. Marie H. Law writes of the romantic qualities of Lamb in *The English Familiar Essay in the Early Nineteenth Century* (1934), but her understanding of romanticism rarely gets below a few obvious surface qualities. Lamb is occasionally spoken of as one of the pioneer romantics, most adequately by Blunden in *Charles Lamb and His Contemporaries*; and he is sometimes credited with an innovative importance in prose comparable to Wordsworth's and Coleridge's in poetry, but there has been no study of the subject. Ian Jack's account in *English Literature, 1815–1832* (1963; Vol. x, of the *Oxford History of English Literature*) sees Lamb as "a most significant figure" because of his characteristic nineteenth-century interest in the past; Jack attempts briefly to relate Lamb to his contemporaries and predecessors. The historical significance of Lamb's criticism is given part of a chapter in Volume II of René Wellek's *History of Modern Criticism* (1955). Wellek credits him with innovative importance, his evocative, metaphorical and personal methods of criticism, and compares him, in this respect, with Hazlitt especially. Most of the account, however, is given not to historical evidences but to Wellek's own reactions to Lamb's criticism, mostly cool. George Watson's *The Literary Critics* (1962) puts Lamb among the less important and least "romantic" critics; D. W. Harding, writing on "The Character of Literature from Blake to Byron" (*From Blake to Byron*), finds Lamb's review of Wordsworth's *Excursion* "a compendium of the Romantic outlook" and returns to it at several key points in his article. Much depends, it becomes evident, on which romanticism and which Lamb one is talking about. More studies are needed like A. P. Hudson's "Romantic Apologiae for Hamlet's Treatment of Ophelia" (*ELH*, 1942) and Sylvan Barnet's "Charles Lamb and the Tragic Malvolio" (*PQ*, 1954), each of which examines closely one point in Lamb's relationship to the Shakespearean criticism of his day. Among other studies we have George Goodin's compendious dissertation on "The Comic Theories of Hazlitt, Lamb, and Coleridge" (Univ. of Illinois, 1962); G. H. Daggett's article on a subject important to Lamb and to many of his contemporaries, "Charles Lamb's Interest in Dreams" (*CE*, 1942); and Josephine Bauer's *The London Magazine, 1820–29* (1953), which has some material on Lamb's literary companionship with the *London* writers. Perhaps the largest claim for Lamb's influence on a contemporary is George Whalley's "Coleridge's Debt to Lamb" (*E&S*, 1958), when he says that young Coleridge was launched on his marvelous year as a poet with vision clarified and energies redirected by his fruitful correspondence with Lamb; the article is good, but must remain more suggestive than convincing. Other references to Lamb's relations with his contemporaries are listed above in the earlier portion of this section and in the section on biography.

Lamb's influence on later writers is often spoken of, unfavorably, as by Denys Thompson and Gregory (above), favorably, as by Lucas. Lucas connects Lamb closely with Dickens, in "The Evolution of Whimsicality" (*Giving and Receiving,* 1922) and elsewhere. The relationship has long been noted—Percy Fitzgerald devotes to it the closing pages of his *Charles Lamb* (1866)—and is often referred to; there is a slight article on it by F. C. Dance (*Dickensian*, 1939). In the course of an excellent article, "Charles Lamb Sees London" (*Rice Institute Pamphlet*, 1935), Alan D. McKillop compares Lamb and Dickens as Londoners; he places Lamb in the history of literature and art about London. There is a note on "Lamb's Role in Green's Card Table Scenes," (*Rom N*, 1961), by Marilyn Rose; this is Julian Green, the novelist and playwright and, incidentally, author of several essays on Lamb. Lamb's influence on subsequent essayists is often mentioned, but has never been seriously demonstrated. Annemarie Schöne, "Charles Lamb—der Schöpfer des humoristischen Essays" (*Die Neueren Sprachen*, 1956), calls him the real founder of the tradition of the humorous essay as a literary form, but the historical claim is not substantiated. And a good study of the history of his reputation would be informative. Nethery (above, in the section on bibliography) has gathered the materials for the early period in America, up to 1866; the later period, in America and England, is likely to be more interesting.

Lamb and the history of the essay to his day have received more attention. Among the general histories there are Walker's book and Law's (above), and, much better, Melvin Watson's "The *Spectator* Tradition and the Development of the Familiar Essay" (*ELH*, 1946; with another version in his *Magazine Serials and the Essay Tradition*, 1956). Varley Lang is good on "The Character in the Elia Essay" (*MLN*, 1941), though not primarily historical; the subject is resumed by Allie Webb, "Charles Lamb's Use of the Character" (*SoQ*, 1963). W. L. MacDonald (*PMLA*, 1917) is historical and comparative in approach, but neither penetrating nor discriminating. Lamb's relation to Montaigne has been debated occasionally. Pater, for example, finds them close in the desire for self-portraiture, Elwin (above) far apart. Charles Dédéyan, *Montaigne chez ses amis anglo-saxons* (1946), rather oddly, sees Lamb active in a nationalistic and snobbish conspiracy against Montaigne's reputation.

We have also some attempts to amalgamate in full-length book form the total of historical and biographical influences on Lamb and to see their significance in the critical evaluation of his work. Most of the longer studies of him glance at this problem, but the chief interest of their authors lies elsewhere. Edith C. Johnson (*Lamb Always Elia*, 1935), under the immediate stimulus of F. V. Morley's escapist interpretation, tried to demonstrate that the evolution of young Charles Lamb into the author of the Elia essays was a regular, inevitable process, the stages of which are all essentially visible and understandable. She sees Lamb as a man of keen,

discriminating intellect, and traces his development through the
various steps of his life, his reading and his earlier writing, to show
the contribution of each to the final product. She has original
material, but lacks the essential critical ability that a book like this
demands. A similar new study is George L. Barnett's *Charles Lamb:
The Evolution of Elia* (1964); the chief distinction of the book is
that it gathers for the first time all available manuscripts of Lamb
into its survey to determine his habits of composition and revision
and the effects he worked for (see also J. M. French, "A Chip from
Elia's Workshop," *SP*, 1940). It is the fullest, firsthand, scholarly
account of the historical and biographical materials and of the
process that produced the essays.

WHAT is probably most lacking in the present state of the criticism
of Lamb is further close analysis of the compositional elements of
his essays. The shyness of Elian criticism, unwilling to handle its
subject too nearly for fear of unweaving the rainbow, has laid its
strongest restraint here.

Lamb's style is everywhere praised to the highest (except, of
course, where it is damned to the deepest), but usually for contradictory virtues. It has been called Elizabethan (S. C. Hill, in his
perceptive Introduction to *Essays of Elia*, 1895), seventeenth
century (Walker, above), eighteenth century (Oliver Elton, *A
Survey of English Literature 1780–1830*, 1912), and conglomerate
(Saintsbury, *History of English Prose Rhythm*, 1912); it is rarely
called nineteenth century, though it has been made the derivative of
his conversational stammer (Ward, above). For those to whom
Lamb is an artless creature, or who prefer the artless, the unre-
hearsed letters are the better part of his work.

The numerous parallels between the letters and the essays have
been gone over many times; Law (above) is useful here; Barnett
(above) is the most thorough in showing the development of idea and
phrasing of the finished essays. Usually, however, the purpose of this
exercise is to underscore the similarities, to illustrate how Lamb
treats his readers as intimately as his friends: he furbishes a phrase
or two, when he moves from letter to essay, rearranges a bit to
improve the art—or spoil the spontaneity, depending on one's
prejudices—but rarely makes any radical adjustments. But George
Williamson ("The Equation of the Essay," *SR*, 1927), by taking
"The Superannuated Man" and comparing it with three letters of
Lamb's on the same subject, has pointed out how different in essence
the essay is. Each of the letters is shaped by the recipient; the essay

is written for "antiquity," and in it alone is Lamb free of the personal equation, free for complete communication, the "terrible intimacy" of art.

The careful artistry of Lamb's style was recognized by many of his early critics; Hazlitt and De Quincey have been mentioned. Among later critics, C. T. Winchester (*A Group of English Essayists of the Early Nineteenth Century*, 1910), like De Quincey, dwells upon the Little Master, high-finish quality of the prose, and there are many others, though they usually limit themselves to generalizations and a few quoted phrases or passages. A remark of J. Middleton Murry's, in "The Meaning of Style" (*The Problem of Style*, 1922), has been picked up by A. G. van Kranendonk (*ES*, 1932), who tries to analyze the "ornateness" of Lamb's style as a necessary expression of his uncommon, complex vision, and to point out the variety of effects that Lamb is capable of. He is answered by T. B. Stroup (*ES*, 1932), to whom the remarkable quality of Lamb is his studied negligence and informal manner. Each critic pitches on a different essay to make his point. The variety of Lamb's style, recognized by van Kranendonk, still awaits full study.

Stroup insists, presenting a single example, that Lamb sought only those archaisms that survived in colloquial usage. The problem of Lamb's diction, often discussed, has never been adequately handled. There is an article by Louise Griswold, "The Diction of Charles Lamb" (*Quart. Jour. of the Univ. of N. Dakota*, 1927), which deals chiefly with word lengths. W. D. Howe gives a list of some of Lamb's archaisms and coinages in *Charles Lamb and His Friends* (1944). A couple of recent Japanese studies—T. Miyagawa, "Some Notes on the Style of the *Essays of Elia*" (*Anglica*, 1960), and, much more ambitiously, Tsutomu Fukuda, in the first part of *A Study of Charles Lamb's Essays of Elia* (1964)—have offered classified lists of archaisms, alliterations, repetitions, figures of speech, allusions, and the like; the specific examples that are given do not inspire confidence in the general accuracy of the compilations and nothing much emerges, but others may be able to use some of the material.

Lamb's essays have been called poems—the comparison of the familiar essay and the lyric is common—by Bulwer-Lytton in *England and the English* (1833) and the *Quarterly Review* (1867), by Oliver Elton in his useful essay (above), and by May (above), for example; the lyric quality is what most impresses an Italian critic, Carlo Izzo, writing on "Gli 'Essays of Elia' di Charles Lamb" (*Convivium*, 1959). The essays would stand up under close textual analysis of the type we have become familiar with in modern poetic criticism. The structure of the essays, Lamb's use of imagery and metaphor, his rhetoric, "his highly original sentence-structure, which throws overboard all formal rhetoric" (J. M. French, *JRUL*, 1948), are all open to study. C. E. Whitmore, in "The Field of the Essay" (*PMLA*, 1921), has touched lightly on Lamb's device of inverting normal expository forms; further study of this and similar techniques would be useful. An article published since the first edition of this volume which takes up the challenge of applying to the essays the same kind of serious critical attention that in recent years has been given to poetry is Richard Haven's "The Romantic Art of Charles Lamb" (*ELH*, 1963). His particular examples are "Old China" and "The Old Benchers" and he does a good job; even if some of the things that he says can be argued with, the argument will be valuable. Mulcahy's article (above) is especially good on "Witches, and Other Night-Fears" and "Blakesmoor in H———shire"; Barnett's book (above) has essential material on a number of essays.

Strangely enough, the book that makes the fullest attempt to come to close grips with Lamb's artistry in language was written by a Frenchman over half a century ago. A deep admirer of Lamb, but not a blind one, Jules Derocquigny (*Charles Lamb*, 1904), has offered more examples from the text, and more perspicacious comment on them, than any other critic. He is finely aware of the quality of Lamb's mind, its subtlety and its limitations. For critical intelligence his work remains one of the best things we have.

CRITICISM of Mary Lamb's writings, of course, is scattered throughout the books and articles on Charles, especially in those that discuss the tales and poetry for children, like Elton (above) and Howe (above). There are also a number of general accounts of children's literature that locate the work of the Lambs in its history; Florence V. Barry's *A Century of Children's Books* (1922) is the most useful in this respect. Among the items devoted to Mary Lamb which are listed in the section on biography, E. C. Ross's book and the *Times Literary Supplement* article contain criticism.

Douglas Grant identifies a source of one of Mary's poems, in "Mary Lamb and Penny Ballads" (*TLS*, 20 Sept. 1947).

3

William Hazlitt

By Elisabeth W. Schneider

UNIVERSITY OF CALIFORNIA
AT SANTA BARBARA

I. BIBLIOGRAPHIES

B IBLIOGRAPHICAL study of Hazlitt is of two sorts. In addition to the formal bibliographical description of his books, there is the less strictly bibliographical and more difficult task of identifying his unsigned and uncollected periodical articles. Early lists attempted to serve both functions.

The first undertaking was a "Chronological Catalogue" printed by W. Carew Hazlitt in the first volume of his *Memoirs of Hazlitt* (1867); it is occasionally worth consulting still, though for most purposes it has long been superseded. P. P. Howe, the acknowledged modern authority, gives it a certain weight, believing that some articles were included on the authority of the biographer's father, Hazlitt's son. But as the latter is known to have been an extremely unreliable source of information and as the ascriptions have all been closely scrutinized by Howe, there is little profit for most students in traversing that ground again unless new information should come to light that might unsettle Howe's conclusions. A *List of the Writings of William Hazlitt and Leigh Hunt*, published in the following year (1868) by Alexander Ireland, is unlikely to be of any value to the student today. For authenticating and dating individual articles, the *Liste chronologique des œuvres de William Hazlitt* by Jules Douady (1906) offers the convenience of a compact chronological arrangement, though it is neither complete nor free of errors.

The standard descriptive work is that of Geoffrey Keynes (*Bibliography of William Hazlitt*, 1931). Dealing with books only, it excludes the ticklish problems of authorship. Keynes not only describes books and editions published during Hazlitt's lifetime, but follows the history of later editions, including single volumes of selections, down to 1930. For the books published by Hazlitt himself Keynes adds to the usual data a full account of what he calls "transfers," as well as cancels (a few of which are of more than bibliographical interest), paper, and watermarks. As a rule, for works of this period bibliographers ignore the paper; but the value of taking it into account is demonstrated not only by Keynes's example but also by one perhaps hasty deduction he makes. Observing the date 1817 in the watermark of part of the suppressed first issue of *Select British Poets*, he suggests that though the book was not published till 1824, it had been in preparation before 1820. Sir Edmund Chambers, however, once noted that paper of 1795 was used in the 1800 edition of the *Lyrical Ballads*. Occasional observations such as these indicate a need to know more, and to deduce less until we do know more, about paper and watermarks of the period. Keynes aims at completeness, within the limits set by his plan, and has probably achieved it for all practical purposes. One unimportant omission is a limited edition of the *Life of Napoleon* (6 vols., 1895), published by "The Napoleon Society, Paris and Boston." Two minor additions to his information are printed in the *Times Literary Supplement* for 19 August 1939 and 14 August 1943; and he himself in *Library* (1932) corrected his earlier date for Hazlitt's *Grammar* and described an unrecorded abridgment of it by Godwin.

The major task of identifying Hazlitt's uncollected writing has been accomplished by editors of the modern collected editions, Waller and Glover (q.v.) and, subsequently, Howe. The latter's numerous articles on the subject need not be listed, since their results were all incorporated in his edition. Geoffrey Carnall, however, in the *TLS* for 19 June 1953, uncovered one more article in the files of the *Monthly Magazine*; E. L. Brooks, under the misleading title "Was Hazlitt a News Reporter?" (*N&Q*, 1954), finds very probable traces of his hand in the department of "Literary and Scientific Intelligence" in the *London Magazine* in 1820; and Herschel M. Sikes ("Hazlitt, the *London Magazine*, and the 'Anonymous Reviewer,'" *BNYPL*, 1961) prints and offers persuasive reasons for ascribing to Hazlitt a review of Allan Cunningham's *Sir Marmaduke Maxwell*. On Hazlitt's contributions to the *Edinburgh Review*, the article by P. L. Carver (*RES*, 1928) may be consulted along with the notes to the centenary edition, in which Howe took account of the study by Carver without admitting all of its conclusions. Certainly Carver is wrong in accepting from Ireland's list a review of *Histoire de la peinture en Italie* by "B.A.A." in 1819 (the article has also been ascribed, without certainty, to Brougham [see appendix to Chester New, *Life of Henry Brougham to 1830*, Oxford, 1961]). The connection of this article with Hazlitt's name offers matter for speculation, since the work under review was by Stendhal, published without his name but even then reputed to be his, and the links connecting Hazlitt and Stendhal have been multiplying of late. The article is unlike Hazlitt's work in style and language, and in nearly all the views expressed or implied. William H. Marshall ("An Addition to the Hazlitt Canon: Arguments from External and Internal Evidence," *PBSA*, 1961), reprints and ascribes to Hazlitt an article, "Pulpit Oratory. No. IV" (on the Bishop of Llandaff) in the *Yellow Dwarf* in 1818. John Hamilton Reynolds had written the first three sketches in the series, but Marshall thinks illness and other preoccupations would have prevented his writing this one and finds internal reasons for assigning it to Hazlitt. The most controversial of the problems of attribution, that concerning the review in the *Edinburgh* of Coleridge's *Christabel*, will be discussed later, since it hinges upon biographical and critical questions.

II. EDITIONS

THE TASK of the editor of Hazlitt is not primarily that of establishing a text. Once the writing has been identified as his, there is little choice of what to print because few manuscripts survive. For periodical articles that Hazlitt himself republished in book form, the later text is almost always preferable, since it represents his final version and is more likely to be his own writing, free from editorial tampering. The articles that he did not reprint offer, as a rule, no choice but to accept the existing text with indication, where the occasion warrants, of passages that may have been an editor's insertion. This practice has been followed in the two collected editions of Hazlitt's works published during the present century. The chief problem of modern editors is the difficulty of identifying Hazlitt's uncollected articles. The *Collected Works*, edited by A. R. Waller and Arnold Glover in thirteen volumes issued between 1902 and 1906, represented a standard of scholarship far beyond the average of that day. Its text was nearly unexceptionable, its notes full and helpful. In the 1920's, however, it was out of print. Meanwhile, P. P. Howe had discovered a quantity of unknown writing by Hazlitt, which he published in two independent volumes, *New Writings* (1st Ser., 1925; 2d Ser., 1927). The modern definitive edition is his, edited, according to his modest title page, "after the edition" of Waller and Glover, the *Complete Works of William Hazlitt* (centenary ed., 1930–34; Vol. XXI, comprising the general index and the useful index of quotations, compiled by James Thornton). The text of the old edition is followed for the most part;

but the arrangement has been improved, the notes corrected and augmented, and much new matter added. Hazlitt's *Life of Napoleon* and his *English Grammar*, omitted from the earlier edition, are included; newly identified articles and the Preface and Critical List of Authors from *Select British Poets* are added; the long and important critique of Wordsworth's *Excursion*, hitherto available only in the much-altered version in the *Round Table*, is here reprinted in its original form from the *Examiner;* and some improved texts, as well as new material, have been printed, chiefly from the Hazlitt manuscripts of Colonel A. Conger Goodyear (now in the collection of the Lockwood Memorial Library of the University of Buffalo). The edition is a model of its kind. Further discoveries may unsettle a few of Howe's additions to the Hazlitt canon or his rejection of work formerly included in it; even now one may occasionally doubt certain of his conclusions. No scholar or critic of the present day, however, possesses a knowledge of Hazlitt, accompanied by literary tact, comparable to Howe's; one differs from him only at considerable risk.

Of the numerous volumes of selections, only one comes within the scope of this survey. Jacob Zeitlin's *Hazlitt on English Literature* (1913) has independent value for its notes, which contain information not available elsewhere, particularly on the interrelations of Hazlitt, Coleridge, and Schlegel, and for its introductory essay, the most elaborate account that has been published of Hazlitt's criticism.

Several editions of individual works deserve mention. The *Liber Amoris*, privately printed in 1894 with an introduction by Richard Le Gallienne and an unsigned second essay, "Hazlitt from Another Point of View," by W. C. Hazlitt, contains material not available in print earlier. To the original published text is added another draft from a manuscript not in Hazlitt's hand but with his notes, as well as certain of the letters used for the book, the journal kept by Hazlitt's wife during her stay in Scotland, and a few of her letters. The introductory essays in the volume are negligible and inaccurate, but some of the added material is of biographical interest. More valuable than the introductions to this edition is a later one by Charles Morgan (in *Liber Amoris and Dramatic Criticisms*, 1948, reprinted in Morgan's *The Writer and His World*, 1960), of which something will be said hereafter.

The *Reply to Z* was first published in a limited edition for the First Editions Club (1923). Charles Whibley, who then owned the original manuscript (now in the British Museum), wrote an intemperate and misleading introduction, adapted from an earlier article in *Blackwood's Magazine* (1918), castigating Hazlitt and the Whig party as if the latter were still an issue, and defending not only the Tory cause but even the methods employed by its most virulent writers in the early years of *Blackwood's*. He described Hazlitt as in politics a "Jacobin" but in literature a "violent anti-Jacobin" who hated modern trends in the poetry of his day and ignored Keats in his lecture upon living poets. Whibley seemed unaware that Hazlitt's lecture had preceded the publication even of *Endymion*.

In 1925, Elbridge Colby published a limited edition in two volumes of the *Life of Thomas Holcroft*, which for certain purposes has not been superseded by that of Howe in the *Complete Works*. Interested in Holcroft rather than Hazlitt, Colby added much new material, some in the form of notes, some incorporated, with due notice, into the text itself. He corrected dates in the autobiographical parts written by Holcroft and to some extent reorganized Hazlitt's chapters. The product of painstaking research, this edition should be consulted by those interested in biographical facts about Holcroft. Those seeking the actual text of Hazlitt will avoid it. More recently, an article by Virgil R. Stallbaumer, "Hazlitt's *Life of Thomas Holcroft*" (*ABR*, 1954) discussed conditions under which the *Life* was produced and offered a possible explanation of the "missing" fourth volume.

The *Conversations of Northcote* has been published in separate editions by W. C. Hazlitt (along with the *Round Table*, in 1871); Edmund Gosse (1894), who introduced it with a perfunctory essay on "Hazlitt as an Art-Critic"; and Frank Swinnerton (1949). The first two of these are out of date, the discovery of Northcote's own marked copies, with canceled leaves and manuscript correspondence bound in, having enabled Howe, in the centenary edition, to supply missing information.

No collection of Hazlitt's letters has ever been published, but an edition by Herschel M. Sikes is in preparation.

III. BIOGRAPHIES

Materials for the life of Hazlitt are in some respects meager and in others embarrassingly copious. Of letters, usually a prime source for the biographer, there are not a great many, and few even of these tell us much more than that he was in London, or out of London, at a given time, or that he needed money. During his adult years Hazlitt wrote possibly fewer personal letters than any other English author of modern times; when he wrote, it was usually from necessity —a matter of business with his publisher or editor, an appointment, more rarely a personal communication as brief as decency permitted. Only once did he break his habitual silence for an extended time; that was during the period of his feverish passion for Sarah Walker in 1822. For the rest, biographers have had to depend upon such indirect sources as the recollections of Talfourd, Bulwer, Procter, and Patmore, and upon incidental reports in the letters and journals of friends and acquaintances, especially Lamb, Haydon, and Crabb Robinson.

The one important repository that almost supplies the place of private correspondence is the mass of published essays in which Hazlitt recorded past or passing events of his life. Ordinarily, familiar essays written for the periodical press are not the most trustworthy source of biographical information. Hazlitt's, however, are an exception, for his memory was remarkably faithful. The comfortable memory that allows most of us to improve our past had not been bestowed upon him; on the contrary, his memory exhibited the same stubborn inveteracy that characterized his opinions—a sign, perhaps, of an inflexible temperament but a gift to the biographer. Wherever Hazlitt's recollections can be tested against other evidence, they show almost no distortion and very few errors. The point is emphasized here because some writers have made much of two or three slips. He was accused of malicious distortion because he reported, twenty-five years after the event, that Wordsworth had lived rent-free at Alfoxden. He should have said Racedown, Wordsworth's previous residence. There are occasional mistakes of this sort in Hazlitt's essays, but very few. Even at best, however, a reminiscent essay lacks the immediacy of letters in recording the daily event; it is not raw, but already selected, material. These are the conditions under which the biographer of Hazlitt works.

Until recently, the best biography has been P. P. Howe's *Life of William Hazlitt* (1922; rev. ed., 1928; new ed., 1947, with an introduction by Frank Swinnerton containing a sketch of Howe's life and character as well as an appreciation of Hazlitt). The services rendered by Howe to the student of Hazlitt are greater than those of all other writers together, and his biography superseded for most purposes, though not quite all, the volumes published by Hazlitt's grandson, William Carew Hazlitt, the *Memoirs of William Hazlitt* (2 vols., 1867), *Four Generations of a Literary Family* (2 vols., 1897), and *Lamb and Hazlitt* (1900). Howe excluded all but the most significant facts of Hazlitt's ancestry, his early life in America, and his father's occupations and correspondence. The volumes of W. C. Hazlitt contain this material and a text (not always accurate) of some of Hazlitt's surviving correspondence and are therefore still to be consulted for occasional purposes. They are shapeless compilations, however; and they must be used with caution. Much of the material they contain reached the biographer through Hazlitt's son, whose scarcely disguised hostility to his father, mingled with family pride and a squeamish defensiveness, warped both the biographical sketch with which he prefaced Hazlitt's *Literary Remains* (2 vols., 1836) and the accounts he transmitted to his own son. The grandson's volumes, for this and other reasons, contain numerous errors of fact and much unsubstantiated hearsay. They are further disfigured by lack of taste and the conflicting impulses to bask in his grandfather's fame and at the same time to dissociate himself from the same grandfather's unpopularity.

Within its limitations of space and aim, Howe's *Life* is a model of biographical writing. Not only did it correct W. C. Hazlitt on many points of both fact and interpretation; it presented for the first time a convincing and lifelike portrait. As the first life written in conformity with standards of modern scholarship, it is primarily factual; eschewing criticism and psychological speculation, Howe undertook primarily to set forth the record of Hazlitt's controversial life and let it speak for itself. He spared no pains in ascertaining facts, yet kept his pages uncluttered by meaningless detail. He wrote with undisguised sympathy for Hazlitt and some severity toward his enemies. But he warped no evidence and scanted no difficult questions. His was the first work to treat Hazlitt without patronage or apology.

Aside from the volumes of Carew Hazlitt and some brief early sketches, Howe's biography had been preceded by two others. Augustine Birrell wrote a short life for the English Men of Letters series (1902) which, though it corrected a few earlier misconceptions, is on the whole negligible, a popular biography in a now-outmoded vein. It is marred by a tone of condescension, which today sounds odd, coming from the almost forgotten Birrell; and it perpetuates more errors than it corrects. Jules Douady's *Vie de William Hazlitt, l'essayiste* (1907) is a sympathetic account addressed particularly to a French audience, by whom Hazlitt had been little known. The best biography in its day and the fruit of independent research, it corrected W. C. Hazlitt on a number of points, particularly dates. It may still be consulted for the evidence justifying those corrections, since Howe sometimes gives only the conclusions. For the rest, its interpretations are uncritical and space is taken up with explanatory matter not required by English-speaking readers.

Howe's *Life* was followed by Hesketh Pearson's *The Fool of Love* (1934) and Catherine Macdonald Maclean's *Born under Saturn* (1943). The first is a popular, undocumented biography; its limitations are those of its genre with a few others added. Pearson set out primarily to explore—perhaps to exploit—the love affairs of Hazlitt. In doing this, he presented the fullest account we have of Hazlitt's relations with women. More than a third of the volume is given over to a section called "The Lover," and of this the major part deals with the divorce and the Sarah Walker affair. Hazlitt's own account in the *Liber Amoris* had been used to discredit him in the eyes of his contemporaries, and Pearson maintains that that book remains even now an injury to his reputation. He thinks the passion for Sarah Walker was Hazlitt's deepest emotional experience and that to understand either the man or the writer we must understand this story fully. Pearson's material is drawn mainly from the *Liber Amoris*, the correspondence with Patmore, the diary kept by Mrs. Hazlitt in Scotland, and the record of legal proceedings in the Scottish divorce. His use of sources is occasionally careless; he assumes omniscience without pausing to distinguish between fact and conjecture, recounting, for example, as established inner experiences of Hazlitt's youth what can only be gratuitous surmises founded on recent doctrines of adolescent psychology. His interpretations of motives and character are generally superficial. His passing critical judgments, on the other hand, are independent and often acute.

If Pearson is all for love, Catherine Macdonald Maclean is all for liberty. *Born under Saturn* is composed from thorough firsthand knowledge, as well as from an obviously strong personal devotion to her subject. Her major theme is Hazlitt as the courageous advocate of political freedom and the ideals of the French Revolution during the long period of Tory rule that preceded the enactment of the Reform Bill. She provides an especially valuable account of his Nonconformist religious background. No previous study had brought out so clearly the connection between his temperamental predisposition to a sense of injury and the strong public prejudice at the close of the eighteenth century against Unitarians and their ministers, of whom his father was one. The burning of Priestley's house, upon which at the age of thirteen Hazlitt wrote a letter of protest to the *Shrewsbury Chronicle*, is noted as a single incident by other biographers; in Miss Maclean's book this is shown as merely one of the more conspicuous events in the history of a mild but insistent persecution that followed these dissenters and helped to set them apart from the main current of English life in a narrow and defensively self-righteous isolation. Other writers have emphasized from time to time the positive side of this inheritance, the courageous independence of thought, the firmness of principle. But the reverse side is there too. The paranoid and almost priggish strain in Hazlitt, his least attractive quality, is shown for the first time in Miss Maclean's book in relation to what probably was its origin. Her treatment of Hazlitt's political thought is full, though it does not take the place of his own political essays, which set forth even more clearly his love of liberty as well as his detestation of the cant and inhumanity of the extreme right and the doctrinaire left of that era. Miss Maclean illuminates many particular points in his life and writings through her unusual familiarity with day-by-day political events. On the interpretive side the book is more open to criticism. The author subjects every action of Hazlitt to an intense imaginative scrutiny to determine the motive behind it, and her imagination is not always equal to the task. She presents her own intuitions as facts more freely than even the avowedly Stracheyan biographer is apt to do. Sometimes a quotation from Hazlitt is used in support of these interpretations, but the quoted passage may prove to have been written long afterward in different circumstances or even with reference to a different subject. Miss Maclean's liberties obviously do not derive from any wish to popularize (in the sense of vulgarize), as may have been the case with Hesketh Pearson; they seem rather to arise out of a passionate identification with her subject. When it appeared, her biography contained information not available in any other. It is written in an emotional and somewhat archaic style reminiscent of the Carlyle of the *French Revolution* and the *Life of Sterling*.

Miss Maclean experimented with a different form of biographical writing in *Hazlitt Painted by Himself and Presented by Catherine Macdonald Maclean* (1948). Using the first person singular throughout, she rewrote Hazlitt's own story almost—but not quite—in his own words. The *not quite* is the rub. The author wished to present Hazlitt's "feeling as closely as possible in his own words," and the great bulk of reminiscence in his essays furnished inviting material for such an experiment. But, despite the use of the first person, "his own words" are precisely what are often lacking; they are subjected to constant alteration that destroys their character. His "I got there" is elevated to "I arrived"; "in the dim light . . . I thought Coleridge pitted with the smallpox" is reduced to "his face appeared dark and scarred." The wry comments with which Hazlitt brought his flights to earth are regularly absent. His variety and sweep of language, the gusto supported by intellect and spiced by bitterness disappear in insipidity. The work is sprinkled with tags of modern diction ("definitely," "personality") that, placed in Hazlitt's mouth, sound slightly outlandish; only now and then is the reader aware of Hazlitt's own voice. The book is a trap for cataloguers, bibliographers, and unwary readers, falling as it does, in authorship, in a limbo somewhere between Miss Maclean and Hazlitt. It has been advertised in booksellers' catalogues as a work by Hazlitt "edited" by Miss Maclean—which it is not.

The latest, and very likely for this century the definitive, biography is the large-scale and handsomely printed *William Hazlitt* by Herschel Baker (1962). The first quarter of this impressive work is mainly historical: it presents a full survey of the climate of English political thought in the days of Burke, Paine, and Godwin; of the long Tory reign, the treason trials, and the Malthusian and other controversies. There is a full account of the background of Dissent out of which Hazlitt grew, with more information than we have had before about the social and religious opinions of his father and a more thorough and impartial account of Hazlitt's own views on religion. His attempts to become a painter, his unsuccessful philosophical writing, hack work, and subsequent career as a periodical writer, all are set forth in detail in a work of admirable scholarship. Baker prints a good deal of new material, including a number of letters of Hazlitt, some of them important and, as Hazlitt letters go, revealing. If Howe and Miss Maclean are felt to have been too sympathetic with their subject, however, Baker more than redresses the balance. Though he praises Hazlitt's best work, in general he gives the impression of disliking, and certainly of condescending to, his subject. His judgments, expressed or implied, are presented in harsh terms: Hazlitt was "ill-bred" and vulgar, his love of art was "feverish," his style "febrile" or marked by "jaunty ease." As a whole, it is an unsympathetic and condescending biography, but thorough and scrupulous in its facts.

The full-length biographies are supplemented by a number of briefer studies. H. W. Stephenson's pamphlet, *William Hazlitt and Hackney College* (1930, a reprint from *Trans. of the Unitarian Historical Soc.*), furnished part of the material for Miss Maclean's account of Hazlitt's early Unitarian connections but contains additional information. It presents from the periodical press of the day and the correspondence of Priestley, Price, and others, the story of the collapse of the Unitarian school at Hackney in consequence of attacks from without and the growth of skepticism within. The author cites contemporary denunciations of Hackney College as one of the "volcanoes of sedition and nurseries of riot," and quotes a melancholy report by Thomas Belsham, under whom Hazlitt studied divinity there, that many of the students had declared "their unbelief in the Christian religion" and deserted the ministry. That was in 1795, the year Hazlitt left the school and abandoned his intention to enter the ministry. Miss Stephenson's pamphlet thus provides additional evidence of the cloud of social disapproval under which Hazlitt lived in childhood and youth; it also adds weight to the disputed statement of Crabb Robinson that Hazlitt was "one of the first students" to leave Hackney College "an avowed infidel." Still earlier background is provided by Ernest J. Moyne in "The Reverend William Hazlitt and Dickinson College" (*PMHB*, 1961), which presents new details about the Hazlitt family's stay in America. The elder Hazlitt, it seems, had been recommended for the presidency of the newly founded Dickinson College but fell victim to the quarrel between Benjamin Rush and John Ewing. Moyne has also uncovered a new letter from Hazlitt to his father describing the Lamb's visit to him at Winterslow in 1809 (*PMLA*, 1962).

Three particular points in the life of Hazlitt have received special attention because of their bearing upon his literary reputation during his lifetime and afterward. They are the estrangement from Coleridge and Wordsworth, the personal attacks upon him in *Blackwood's Magazine*, and the Sarah Walker affair. The beginning of his friendship with Coleridge and Wordsworth also has received attention; the precise date, in the spring of 1798, of his first visit to Nether Stowey is important in dating other events in the lives of all three men. Earlier biographers had placed the visit in April; George W. Whiting (*MLN*, 1927) argued for the latter half of May or June; Abbie Findlay Potts (*MLN*, 1929) supported Whiting's date with evidence from records of theatrical performances in Bristol. Other circumstances also point to the three weeks from about 20 May to 10 June. For the complete evidence the reader must consult Howe's *Hazlitt*, Harper's *Wordsworth*, the biographies of Coleridge by Sir Edmund Chambers and Lawrence Hanson, Chambers' "Some Dates in Coleridge's *Annus Mirabilis*" (*E&S*, 1934), H. M. Margoliouth's "Wordsworth and Coleridge, Dates in May and June 1798" (*N&Q*, 1953), Malcolm Elwin's *The First Romantics*, and my *Coleridge, Opium, and Kubla Khan*, as well as the articles of Whiting and Miss Potts and the Wordsworth and Coleridge correspondence.

Most accounts of the later estrangement are partisan in spirit, the animosities of the principals having descended to biographers and scholars. Discussions in the standard biographies and published letters are supplemented by special articles by Robert S. Newdick ("Coleridge on Hazlitt," *Texas Rev.*, 1924), Earl Leslie Griggs ("Hazlitt's Estrangement from Coleridge and Wordsworth," *MLN*, 1933), and B. Bernard Cohen ("William Hazlitt: Bonapartist Critic of *The Excursion*," *MLQ*, 1949), and by a long letter of Wordsworth to John Scott, first published in full by W. M. Parker in the *Times Literary Supplement* for 21 December 1941. Newdick surveys Coleridge's well-known statements about Hazlitt and observes that the two were apparently still friendly in 1811 but were at odds by 1815; he attributes their break to political and temperamental differences, particularly suspicion, envy, and stupid failure of understanding on Hazlitt's part. Griggs discusses the estrangement chiefly in the terms set forth by Wordsworth, who between 1814 and 1816 communicated to a number of friends and acquaintances as the reason for the estrangement his moral disgust at a scandalous affair of Hazlitt's during a visit to the Lakes in 1803. Griggs's full acceptance of this late version of the affair leaves unexplained the evidence of friendly interchanges after 1803, noted by Newdick and others. The article by Cohen traces the history of Hazlitt's references to Wordsworth from the review of *The Excursion* in the *Examiner* to the publication of the *Round Table*. Cohen wrote, however, without reference to the letter of Wordsworth published by Parker, and his article should therefore be read in conjunction with both that letter and the chapter "The Aftermath of Victory" in *Born under Saturn*. Correspondence reflecting a late stage of the quarrel, chiefly from the unreliable Charles Lloyd, was published by Paul M. Zall (*MLN*, 1956), and manuscript remains of Talfourd published by Vera Watson (*TLS*, 20 and 27 April 1956) add one or two peripheral details on the subject. These records, along with an earlier communication by Joanna Richardson (*TLS*, 19 June 1953), incidentally give a bleaker picture than we have had before of the final year of Hazlitt's life.

A perennial question in the accounts of the quarrel is that of the authorship of the notorious review of Coleridge's *Christabel* in the *Edinburgh Review*. It was often ascribed doubtfully to Hazlitt, but the evidence was first debated at length in the columns of *Notes and Queries* (1902, passim) by Thomas Hutchinson and Col. W. F. Prideaux, the first convinced that Hazlitt was the author, the second equally certain that he was not. Most authorities on Hazlitt since that time have agreed with Prideaux. The fullest discussions will be found in the biographies of Miss Maclean and Howe, in Howe's later notes to the *Complete Works*, P. L. Carver's "The Authorship of a Review of *Christabel* Attributed to Hazlitt" (*JEGP*, 1930), my article "The Unknown Reviewer of *Christabel:* Hazlitt, Jeffrey, Tom Moore" (*PMLA*, 1955), and Hoover H. Jordan's "Thomas Moore and the Review of *Christabel*" (*MP*, 1956). Howe found no traces of Hazlitt's writing in the review and believed the opinions expressed were those of Jeffrey; the article, he said categorically, as printed, was "demonstrably" not Hazlitt's, though he supposed that a manuscript might have been submitted and been rewritten out of all recognition by Jeffrey. Miss Maclean and Baker agree that the writing is not Hazlitt's. Meanwhile, Carver had introduced a new candidate, giving cogent reasons against Hazlitt's authorship and speculating that Brougham might have been the culprit. His negative argument is stronger than his positive, for the tentative evidence offered for Brougham—internal evidence of language and allusion—points as readily to Jeffrey and not convincingly to either. Much of his argument turns upon whether either Hazlitt or Brougham was familiar with the *Art of Sinking in Poetry*, which the reviewer of *Christabel* obviously had in mind. But as Carver could find nothing conclusive on this point, his attribution remained a pure guess. I agreed with Howe that the writing is not Hazlitt's, but did not think it Jeffrey's either. Observing that Dibdin's *Reminiscences*, in a passage that seemed to imply firsthand knowledge, ascribed the review to Thomas Moore (an ascription partly supported by other testimony), that the opinions expressed in the article corresponded with those of Moore, and that it resembled his other reviews for the *Edinburgh* in a number of points in which it was unlike the work of either Hazlitt or Jeffrey, including a strikingly idiosyncratic use of the term "couplet," I suggested that Moore was almost certainly the author though he was unlikely to have acknowledged, and might well have denied, having written it. Jordan took exception to this conclusion. Limiting his discussion to questions of internal evidence, he assigned the review to Hazlitt and Jeffrey on grounds of style and thought. Two subsequent articles, Wilfred S. Dowden's "Thomas Moore and the Review of *Christabel*" (*MP*, 1962) and my "Tom Moore and the *Edinburgh* Review of *Christabel*" (*PMLA*, 1962) presented further evidence and arguments on both sides of the question, including the almost but not quite categorical denial by Moore, printed by Dowden. To arrive at a sound conclusion, all these discussions and all the sources they cite need to be studied with close attention.

The beginning of *Blackwood's* campaign of abuse against Hazlitt followed circulation of the report of the scandal of 1803 by Wordsworth and Coleridge and has been traced to it by some writers, Swinnerton (in his introduction to Howe's *Hazlitt*) going so far as to assert that "all the evil report of Hazlitt was circulated by Wordsworth." This conjecture was shared, less categorically, by Howe and Miss Maclean, both of whom discussed the *Blackwood* affair fully. In the *Fortnightly Review* ("Hazlitt and *Blackwood's Magazine*," 1919), Howe gave some details not included afterwards in his *Life* and incidentally corrected Whibley's statements in *Blackwood's* of the preceding year. He thought that Wordsworth probably reported the scandal to John Wilson and that this was the origin of the threats in *Blackwood's* to "expose" Hazlitt. Howe's article contained some inaccuracies that subsequent information enabled him to mend. Other articles add minor points to the record of the *Blackwood* campaign. In 1936 Howe printed a group of newly discovered letters (*TLS*, 21 March), one of which, to Constable in 1818, is important for the light shed upon Hazlitt's state of mind and the circumstances surrounding his *Reply to Z*. Theodore Besterman (*TLS*, 22 Aug. 1935) printed evidence of a second threat from Hazlitt of action for libel. Ralph M. Wardle (*MLN*, 1942) described a hoax perpetrated by Maginn that seems to have saved the publishers from this second suit and that has continued to fool critics and scholars. Alan Lang Strout, in "Hunt, Hazlitt, and *Maga*" (*ELH*, 1937), traced the personal attacks in *Blackwood's* and commented upon the lasting damage done to Hazlitt's reputation by the repeated epithet "pimpled," which, under threat of proceedings for libel, was ostentatiously transferred from his person to his literary style.

Overlapping this in time is the episode of Hazlitt's unreturned love for Sarah Walker and the Scottish divorce from his first wife, from whom he had separated two years earlier. The unsuitability of that marriage has been noted by all biographers, and in an article, "Some Early Correspondence of Sarah Stoddart and the Lambs" (*HLQ*, 1960), John R. Barker prints letters showing what he describes as the future Mrs. Hazlitt's "meanly calculating" spirit in money matters as well as her already well-known desperate rashness in the search for a husband. William Hallam Bonner's *The Journals of Sarah and William Hazlitt* (Univ. of Buffalo Studies, 1959) prints the journal in which Mrs. Hazlitt recorded the divorce proceedings and her simultaneous sightseeing excursions in Scotland, along with some of her letters and a short journal kept by Hazlitt for twelve days in 1823. Sarah's portion had been published, less accurately, in Le Gallienne's edition of *Liber Amoris* and much of the Hazlitt journal, freely altered, in *Lamb and Hazlitt*. Bonner prints a full and corrected text. He takes the side of the wife avowedly, and in his introduction undertakes to paint a more favorable picture of her than we have commonly had. In his introduction to the *Liber Amoris,* Le Gallienne had surveyed the history of the Sarah Walker affair and all the other of Hazlitt's reputed romances, but his account is unreliable. That of the episode of 1803 is not in accord with more recent findings, incomplete as these are; and the other two chief loves, "Sally Shepherd," the supposed daughter of Dr. Shepherd of Gateacre, and a supposed Miss Windham, heiress of the Hon. Charles Windham of Norman Court, who was said afterward to have married Charles Baring Wall, M.P., have evaporated entirely. Howe noted that Dr. Shepherd was too young to have been the father of a grown daughter at the time in question; and J. Rogers Rees (*N&Q,* 8 Feb. 1908) destroyed Miss Windham by discovering that no Windham with an only daughter or heiress ever owned Norman Court and that the supposed Miss Windham's supposed husband, Baring Wall, lived and died a bachelor. Both the *Liber Amoris* itself and the love affair it records were dismissed by Le Gallienne as the absurdities of a "maudlin sentimentalist." The second essay in the volume, by W. C. Hazlitt, defended Hazlitt by apologizing for him.

A more sympathetic account is that of Walter Sichel in the *Fortnightly Review* (1914). Regretting that "scarcely anyone now reads" Hazlitt, Sichel wrote one of the most appreciative general essays that had appeared up to that time, dwelling at some length and with more than common tolerance upon the *Liber Amoris* episode. Resuming the subject in the same journal in 1916 ("Hazlitt and 'Liber Amoris' "), Howe took to task the critics who rejected the book as ungentlemanly, criticizing most severely among these Leslie Stephen, Le Gallienne, and W. C. Hazlitt. *Liber Amoris* should be read, he urged, not as "a biographical lapse from virtue" but as a novel, like other novels founded on autobiographical material. He considered it a "highly characteristic work of art" and a good one. Hazlitt wrote and published it, he believed, not only to rid himself of an obsession but also because he had something to say. This is essentially the view expressed afterward in the introduction to the edition of 1948, in which Charles Morgan placed the book beside Stendhal's *De l'amour* and among the literary descendants of Rousseau's *Confessions.* But the former view is still sometimes heard. Myron F. Brightfield ("Some English 'Confessions' of the Early Nineteenth Century," *Univ. of California Chron.,* 1931), described the book with evident distaste as fit only for "the annals of psychopathology," adding that a modern psychiatrist could "have reasoned Hazlitt quickly out of this obsession." In a more recent article ("Hazlitt's 'Liber Amoris,' " *London Mag.,* 1954), Cyril Connolly characterized the affair itself as "the most unfortunate

love story in literature from Propertius' meeting with Cynthia to
Baudelaire's with Jeanne Duval" and the book as a work containing
"some of the loveliest pages in English and some of the silliest." A
minor addition to contemporary gossip on the subject was published,
along with much other gossip, in the *Times Literary Supplement for
7 June 1947*, by W. M. Parker, in a series of letters to Blackwood
from Charles Ollier, who appears to have stood with a foot in either
camp during the *Blackwood's-London Magazine* fray. Stanley
Jones ("Hazlitt as Lecturer: Three Unnoticed Contemporary Accounts," *EA*, 1962) reprinted accounts from two Glasgow newspapers of lectures delivered by Hazlitt during his divorce proceedings
(nearly if not exactly a repetition of already published ones), noting,
without surprise, that the account in the Whig paper was favorable,
that in the Tory paper hostile; and in "William Hazlitt at Renton
House" (*College Courant* [a Glasgow University journal], 1963) he
fills in details that give us a more vivid sense of Hazlitt's state of
mind and circumstances during these desperate months.

IV. CRITICISM

1. GENERAL DISCUSSIONS

N O FULL-LENGTH critical studies deal with Hazlitt's work as a
whole, and perhaps none should be looked for, since the clarity
and consistency of his writing offer little challenge to the critic who
might undertake to follow patiently through all the phases of his
work. The numerous short surveys intended for the general reader
are outside the scope of the present chapter, except for a few that
deserve passing notice because of the distinction of the author or the
essay, or because they illustrate the history of Hazlitt's reputation.
Among nineteenth-century accounts, the two by Sir Leslie Stephen
(*D.N.B.* and *Hours in a Library*, 2d Ser., 1876) still have some
currency though they are unreliable in the facts presented and
obtuse in their critical evaluations. Saintsbury at about the same
period found Hazlitt as a man contemptible but was disposed to
think him the greatest critic England had yet produced (*Collected
Essays and Papers*, 1923; the essay on Hazlitt dates from 1887).

He found in Hazlitt's style the germ of those of Macaulay, Thackeray, Dickens, Carlyle, and Ruskin, all of whom, however, he considered better stylists than Hazlitt. Like other critics who had to depend on Carew Hazlitt, Saintsbury gave currency to a certain amount of erroneous and misleading information.

Early in the present century, Paul Elmer More took the publication of the Waller and Glover collected edition as the occasion for a general evaluation of the work of Hazlitt (*Shelburne Essays*, 2d Ser., 1905). The key to his quality, according to More, was the fusion of passion and insight; passion accounted for the contradictions in his writing, for the keenness as well as the limitations of his psychological insight, for the rapidity of style and even the zest of his quotations. On the same occasion, the *Quarterly Review* ("Hazlitt and Lamb," 1906), in an article by Sidney T. Irwin, made partial amends for its former abuse, bestowing high praise upon Hazlitt and quoting some of his finer phrases. On the other hand, H. A. Beers wrote in the *Yale Review* (1923) that Howe's biography was supererogatory: the world already knew as much of Hazlitt as it would ever care to know, for he had led a dull life and as an essayist was no more than "a good third to Lamb and Leigh Hunt" in his century. By far the best general essay on Hazlitt is still the well-known chapter by Oliver Elton in his *Survey of English Literature, 1780–1880* (1912). Within the space of twenty pages he compressed a greater amount of significant information and a greater number of perceptive comments than most critics have been able to do in unlimited space. Almost every aspect of the life and work of Hazlitt is touched upon: his development as a writer, his personal idiosyncrasies, his criticism, his descriptions of nature, his skill in portraying his contemporaries, the *Liber Amoris* episode, his style, his love of quotations, and much else. Elton's is perhaps the only general essay that cannot safely be ignored by the serious student of Hazlitt.

Virginia Woolf may stand as representative of the next generation's criticism. Her essay on Hazlitt in the *Second Common Reader* (1932) is more perceptive, as well as more favorable, than her father's accounts had been in a former day; still, it is a piece got up for an occasion, and though conscientiously done, the outcome is not her most distinguished critical writing. She was perhaps too "creative" for her task; her portrait comes to life but is someone who is not quite Hazlitt. The recent *William Hazlitt* (1960), J. B. Priestley's contribution to the *Writers and Their Work* series, is a pleasant, enthusiastic essay full of quotations (well chosen) from Hazlitt, who is here said to be the greatest of all essayists. Bonamy

Dobrée ("William Hazlitt, 1778–1830," *REL*, 1961) also ranks Hazlitt high, maintaining that he possessed a "centrality of mind" that made him an exceptionally sane and discriminating critic.

2. PHILOSOPHY, POLITICS, AND POLITICAL ECONOMY

Though Hazlitt prided himself on being a thinker, no full-dress study of his philosophical writing has been published. It may be supposed that none is needed, since his avowedly philosophical works had no influence when they appeared and are of little significance today. His philosophical views, however — or, if one reserves the term "philosophical" for systematic constructions of thought, his fundamental beliefs and attitudes — have such important bearing upon his writing as a whole that they deserve to be fully set forth. René Wellek, in *Immanuel Kant in England, 1793–1838* (1931), dealt briefly with Hazlitt's remarks on Kant. He found Hazlitt naturally inclined toward Kantian ideas, and thought he missed becoming a genuinely Kantian philosopher from ignorance of the German language and a consequent dependence upon the unreliable interpretation in the English version of Willich. My study *The Aesthetics of William Hazlitt* (1933) contains a chapter on his philosophical ideas; James Noxon has a short paper on "Hazlitt as Moral Philosopher" (*Ethics*, 1963); and three dissertations deal with particular aspects of the subject, Horace Williston's "Hazlitt as a Critic of the 'Modern Philosophy'" (Univ. of Chicago, 1938), Edmund Gillmore Miller's "The Intellectual Development of the Young William Hazlitt" (Columbia Univ., 1955), and John William Kinnaird's "William Hazlitt's Philosophy of the Mind" (Columbia Univ., 1959), a study of his philosophical thought down to 1812. Recently, in "Sources of Hazlitt's 'Metaphysical Discovery'" (*PQ*, 1963), Leonard M. Trawick III, has produced an excellent short article that does more than its title promises. He shows with precision and succinctness not only what the "sources" were but also Hazlitt's departure from them; the "discovery," he concludes, owes much to earlier thinkers but is also a "genuine innovation" in philosophical thought. One other item deserves mention, W. U. McDonald, Jr.'s "Notes to Hazlitt's Writings Against the Phrenologists" (*N&Q*, 1960), supplementing the notes in Howe's edition of Hazlitt's writing on this subject. Hazlitt's religious opinions have been touched upon but never fully explored. Miss Maclean passionately denied the possibility that he was a skeptic; others less convinced of his attachment to religion have not felt compelled to discuss the question, since he made no attack upon Christianity.

His political views are clearly set forth in the biographies of Howe, Miss Maclean, and Baker. A central chapter in Crane Brinton's *Political Ideas of the English Romanticists* (1926) is given over to an account of Sir Walter Scott and Hazlitt as the prime literary representatives, for their time, of Tory and Radical beliefs and temperament. Brinton discusses Hazlitt's conception of "rights" as set forth in the "Project for a New Theory of Civil and Criminal Legislation," showing the principles by which Hazlitt would avoid the extremes of statism at one end and anarchic individualism at the other. He discusses Hazlitt's critical differences with the schools of Bentham, Godwin, and Owen; shows his belief in natural "benevolence" but also his disagreement with the Rousseauist assumption of the entire natural goodness of man; and remarks upon the balance maintained between his sympathy with the French Revolution and his belief in the values and achievements of the past. He finds Hazlitt, in short, a realistic rather than a utopian political thinker, who saw the weakness of extreme views so clearly that his own radicalism may be thought not far from the Aristotelian golden mean. Though most readers will be slow to associate the "golden mean" with Hazlitt, Brinton's account helps to correct the impression fostered by his political opponents that he was a mad Jacobin, impractical at best and malevolent at worst.

Brinton ignores the subject of Napoleon, upon which Hazlitt was least rational, but on which nevertheless he has been defended by Jules Deschamps in "Hazlitt et Napoléon" (*Rev. des études napoléoniennes*, 1939). In "Scott, Hazlitt, and Napoleon" (*Essays and Studies*, Univ. of California Pubs. in English, 1943), M. F. Brightfield started from the same contrast between Scott and Hazlitt as Tory and Radical. Writing, however, with his eye upon the Second World War as much as on the Napoleonic struggle, he undertook to assess the values and weaknesses of those Tory and Radical attitudes for our own time. He was not concerned with Hazlitt's actual opinions as such and did not set out to discuss them specifically, but took Hazlitt merely as representative of the utopian radicalism of Godwin, Hunt, Shelley, Keats, and others. This classification, very different from Brinton's, is merely incidental to Brightfield's main theme. William C. Hummel in "Liber Amoris: Hazlitt's *Napoleon*" (*KM*, 1963) also discusses the political aspects of the *Life*. *William Hazlitt's* LIFE OF NAPOLEON BUONAPARTE: *Its Sources and Characteristics* (1959), a monograph by Robert E. Robinson, is the only extended study of the work. Robinson points out errors and omissions in Howe's account. Hazlitt's use of sources he considers so close as to amount to "virtual plagiarism." The charge is illustrated by parallel passages quoted from Mignet, Ségur (a debt noted earlier by K. B. Schofield in *TLS*, 16 Dec. 1926), and Scott, and by further detailed textual comparisons. It is followed by a thoroughly unfavorable description of the *Life* as a whole and by nearly seventy pages of appendixes tabulating Hazlitt's use of sources line by line, as well as his passages of independent commentary.

Hazlitt's political writings as a whole—their range of ideas, scope, method, and style, their antecedents, their influence, and much else—still await published authoritative treatment, though Robinson wrote a dissertation, "William Hazlitt as Social Controversialist and Propagandist" (Univ. of California, 1942), two other dissertations have dealt with certain aspects of the subject (by Eric A. Eckler, 1937, and William C. Hummel, 1947, both Univ. of Pittsburgh), and Joseph J. Reilly in "Hazlitt, Liberal and Humanitarian" (*Cath W*, 1944) published a short appreciative study. W. P. Albrecht's "Liberalism and Hazlitt's Tragic View" (*CE*, 1961) discusses the theory that, as the concept was evolved by English philosophers from Hobbes to Godwin, political liberalism, because it was essentially optimistic, allowed no ground for a tragic view of life. Albrecht distinguishes from this position that of Hazlitt, whose insistence upon the importance of imagination and whose conviction that "evil is inseparable from the nature of things" did provide a basis for his "tragic view of life."

Hazlitt appears to have been the only amateur whose writings on the Malthusian controversy retain a place beside those of professed political economists in the main stream of that argument. Alfred Cobban, writing the article on him in the *Encyclopedia of the Social Sciences*, described his *Reply to the Essay on Population* (1807) as a serious, though intemperate, contribution to the subject. *The Malthusian Controversy* (1951), by the economist Kenneth Smith, begins and ends with a quotation from Hazlitt. Smith gives a closely reasoned account of his anonymously published *Reply to the Essay on Population;* discusses the criticism of this in the *Edinburgh Review*, which denounced the *Reply* and defended Malthus (in a review perhaps written by Malthus himself) ; summarizes the rejoinder published by Hazlitt in Cobbett's *Political Register* (1810) ; and cities, more briefly, other arguments from his later writings. Smith pays more attention to Hazlitt than do some other historians of the controversy because he himself is critical of certain of Malthus' doctrines. In general he upholds the soundness of Hazlitt's criticism.

The full exposition of this aspect of Hazlitt's thought will be found in a monograph by William P. Albrecht, *William Hazlitt and the Malthusian Controversy* (Univ. of New Mexico Pubs. in Lang. and Lit., 1950). Albrecht is less critical of Malthus and correspondingly more critical of Hazlitt than is Smith. Thoroughgoing Malthusians as a rule have attributed errors or inconsistencies in the application of the theory, and even in the theory itself, to the followers of Malthus rather than to the master. Smith maintains — and quotes passages which, to a layman, seem to bear him out — that Malthus himself expressly gave out almost all the ideas, including the contradictions and the somewhat embarrassing baggage of corrollaries and flinthearted applications of the theory to problems of poor relief and the like, which followed in the wake of his primary doctrines concerning population. Agreeing with the more favorable expounders of Malthus, Albrecht finds Hazlitt's criticisms not only violent, as Hazlitt admitted they were, but unsound and unjust at many points. He notes, among other things, Hazlitt's unwillingness to give Malthus credit for major advances over the theories of Wallace and his neglect of other points in favor of Malthus' "ratios." On the other hand, he points out what he regards as one of the most telling criticisms of Malthus, Hazlitt's defense of the right of the laboring population to strike and his attack upon the injustice of laws that permitted employers to combine against labor while forbidding combinations of the poor. Malthus had recognized injustice in the employers' combination but had left this out of account in his actual recommendations for achieving a "natural" wage. Albrecht shows also that Hazlitt anticipated important arguments that were afterward brought forward by Francis Place and J. S. Mill; and he shows how Hazlitt's critical analysis of Malthus' thought enabled him to foresee, as others did not, one notably un-Malthusian phenomenon of the later nineteenth century, the great rise in population attended by a rise, instead of what should by Malthusian theory have been a decline, in the general standard of living. Hazlitt opposed Malthus' theories, Albrecht concludes, because of his revolutionary philosophy "as both modified and supported by his explanation of human behavior"; his opposition was similar to that of Godwin though he did not share Godwin's belief in "perfectibility." Albrecht analyzes Hazlitt's arguments in detail and presents them against the background of the economic thought and the social conditions of the period. Whether the reader accepts his or Smith's evaluation of Hazlitt's part in the controversy will depend upon the reader's own disposition toward Malthusian theory, a subject on which economists themselves are not agreed. Albrecht's work, at any rate, is the one indispensable to students of Hazlitt; Smith's treatment is incidental to his survey of the whole controversy. An earlier paper by Albrecht, partly but not entirely incorporated into his monograph ("Hazlitt's *Principles of Human Action* and the Improvement of Society" in *If by Your Art: Testament to Percival Hunt,* 1948), discusses Hazlitt's theories of human nature and economics as set forth in the *Principles* and the *Reply to Malthus.*

3. AESTHETIC THEORY, LITERATURE, AND THE ARTS

In *The Aesthetics of William Hazlitt* (1933) I made an attempt to explore the philosophical basis of his writing on literature and the other arts. Though not disagreeing with the common opinion that the greatest contribution of Hazlitt to English criticism rests in his account of individual writers and individual works, I maintained that the theoretical principles are there, that awareness of them is essential to a full understanding of Hazlitt's work, that they shed light upon his individual judgments, and that they amount to something more than mere parroting of the opinions of Coleridge, as they have often been thought to be. A chapter on Hazlitt's philosophy is followed by accounts of his aesthetic theory with reference, first, to the aims and problems of painting, and afterward, in somewhat more detail, to literature. Particular emphasis is laid upon Hazlitt's dislike of the single-valued answer to all questions, his insistence that "truth is not one but many," a belief related to the catholicity of his tastes and the disinterestedness of his criticism.

An important further study of his theory appears in an article by John M. Bullitt, "Hazlitt and the Romantic Conception of the Imagination" (*PQ*, 1945). Avoiding most of the familiar statements of Hazlitt on the subject, Bullitt extracts from the wealth of little-known material in Howe's edition some neglected statements on the constitution of the imagination, on its relation to the ethical life, and on its function in painting, drama, and poetry. The article is made up largely of direct quotations from Hazlitt—which is all to the good, for they are so well chosen and often so unfamiliar that even the expert will find himself illumined. Bullitt discusses the associationist theory of the mind as it was used by Hazlitt and brings out the close connection between his thought and that of Keats, citing unfamiliar parallels. On two points, however, Bullitt may be thought to misinterpret or strain Hazlitt's meaning. In writing of Turner's landscapes as "abstractions of aerial perspective, representations not so properly of the objects of nature as of the medium through which they are seen," Hazlitt was surely using the term "medium" to mean the air or atmosphere, not, as Bullitt reads it, the technical "medium" of line and color. Bullitt also interprets Hazlitt's theory of the "ideal" in such a way as to make it almost identical with the theory of Reynolds that Hazlitt was undertaking to refute. A later contribution to the subject is an important essay, "Hazlitt the Associationist" (*RES*, 1964), in which J.-C. Sallé shows the full extent of Hazlitt's eighteenth-century associationism. A paper by Tommy G. Watson, "Johnson and Hazlitt on the Imagination in Milton" (*SoQ*, 1964), summarizes relevant passages from Hazlitt's lecture on Shakespeare and Milton.

The most widely known accounts of Hazlitt's literary criticism are those of Saintsbury in his *History of Criticism* (1904) and H. W. Garrod ("The Place of Hazlitt in English Criticism," 1925; reprinted in *The Profession of Poetry and Other Lectures*, 1929). Saintsbury charged Hazlitt with vast ignorance, errors, prejudice, and an unpleasantness of temper amounting almost to insanity; then turned about and declared himself unable to decide whether Coleridge or Hazlitt is the greatest of English critics (cf., however, his earlier essay on Hazlitt, mentioned above, and, on the other side, his chapter on Coleridge in the *History of Criticism*). He considered the theoretical criticism of Hazlitt interesting but believed that it is his discussions of individual writers and works that are truly great. Nearly a quarter of a century later, Garrod found Hazlitt's reputation as a critic increasing yearly but still below what it should be; Saintsbury's high, if erratic, praise had not "taken." Garrod predicted that when critical accounts are made up in another hundred years, *Hazlitt's Spirit of the Age* may be found the brightest gem of English criticism. The pre-eminence of Hazlitt, according to Garrod, derives first of all from the fact that literature meant more to him than to the other great critics; but Hazlitt had also a "flair for truth in which no English critic rivals him," a finer sense than anyone else possessed for distinguishing between "the genuine and tinsel," and a sounder judgment of his contemporaries than has been made by any other. His criticism, Garrod maintained, was notable for disinterestedness in spite of some injustice to his former friends who had turned Tory. Like Saintsbury, but more emphatically, Garrod considered the *Characters of Shakespeare's Plays*, Hazlitt's earliest volume of sustained criticism, as the least satisfactory though it remains the most widely known of his critical works; the *Lectures on the English Poets* is far better; and still better, "principally as being more courageous," is the *Lectures on the English Comic Writers*. Garrod singled out also in passing the "admirable" critique of *The Excursion* in the *Round Table*.

Saintsbury, however, and to a lesser extent Garrod also, will no doubt be superseded by the much more solid account of Hazlitt's criticism in the second volume of René Wellek's *A History of Modern Criticism: 1750–1950* (1955). In contrast to Saintsbury's caprices, Wellek supplies an informed and reasoned analytical survey, too succinct to be summarized here but not in itself a mere summary. Wellek covers satisfactorily all the important aspects of Hazlitt's criticism but is particularly valuable as a historian of ideas, where his remarkably wide and exact knowledge enables him to place Hazlitt in relation to earlier and contemporary thought without losing sight of the individual character of his writing. Since Wellek makes few unsupported statements of any kind, a reader must respect even the occasional opinions that he may not share.

The most extensive account of Hazlitt's criticism is that of Jacob Zeitlin in the introduction to his volume of selections, *Hazlitt on English Literature.* Beginning with a sketch of the intellectual history, tastes, character, and general qualities of Hazlitt's mind, he proceeded to consider the assumptions underlying his criticism. An "implicit basis of sound theory" (Coleridge's), Zeitlin thought, sets Hazlitt apart from the later impressionist critics with whom he has often been compared. Zeitlin emphasized the breadth of Hazlitt's tastes, his power of generalization, his gift for distilling in a paragraph the essential spirit of a historical period or fashion, and his power to present an old subject freshly without falling into eccentricity. After discussion of the separate critical volumes, he closed with a description of Hazlitt's style and some brief remarks concerning his influence on later critics, noting particularly parallels from the writing of James Russell Lowell. The study is solid and useful. In considering Hazlitt's admiration for Rousseau, however, Zeitlin falls into a misconception common among students of romanticism; it is the failure to distinguish between Rousseau's own insistence upon feeling or emotion as an ultimate good to be encouraged, increased, and indulged, even to be proud of—an attitude which is not only "romantic" but sentimental also—and the insistence of such writers as Hazlitt that feeling, "custom," passion, and imagination, being fundamental to the constitution of man, cannot and should not be ignored in life or literature. Much of the attack upon the romantic writers in the present century stems from confusion between these two very different things, the urging of something as a value and the acceptance of it as a fact. Zeitlin also supported the widely held opinion that in criticism Hazlitt played the Huxley to Coleridge's Darwin. He thought Coleridge established the principles but spoke only to the few, whereas Hazlitt took over these principles, applied them to literary works, and interpreted them for the many. The ironical commentary on this view is René Wellek's statement (in *English Romantic Poets*) with respect to Coleridge that *his* "main theoretical ideas are derivative and second-hand, and that his specific merit as a critic is in the practical application of the principles."

Like Garrod, Zeitlin considered Hazlitt's criticism of his contemporaries remarkably sound. Though Hazlitt was perhaps the only English writer of genius who regularly addressed himself to the task of portraying his contemporaries, neither Zeitlin nor anyone else has much more than glanced at this aspect of his writing. Hazlitt stands alone in the number and possibly also in the soundness and brilliance of his portraits of literary men of his age, and is approached only at a distance even by Clarendon in his characters of public men, especially political figures. The portrait painting in which he had failed with pigment came to life in his mature character writing. This part of his work has been ransacked for evidence concerning quarrels, personal or political, but surprisingly little has been written about it from the standpoint either of character drawing as an art or of historical accuracy and insight. It cost him a good deal in friendship and favor during his lifetime and has often been condemned because so many of the portraits were of his present or past friends. To what extent this writing stemmed from the artist's creative passion for drawing a "true" living portrait at whatever personal expense and to what extent from malice is a question no doubt insoluble but nevertheless still open for exploration. It would be agreed, at any rate, that when he drew Gifford, malice colored the ink; on the other hand, in a discussion of his criticism of Wordsworth's poetry, Albrecht maintains that even his hatred of Wordsworth's and Coleridge's later political views did not warp his critical judgment of their work ("Hazlitt on Wordsworth; or, The Poetry of Paradox," *Six Studies in Nineteenth-Century English Literature and Thought*, ed. H. Orel and G. J. Worth, *UKPHS*, No. 35, 1962). R. K. Gordon touched upon the subject in "William Hazlitt on Some of His Contemporaries" (*TRSC*, 1948, the presidential address).

Another general estimate of Hazlitt's place in criticism is that of G. D. Klingopulos ("Hazlitt as Critic," *Essays in Criticism*, 1956). Though he does not fail to point out Hazlitt's deficiencies, the writer concludes with the assertion that as a literary critic Hazlitt is "at least as interesting, as useful and as important as Matthew Arnold." A still later article that says a great deal in limited space is John Kinnaird's "The Forgotten Self" (*PR*, 1963), nominally a review article (unfavorable) on Baker's biography but in substance a concentrated analysis of certain ideas concerning the nature of man that underlie Hazlitt's criticism. In "Hazlitt's Preference for Tragedy" (*PMLA*, 1956), Albrecht discussed Hazlitt's ideas of the function of imagination and "gusto" with reference to the tragic poet, finding the key to the critic's preference in the sympathetic identification with others, which tragedy arouses and comedy limits. The paper was followed by an argument between the author and Sylvan Barnet (*PMLA*, 1958) and by another article by Albrecht (*PMLA*, 1960), distinguishing, among other things, Hazlitt's use of certain terms: "imagination" and the "poetry of wit," of "common places," and of "paradox." The substance of Albrecht's various studies is brought together and amplified in *Hazlitt and the Creative Imagination* (1965), a survey of Hazlitt's major writings, with imagination presented as a key conception in Hazlitt's thought. A number of dissertations have been concerned with miscellaneous aspects of Hazlitt's criticism: by Leon Cogswell Wilkerson (Vanderbilt Univ., 1954), Herschel M. Sikes (New York Univ., 1957), Elaine Plasberg (Boston Univ., 1961), Alice E. Meyer Linck (Univ. of Kansas, 1961), Martin Boris Friedman (Yale Univ., 1962), George Vincent Goodin, 1962, and Kathryn Floyd Douglass, 1963 (both Univ. of Illinois).

The Shakespearean criticism of Hazlitt has attracted more notice than his other critical writing, not so much from its superiority as because of the fame of the subject and the compactness of the material. Surveying it in 1932 (*PMLA*), Harry T. Baker cited Heine's opinion that Hazlitt had produced the only Shakespearean criticism of consequence in England and proceeded to compare him briefly with Johnson, Coleridge, Arnold, Swinburne, Dowden, and Bradley. He ascribed to him, incidentally, the first use of the term "dramatic romance" in the account of *Cymbeline*. R. W. Babcock in "The Direct Influence of Late Eighteenth-Century Shakespeare Criticism on Hazlitt and Coleridge" (*MLN*, 1930) undertook to show that, contrary to the belief of other scholars, the late eighteenth-century critics, particularly Morgann and Richardson, were known to their successors and influenced them. He noted that the *Monthly Magazine* in 1810–12 referred to Morgann's essay as "celebrated" and that both Hazlitt and Coleridge were readers of the *Monthly*. He maintained that Hazlitt's analytical comparison of Richard III and Macbeth is "practically a direct repetition of Whately," that in other remarks Hazlitt seems to be controverting the views of other earlier critics, and that his "psychologizing" shows both imitation of and reaction against Richardson. Babcock's argument must be taken seriously though it is not conclusive. In the same year P. L. Carver ("The Influence of Maurice Morgann," *RES*, 1930) presented evidence that seemed to indicate that Hazlitt knew Morgann's work. Stuart M. Tave, however, in an exceptionally well-reasoned and well-documented brief history of the reception of Morgann's essay, "Notes on the Influence of Morgann's Essay on Falstaff" (*RES*, 1952), shows that, though Hazlitt may have known it, his one quotation probably came not directly from the essay but from a review of a new edition of it in the *London Magazine* for February 1820, where the passage was quoted. There is every reason, as Tave shows, to think that Hazlitt read this number of the magazine, and his own quotation from the same passage appeared only a few months later in the *Edinburgh*.

Hazlitt's debt to Schlegel was made the subject of a German dissertation by Georg Schnöckelborg, *August Wilhelm Schlegels Einfluss auf William Hazlitt als Shakespeare-Kritiker* (1931). Hazlitt had written a long and sympathetic review of John Black's translation of Schlegel's lectures for the *Edinburgh Review* in 1816, and in the following year published his *Characters of Shakespeare's Plays*, during the writing of which he obviously had Black's *Schlegel*, as well as his own review of it, before him. Schnöckelborg studied this material closely and pointed out the resemblances between Hazlitt's book and its predecessor, particularly in the accounts of individual plays. In this earliest critical book Hazlitt was obviously feeling his way at first with the aid of Schlegel, whom he named, quoted, and often followed. In the latter part of the book, however, he ceased almost entirely to cite the German critic's opinions and no longer modeled his own interpretations after them. Schnöckelborg ignored this petering out of Schlegel's influence; he wrote, incidentally, under the misapprehension that the *Characters* had originally been given to the public as lectures. Discussing the influence of Schlegel on Hazlitt's subsequent *Lectures on the Dramatic Literature of the Age of Elizabeth*, Schnöckelborg printed certain passages in parallel columns to show that Hazlitt followed closely Schlegel's distinction between the classic and the romantic spirit in literature. He failed to notice that Hazlitt was merely quoting from his own earlier review of Schlegel in the *Edinburgh*. To urge this as an important "influence" may be going too far, since the ideas do not appear again in Hazlitt's writings. In other respects Schnöckelborg's conclusions seem well grounded. Two later and more inclusive studies are the dissertations, "Some Chapters on Shakespearean

Criticism: Coleridge, Hazlitt, and Stoll" (Univ. of Michigan, 1945) by Yao Shen, and "William Hazlitt's Shakespeare Criticism" (Johns Hopkins Univ., 1947) by Lynn B. Bennion.

Several writers have observed in passing that, partly perhaps because of his interest in individual character and portraiture, Hazlitt was the first great critic to undertake a serious account of prose fiction. Charles I. Patterson in "William Hazlitt as a Critic of Prose Fiction" (*PMLA*, 1953) points out that Hazlitt's judgments of individual works were in harmony with his theory, which calls for a balance between the actual and the "ideal." Patterson cites Hazlitt's criticism of Fenimore Cooper as a writer who described an Indian chief "down to his tobacco stopper and buttonholes" but who failed to master his materials and therefore failed "in massing and impulse." He summarizes Hazlitt's judgments of the major eighteenth-century English novelists, Fielding, Richardson, Sterne, Smollett; also of Scott, Godwin, a number of minor figures, and finally Cervantes, whom Hazlitt ranked perhaps above them all (W. U. McDonald, Jr. [*Rom N*, 1960] counted fifty or more affectionate references in Hazlitt's works to *Don Quixote*). Patterson emphasizes more than some writers would do the moral side of his subject though he makes quite clear Hazlitt's dislike of didacticism.

In 1837 the reviewer of Hazlitt's *Literary Remains* in the *Edinburgh Review* described Hazlitt as a writer "even now more read than praised, more imitated than extolled." Only in recent years, however, has attention been given to the influence of Hazlitt on other writers. Most of what has been written concerns Keats and Stendhal. The admiring references to Hazlitt in Keats's letters furnished the starting point for observations on the influence of the elder writer upon the poetry, taste, and intellectual development of the younger. The subject was broached during the 1920's in Amy Lowell's *Keats* (1925) and Clarence D. Thorpe's *The Mind of John Keats* (1926). Claude Lee Finney in *The Evolution of Keats's Poetry* in 1936 carried it further; he traced the poet's "empiricism" to Hazlitt, remarked upon Keats's annotated copy of the *Characters of Shakespeare's Plays*, and connected it and Hazlitt with Keats's ideas of "negative capability" and poetic intensity. Stephen A. Larrabee ("Hazlitt and the Augustan 'Rocking Horse,'" *TLS*, 14 March 1935) thought the earliest sign of influence was an image from Hazlitt's paper on "Milton's Versification" (1815), which appeared in Keats's attack on Augustan poets in "Sleep and Poetry" (1816).

On a much larger scale, James R. Caldwell dealt with the relationship of the two men as a whole. In "Beauty Is Truth . . ." (*Five Studies in Literature*, Univ. of California Pubs. in

English, 1940), he argued that the most famous pronouncement of Keats, the "beauty is truth" passage, represents "part of a definite system of aesthetics" formulated by Hazlitt. Caldwell discussed the system with particular reference to the "Grecian Urn" and other poems that he thinks deal with the same theme. Much of this discussion was later incorporated into his *John Keats' Fancy* (1945). Kenneth Muir, in "Keats and Hazlitt" (*Proceedings of the Leeds Philosophical and Literary Society*, 1951; reprinted in *John Keats: A Reassessment*, ed. Muir, 1958) treated the question at some length, asserting that nearly all the critical opinions of Keats "originated in Hazlitt's essays" but that the poet's more subtle mind refined upon them: "Hazlitt is a good critic; Keats is a great one." The subject has been treated also by W. Schrickx in "Keats en Hazlitt" (*HZM*, 1956 [I have not read this paper]), R. T. Davies in "Keats and Hazlitt" (*KSMB*, 1957), and Herschel M. Sikes in "The Poetic Theory and Practice of Keats: The Record of a Debt to Hazlitt" (*PQ*, 1959); and there have been two dissertations: Bertram L. Woodruff's "Keats and Hazlitt: A Study of the Development of Keats" (Harvard Univ., 1956) and Rotraud Müller's "Keats and Hazlitt: Parallels and Influences" (Freiburg Univ., 1957). In a paper related to these studies, William Garrett (*KSMB*, 1964) described Hazlitt's debt to the *Introduction to the Continuation of Dodsley's Old English Plays* written by Keats's friend C. W. Dilke.

Janet Spens, in "A Study of Keats's 'Ode to a Nightingale' " (*RES*, 1952), argued that "the principal clue to Keats's experience and the structure of the *Ode* is to be found in Hazlitt's *Lectures on the English Poets*." For the lines connecting the nightingale with "ancient times," Miss Spens found the key in an account of the "transferable" associations of nature which Hazlitt illustrated from birds, the voice of the cuckoo and the lapwing, Tereus and Philomela. She showed that Hazlitt's quotations from Spenser and from "Chaucer's" *Flower and the Leaf*, as well as his ideas, found their way into the ode. Other points concerning Keats and Hazlitt are made by Harold Briggs (*PMLA*, 1944) and by Bullitt in the article already discussed on imagination. Clarence D. Thorpe, in "Keats and Hazlitt" (*PMLA*, 1947), discussed the acquaintance and the mutual respect of the two men. He told first the better-known side of the story, that of Keats's admiration for Hazlitt. His concern was not with specific borrowings or influences, though he expressed the belief that Hazlitt helped "as much as any other man, including Wordsworth," in the development of an aesthetic philosophy that was still in process of change when Keats died. The major part of

Thorpe's article was devoted to a less familiar subject, Hazlitt's appreciation of Keats; and on this he marshaled a surprising number of passages, observing also that Hazlitt was the first to give a place to Keats in an anthology of English poetry, the *Select British Poets* of 1824.

A footnote to this subject, in the form of an exceptionally readable and well-reasoned article, was furnished by Payson Gates in "Bacon, Keats, and Hazlitt" (*SAQ*, 1947). A copy of the 1629 edition of Bacon's *Advancement of Learning* in the Keats house at Hampstead contains copious marginalia hitherto supposed to have been made by Keats. Gates proves conclusively that the notes are by Hazlitt instead, and quotes interesting extracts from them. It is to be hoped that the remainder may be published, for Hazlitt's temperamental kinship with the thought of Bacon lends unusual interest to the material. Gates's article throws light upon more than one side of Hazlitt. Jeanne Andrews, in "Bacon and the 'Dissociation of Sensibility'" (*N&Q*, 1954), writes of "Hazlitt's remarkable anticipation" of a famous passage in T. S. Eliot's essay on the metaphysical poets. In both *The Eloquence of the British Senate* and the *Lectures on the Age of Elizabeth*, she says, Hazlitt remarked in Bacon and other writers of the late sixteenth and seventeenth centuries a unification of sensibility in which thought and experience were simultaneous and "facts and feelings went hand in hand." She proceeds to defend Hazlitt's view of Bacon in opposition to the recent interpretation of L. C. Knight.

Howe observed that in 1817 Stendhal had visited England and in the following year had come to know and admire Hazlitt's *Characters of Shakespeare's Plays*. The two had some correspondence and eventually met in 1824. In a valuable article "Stendhal et Hazlitt" (*MP*, 1938), Robert Vigneron uncovers a remarkable record of unacknowledged borrowings by Stendhal from Hazlitt, as well as what appears to have been a natural affinity on the part of the Frenchman for Hazlitt's writings even when these were unsigned. Vigneron records borrowings by Stendhal in his *Rome, Naples, et Florence en 1817* and *Histoire de la peinture en Italie* (both 1817) from Hazlitt's anonymous reviews in the *Edinburgh* of Sismondi's *Littérature du midi de l'Europe* and Schlegel's *Lectures*, and from his *Memoirs of Thomas Holcroft*. Hazlitt's article on Schlegel, according to Vigneron, had a great deal to do with Stendhal's final rejection of the German aspects of romanticism. Stendhal borrowed from other articles of Hazlitt also, as well as from a review of Byron by Jeffrey and one of Goethe by an unknown hand. The discovery of the *Edinburgh* he himself declared was a landmark in his intellectual development, and the greatest attraction in it for him, evidently, was the work of Hazlitt. In his manuscript of *De l'amour* a passage is quoted from the review (again by Hazlitt) of Mme. d'Arblay's *Wanderer*. He wrote a letter to Hazlitt, evidently in 1819. Vigneron gives an account of what seems to have been their first meeting in September 1824 and records the subsequent comments and reflections in the works of both writers. After the opening of personal acquaintance, Stendhal seems generally to have acknowledged Hazlitt as his source when he borrowed. The debts were in some degree reciprocal. Vigneron cites a number of occasions on which Hazlitt credited to "my friend Mr. Beyle" or a less specifically identified "informant" observations on French taste or literature, and thinks Beyle, who himself had embarked upon a life of Napoleon as early as 1817–18, may have helped and encouraged Hazlitt in his work on the same subject. Vigneron notes opinions shared by the two writers on this and other matters, particularly French painting, but does not mention the resemblance later discussed by Charles Morgan between *De l'amour* and *Liber Amoris*, though this becomes more rather than less puzzling in the light of his information. Stendhal's book appeared late in the summer of 1822, *Liber Amoris* early in May 1823, though the conversations that went into it were being recorded as early as January 1822. Hazlitt was reading *De l'amour*—Morgan thinks almost certainly for the first time—after the two writers met in 1824. However, though the book received no attention even in France and was said to have had just seventeen readers in ten years, it was reviewed in England in the *New Monthly Magazine* (1822). Vigneron speculates upon the possibility that Hazlitt may have been the reviewer but finds no proof. François Michel's "Stendhal chroniqueur clandestin au *New Monthly Magazine*" (*Nouvelles soirées du Stendhal-Club*, ed. Henri Martineau and François Michel, 1950) shows numerous details of Stendhal's connections not only with this periodical but, a little later, with the *London Magazine* as well. In view of Hazlitt's close association with both magazines and the earlier letter or correspondence, it seems quite possible that he may have been one of the seventeen readers before his own book was published. The observations of Vigneron and Morgan, at any rate, open a new range of speculation concerning these two nineteenth-century post-Rousseauist works on love.

Several notes and studies record other borrowings from Hazlitt. P. L. Carver, in "The Sources of Macaulay's Essay on Milton" (*RES*, 1930), after showing how Macaulay used and reused his own earlier writing, points out a number of passages in various works, particularly the "Essay on Milton," which owed a great deal in ideas, style, and language to the *Edinburgh* articles and the *Lectures on the English Poets* of Hazlitt. Carver's demonstration is convincing, though he must be wrong in attributing to Hazlitt the review in the *Edinburgh* of Maturin's *Melmoth*. Kenneth Hayens (*MLR*, 1922) describes Heine's borrowings from Hazlitt's *Characters of Shakespeare's Plays;* Paul Turner (*N&Q*, 17 May 1947) argues in favor of Hazlitt's lecture "On Chaucer and Spenser" as a source of the imagery in Arnold's "Memorial Verses"; Donald K. Adams ("Swinburne and Hazlitt," *N&Q*, 1959) has a note recording Swinburne's close reading of the *Conversations of Northcote* (not, however, a borrowing), and Archibald C. Coolidge, Jr., a brief one on "Dickens's Use of Hazlitt's Principle of the Sympathetic Imagination" (*Miss Q*, 1962).

A few other miscellaneous papers dealing with various aspects of Hazlitt's criticism make points not elsewhere mentioned. W. R. Niblett (*DUJ*, 1940–41) suggests that Hazlitt's criticism gains particular excellence from "the penetration of his own self-knowledge, which enabled him to enter into the minds of a great variety of writers." He notes also the disinterested spirit of the criticism and observes that, seen as a whole, it forms the "first important survey of English literature after Johnson's *Lives*." Herbert Weisinger's "English Treatment of the Classical-Romantic Problem" (*MLQ*, 1946) discusses the views of Coleridge, Hazlitt, and De Quincey on this subject. Arthur Palmer Hudson's "Romantic Apologiae for Hamlet's Treatment of Ophelia" (*ELH*, 1942) considers Hazlitt's comments on the Hamlet-Ophelia scenes but throws more light on *Christabel* than on Hazlitt. Donald J. Rulfs, in "The Romantic Writers and Edmund Kean" (*MLQ*, 1950), and Harold N. Hillebrand, in *Edmund Kean* (1933), survey the criticism of Kean by Hazlitt and other writers of the time. In a later work, however, more important for the study of Hazlitt ("Hazlitt and the Theatre," *UTSE*, 1955), Alvin Whitley discusses the whole range of his theatrical criticism. David L. Jones, in "Hazlitt and Hunt at the Opera House" (*Symposium*, 1962), fills a small gap among critical studies by surveying Hazlitt's relatively few, and in general not very sympathetic, pronouncements on opera and opera singers.

In his brief remarks on Hazlitt's criticisms of art, Elton pointed out that these are among the first of any length in English to be concerned with actual pictures and statues rather than with theorizing on such subjects as "the picturesque" or "beauty." Two or three other writers on Hazlitt, however, have taken an equivocal or unfavorable view of his writings on art. The earliest account is the brief essay by Edmund Gosse printed as an introduction to the

Conversations of Northcote in 1894. Gosse thought Hazlitt's art criticism already outdated: the theoretical part was dull and ignorant; the criticism of individual pictures, on the other hand, was too lively and overluscious, too loaded with "sweetness" (probably a unique epithet as applied to Hazlitt); the critical method was "primitive." Thirty years later Stanley P. Chase covered the subject more fully in "Hazlitt as a Critic of Art" (*PMLA*, 1924). In his opinion, too, Hazlitt has little value today for students of aesthetic theory: his ignorance of the writing of Lessing and Winckelmann, later archaeological discoveries of the nineteenth century, impressionist painting, and other circumstances have rendered many of Hazlitt's theoretical discussions archaic. Chase discussed the main ideas of Sir Joshua Reynolds' *Discourses* and Hazlitt's criticism of them. The central argument concerns the conception of the Ideal which in neoclassical theory means correcting by art the imperfections of Nature or "imitating" the unfulfilled intention of Nature rather than actual visible nature. Hazlitt took issue with this view, insisting that great art is "scrupulously faithful" to what is fine in nature and that the painter does not produce great works by avoiding all particulars in order to paint the general. Chase proceeded to explain Hazlitt's belief that the Ideal is not merely the avoidance of individual deviations from an average or mean form but is something positive, an extreme, not a mean: it is "carrying an idea as far as it will go." This theory, Chase argued, leaves out of account the element of composition and therefore begs the whole question of idealization. Hazlitt does, it is true, neglect questions of composition, unity, and organic form in his critique of Reynolds' discourses; and the gap is only partly filled by comments scattered elsewhere in his work. Historically, Chase considered that Hazlitt's theory pointed toward later realism and his appreciations of individual pictures toward impressionism, thus in both directions anticipating the teachings and the revolution in taste brought about in the following generation by Ruskin. More recently, Eugene Clinton Elliott, in "Reynolds and Hazlitt" (*JAAC*, 1962), has compared the theories of the two men, which he finds a good deal alike except for their notions of the "ideal," which in Reynolds was social, he thinks, and in Hazlitt individual.

Two other essays consider many of the same points. G. M. Sargeaunt ("Hazlitt as a Critic of Painting," *The Classical Spirit*, 1936) discusses again certain critical terms used by Hazlitt—the *ideal, truth, nature, beauty*—which Sargeaunt says are now as meaningless as our present terms may come to be in their turn, though he thinks the modern emphasis on design and color intrinsically better, because more concrete, than Hazlitt's "truth and beauty." Sargeaunt's most distinctive point is the observation that when Hazlitt used the word "pleasure" to describe the aim of art, he knew the power of art to "stir the center" of one's being and therefore attached to the word a deeper and more serious meaning than was current among the fashionable amateurs who, in the era before the founding of public galleries in England, were almost the only persons, except for practicing artists, with a knowledge of pictures. Hazlitt's criticism thus struck a blow at the conventional drawing-room view of art. Larrabee's study "Hazlitt's Criticism and Greek Sculpture" (*JHI*, 1941) notes that, for a painter, Hazlitt was slow in coming to an appreciation of sculpture: that in Paris in 1802 he was unimpressed by the admired figures of the Venus de Medici and the Apollo Belvedere and by the productions of the favorite modern sculptor Canova. His enthusiasm was aroused only a dozen or so years later, when he became acquainted with the earlier Greek figures from the Parthenon in the collection of Lord Elgin. Larrabee sums up Hazlitt's reasons for admiring these but gives the impression, whether intentionally or not one cannot be sure, that he considers Hazlitt's preference for the older sculpture an error in taste. He devotes a final section to showing how often Hazlitt's criticism of literature was enriched by his interest in classical art, illustrating from the essays on Schlegel, Milton, Chaucer, Wordsworth, and on such actors as Kemble, Mrs. Siddons, and Miss O'Neill. In "Two Critics of the Elgin Marbles: William Hazlitt and Quatremère de Quincy" (*JAAC*, 1956) Frederick Will holds that Hazlitt's and De Quincey's judgments of the Elgin marbles constitute a minor movement, within the romantic movement, of reaction against Winckelmann and Reynolds.

Other references to the views of Hazlitt on art appear in Larrabee's *English Bards and Grecian Marbles* (1943) and C. H. Salter's "The First English Romantic Art-Critics" (*Cambridge Rev.*, 1956); and there is a recent dissertation, James Donald O'Hara's "William Hazlitt and the Fine Arts" (Harvard Univ., 1963). Peripheral matter will be found in two articles by Clark Olney, "William Hazlitt and Benjamin Robert Haydon," (*N&Q* 5 and 12 Oct. 1935), which trace the relations of the two men, mainly through the published accounts of Haydon and Bewick. "The Devil's Visits," a long general article (*TLS*, 19 Oct. 1946), calls attention to the merits of the *Conversations of Northcote;* and Stewart C. Wilcox ("Hazlitt and Northcote," *ELH*, 1940), drawing mainly on the accounts by Allan Cunningham and Cyrus Redding and on Howe's notes, presents the evidence of Northcote's duplicity concerning his part in Hazlitt's book. Northcote had co-operated in the actual conversations and obviously liked the fame or notoriety brought him by the published work but was loath to antagonize his old friends the Mudges of Plymouth. The correspondence shows the failure of his attempt to carry water on both shoulders: the Mudges were not placated. All this furnishes some background for interpreting cancels in the *Conversations* when it appeared in book form.

4. FAMILIAR ESSAYS AND STYLE

Both the familiar essays and the prose style of Hazlitt have been remarkably unfruitful as subjects of scholarly investigation. There are the usual brief accounts in historical sketches of the essay and in general works on Hazlitt, most notably, as on so many other points, in Elton's chapter. Particularly on Hazlitt's style there have been good brief passages, often of only a sentence or two. Longer studies have not flourished. More than thirty years ago Mario Praz raised the question "Is Hazlitt a Great Essayist?" (*ES*, 1931). His answer was "no": Hazlitt is "correct without distinction, virile without pithiness," his style "lacks bouquet," his "tea" is too "weak," his ideas are platitudes. All that can be said for him—all that Praz could say—is that he had common sense. Perhaps belatedly, Praz confessed to some rashness, as a foreigner, in making his sweeping judgment.

A published dissertation by Marie Hamilton Law, *The English Familiar Essay in the Early Nineteenth Century* (1934), deals with Hazlitt at some length but does not undertake to do more than expand what is usually said of the "romantic" essay. Apparently inspired by the admiration of Hazlitt so frequently expressed by Robert Louis Stevenson, and by the eminence of both as familiar essayists, Evert Mordecai Clark made a study of resemblances and influence in "The Kinship of Hazlitt and Stevenson" (*UTSE*, 1924). He quoted parallel passages, most of them not very striking, and followed these with personal parallels, chiefly a similarity of temperament and appearance, which few readers will see, and the observation that each had rejected his father's profession. The essay "Of Persons One Would Wish to Have Seen" became the center of animated correspondence, printed under the head of "The Text of Hazlitt" in the *Times Literary Supplement* (Feb.–June 1953). The main question at issue was the identity of the actual persons behind the initials in the essay and, indirectly, the proportions of truth and fiction in the conversation it purports to record. Heat was generated by concern over whether Charles Lamb must be believed to have introduced the Saviour into an otherwise secular conversation. The chief participants were Henry Tyler and R. W. King (who had the best of the argument).

On Hazlitt's style only one study of any length and pretension to completeness has been published, Zilpha E. Chandler's *An Analysis of the Stylistic Technique of Addison, Johnson, Hazlitt, and Pater* (Univ. of Iowa Humanistic Stud., 1928). This is an early example of the attempt to use scientific method, mainly quantitative, in the study of English prose. A fifteen-hundred-word passage was chosen from the criticism of each of the four writers, and a count made of parts of speech, abstract and concrete terms, Latin and Saxon words, length and construction of sentences, "rhythmic units," rhetorical devices, grammar, and "logic." The conclusions reached about the style of Hazlitt were obviously in the author's mind from the start and bear little visible relation to her statistical analysis. The analysis itself, moreover, is vitiated by naïve unawareness of historical changes in language. Along with Addison and Johnson, Hazlitt is found guilty of incorrect parallel constructions, the assumed standard of correctness being that of a twentieth-century American classroom. The book is an object lesson in how not to be scientific, for there is no "control" study, nothing to ensure that by the same analysis a different passage of Hazlitt might not be proved (statistically) to have been written by Addison or Pater. Statistical studies of prose have sometimes been profitable, but a respect for charts and tabulations need not blind literary students to the profound naïveté that often underlies an imposing statistical surface. A more recent unpublished study is a dissertation by John Raymond McCormick, "The Language of William Hazlitt: A Study of Prose Techniques in *The Spirit of the Age*" (Univ. of Alabama, 1961).

Most critics have had something to say concerning Hazlitt's habit of "interlarding" (to use his own word) his prose with quotations, often inexact ones. The consensus—though there is an occasional dissent—is that for the reader as, obviously, for the author the quotations endow what he is saying with a richness of association that justifies their presence; they were, moreover, his natural way of thinking and not usually a deliberate adornment. Separate notes or articles on the subject have been published by Harry T. Baker (*TLS*, 9 Dec. 1926; *MLN*, 1927); Wayne D. Clark (*MLN*, 1945); J. C. Maxwell (*N&Q*, 15 Sept. 1951); Stewart C. Wilcox (*N&Q*, 1952); F. V. Bernard, G. Thomas Fairclough, and J. C. Maxwell (all in *N&Q*, 1964); and Stanley Jones (*ES*, 1964), who makes comments of more than routine critical interest on a misquotation from *Cymbeline*.

Finally, several studies by Wilcox throw light on both Hazlitt's style and his practice as a familiar essayist. The chief of these is *Hazlitt in the Workshop* (1943), in which Wilcox prints the original (incomplete) manuscript of "The Fight." This little volume, which has considerable interest because of the rarity of Hazlitt manuscripts, provides an unusual opportunity to observe Hazlitt's method of writing and revision, though whether this sample is typical or not we cannot be sure, for the essay was written during the most agitated period of Hazlitt's life and the main alterations consisted in the removal of passages relating to this. Wilcox comments on the revisions and carefully collates the manuscript with the printed text of the essay. He has also written briefly on "A Manuscript Addition to Hazlitt's Essay 'On the Fear of Death'" (*MLN*, 1940), "Hazlitt on Systematic in Contrast to Familiar Composition" (*MLQ*, 1941), and "Hazlitt's Aphorisms" (*MLQ*, 1948).

4

Sir Walter Scott

By James T. Hillhouse

Revised by
Alexander Welsh
YALE UNIVERSITY

I. BIBLIOGRAPHIES

B Y ALL ODDS the main bibliographical item for Scott study is
J. C. Corson's *A Bibliography of Sir Walter Scott: A Classified and Annotated List of Books and Articles Relating to His Life
and Works, 1797–1940* (1943). As the title hints, Corson does not
deal with editions of Scott, but he covers practically everything else.
He lists some three thousand items, about half the bulk which he had
collected. It would seem safe to say that he has omitted little or
nothing of importance. Considering the huge mass of matter published on Scott during the nineteenth century, one would hope that a
bibliographer with such a task would be a judicious selector. The
work is, moreover, excellently compiled; the divisions and subdivi-
sions of the table of contents and the full index save the reader a
great deal of time. The frequent succinct and pointed annotations,
sometimes overastringent, reveal a close examination of the items
Corson is listing. Within the limits indicated above, this work makes
the use of the annual bibliographies and *The Cambridge Bibliography of English Literature* unnecessary, except for the comments
and reviews they may contain, up to 1939 or 1940.

The life of Scott by C. D. Yonge (1888) contains an extensive
bibliography by J. P. Anderson of the British Museum, and the one
in *CBEL*, useful for the editions of Scott (omitted by Corson), has
evidently made full use of the Anderson, some of the dating in which
should be checked. For a short and highly selective, but well-chosen
general bibliography, one may consult Ernest Bernbaum's *Guide
Through the Romantic Movement* (2d ed., 1949). There is also the
general bibliography in *The Cambridge History of English Literature*, now completely superseded by the one in *CBEL*. Corson's note
that the bibliographies in these last two works are of no value is an
overstatement, at least as far as it applies to *CBEL*. A full
description of the original editions of the poems is provided in
W. Ruff's "A Bibliography of the Poetical Works of Sir Walter
Scott, 1796–1832" (*Edinburgh Bibliographical Soc. Trans.*, 1937–
38), and of the novels in Greville Worthington's *A Bibliography of the
Waverley Novels* (1931). J. Thomson's *A Descriptive Catalogue of
the Writings of Sir Walter Scott* (1898) is merely a fairly detailed
analysis, volume by volume of the Cadell collected edition of Scott's

117

work (see below), but might be useful to some readers, especially of
the miscellaneous prose works. R. Caplan's *Bibliography of Sir
Walter Scott, Bart.* (1928) is not a work on the level of Ruff or
Worthington, but does afford a chronological list of Scott's publications.

Information on Scott's manuscripts and proof sheets (the two
chief centers for study, the Morgan Library in New York and the
libraries in Edinburgh) is contained in the *Catalogue of Manuscripts Acquired since 1925,* I (1938) of the National Library of
Scotland. W. C. Van Antwerp's *A Collector's Comment on His First
Editions of the Works of Sir Walter Scott* (1932) gives a good deal
of information about manuscripts and proof sheets (as well as
editions)—prices they have brought, and their present location.
Chambers's Journal (1898) records "The Fate of Sir Walter
Scott's Manuscripts," and J. M. Collyer in " 'The Catastrophe' in
Saint Ronan's Well" (*Athenaeum,* 4 Feb. 1893) reports on a
canceled sheet which reveals the original ending, altered by Scott
under pressure from his friends.

II. EDITIONS

THE LIST of the separate original editions of Scott's poems and
novels, with later editions and reissues, American editions and
translations, speaks eloquently of Scott's popularity. Note, for
instance, the record of such works as *The Lady of the Lake* or
Waverley in *CBEL*. The first editions of the novels (not in original
boards) are still not hard to come by. Most of the novels were
originally published in three volumes (the famous nineteenth-century
three-deckers), though some, because of length (e.g., *The Heart of
Midlothian*) or in combination with a short novel (e.g., *The Black
Dwarf* and *Old Mortality*) were issued in four. Collected editions,
moreover, appeared early (e.g., *Poetical Works,* 6 vols., 1806–08;
Novels and Tales of the Author of Waverley, 12 vols., 1820). The
less popular prose works were also collected before Scott's death—
Miscellaneous Prose Works of Sir Walter Scott (6 vols., 1827).

In 1828, near the end of his life, Scott undertook at the instance of Cadell a new edition of the novels and poems, writing biographical introductions to the various works to give the circumstances of composition and publication, adding many explanatory notes, chiefly of a historical or antiquarian nature, and revising the text itself. To the new edition of the novels, which began to appear in 1829, he was accustomed to refer as the "Magnum Opus." The introductions in the new editions of the poems are dated 1830 and 1831. Of extensive or major rewriting there are no signs; he did reread all the text, and there are numerous changes, but they are practically all stylistic, really the result of his rapid original writing and not very laborious changes in page proof. But these alterations in text, together with the new introductions and notes, did establish a thoroughly new edition, which has been the basis of later editions of the novels and poems. (Worth noting here is M. H. H. Macartney's "Sir Walter Scott's Use of the Preface" [*Longman's Mag.*, 1905], contending that Scott gave the preface an importance it had never had before and has not had since.) To this, Cadell added in the same format twenty-eight volumes of collected prose works (edited by Lockhart, 1834–40) and, on the publication of Lockhart's *Life*, the second edition of that work in ten volumes, making altogether a total set of ninety-eight volumes. This set was kept in print for forty or fifty years after Scott's death. A. and C. Black succeeded Cadell in the ownership of the Scott copyrights after 1851. In advertisements to late nineteenth-century editions they claim to have collated the "Magnum Opus" edition with Scott's own interleaved edition of the novels.

The demand for the novels and poems forced their publication in new collected editions all through the century. *CBEL* lists eleven distinct editions of *Poetical Works* after Scott's death and twenty of the *Waverley Novels*, and it is hard to believe that these lists are exhaustive. In addition, there are innumerable separate editions of the more popular poems (e.g., *The Lay, Marmion, The Lady of the Lake*) and of individual novels, latterly edited, many of them extremely well, for use in school and college. *CBEL* lists six editions of the *Waverley Novels* between 1890 and 1900, but only four since 1900; and these include such inexpensive ones as the Everyman and Oxford. In the last half century there have been no important new editions of either the collected poems or the collected novels.

The publication of Scott in the United States—really the pirating, or close to it—is described in Capt. Basil Hall's *Travels in North America* (1829) and more exactly in **D. A. Randall's**

"Waverley in America" (*Colophon*, 1935). Publication in France is recounted in D. Cook's "The Waverleys in French" (*TLS*, 17 July 1937). *CBEL* has many entries of foreign editions.

Attention may be called to a small miscellaneous group of novels consisting of *Queenhoo Hall* (1808), the antiquarian novel begun by Joseph Strutt and finished by Scott, *The Siege of Malta*, and certain forgeries. *The Siege of Malta*, which Scott began and for which he wrote a summary historical sketch, has been developed into a full-length novel by S. Fowler Wright (2 vols., 1942). The best known of the Scott imitations is the German *Walladmor*, exposed by De Quincey as a "hoax" and as "trash" (see Masson ed., Vol. XIV, and a Marburg thesis by Hedwig F. Kohler, *Walladmor von Willibald Alexis*, 1915, a routine study). *Moredun* and *Pontefract Castle* are frequently mentioned too, as in J. A. Farrer's *Literary Forgeries* (1907), where there is also an account of several obscure French forgeries, and in Corson.

The first considerable collection of the letters came only in 1894 —*Familiar Letters of Sir Walter Scott*, edited by David Douglas. These had to do as Sir Walter's correspondence until 1932, when there appeared a compilation of letters in the Brotherton Library by J. A. Symington and the first of the twelve volumes of H. J. C. Grierson's monumental collection, *The Letters of Sir Walter Scott, 1787–1832*, which was finally complete in 1937. Here is to be found the great bulk of the letters Scott wrote, though a few omissions have been discovered and there is still, since 1937, a trickle of letters that never came to Grierson's hand and which are noted in the annual bibliographies since his work was finished. Grierson and his helpers collected this mass of letters from all over the world and edited them with skill and judgment. In general, they are meticulously accurate; perhaps the only lapses came when they had to work at a distance and apparently with insufficient funds for complete photostats. (See Mildred Lambert and James T. Hillhouse, "The Scott Letters in the Huntington Library," *HLQ*, 1939.) The twelve volumes of letters still lack an index, however.

Selected letters *to* Scott appear in Wilfred Partington's two collections, *The Private Letter-Books of Sir Walter Scott* (1930) and *Sir Walter's Post-Bag* (1932). Other scattered items are listed in Corson. Among correspondence which has come to light since Corson, the most interesting are "Scott Letters Discovered in Russia" (*BJRL*, 1944, reprinted in book form, 1945) and "Russian Friends and Correspondents of Sir Walter Scott" (*CL*, 1950), both by Gleb Struve.

Scott's journal was first published in 1890 by David Douglas.

As Douglas' work on the letters and journal came to be closely examined, dissatisfaction with it was expressed, to be met by Grierson's edition of the letters and a careful re-editing of the journal in three installments by J. G. Tait, *The Journal of Sir Walter Scott, 1825–26* (1939), *1827–28* (1941), and *1829–32* (1947).

III. BIOGRAPHIES

THE BIOGRAPHICAL materials for Scott are overwhelming. He was a great public figure for two decades or more, a person whom everyone, both British and foreign, wished to meet; he was an unbelievably voluminous correspondent and received more letters than he wrote; there is an autobiography of his early years; he kept a journal. On top of all this, those who knew him well, and many who knew him less, were eager, especially after his death, to capitalize on their acquaintance with reminiscences, descriptions, sketches. The great bulk of this material is made evident in the listings in Corson, methodically subdivided.

As for autobiography, Scott wrote an account of his first twenty-one years which Lockhart used to introduce his *Life;* and the very considerable amount of personal information embodied in the introduction to the collected edition of the poems and novels was compiled and published separately at the time. Later it was absorbed into Lockhart, and so into the less extensive biographies which subsisted on Lockhart.

Scott's reading is an important matter. A great deal can be learned of it by his constant allusions in the letters and journals, and also from the catalogue of his library at Abbotsford, which was published at Edinburgh in 1838, and is at present not a rare item.

In addition to all this material originating in Scott himself, there was a great mass of biographical material from friends and acquaintances. The most famous of these items is probably *Familiar Anecdotes of Sir Walter Scott* by James Hogg, "the Ettrick Shepherd" (1834; published with slight additions as *The Domestic Manners and Private Life of Sir Walter Scott,* 1834). There are also, to note the most important, *Letters and Recollections of Sir Walter Scott* by Mrs. Hughes of Uffington (1904); the record of Washington Irving's famous visit in his essay "Abbotsford"; *New Love-Poems of Sir Walter Scott* (ed. Davidson Cook, 1932); *Journal of a Tour to Waterloo and Paris*, J. Scott of Gala (1842); on the same tour, A. F. Steuart, "A Journey with Sir Walter Scott in 1815" (*Chambers's Jour.*, 1905); Capt. Basil Hall, *Fragments of Voyages and Travels*, Third Series (1833); "The Funeral of Sir Walter Scott" (*Tait's Edinburgh Mag.*, 1832); Mrs. Margaret Oliphant, *Annals of a Publishing House* (1897), for Scott's relations with Blackwood's; T. Constable, *Archibald Constable and His Literary Correspondents* (1873); John Gibson, *Reminiscences of Sir Walter Scott* (1871), relating especially to financial affairs before and after the crash of 1826; W. F. Gray, "Abbotsford since Scott's Time" (*Sir Walter Scott Quart.*, 1928), for the history of Scott's descendants; W. F. Gray, *Scott in Sunshine and Shadow* (1931) and F. A. MacCunn, *Sir Walter Scott's Friends* (1909), these last two, accounts of Scott's relationships with his closest and most important friends; Lord Sands, *Sir Walter Scott's Congé* (3d ed. rev., 1931), on Scott's early unhappy love affair; M. G. Garden, *Memorials of James Hogg* (1884); *The Correspondence of Sir Walter Scott and C. R. Maturin* (ed. F. E. Ratchford and W. H. McCarthy, 1937); L. A. Bisson, *Amédée Pichot, A Romantic Prometheus* (1942) — Pichot was a most enthusiastic devotee and translator of Scott, and visited Abbotsford in 1822; Sir William Gell, *Reminiscences of Sir Walter Scott's Residence in Italy, 1832* (rev. ed., 1957); for Lady Louisa Stuart, see below.

Biographical sketches of Scott began to appear as early as 1816. At his death in 1832 they swelled into a flood of notices, sketches, and personal reminiscences of friends and acquaintances. The most important early *Life* was by Robert Chambers in *Chambers's Edinburgh Journal* (1832). (See also *The Letters of Sir Walter Scott and Charles K. Sharpe to R. Chambers, 1821–45, with Original Memoranda of Sir Walter Scott*, 1904.) Chambers had numerous sources of information about Scott, and was able to identify the originals of many characters in the novels. His *Life* was frequently reprinted, and was finally enlarged by W. Chambers (his brother) in 1871 and given an appendix of "Abbotsford Notanda" by Robert Carruthers, dealing especially with Scott's relations with his steward, William Laidlaw. This is the only early (or pre-Lockhart) *Life* on which Grierson draws for his biography of 1938.

Then in 1837–38 appeared the official *Life* by Lockhart. It came out serially in seven volumes (six in 1837, one in 1838) and was followed in 1839 by a ten-volume second edition which has become standard and has been reprinted ad infinitum. A decade later (1848) Lockhart published a two-volume abridgment with additional notes revealing names which had not appeared in the first two editions.

Lockhart's *Life* is recognized as one of the great English biographies. Lockhart was himself a man of real literary distinction, he had known Scott since 1818, and as his son-in-law since 1820 he had been in the very center of Scott's life, both private and public; he was highly regarded and trusted by Scott except for his dangerous tendency toward vindictive "satire" and condescending superiority; and he was clearly designated by Scott as the author of the *Life* which was bound to be written. Of course he had access to the bales of correspondence and other papers which had accumulated at Abbotsford. The result was a magnificent biography—a biography, however, which, as time went on, has shown itself to have certain failings. This was to be expected in view of Lockhart's place in the very heart of the family and of the common practices of nineteenth-century biographers. Lockhart was concerned to present Scott and everything about him in a favorable light, and he did not hesitate to take the steps biographers of the time commonly took, especially suppression and actual revision, but also manipulation of letters and other documents, including telescoping or "contamination." This process has been sharply illuminated by F. R. Hart's study of the corrected proofs of Lockhart (*SB*, 1961). Before one's indignation boils over, it is best to realize that many of Lockhart's contemporaries felt that he had not sufficiently *concealed* some aspects of Scott's life. Latterly he has also been accused of carelessness, and there have been demands for a new and thoroughly edited version of the biography. (See especially Vernon Rendall and W. M. Parker in *TLS*, 10 and 24 July 1930, 20 March 1937, and 1 Oct. 1938, and Rendall again, on Lockhart's careless and misleading citations from Scott's journal, in *TLS*, 8 Jan. 1944.) This revised edition, understandably enough when one considers the scope and expense of the work, has not been forthcoming. At least a definitive text of the *Life* is now being prepared by John Cameron and F. A. Pottle.

There has been no dearth of other lives of Scott. Corson lists twenty-eight of book length, excluding several written especially for children. Their authors generally admit that they have little to add to Lockhart or say that Lockhart is simply a quarry for them to cut stones from, or that they wish to tell Scott's story in narrower compass or from a special point of view, as, for instance, R. H. Hutton in the English Men of Letters series (1878), C. D. Yonge in the Great Writers series (1888), Andrew Lang in the Literary Lives series (1906), and John Buchan (1932). Buchan's *Life* is a brilliant account admittedly drawn from the materials of Lockhart; Grierson in his own *Life* calls it "delightful." Certain lives or biographical studies written to develop special theories or controversial issues will be mentioned later.

Very important is H. J. C. Grierson's *Sir Walter Scott, Bart.* (1938), a substitute for the revision of Lockhart which was probably too elaborate and expensive an undertaking. Grierson's purpose was to correct the omissions, misrepresentations, and errors in Lockhart in a running account of Scott's life. Since the most significant of these concern money matters, which were in crisis or at least on the verge of crisis off and on all through Scott's career and long before the great disaster of 1826, Grierson's *Life* tends to become a financial one, a history of Scott's relations with his publishers and his creditors. These matters are inextricably involved with the interpretation and criticism of the novels and poems, and with Scott's motives as a poet and novelist. Grierson was uniquely qualified for this task. He had just finished the monumental edition of Scott's letters and thus had probably more information and more comprehension based on actual data than anyone who had dealt with the subject before. At any rate, Lockhart as supplemented by Grierson is the core prescription in biography for the Scott student.

Hesketh Pearson's *Walter Scott, His Life and Personality* (1954) is packed with fresh anecdotal material drawn from the new editions of the letters and journals. The style is rather jaunty and gossipy, and the criticism, which is kept to a minimum, is definitely personal. Pearson makes Scott an extremely engaging character. For general background this life does not supersede John Buchan's. However, Edgar Johnson's life of Scott, comparable to his two-volume life of Dickens, is now nearing completion. A chapter on the year 1815 has appeared in *Nineteenth-Century Fiction* (1963).

Much biographical matter on Scott can be best taken up under "Criticism" below, but one set of documents clearly comes under biography—the Lockhart-Ballantyne controversy (1838–39), growing out of Lockhart's treatment of the financial disaster of 1826 and the events following. This resulted in a "Refutation" from the Ballantynes and a reply by Lockhart, "The Ballantyne Humbug Handled," which was answered in turn by the Ballantynes, "A Reply to Mr. Lockhart's Pamphlet." These and other associated items, including one by Dickens, who was violently pro-Scott and anti-

Ballantyne, are covered in Corson. The history of Scott biography in general has been reviewed by Corson in his recent Scott lectures (*UEJ*, 1955–56).

IV. CRITICISM

1. POEMS

WITH TIME, Scott has become the novelist. Even in his own time the novels threw the poems into the shade, and in later periods the bulk of writing about him, critical, biographical, scholarly, has been about the novelist; his literary career before 1814 assumes the appearance of a preparation for or an approach to the novels. The poems, however, had made him famous and prosperous, and three of them at least, *The Lay, Marmion,* and *The Lady of the Lake,* became English classics. The writing of these had been prepared for in turn by his work with the ballads and by his more superficial interest in the 1790's in the German Gothic. These early phases are well covered in many of the biographies, generally from a critical as well as a biographical point of view, and in various histories of literature; but the number of special articles on Scott's work before the novels is surprisingly small.

The years up to 1810 are covered by a series of three long articles by O. F. Emerson, "The Early Literary Life of Sir Walter Scott" (*JEGP*, 1924), where Emerson carefully re-examines the known facts. He had also published earlier several articles on special details in this period. G. P. Johnston, "The First Book Printed by James Ballantyne: Being an Apology for Tales of Terror" (*Pubs. of the Edinburgh Bibliographical Soc.*, 1893–94, 1896), cleared up long-standing confusion over *Tales of Terror* and *Tales of Wonder.* This article is now difficult of access, but is dealt with by Elizabeth Church in "A Bibliographical Myth" (*MP*, 1922), and is also described in the *Times Literary Supplement* by M. Sadleir on 7 January 1939, with additional information by W. Beattie the following week.

For Scott's first important literary work, *The Minstrelsy of the*

Scottish Border (2 vols., 1802; 3 vols., rev. throughout and with additions, 1803), there is a highly praised modern edition by T. F. Henderson (1902, reissue 1932), with full editorial treatment, especially as to the vexed questions of authenticity, Scott's manipulation of original materials, and the concoction of original ballads. This edition led to a controversial discussion in reviews and in later articles. Notable among these are W. F. Elliot's *The Trustworthiness of Border Ballads* (1906) and his *Further Essays on Border Ballads* (1910), answered militantly by Andrew Lang in "The Mystery of Auld Maitland" (*Blackwood's*, 1910) and in *Walter Scott and the Border Minstrelsy* (1910). Alfred Noyes also published an edition of *The Minstrelsy* (1908), attacking Scott's methods as a ballad collector. (For the ramifications of this controversy, see Corson.) Later articles on this subject are W. E. Wilson's "The Making of the 'Minstrelsy': Scott and Shortreed in Liddesdale" (*Cornhill Mag.*, 1932); Alan L. Strout's "An Unpublished Ballad Translation by Scott" (*MLN*, 1939), amplified and corrected by J. C. Corson (*MLN*, 1939); M. R. Dobie's "The Development of Scott's *Minstrelsy:* An Attempt at a Reconstruction" (*Trans. of the Edinburgh Bibliographical Soc.*, 1940). Lockhart, in his preface to the *Minstrelsy*, written in 1833 for the collected edition of Scott's works, says that the origin of practically every poem or novel on Scottish subjects can be discovered in the poems Scott collected here or in his notes on them. Grierson repeats this idea in his *Life*.

Of the scholarly notes, articles, and books on Scott's poems, the following are the most important (the contemporary reviews of his poems, the critical evaluation of them, and the poetry in the *Waverly Novels* are dealt with later): "Walter Scott" (*Courier*, 15 Sept. 1810; see an important note by Corson, No. 826); "Recent Poetical Plagiarisms and Imitations" (*London Mag.*, 1823–24); "Sir Walter Scott's Manuscripts" (*Literary Gazette*, 1833), a comparison of a part of the manuscript of *The Lay* with the printed version; E. Franke, *Quellen des Lay of the Last Minstrel* (*Archiv*, 1898), systematic but perfunctory; Hugo Hertel, *Die Naturschilderungen in Walter Scotts Versdichtungen* (1900), very thin, the body consisting of about fifty small pages, chiefly quotation; Alfred Ainger, *Lectures and Essays* (1905), principally on the influence of Scott's reading of plays on his style; P. W. Franke, *Der Stil in den epischen Dichtungen Walter Scotts* (1909); J. Möller, *Die romantische Landschaft bei Walter Scott* (1936), on the novels also, where one may, if he wishes, find Scott's landscapes dissected into tabulations of mountains, rocks, cliffs, and so on; J. C. Jordan,

"The Eve of St. Agnes and the Lay of the Last Minstrel" (*MLN*, 1928), on the possibility that certain lines in *The Lay* may be reflected in Keats's poem; T. Larsen, "The Classical Element in Scott's Poetry" (*TRSC*, 1938), an argument that Scott's poetry is only superficially romantic, and is essentially classical; and on the same subject, J. C. Shairp, "The Homeric Spirit in Walter Scott" (*Aspects of Poetry*, 1881); and W. M. Parker, "Suggestions for Scott's Muse" (*TLS*, 23 March 1940), subjects suggested to Scott for long poems, notably one by Warren Hastings, with Scott's comments. Recent defenses of Scott's poetry are lectures by D. Nichol Smith (*UEJ*, 1950) and Donald Davie (*PBA*, 1961). The transition from the poems to the novels is covered in J. T. Hillhouse, "Sir Walter's Last Long Poem" (*HLQ*, 1952), and by Karl Kroeber in a strong chapter on Scott in *Romantic Narrative Art* (1960).

Corson supplies an ample list of contemporary reviews of the poems. The most significant point about them is the large amount of critical disapproval in the face of the great popularity of the poems. These contemporary critics saw many of the same flaws in the poems that have displeased later writers, especially the loose, careless writing, and the equally rambling, carelessly constructed plots. Most important, perhaps, is the criticism of Jeffrey in the *Edinburgh Review*. Jeffrey found the novelty of the poems hard to accept, approaching them from an eighteenth-century, neoclassic point of view; but his later comments in his *Contributions to the Edinburgh Review* (1844) have a definitely favorable cast, with reservations. For this volume he selected his reviews of *The Lay*, "the first and most strikingly original," and of *The Lady of the Lake*, "the best" of the poems. Jeffrey's reviews, especially the one of *Marmion*, along with the Whig politics of the *Edinburgh*, stirred Scott to the establishment of the *Quarterly Review*. With Jeffrey's articles on the poems might be compared those of George Ellis in the *Quarterly*. Two especially unfavorable comments at the time or close to it are the review of Byron's *English Bards and Scotch Reviewers* in the *Antijacobin Review* (1810), and "Scott, Byron, and Their Imitators" in *Tait's Edinburgh Magazine* (1841). "Sir Walter Scott and One of His Reviewers" (*Chambers's Jour.*, 1905) describes a review of *The Lay* written for the *Edinburgh Review* (1806) that was laudatory in parts but also accused Scott of plagiarism and anachronism. It was finally withdrawn by the author.

Criticism of Scott's poetry since his own time frequently starts with the assumption, often stated explicitly, that the poems are far less important than the novels, that Scott's greatness appears fully in the novels and only partially and comparatively dimly in the poems. The critic may even say that he is really great only in prose. An early instance of this appears in Jeffrey's editorial remarks in the 1844 selection of his *Edinburgh Review* critiques (above), where he says that the novels unquestionably throw the poems into the shade, though he leaves no doubt that he thought Scott a real poet, even, it would seem, the most distinguished poet of the age.

Many historians of literature, most of them academic, speak up strongly for the poems, as the following list demonstrates. F. T. Palgrave in his *Landscape in Poetry from Homer to Tennyson* (1897) sets Scott among the great poets because of his Homeric simplicity, directness, and objectivity. Andrew Lang is of course a strong Scott partisan (*Lyrics and Ballads of Sir Walter Scott*, 1894, and introd. to the poems in the Dryburgh ed., 1892–94). Saintsbury (*History of Nineteenth-Century Literature*, 1896) declares it "impossible to rank [Scott] low as a poet"; although he has admitted limitations and his rapidity is especially bad in poetry, he should not be put below Byron. T. S. Omond (*The Romantic Triumph*, 1900) praises the poems highly, again with the claim of Homeric qualities. H. A. Beers (*History of English Romanticism in the Nineteenth Century*, 1901) calls Scott's poetry "the middle point and the culmination" of English romanticism, and while clearly admitting limitations, does not hesitate to enter into comparisons of Scott with Wordsworth and Coleridge. R. H. Hutton (*Brief Literary Criticisms*, 1906), though unwilling to set Scott beside Homer and Wordsworth, discovers fine passages of a meditative sort which most critics declare Scott incapable of, and thinks his battle scenes unsurpassed even in Homer. Stopford Brooke (*Studies in Poetry*, 1907) maintains that no one would place Scott among the greater poets, but is obviously affectionate and sentimental and makes a number of specific points about the historical place of the poems. G. E. Woodberry (*Great Writers*, 1907) calls Scott's poetry the best of its kind, and its kind one well worth having; there is nature in it, and certainly Wordsworth's is not the only way to deal with nature in poetry; the life he depicts "is not only the life of a past age, but it is one of the great permanent types of life." W. J. Courthope (*History of English Poetry*, 1910) declares that Scott met a fundamental demand of the people at large for a new form of poetic expression, blames Jeffrey for not grasping this fact and explaining it to his contemporaries, and sees in *The Lady of the Lake* "a triumph . . . which can hardly be repeated." J. C. Bailey (*Poets and Poetry*, 1911) from more or less the same point of view praises Scott as a poet of action and of patriotism who appealed deeply to all people with a pervasive power such as no poet since his time has had. Oliver Elton (*Survey of English Literature, 1780– 1830*, 1912), after defending Scott's handling of the ballads, and making it clear that he is only mildly favorable to the long poems, even the best of which seem to be *Waverlies* in verse, finds him the best lyric poet between Blake and Shelley, and thinks he could have been remembered as a poet on the basis of his short poems alone. Louis Cazamian, in the literary history (Legouis and Cazamian, 1927), says that Scott's poetry has a "persisting charm" and that "he has too sure a touch not to be a born poet"—yet the poems suffer from too close proximity to the novels. H. N. Fairchild (*The Romantic Quest*, 1931) insists on the importance of the poems, which are mistakenly called superficial, but are really deep and true, "native and instinctive"; Scott's tremendous influence as a popularizer of the Middle Ages was due not only to the positive merits of his poems but to the fact that he could attract "normal" readers of his day who would have recoiled from the queerness of "Christabel." J. W. Oliver (in *Scottish Poetry, a Critical Survey*, ed. James Kinsley, 1955) summarizes Scott's achievement in a discussion that includes some of Scott's contemporaries. W. L. Renwick (*English Literature, 1789–1815*, 1963) offers a brief assessment of Scott that includes a comparison with Wordsworth.

Despite such favorable criticism as this, one must conclude that there has been for some time little critical interest in Scott's poetry. The references of modern critics are likely to be sidelong glances, chiefly to contrast him unfavorably with his contemporaries. The comment is in general disparaging. C. H. Herford (*Age of Wordsworth*, 1897) speaks coolly of the poems: Scott was very good only at moments and within a limited sphere; in the epic quality he aimed at, he was far below Homer and Dante, and for his greatness he had to wait for the novels. Arthur Symons denies that Scott was a poet (*Atlantic Monthly*, 1904), a point of view retained in his *Romantic Movement in English Poetry* (1909), and asserts that the qualities that produced Scott's popular success were not poetical ones, that popularity (that of Byron too) in itself is not a sound criterion, and that the judgments of various favorable critics are to be challenged. This essay was answered by Goldwin Smith (*Atlantic Monthly*, 1905), who admits that the poetry by no means equals the novels, and is distinctly lame and impotent in his rejoinder. Edmund Blunden in "The Poetry of Scott" (*QQ*, 1932) more or less echoes Symons. He writes a goodnatured depreciation of the poems as "journalism"; Scott merely had the gift of appealing to current taste. About as damning as any modern critic is Benedetto Croce (see below). But the most significant point to note is the almost total indifference to the poems; they are now practically ignored except in the histories.

2. THE NOVELS

Scott published his novels anonymously for reasons that may only be surmised, he himself never having explained them. At first, his purpose was clear: to protect the valuable reputation he had gained as the author of *The Lady of the Lake* and other poems from the damaging effect of possible failure in a new field. But this motive evaporated upon the huge success of *Waverley* and its immediate successors, and still he persisted in his anonymity. If hard pressed he would refuse to admit his authorship, or would even flatly deny it. Biographers have guessed at his possible motives, the most probable being his love of mystery, the pleasure of hiding himself in a cloud. The group of those who were actually in on the secret was small: the Ballantynes, Constable, and a few very intimate friends, notably Lady Louisa Stuart and J. B. S. Morritt, with whom he carried on a good deal of correspondence about his problems in the writing of the novels and about his own critical ideas. Actually the authorship was an open secret. Most cultivated readers assumed that "the author of *Waverley*" or "the great Unknown" was Walter Scott. However, there appeared in 1821 the *Letters to Richard Heber, Esq., M. P.* by J. L. Adolphus (for a summary, see W. F. Gray, "An Early Critic of Scott," *Sir Walter Scott Quart.*, 1927), the ostensible purpose of which was to prove by a comparison of the novels with the poems, of which Scott was the acknowledged author, that both came from the same pen. As a piece of analysis based on internal evidence, these letters were extremely convincing, had conviction been needed; they showed by a dissection of language and style, as well as by the actual materials and attitudes, the common authorship. The value of the *Letters*, however, went far beyond this. They constitute one of the best critical appraisals of the novels ever to appear, and are especially important as illustrating the fact that Scott's own contemporaries were fully conscious of his deficiencies as well as of his gifts as a writer. Far from resenting this penetrating attack on his anonymity, Scott was delighted by it, and invited the young Adolphus to be his guest at Abbotsford, although he still refused to admit the truth. This finally came out as a result of the 1826 financial crash, when Scott was forced to make an accounting for his creditors. Nevertheless, rumors circulated almost from the beginning that there were other authors, particularly his black-sheep brother Thomas, or Thomas and his wife. As late as the 1850's W. J.

Fitzpatrick and G. J. French published pamphlets to prove that Thomas Scott and his wife had written some of the *Waverley Novels.* Fitzpatrick (*Who Wrote the Waverley Novels?* 1856; an enlarged 2d ed. *Who Wrote the Earlier Waverley Novels?* also 1856) maintained that Scott was at most a sort of editor. French (*An Enquiry into the Origin of the Authorship of Some of the Earlier Waverley Novels*, 1856), sorted out the authorship of Walter from that of Thomas and Mrs. Thomas. Summaries of these two items as well as replies to them are covered in Corson.

In criticism of the novels that is biographically orientated, probably the single most pervasive theme is Scott's motive in writing them. Did he write for money? Did he write *merely* for money? The question comes up very early in the contemporary criticism and echoes through the biographies, both the early and the late; it may appear in almost any connection in criticism of him and his work. Carlyle says flatly, "The great fact about [the *Waverley Novels*] is that they were faster written and better paid for than any other books in the world." Croce, nearly a century later, thinks of Scott first of all as a captain of industry, and between Carlyle and Croce, and later, such statements echo and re-echo. They involve not only biographical matters (notice, for instance, the strong financial coloring of Grierson's 1938 biography, the analysis by James Glen of Scott's financial affairs in Grierson's *Letters*, and the Lockhart-Ballantyne controversy mentioned earlier), but such critical matters as slapdash style, errors and weaknesses in all sorts of detail as well as in broad construction. The facts are there, but the interpretation is controversial and produces a wide range of conclusions. For the most sympathetic and at the same time most sensible and unbiased opinion one should turn to the work of Grierson, if not to the declarations of Sir Walter himself in letters and journals for his feeling on such subjects as painstaking writing and the deliberate construction of novels. Scott's ideas about his own writing as well as his critical opinions on other writers are collected in Margaret Ball's *Sir Walter Scott as a Critic of Literature* (1907), a very useful work. On the same general subject are A. Brandl's "Walter Scott über sein dichterisches Schaffen," in *Sitzungsberichte der Preuss-ischen Akademie der Wissenschaften* (1925); an unpublished Cornell University dissertation (1934) by G. E. Smock, "Sir Walter Scott's Theory of the Novel"; and John Lauber, "Scott on the Art of Fiction" (*SEL*, 1963).

J. T. Hillhouse, *The Waverley Novels and Their Critics* (1936), reveals the pervasiveness of such questions of motive and attitude. This survey also shows that the novels were widely read until about 1900, and that through the nineteenth century Scott was regarded as the greatest of English novelists, chiefly because of his wide romantic sweep and the feeling that his national scope elevated him above the other novelists, who dealt with private life. Comparisons with Shakespeare are frequent, as also with Cervantes and Le Sage. It becomes obvious too that the limitations now charged to him were emphasized by the original reviewers. Scott's politics have always been a warmly debated issue, the interpretation depending on the point of view of the critic. There has always been a sharp line drawn between the "Scotch Novels" and the "romances" with practically universal agreement that the first group are far the more distinguished. And finally, there has been increasing stress since Carlyle's time on the matter of ideas and philosophy: Did the novels serve merely for amusement or did they indirectly through character offer their readers an admirable ideal of human behavior? These are the dominating themes in the critical discussion of the novels since 1814; with them are interwoven many other, but relatively minor ones. Other essays that cover specifically the reputation of the novels are P. N. Landis, "The *Waverley Novels*, or a Hundred Years After" (*PMLA*, 1937), which attributes the decline of interest in Scott to a modern shift in emphasis from the individual to mankind in general, and S. C. Roberts, "The Fate of a Novelist" (in *Sir Walter Scott Lectures, 1940–1948*, 1950). J. H. Raleigh reviews the entire question of Scott's reputation, both as a novelist and as a "historian-thinker," in an important and heavily documented article, "What Scott Meant to the Victorians" (*VS*, 1963).

Doubtless the most famous piece of criticism on Scott is Carlyle's essay in the *Westminster Review* (1838), provoked by Lockhart's *Life*. Actually Carlyle found the novels mediocre; the characters were superficial, the whole tone worldly, not spiritual, there was no message, they were not "profitable for doctrine, for reproof, for edification." Certainly these judgments, presented with all the force of Carlyle's dramatic style, have had great influence on later critics, who have either echoed them with approval or tried to argue them away in part or in whole. (F. W. Roe, *Thomas Carlyle as a Critic of Literature*, 1910, and H. J. C. Grierson, "Scott and Carlyle," *Essays and Addresses*, 1940, both attack Carlyle's judgment of Scott.) Of other significant critics of Scott, the earliest is Lord Jeffrey, who reviewed the novels in the *Edinburgh Review* as they came out, and whose Scottish patriotism made him an especially understanding critic. Surprisingly enough, considering the "plagiarism" of "Christabel" in *The Lay of the Last Minstrel*, Coleridge was one of the finest of all Scott's critics. His ideas are not organized in any set essays, but are scattered through his letters and recorded conversations. Also important is the criticism of Hazlitt, whose enthusiasm for Scott was as strong as was his detestation of Scott's Toryism. Hazlitt wrote notable reviews of *The Pirate* and *Peveril of the Peak* in the *London Magazine* (1822–23), and also dealt with Scott at length in his lecture "The English Novelists" (1818), in his essay for Colburn's *New Monthly Magazine* in 1824 (included in *The Spirit of the Age*, 1825), and in "Scott, Racine and Shakespeare" in *The Plain Dealer* (1826). In addition, numerous allusions occur in Hazlitt's collected works. *Blackwood's Magazine* (1824) reprints a suppressed passage in Hazlitt's review of *Peveril* in the *London Magazine*, where Scott was attacked politically; Charles I. Patterson's "William Hazlitt as a Critic of Fiction" (*PMLA*, 1935) might allow Hazlitt a stronger enthusiasm for Scott than it does.

Scott's own discussion of his work and his methods of writing is valuable (in letters, journal, and prefaces and notes passim, or see Ball or Hillhouse, above). Especially important is his own famous review of his *Tales of My Landlord* in the *Quarterly* (1817). Widely read in their own time and highly esteemed by Lockhart were a group review by Nassau Senior in the *Quarterly* (1821) and, later, individual articles on *The Pirate* and *The Fortunes of Nigel* (both 1822) and another group review in the *London Review* (1829), all reprinted in his *Essays on Fiction* (1864). Lockhart's judgment of Scott in his review of *Lives of the Novelists* (*QR*, 1826) and his voluminous comments throughout the *Life* are of first importance. Another significant group review in the *Quarterly* (1827), entitled "Historical Romance," compares Scott, greatly to his advantage, with some of the imitators who were now swarming about his head. There should be included here a preface by "Christopher North" to a review in *Blackwood's* (1827) of *Chronicles of the Canongate;* as also the penetrating criticism of Lady Louisa Stuart, one of Scott's most intimate friends and shrewdest critics. (See *The Letters of Lady Louisa Stuart*, ed. R. B. Johnson, 1926, and Lady Tweedsmuir, *Lady Louisa Stuart: Her Memories and Portraits*, 1932.) Two essays by Harriet Martineau in *Tait's Edinburgh Magazine* (1832), republished in her *Miscellanies* (1836), are representative of a very special utilitarian point of view. One might also cite *The Autobiography of John Galt* (1833), since Galt was one of the most popular contemporary novelists. His comments are notable chiefly for his preference of the "romances" over the Scotch Novels. Other opinions are cited in C. W. Collins' "Sir Walter Scott: His Friends and Critics" (*Blackwood's Mag.*, 1910), and in Amy Cruse's *The Englishman and His Books in the Early Nineteenth Century* (1930).

In the Victorian period, a time of continued hero worship, Walter Bagehot in an essay in the *National Review* (1858; reprinted in *Literary Studies*, 1879), and Leslie Stephen in the *Cornhill Magazine* (1871) produced the two most distinguished landmarks of Scott criticism. Neither one, however, has the strong personal feeling and enthusiasm of Scott's contemporaries, and by contrast they seem cool and detached, although Stephen contributed to the *Critic* (1888) a much warmer appreciation of Scott. See also his essay on Disraeli in *Hours in a Library* and the *Cornhill Magazine* (1897).

Other pieces of criticism notable for the distinction of their authors are those of the young Henry James in the *North American Review* (1864); Edward FitzGerald in his letters; R. W. Emerson in his *Works* (1903–21) and *Journals* (1909–14); Bulwer-Lytton, whose Victorian prestige, now sadly faded, should be remembered, in the *New Monthly Magazine* (1832), "Caxtoniana" (*Blackwood's*, 1863); and his essay "On Art in Fiction" (*Monthly Chron.*, 1838); and Ruskin in "Fiction—Fair and Foul" (*Nineteenth Century*, 1880), and in allusions in *Fors Clavigera, Modern Painters*, and elsewhere. An article on Ruskin by H. H. Carter (*SR*, 1922) is relevant. To these memorable names should be added that of Julia Wedgwood, who contributed to the *Contemporary Review* (1878) "Sir Walter Scott and the Romantic Reaction," one of the soundest considerations of Scott's genius in this period. Swinburne also was an ardent partisan of Scott in his review of the *Journal* in the *Fortnightly Review* (1891). For a slashing attack, unusual in this period, one might turn to J. C. Jeaffreson's *Novels and Novelists* (1858). Taine, too, in his famous history of English literature could find little good to say of Scott; even at his best, in the more realistic novels, to Taine he seemed second-rate, a producer of bourgeois realism; and another highly influential continental critic, Georg Brandes, though granting Scott certain gifts, condemned him because of his haste, carelessness, and prolixity, which he thought would finally doom him to oblivion (*Naturalism in England*, 1875; rev. in *Main Currents in Nineteenth-Century Literature*, 1901–05). As violent an attack on Scott as was ever written is that of D. F. Hannigan, a translator of French novelists and a partisan of Flaubert, in the *Westminster Review* (1895).

After 1880 the champions of Scott give the impression of being on the defensive, of answering charges, of explaining away indifference, and in general of writing in an apologetic tone, often robust

enough, but still apologetic. Early in the period Andrew Lang served
as a sort of high priest of Scott. (See, *inter alia*, his *Sir Walter
Scott*, 1907. For interesting attacks on the enormous critical
influence of Lang and of W. R. Nicoll in the late nineteenth century,
see Q. D. Leavis, *Fiction and the Reading Public*, 1932, and Donald
and Catherine Carswell, "The Crisis in Criticism," in the *Nineteenth
Century*, 1933.) R. L. Stevenson, though highly critical of Scott in
matters of form, could also praise him highly (Graham Balfour, *The
Life of Robert Louis Stevenson*, 1901; *The Letters of Robert Louis
Stevenson*, ed. Sidney Colvin, 1911). Stevenson's "Gossip on Romance" (*Longman's Mag.*, 1882, reprinted in *Memoirs and Portraits*, 1887, and elsewhere) contains a brief psychological insight on
the reading of fiction that is remarkable in a pre-Freudian essay.
C. A. Young's *The Waverley Novels: An Appreciation* (1907) is a
striking and memorable little volume. G. K. Chesterton was a shrewd
defender of Sir Walter in his essay in *Varied Types* (1903). In
general, professional critics have been very kind to Scott, possibly
because of a tendency to conservatism, but especially, it would seem,
because of the value they set on his power as an innovator and his
influence on later novelists, and even on historians. This is revealed
by a survey of such well-known handbooks as those of Saintsbury,
Sir Walter Raleigh, W. L. Cross, Harold Williams, W. L. Phelps,
R. M. Lovett and H. S. Hughes, Edward Wagenknecht, and Gordon
Gerould, and of more general historians, such as W. R. Nicoll and
Thomas Seccombe, Oliver Elton, and Louis Cazamian (in Legouis
and Cazamian). In the history edited by A. C. Baugh (1948) the
chapter on Scott by Samuel Chew is distinctly chilly. On the other
hand, E. A. Baker, in a most thoroughgoing analysis of the
Waverley Novels, sets Scott very high, in some points comparing
him with Shakespeare. Like many other critics in Scott's own time
and since, Baker finds Scott's genius most fully revealed in the more
realistic Scotch Novels. Among other notable professors who have
praised Scott highly are A. A. Jack, who still (1897) contended that
Scott is our greatest novelist because of his volume and range and
the power of character demonstrated in the Scotch Novels (*Essays
in the Novel*, 1897); G. E. Woodberry in *McClure's Magazine*
(1905; reprinted in *Great Writers*, 1907); C. W. Collins (*Blackwood's*, 1910), who has high praise for Scott on patriotic grounds—
his permeation of British national life and his drawing together of
England and Scotland into one country; Thomas Seccombe, not only
in the history just mentioned but in the *Contemporary Review*
(1914) on the centenary of *Waverley*, and in ten other essays on
centenaries of succeeding novels, published originally in the *Times*

Literary Supplement and later collected in *Scott Centenary Articles* (1932); John Erskine, who eloquently defended the philosophy implied in the novels, in the *Columbia University Quarterly* (1914); and W. P. Ker, in several short but valuable essays (*Collected Essays*, 1925; *On Modern Literature*, 1955).

Later in the period, especially because of the stimulus of the centenary (1932) of Scott's death, which brought out a considerable volume of critical, biographical, and scholarly material, one can still find enthusiastic defense of Sir Walter as a great novelist. The two most prominent names are those of H. J. C. Grierson and John Buchan. Grierson published the edition of Scott's letters and the *Life* already noted, and he was in both these works a consistent apologist, highly effective because of his vast reservoirs of information and his sympathetic but not extravagant interpretation. In these two works are subsumed his final ideas about Scott as a man and as a writer, but one might note also his essay "Scott and Carlyle" (*E&S*, 1928), a centenary address reprinted in the *Columbia University Quarterly* (1933), and the preface to *Sir Walter Scott Today*. Similarly, one may get the sum total of Buchan's attitude toward various facets of Scott's personality and genius in his biography (mentioned above), but may also turn to his article "Some Notes on Sir Walter Scott" (*English Association, Pamphlet No. 58*, 1924, with which compare Ch. xiii of his biography). To the names of Grierson and Buchan may be joined that of Hugh Walpole, the novelist and the owner of Scott's letter books, who released some of the most interesting letters to Sir Walter in volumes mentioned above under "Biography," and who attempted (vainly, it is to be feared) to bring Scott's fine qualities into sharp focus by publishing *The Waverley Pageant* (1932), a selection of what he considered the most brilliant and striking passages in the novels. Walpole has a number of essays on Scott: "A Note on Sir Walter" (*Nation and Athenaeum*, 17 May 1924); "A Centenary Estimate" (*English Rev.*, 1932); and a Rede Lecture, published as *The English Novel* (1925).

Certain other distinctly favorable criticisms of the novels may be added. For perhaps the most eloquent and persuasive praise, Scott is indebted to Virginia Woolf (*New Republic*, 3 Dec. 1924), who couples his name with Shakespeare's, and declares that "his transparent stream . . . becomes without warning . . . the universal ocean on which we put out with the greatest only." Agnes M. Mackenzie in a brilliant centenary essay in the *London Mercury* (1932) undertakes to demonstrate the greatness of Scott's genius by comparing him with a long list of Victorian and modern novelists; Lord David Cecil has published a long and carefully studied two-part essay on Scott (*Atlantic Monthly*, 1932; in book form, *Sir Walter Scott*, 1933) in which Scott is superlatively praised for his powers of style when he is at his best, as well as for his great scope and his power to create character. (See also Lord Cecil's introduction to *Short Stories by Sir Walter Scott*, 1934.) Stephen Gwynn in his biography (1930) presents a striking defense of the depth and power of Scott's best characters. V. S. Pritchett has a two-part article in the *New Statesman and Nation* (10 June and 1 July 1944; reprinted, revised, in *The Living Novel*, 1947), praising Scott highly as primarily a realistic and comic writer, rather than a romantic. Two articles implying a high regard for Scott's genius are Jared Wenger's "Character-Types of Scott, Balzac, Dickens and Zola" (*PMLA*, 1947), an elaborate and perhaps oversubtle study, not strongly convincing; and S. Stewart's "*Waverley* and the 'Unified Design'" (*ELH*, 1951), a not too persuasive attempt to endow Scott with a gift for organization that has generally been denied him. J. R. Sutherland's Scott lectures (*UEJ*, 1953) are on the composition of the novels and the use of dialogue. C. S. Lewis has contributed some suggestive remarks on the personality and style of Scott (*They Asked for a Paper*, 1962).

There have been, of course, some articulate expressions of disapproval. W. D. Howells, for instance (*Harper's Bazaar*, 1900; reprinted in his *Heroines of Fiction*, 1901), finds much to admire in the Scotch Novels, if not in the romances, but he cannot escape the feeling of what they might have been had Sir Walter been an assiduous craftsman—a point of view not unlike that of Brandes and one which shows, as does the criticism of D. F. Hannigan already cited, the influence of the criteria established by French and Russian models, now beginning to be widely accepted. Another distinguished continental critic, Benedetto Croce, writing with these same criteria in mind (*Dial*, 1923; see also *European Literature in the Nineteenth Century*, 1924), declares that Scott's great glory is a thing of the past; he flatly denies that Scott is a poet at all, and asserts that as a novelist he is only mediocre. The two later British writers who have seemed most critical of Scott are Archibald Stalker and Donald Carswell. Stalker, in his *Intimate Life of Sir Walter Scott* (1921), finds little to admire in Scott as a man and is equally cool toward his books. Carswell's criticism involves a strange contradiction: after an annihilation of both Scott's character and his work, he produces an equally eloquent but glorifying defense of his epoch-making powers (*Scott and His Circle*, 1930). E. M. Forster (*Aspects of the Novel*, 1927) says simply that he does not care for Scott, whose technique seems to him amateurish and naïve. Edwin Muir praises Scott's

power of creating characters as opposed to his depth of characterization, and finds his technique, especially his failures in plot
structure, extremely damaging. Muir explains Scott's life, as others
have, by the opposition between his practical and imaginative,
idealistic sides. His essays on Scott are important and influential but
tend to repeat themselves: *The Structure of the Novel* (1928); *Scott
and Scotland* (1936); and essays in the *Spectator* (24 Sept. 1932),
The English Novelists, ed. Derek Verschoyle (1936), *From Anne to
Victoria: Essays by Divers Hands* (1937), and *Sir Walter Scott
Lectures, 1940–1948* (1950). Two articles on *The Heart of Midlothian* in *Essays in Criticism*, by Robin Mayhead (1956) and David
Craig (1958), tend to damn Scott indirectly by implying that he
wrote only one good book. In general, *The Heart of Midlothian* has
been taken more seriously by modern critics than any other novel of
Scott.

Recent criticism of the novels has frequently combined a new
respect for Scott with determined objectivity. In much of this
criticism there is great precision and awareness of what kind of
discussion the critic is himself conducting. The primary concern is
not to praise or blame Scott but to understand his novels. Dorothy
Van Ghent's essay on *The Heart of Midlothian* is *not* very respectful, and not up to the general standard of her excellent book (*The
English Novel: Form and Function*, 1953); she uses *The Heart of
Midlothian* to demonstrate the "implications of incoherence in the
work of art" but seems generally uninformed about the rest of
Scott's works. Nevertheless, there is little the matter with Mrs. Van
Ghent's logic, and her essay helps to clarify the central moral issue
of this novel. W. H. Marshall, "Point of View and Structure in *The
Heart of Midlothian*" (*NCF*, 1961), is just as precise on another
subject and much less offensive to admirers of Scott. *Ivanhoe*, the
last of the novels finally to disappear from the American school
curriculum, has been suddenly fortunate to find a critic in Edgar
Rosenberg (*From Shylock to Svengali: Jewish Stereotypes in
English Fiction*, 1960). His study of the Jew as comic miser, the use
of historical environment, and Rebecca as the noble Jewess adds up
to an excellent and unorthodox critical essay on the novel itself; it is
supplemented by some pages on *The Surgeon's Daughter*. A short
chapter on Scott in Mario Praz, *The Hero in Eclipse in Victorian
Fiction* (trans. 1956), makes a suggestive comparison between
passages in the novels and the paintings of Sir David Wilkie. Ian
Jack has written a useful introduction to Scott in the Writers and
Their Work series of the British Council (*Sir Walter Scott*, 1958),
but this pamphlet is far excelled by his chapter on "The Waverley

Romances" in *English Literature, 1815–1832* (*Oxford History of English Literature*, x, 1963), a description and analysis of the novels reminiscent of Adolphus in its power to generalize without any pronounced bias.

Two recent books by distinguished critics of English poetry devote substantial chapters to the novels. In *The Epic Strain in the English Novel* (1958) E. M. W. Tillyard appeals for a general revaluation of Scott and admires "three epicising novels," *Waverley, Rob Roy*, and *The Heart of Midlothian*. Donald Davie, in *The Heyday of Sir Walter Scott* (1961), shares Tillyard's enthusiasm for *Waverley*—"one of the greatest novels of the language"—and singles out Scott's feeling for the "community" of society. His book also includes chapters on Pushkin, Mickiewicz, Cooper, Maria Edgeworth, and lesser figures and is in part an informal exercise in comparative literature. To a reader familiar with their criticism of poetry, however, both Davie and Tillyard are disappointing on Scott's novels. They hold diametrically opposed views of *Rob Roy*, for example, and there is no apparent way of reconciling them.

Alexander Welsh's *The Hero of the Waverley Novels* (1963) is a thematic study organized around the passive young gentleman who stands at the center of virtually every novel of Scott. Though this hero is not even recognized as such by many critics—including Scott himself—he is probably the most consistent important feature of the novels and the object of sore neglect. The study explores his inactivity in detail, stressing the projection of certain moral ideals rather than the exigencies of the narrative. The hero is associated with a passive ideal of property in land and a corresponding ideal of honor; this ideal, which is not limited to Scott, is in some ways an uncomfortable and distressing burden. The dualism of past and present, of nature and civilization in the Waverley Novels is shown to be also psychological.

Much of the best criticism of the novels has focused on Scott's treatment of historical themes. One of the sweeping differences between the eighteenth and nineteenth centuries is a difference of historical awareness. The nineteenth-century attitude—still a part of our daily consciousness—may be called historicism, which means the awareness of man and events as a part of continuing history, not as a manifestation of something more or less unchanging called "human nature." Scott is a transitional figure in this discovery, and critics examining his treatment of history ordinarily indulge in a certain legitimate exaggeration of his position. For in this area Scott could not possibly have appreciated his own importance. The problem can be partly resolved by observing that Scott's conscious theory of history belongs to the eighteenth century, but that his concrete depiction of the past, whether historically "accurate" or not, contributed immeasurably to the historicism of the nineteenth century.

One complicating factor is that in England the historical novel as such did not—at least not qualitatively—become a major literary genre, so that the impact of Scott is more obviously important to the writing of history itself. Two most impressive comments on Scott and history are, because of the eminence of their authors as social historians, those of G. M. Trevelyan (*Times*, 21 Sept. 1932) and G. M. Young, in *Sir Walter Scott Lectures, 1940–1948* (1950), a collection which also contains a lecture on this subject by Grierson. Trevelyan has tremendous praise for Scott, declaring that he was more influential in developing the modern conception of history than any professional historian, and that his history of seventeenth- and eighteenth-century Scotland is sound and shows his great learning, balance, and wisdom. Young's lecture throws new light on Scott's handling of history and gives many fresh illustrations. It is significant that both these historians base their arguments on the Scotch Novels, and find the "romances" unreal and inferior. In a distinguished paper, "The Rationalism of Sir Walter Scott" (*Cambridge Jour.*, 1953), Duncan Forbes sees Scott as fundamentally a product of eighteenth-century "philosophical history," of the "philosophes," and as a disciple of Adam Ferguson and Dugald Stuart, and, behind them, of Montesquieu. He contends that Scott was as much a "triumph of the historical thought of the rationalist eighteenth century" as he was a "triumph of Romanticism." To these may be added D. Munroe's "Sir Walter Scott and the Development of Historical Study" (*QQ*, 1938); and Max Korn's "Sir Walter Scott und die Geschichte" (*Anglia*, 1937), in which the most significant point is the similarity between Scott's attitude toward the French Revolution and Burke's.

The historical material in the novels is naturally discussed in the various histories and handbooks of the novel, notably in E. A. Baker, *The History of the English Novel* (1935) and Lovett and Hughes, *History of the Novel in England* (1932). Useful contributions are also made in such essays as G. H. Maynadier's "*Ivanhoe* and Its Literary Consequences" (*Essays in Memory of Barrett Wendell*, 1926); P. E. More's "The Scotch Novels and Scotch History" (*Shelburne Essays*, 3d Ser., 1905); R. S. Rait's "Sir Walter's Pageant of Scottish History" (*Sir Walter Scott Quart.*, 1927), and "Walter Scott and Thomas McCrie" in *Sir Walter Scott Today;* and, perhaps most important, H. J. C. Grierson's editorial introduction to *Sir Walter Scott Today*. Also to be mentioned is the work on the historical novel as a form: George Saintsbury's "The Historical Novel" (*Essays in English Literature, 1780–1860;* 2d Ser., 1895); Herbert Butterfield's *The Historical Novel* (1924); Ernest Bernbaum's "The Views of the Great Critics on the Historical Novel" (*PMLA*, 1926), and Alfred T. Sheppard's *The Art and Practice of Historical Fiction* (1930).

David Daiches' "Scott's Achievement as a Novelist" (*NCF*, 1951; reprinted in *Literary Essays*, 1956), an excellent two-part study, systematically develops the thesis that Scott's historical novel is of the highest type of that genre, using "a historical situation to illustrate some aspect of man's fate which has importance and meaning quite apart from that historical situation"; and that altogether the Scotch Novels dramatize "the relations between the old heroic Scotland and the new Anglicized, commercial Britain," the characters "playing their parts in an interpretation of modern life." Daiches' argument is continued in an essay on *Redgauntlet* in *From Jane Austen to Joseph Conrad: Essays Collected in Memory of James T. Hillhouse* (ed. R. C. Rathburn and M. Steinman, Jr., 1958), an essay that recalls Muir in *Scott and Scotland*. Daiches' view of the Scottish novels in general is summarized in his *Critical History of English Literature* (1960). P. F. Fisher, "Providence, Fate and the Historical Imagination in Scott's *Heart of Midlothian*" (*NCF*, 1955), is an important interpretation of that novel as an "exemplum" of a central conception of Scott's in which "the ordered movement of history is represented as providential, and the chaos of accident and destruction is attributed to the fate that man brings on himself." J. E. Duncan, "The Anti-Romantic in *Ivanhoe*" (*NCF*, 1955), attempts to demonstrate that Scott has a sound historical point of view in *Ivanhoe;* and that "his main concern . . . was with the difficult but necessary transition from a romantic, heroic era to a comparatively drabber period of unity, peace, and progress." R. C. Gordon, "*The Bride of Lammermoor:* A Novel of Tory Pessimism" (*NCF*, 1957), treats the Master of Ravenswood as "nothing if not a victim of history" and argues that this novel is much more pessimistic than the others on the question of social change: "there lay within [Scott] a deep hatred of historical change." The second of Mary Lascelles' recent Scott lectures (*UEJ*, 1961) is entitled "Scott and the Sense of Time" and argues that Scott interprets the present in terms of the past. Another article on *Redgauntlet* that discusses Scott's interpretation of history is D. D. Devlin, "Scott and Redgauntlet" (*REL*, 1963). And a much-neglected novel, *The Fair Maid of Perth*, is brought to prominence by F. R. Hart in *"The Fair Maid,* Manzoni's *Betrothed,* and the Grounds of Waverley Criticism" *(NCF,* 1963). Hart compares Scott favorably to Manzoni and suggests that Scott's historical novels do not contrast the past with the present so much as they expose the irrelevance of "romantic heroism" in any age and treat "heroic rigidity" as "perennially anachronistic"—an important qualification of the theme of most of the recent essays on this subject.

Ironically, the most comprehensive and compelling study of Scott as a historical novelist—and the most persuasive theory of Scott's originality and influence—is that of the Hungarian Marxist Georg Lukács, in a book that first appeared in Moscow in 1937 *(The Historical Novel,* trans. 1962). A long chapter is devoted to the Waverley Novels, but the entire book is based on this chapter and interrelated with it. A distinguished thinker in his own right, Lukács is both more learned and more liberal than most Marxist critics. Some of his reasons for the rise of historical consciousness do not apply in England and the basically Hegelian interpretation of history sits uneasily with Scott. But "Scott ranks among those great writers whose depth is manifest mainly in their work, a depth which they often do not understand themselves" and "the change which Scott effects in the history of world literature is independent of the limitation of his human and poetic vision." Lukács analyzes the differences between epic and novel and between novel and drama, and he accounts for the treatment of both the historical personages in the novels and the gentlemanly hero. His most important service to Scott is to relate him to the history of the novel in general: the classical form of the historical novel (Scott's) "arises out of the great social novel and then, enriched by a conscious historical attitude, flows back into the latter. On the one hand, the development of the social novel [in the eighteenth century] makes possible the historical novel; on the other, the historical novel transforms the social novel into a genuine history of the present." For a review of Lukács, see Welsh, "Fiction, Society and History" *(New Republic,* 2 March 1963).

3. SPECIAL PROBLEMS

In 1932 began a controversy over the sequence in which the novels were written. On the evidence of style and construction or of identifiable early episodes in Scott's life, Dame Una Pope-Hennessy and Donald Carswell advanced the theory that a number of the novels always supposed to have been written in the order of publication were actually written much earlier. Dame Una suggested

St. Ronan's Well as Scott's first novel in the *Scotsman* (16 March 1932) and shortly after (*TLS*, 28 April 1932), she added *Guy Mannering* and *Redgauntlet* as novels written very early. On 5 May 1932 (*TLS*), Carswell added *The Black Dwarf* and *The Monastery*, also suggesting that *The Surgeon's Daughter* was actually written long before 1827. (See also Carswell, "Sir Walter's Secret," *Scots Mag.*, 1933.) In the *Glasgow Herald* (3 July 1937) they both argued that the first part of *Rob Roy* had been written very early. An article by Mody Boatright (*PMLA*, 1935) supported the new theory as far as *The Black Dwarf, Guy Mannering, Redgauntlet*, and *The Monastery* were concerned, on the ground that Scott's use of the supernatural in them revealed early attitudes.

This striking theory, which runs counter to all the evidence in Lockhart and to Scott's own statements in his letters, naturally called forth remonstrances, which are listed in Corson. As a matter of fact, the theory was completely undermined by simply referring to the manuscripts themselves and by taking into account watermarks. Grierson never accepted it, and out of his vast knowledge of Scott materials was able to refute it with external evidence (note, e.g., his allusion to the manuscript of *Redgauntlet* in his *Sir Walter Scott, Bart.*, p. 232). Dame Una never surrendered, however; she still stuck to her guns in a short life of Scott. For those who still believe it, one would think that R. D. Mayo's "The Chronology of the *Waverley Novels:* The Evidence of the Manuscripts" (*PMLA*, 1948) would finally settle the matter.

Another object of a good deal of study is the authorship of the poetry interspersed throughout the novels, including the "mottoes" or epigraphs of the chapters. There is a useful index to these poems by Allston Burr—*Sir Walter Scott: An Index Placing the Short Poems in His Novels and in His Long Poems and Dramas* (1936). The difficulty here rises from two sources: (1) Scott's habit of quoting from memory and his humorous carelessness about accuracy, and (2) his even more humorous tendency to concoct suitable epigraphs and sign them "Anon," "Old Play," "Old Song," or "Old Ballad." The most thorough discussion of this subject is Tom B. Haber's "The Chapter-Tags in the *Waverley Novels*" (*PMLA*, 1930), where two classes are established—true quotations, for which the authors are given, and Scott's own fabrications with such ascriptions as those just noted. A number of other articles deal with the subject, going back to Scott's own time. "Poetry of *The Waverly Novels*" (*Retrospective Rev.*, 1827) traces the sources of many of the poems which the author remembered having read before. Thomas Seccombe, "The Spoils to the Victors" (*Scott Centenary*

Articles, 1932), discusses the epigraphs signed "Anon," etc., branching out into a general (and not very necessary) defense of plagiarism or borrowing, especially when done as well as Scott did it. Davidson Cook, "Additions to Scott's Poems" (*TLS*, 15 and 22 Nov. 1941), points out that Constable had published a collection of lines attributed to Scott and that the supposedly authentic verse in the novels appeared in a new one-volume edition of the *Poetical Works* by Cadell in 1841. Cook shows that in this edition a number of inclusions were spurious but went unchallenged for a century, and reassigns them to their proper authors, to whom many had been correctly attributed by Scott himself. A rejoinder by W. M. Parker (*TLS*, 13 Dec. 1941) raises questions about several poems discussed by Cook. Other contributions, chiefly on single songs or epigraphs, are found in Corson; in M. H. Dodds and E. G. B., "Sir Walter Scott's Quotations" (*N&Q*, 6 May, 3 June, 17 June, 12 Aug. 1944), a reply to questions raised by W. M. Parker; and in J. C. Maxwell, "Lucy Ashton's Song" (*N&Q*, 13 May 1950).

Discussions of Scott's style and language are found in most of the biographies that deal at all with literary criticism. Generally there is deprecation of the stiff, formal "eighteenth-century" side of his style and his wordiness and carelessness, coupled with lavish praise for his brilliant and moving use of Scotch dialect in the more realistic novels of the first six years, the favorite example being Meg Merrilies' great speech in *Guy Mannering*, Chapter viii (e.g., in the work already cited of Oliver Elton, John Buchan, and Lord David Cecil). A few articles, however, have been devoted especially to Scott's language. A. W. Verrall (*QR*, 1910) reveals the attitude just described, analyzing in minute detail certain selected passages to prove that "Scott, in his way and at his hours is a very great stylist, supreme and hardly to be surpassed." Ernest Weekley (*Atlantic Monthly*, 1931) undertakes to show that Scott has probably added more words to English than any other writer except Shakespeare and in several other ways has enriched the language. Weekley's thesis is further supported in an excellent article by Paul Roberts, "Sir Walter Scott's Contributions to the English Vocabulary" (*PMLA*, 1953). Roberts, after a systematic analysis from many angles, concludes, "The *Waverley Novels* and the narrative poems have been a force comparable to Arabic, or baseball, or World War I." Relevant also is Edwin Muir's *Scott and Scotland: The Predicament of the Scottish Writer* (1936), wherein it is argued that Scottish writers are handicapped by having to use a quasi-foreign language, their own Scots language having long since become obsolete, crowded out by English. C. O. Parsons, "Character Names in the *Waverley Novels*" (*PMLA*, 1934), makes the point that many of the characters have humor names not recognizable by those unversed in Scottish dialect, and L. R. M. Strachan, "Queries from Scott's *Pirate*" (*N&Q*, 2 March 1940), answers various questions about allusions and words in *The Pirate*. E. M. W. Tillyard has contributed a brief article on "Scott's Linguistic Vagaries" in *The Monastery* (*EA*, 1958).

Another widely investigated subject is the originals of Scott's characters. Scott himself gives a great deal of information in his prefaces, notes, and letters, much of it taken over by Lockhart, and others have elaborated on and added to it. The most inclusive single discussion is W. S. Crockett's *The Scott Originals* (1912). In general, the most significant characters to be linked with originals are in the Scotch Novels, notably Pleydell and Dominie Sampson in *Guy Mannering*, Edie Ochiltree in *The Antiquary*, the Black Dwarf in the novel of that name, Habakkuk Mucklewrath in *Old Mortality*, Jeanie Deans in *The Heart of Midlothian*, Dugald Dalgetty in *The Legend of Montrose*, and Cleveland in *The Pirate*. To these should be added the connection between the story of Harry Bertram in *Guy Mannering* and the case (very famous at the time) of James Annesley, which Smollett had used in *Peregrine Pickle*, and which Scott doubtless knew well. (See G. J. French, "Foundations of Scott's *Guy Mannering*," *Gentleman's Mag.* 1840.) Among the "romances," the case of Rebecca in *Ivanhoe* is the most important. On these and many others there is a host of short articles and notes easily available in Corson, where they are listed under the individual novels. There is a convenient *Dictionary of the Characters in the Waverley Novels* (1910) by M. F. A. Husband.

On topography and the originals of places in the novels, the material is overwhelming, and is carefully classified by Corson under countries and individual localities. Of single instances, the most notable are "Waverley," the source of the name being Waverley Abbey near Farnham (see Corson) and, more important, the original of St. Ronan's Well.

Throughout Scott criticism there has been interest in his handling of superstition and the supernatural. The original reviewers of the poems and novels generally comment on it, and it comes in for much attention in the more critical biographies. Two scholars have taken special interest in it. M. C. Boatright is the author of "Witchcraft in the Novels of Walter Scott," and "Demonology in the Novels of Sir Walter Scott: A Study in Regionalism" (*Univ. of Texas Bull.*, 1933, 1934), and an article (*PMLA*, 1935), already cited, in which he uses Scott's varying attitudes toward the supernatural to support the Pope-Hennessy thesis as to the dating of the novels. C. O. Parsons has many publications on the subject, among which the following seem the most important: a series of three notes on "Scott's Letters on Demonology and Witchcraft: Outside Contributors" (*N&Q*, 21 and 28 March and 5 Dec. 1942), on offers of help Scott received when his intention of publishing a work on demonology became known, on later supplementary material offered by reviewers, and on his own involvement in "supernatural" incidents; a note (*N&Q*, 19 June 1943) on Scott's steady collection of supernatural materials, and a classification of such materials in the novels; and an article on the *Letters on Demonology* (*N&Q*, 14 Aug. 1943), concerning the general interest of the period in the supernatural and Scott's own division between imagination and common sense, as well as the changes in his attitude due to advancing age. To Parsons' bibliographical material Montague Summers (*N&Q*, 11 Sept. 1943) adds six works. Parsons also deals with "Scott's Fellow Demonologists" (*MLQ*, 1943) and with "The Original of the Black Dwarf" (*SP*, 1943). In D. F. Schumacher, *Der Volksaberglaube in den Waverley Novels* (1935), apart from a systematic but mechanical cataloguing of materials, the most important point made is that Sir Walter's use of them is much more effective in the Scotch Novels than elsewhere.

4. INFLUENCE

Naturally there has been much discussion of the influence on Scott of other writers, both English and foreign, as well as the influence of Scott himself on later writers.

Shakespeare's influence, more pervasive here than that of any other writer, has been studied at length by John W. Brewer in *Shakespeare's Influence on Sir Walter Scott* (1925). Previously, "Scott and Shakespeare" (*TLS*, 7 July 1921) had stimulated a number of contributions. In an excellent study, "Shakespeare and Some Scenes in the *Waverley Novels*" (*QQ*, 1938), R. K. Gordon argues that Scott is continually drawing on the great stores of Shakespeare material in his mind, and that generally the effect is vivid, though on occasion he seems merely to lean on Shakespeare when his own inspiration has failed. In "Shakespeare's *Henry IV* and the *Waverley Novels*" (*MLR*, 1942), Gordon carefully and minutely shows very wide, but not at all slavish, use by Scott of the Hotspur character as well as others. In "Scott and Shakespeare's Tragedies" (*TRSC*, 1945) he concludes that Scott often borrows from the tragedies to bad effect, since the novels cannot always stand the suggested comparison, although in *St. Ronan's Well* and *The Bride of Lammermoor* the results are fairly successful. D. Biggins, "*Measure for Measure* and *The Heart of Midlothian*" (*EA*, 1961), contains much detailed comparison. Mary Lascelles, "Scott and Shakespeare" (*UEJ*, 1961), has the authority of a critic who has written a monograph on *Measure for Measure* (1953).

Connections with other English writers have been pointed out in various notes and articles. R. M. Smith in "Chaucer Allusions in the Letters of Sir Walter Scott" (*MLN*, 1950) lists some two dozen allusions. G. B. Johnston in "Scott and Jonson" (*N&Q*, 25 Nov. 1950) notes the numerous allusions to Jonson, not only in the novels, but in the letters, and elsewhere, adding three not mentioned in Lockhart. R. K. Gordon in "Dryden and *The Waverley Novels*" (*MLR*, 1939) declares that Scott shows greater fondness for Dryden than for any other writer except Shakespeare and Milton, especially in *The Pirate* and in *Peveril of the Peak*, drawing often on *Absalom and Achitophel* and *The Duke of Guise;* in *Peveril*, the Duke of Buckingham is Dryden's Zimri, watered down. John R. Moore in a long article, "Defoe and Scott" (*PMLA*, 1941), maintains that Scott's knowledge of Defoe is surprisingly extensive, and that Scott was very influential in the revival of Defoe. They had many resemblances, notably in the characters of criminals, and Scott made great use in *The Pirate* of Defoe's history of the pirate Gow. Moore also notes (*MLN*, 1944) Scott's use in *The Antiquary* of a passage from Defoe's *History of Apparitions*. R. K. Gordon shows in "Scott and Wordsworth's *Lyrical Ballads*" (*TRSC*, 1943) that when Scott draws on Wordsworth, it is generally from *The Lyrical Ballads*, in which he is especially attracted by Wordsworth's pictures of the old, broken, and helpless. Also Wordsworth apparently had a share in the shaping of two of Scott's most famous characters —Edie Ochiltree and Madge Wildfire. In the relations between Scott and Coleridge the controversial point of Scott's borrowing (or plagiarizing) from "Christabel" in *The Lay of the Last Minstrel* is generally discussed in the biographies. There is likewise a study by Walter Freye, *The Influence of "Gothic" Literature on Sir Walter Scott* (1902), showing Scott's use of the Gothic especially in the long poems, but also in some of the novels.

The strongest foreign influence on Scott, German, has been the subject of much study. The best general discussions are W. Mackintosh's *Scott and Goethe: German Influence on the Writings of Sir Walter Scott* (1925), which describes the German influence from the beginning down through the poems and in some dozen of the novels; and J. Koch's "Sir Walter Scotts Beziehungen zu Deutschland"

(*GRM*, 1927, two parts), which pays most attention to the early period, but also deals with some of the novels. Scott's German reading is discussed by Fritz Sommerkamp in "Walter Scotts Kenntnis und Ansicht von der deutschen Literatur" (*Archiv*, 1925), useful as a compact collection of fact about all phases of Scott's German connections; and F. W. Stokoe devotes considerable space to Scott in his *German Influence in the English Romantic Period* (1926). Stokoe tends, comparatively, to minimize the German influence on Scott. G. H. Needler in *Goethe and Scott* (1950) develops an earlier essay (*QQ*, 1923) into a small book giving a chronological account of German influences (especially Goethe's) and also of Scott's on Goethe, notably in the use made of *Kenilworth* for the character of Helena in *Faust*, Part II. With Needler should be compared, for a more restrained view of Goethe's opinion of Scott, Friedrich Gundolf, "Scott and Goethe" in *Sir Walter Scott Today* (1932). Louis Reynaud (*Le romantisme*, 1926) thinks that both Goethe and Schiller had a very strong influence on the novels. J. Boyd, "Goethe's Knowledge of English Literature" (*Oxford Stud. of Modern Lang. and Lit.*, 1932), summarizes Goethe's comment on Scott's work, both novels and poems.

The breadth of Scott's classical interests is amply demonstrated by Vernon Rendall in "Scott and the Latin Classics" (*Sir Walter Scott Quart.*, 1927). A not too convincing attempt to establish Scott as an "epic" writer, on the basis of his style, is made by Christabel F. Fiske in *Epic Suggestions in the Imagery of the Waverley Novels* (1940). Comparisons of Scott with epic writers, especially Homer, as in J. C. Shairp's "The Homeric Spirit in the Poetry of Walter Scott" (*Aspects of Poetry*, 1881), have been pervasive from the beginning.

Regarding his connections with early Scandinavian literature, P. R. Lieder (*Smith Coll. Stud. in Modern Langs.*, 1920) investigates Scott's chief Scandinavian sources, but makes it clear that Scott was greatly restricted since most of such materials were inaccessible and in foreign languages; and Edith Batho reports on "Scott as a Medievalist" (*Sir Walter Scott Today*). In "Evidence of Scott's Indebtedness to Spanish Literature" (*RR*, 1932), C. S. Wolfe finds the Spanish influence pervasive, with more than one hundred allusions to Cervantes alone; and A. F. G. Bell covers "Scott and Cervantes" (*Sir Walter Scott Today*). There seems to be no modern work of significance on his connections with earlier French and Italian literature, though Corson lists two contemporary items on Scott and Ariosto.

Of Scott's influence on later authors, both English and continental, including the great vogue of the historical novel and the effect of the *Waverley Novels* on the writing of history itself, there has been much discussion. In the handbooks and histories of the novel the tendency to imitate the formula established by Scott is fully recognized, as it is also in the biographical and critical studies of both Scott and the later novelists. In his letters and journals Sir Walter alludes to contemporary novelists and notes the extent to which many of them were imitating him. Of articles specifically on Scott's influence on British and American novelists none require listing here except for J. R. Moore's "Scott and 'Henry Esmond' " (*N&Q*, 1944). Moore believes that *Henry Esmond* depends not only on *Woodstock*, a recognized source, but also, and quite importantly, on *St. Ronan's Well*.

For Germany several studies are valuable: L. M. Price, *English >German Literary Influences: Bibliography and Survey* (1919, 1953); three books on Theodor Fontane—L. A. Shears, *The Influence of Walter Scott on the Novels of Theodor Fontane* (1922), a rather slight work, A. Paul, *Der Einfluss Walter Scotts auf die epische Technik Theodor Fontanes* (1934), and Peter Demetz, *Formen des Realismus: Theodor Fontane* (1964), whose first chapter concerns Scott and the historical novel; and several articles on Wilhelm Hauff, of which the latest is G. W. Thompson, "Wilhelm Hauff's Specific Relation to Walter Scott" (*PMLA*, 1911). The mechanical thoroughness of this article is revealed in the author's discovery of 748 (!) "analogues" between Hauff's *Lichtenstein* and the *Waverley Novels*.

For France, a number of general studies bring out Scott's overwhelming influence on the French romantics: Louis Maigron, *Le roman historique: Essai sur l'influence de Walter Scott* (rev. ed., 1912); F. W. M. Draper, *The Rise and Fall of the French Romantic Drama* (1923), in which are described the many adaptations of the *Waverley Novels* for the French stage; Marion Elmina Smith, *Une anglaise intellectuelle en France sous la restauration, Miss Mary Clarke* (1927), which contains four chapters especially devoted to Scott in French; Fernand Baldensperger, "La grande communion romantique de 1827: Sous le signe de Walter Scott" (*RLC*, 1927), and by the same author, "Les années 1827–28 en France et au dehors" (*Revue des cours et conférences*, 1928); R. W. Hartland, *Walter Scott et le roman frénétique* (1928), which recounts the effect of the Gothic novels and of Scott on early nineteenth-century French novels of sensation, especially Hugo's; and E. P. Dargan, "Scott and the French Romantics" (*PMLA*, 1934). Two studies specifically on Balzac should be noted: H. J. Garnand, *The Influence of Walter Scott on the Works of Balzac* (1926), and R. K. Gordon, "Scott and the comédie humaine" in *Sir Walter Scott Today* (for an earlier version see *MLR*, 1928). An interesting imitation in a detail of action is noted by W. H. J., "A Prisoner's Escape: Scott and Dumas" (*N&Q*, 6 June 1940).

One of the most famous followers of Scott was Manzoni, whose relations with Scott have been studied in M. Dotti, *Delle derivazioni nei Promessi Sposi—dai romanzi di Walter Scott* (1900); in C. M. Bowen, "Manzoni and Scott" (*Dublin Rev.*, 1925)—Manzoni, though by no means a slavish imitator, does follow Scott more closely than some Italian critics are willing to admit; and in T. Abbiati, "Walter Scott e Alessandro Manzoni" (*Revista di lettere*, 1927). A borrowed detail is described by Rudolph Altrocchi, "Scott, Manzoni, Rovani" (*MLN*, 1926).

For Spain there are two extensive studies, both in *Revue hispanique:* P. H. Churchman and E. A. Peers, "A Survey of the Influence of Sir Walter Scott in Spain" (1922); and E. A. Peers, "Studies in the Influence of Sir Walter Scott in Spain" (1926). These show that the Scott vogue followed, though more slowly, the general pattern seen in other countries, and classify Spanish writers into three groups which reveal in varying degrees the Scott influence.

E. J. Simmons, who devotes a chapter to Scott in his *English Literature and Culture in Russia, 1553–1840* (1935), declares that the impact of Scott on Russian readers in general was overwhelming, as it was too on many writers, notably Pushkin and the early Gogol. P. Struve in "Walter Scott and Russia" (*Slavonic Rev.*, 1933) also describes the influence of Scott on Pushkin and summarizes a controversy between Belinsky and Gogol (pro-Scott) and the critic Senkovsky.

The most important single American subject derives from Mark Twain's disgust with Scott as a reactionary and possibly as the cause of the Civil War, a notion supported by H. J. Eckenrode in "Sir Walter Scott and the South" (*North American Rev.*, 1917), and effectively disputed by both G. W. Landrum in "Sir Walter Scott and His Literary Rivals in the Old South" (*AL*, 1930) and G. H. Orians in "Walter Scott, Mark Twain, and the Civil War" (*SAQ*, 1941). Orians argues convincingly that Scott's influence on Southern life was little more than decorative. Maurice Hewlett also attacks Mark Twain's notions about Scott in a note, "Mark on Sir Walter" (*SR*, 1921).

There exist monographs on Scott's influence in the Netherlands, by Hendrik Vissink (1922), and in Sweden, by Erik Lindström (1925). In fact, what is sorely needed, is a full-scale study of his impact on the nineteenth-century novel in England itself. This is a large task, and perhaps it awaits a more substantial agreement on the nature of the Waverley Novels themselves and their relation to their own period. In any case, it is predictable that "influence" will not much longer be defined as narrowly as it has sometimes been in the past. Lukács, for example, who scorns the search for "philological influence," has probably written the most comprehensive study of Scott's relation to nineteenth-century literature. For England and America, studies such as those of Hillhouse and Raleigh on the reputation of Scott need to be followed through with studies of the relation of Scott to the actual fiction of the later period.

5. POLITICAL AND RELIGIOUS VIEWS

Closely involved with the matter of history in general is the subject of Scott's political and religious views, always discussed in the biographies, with a linking of Sir Walter's personal feelings and the religious and political qualities of the characters in the novels. The basis is the dichotomy in Scott himself—his instinctive Tory and Stuart sympathies balanced by his common-sense belief in the efficacy of the house of Hanover; his attraction to medieval and romantic Catholicism balanced by his practical contemporary anti-Catholicism, and also his personal desertion of the Church of Scotland for the more liberal Anglican fold. Excellent analyses of such apparent contradictions not only in Scott's own life, but as reflected in his fiction, are provided in Grierson's *Sir Walter Scott, Bart.*, and Buchan's *Sir Walter Scott*. In Crane Brinton, *The Political Ideas of the English Romanticists* (1926), Scott is presented sympathetically as a natural Tory and an "unrebellious romantic." The fullest discussion of Scott's treatment of religion in his fiction is in K. Bos, *Religious Creeds and Philosophies as Represented by Characters in Sir Walter Scott's Works and Biography* (1932). Other valuable articles on Scott's personal religion from widely varying and even sharply conflicting points of view are H. E. Walton, "A Catholic Tribute to Sir Walter Scott" (*Month*, 1898, two parts) ; T. E. Ranken, "Sir Walter Scott and Medieval Catholicism" (*Month*, 1903) ; W. H. Kent, "Walter Scott and the Catholic Revival" (*Cath W*, 1914) ; L. M. Watt, "The Religion of Sir Walter" (*Sir Walter Scott Quart.*, 1927) ; W. S. Crockett, "The Religion of Sir Walter Scott" (*HJ*, 1929) ; and W. F. Gray, "The Religion of Sir Walter Scott" (*HJ*, 1932). One might also refer to Newman, who was drawn to Scott because of his favorable pictures of medieval Christianity, in his *Apologia* and

Essays, and George Borrow, who admired Scott's literary gifts but hated his political and religious tendencies as reactionary, in *Lavengro.*

Scott was a lawyer by profession, held with great pride the office of Sheriff of Selkirkshire, attended court regularly, and carried over his legal experiences into the novels—in the opinion of many critics, with all too much enthusiasm. The biographers generally describe fully the legal side of Scott's life as well as its infiltration into the novels, and Corson gives an extensive list of special articles on the subject in various law journals, Scottish, English, and American.

Scott's politics have always been controversial, and liberal and radical critics have been influenced in their attitudes by their own political alignments. The issue comes out continually in the contemporary reviews and is echoed in all later generations. Among the biographers, Grierson and Buchan best exemplify the apologetic and sympathetic attitude. For hostile comment one may turn to Hazlitt and George Borrow (above), or among later writers to Archibald Stalker, *The Intimate Life of Sir Walter Scott* (1921) and Donald Carswell, *Scott and His Circle* (1930). The latter speaks, for instance, of Scott as "a Jacobite whose devotion to the House of Hanover became a byword." G. K. Chesterton defends Scott's humanity and democracy brilliantly in an essay in *Varied Types* (1903), where he proclaims Sir Walter a greater democrat than Dickens. In his article on Scott's politics, "Scott, Hazlitt, and Napoleon" (*Essays and Studies,* Univ. of California Pubs. in English, 1943), M. F. Brightfield contrasts Scott's Tory attitude of national patriotism with Hazlitt's radical ideas, and observes that each point of view has its virtues.

6. MISCELLANEOUS WRITING AND EDITING

Scott was the author of four plays, now pretty much forgotten, none of them successful: *Halidon Hill* (1822), *The House of Aspen* (1829), and *The Doom of Devorgoil* and *Auchindrake* (1830), these two last being old experiments, discarded but finally sent to the publishers to swell the bulk of the collected works. There are contemporary reviews of these plays (see Corson) but later critics have paid them little attention except for very casual mention in the biographies. Information about the dramatic versions of the novels is to be found in H. A. White's *Sir Walter Scott's Novels on the Stage* (1927).

Although Scott's miscellaneous prose work was voluminous, the number of notes and articles on it is slight. *Letters on Demonology and Witchcraft* (1830) is the subject of continual casual allusion because of Scott's interest in the supernatural and its importance in the poems and novels, but since the original reviews there has been no work which should be listed here. *The Life of Napoleon* (1827), undertaken after Scott's financial crash as a probable money-maker, which it turned out to be, was regarded in its own time as a failure. It was also highly controversial, leading to a rebuttal by Napoleon's brother Louis and also by the Bonapartist General Gourgaud, who was intent on a duel over the matter. The pronouncements of both Louis Bonaparte and Gourgaud, Scott's reply to the latter, and several other documents are covered in Corson. *Private Letters of King James's Reign*, a fabrication which served as a germ for *The Fortunes of Nigel*, was published in part in *Scribner's Magazine* (1893), and in full, with a disproportionately long introduction, by Douglas Grant (1947); it is discussed by W. M. Parker in "The Origins of Scott's 'Nigel' " (*MLR*, 1939).

Scott was throughout his career a diligent reviewer and writer of periodical articles. Two of these have attracted special attention. Because of the heated controversy over the historical truth of his portraits of the Convenanters in *Old Mortality*, and particularly the attack by Thomas McCrie (see above), Scott himself undertook a defensive review in the *Quarterly* in 1817, which generally receives attention in the biographies. More specific studies are by Andrew Lang, "Scott His Own Reviewer" (*Sketch*, 5 Dec. 1894, and *TLS*, 8 Nov. 1918), Walter Graham, "Scott's Dilemma" (*MLN*, 1926) and R. S. Rait, "Walter Scott and Thomas McCrie" (*Sir Walter Scott Today*).

Scott's famous review of *Emma* in the *Quarterly* (1815) has also aroused controversy. William Reitzel (*PMLA*, 1928), contended that the author was Archibishop Whately, who did write later (1821) a review of *Northanger Abbey* and *Persuasion* for the *Quarterly*. He was answered by Walter Graham ("Scott and Mr. Reitzel," *PMLA*, 1929), who offered objective proof of Scott's authorship, which Reitzel refused to accept (*PMLA*, 1929). The matter was settled, however, by C. B. Hogan in "Sir Walter Scott and *Emma*" (*PMLA*, 1930) with incontrovertible proof of Scott's authorship. W. B. Squire had discussed this point earlier in "Walter Scott and Jane Austen" (*TLS*, 14 Nov. 1918). Correspondence in the *Times Literary Supplement* on the 1821 *Quarterly* review is listed by Corson. R. S. Rait reworked an article, "Scott as Critic and Judge," originally contributed to the *Times Literary Supplement* (7 Nov. 1918) for *Scott Centenary Articles* (1932).

The editions of Dryden and Swift are Scott's most ambitious pieces of editing, but have evoked no special articles of any scope. Scott's editing is considered, in view of the time when it was done, to have been excellent, and Saintsbury's revisions of the Dryden may almost be called negligible. The Dryden, however, has now been largely superseded by later work, and the Swift altogether superseded.

The other most important piece of editing undertaken by Scott (except perhaps the *Minstrelsy*) is *Ballantyne's Novelist's Library*, consisting of Scott's selection from the works of earlier novelists, with introductory biographical and critical essays by Scott. Here again there are no modern articles or notes specifically on this work to be recorded, although Scott is generally cited and quoted in any work on these individual writers, and his critical opinions throw valuable light on his own ideas concerning the novelist's art.

5

Robert Southey

By Kenneth Curry
UNIVERSITY OF TENNESSEE

I. BIBLIOGRAPHIES

S INCE THERE IS no special bibliography of Southey, the student
must begin with the list of editions and studies in *The Cambridge
Bibliography of English Literature*, supplemented by the annual bibliographies in *ELH* (later in *PQ*), *PMLA*, and *Modern Humanities
Research Association Bibliography*. Southey's own published works
are listed (together with brief notes about their first publication and
later editions) in William Haller's *Early Life of Robert Southey*
(1917), and in Jack Simmons' *Southey* (1945). Two additions to
the Southey canon are discussed by me in *SB* (1952–53).

Southey's numerous periodical contributions have never been
completely identified, but a series of articles has succeeded in
bringing some order out of uncertainty. J. Zeitlin (*N&Q*, 1918) has
listed and discussed his contributions to the *Critical Review*, 1798–
1803; K. Curry (*BB*, 1939), those in the *Annual Review*, 1803–09;
R. D. Havens (*RES*, 1932), those in the *Foreign Review* and the
Foreign Quarterly Review. Southey's work for the *Quarterly Review*
represented his most significant periodical writing, for which Hill
and Helen C. Shine's *The Quarterly Review Under Gifford* (1949)
provides the most complete identification of his articles—with many
pertinent quotations from the unpublished correspondence of Gifford
and Murray—for the years 1809–24. For 1825–39 there is the list in
C. C. Southey's *Life and Correspondence of Robert Southey*
(1849–50). Additional notes will also be found in the article by J. D.
Kern, E. Schneider, and I. Griggs, "Lockhart to Croker on the
'Quarterly' " (*PMLA*, 1945). N. L. Kaderly (*MLN*, 1955) has
clearly demonstrated that the article "On the Means of Improving
the People," in the *Quarterly* for April 1818, is Southey's, not
Rickman's.

Southey also contributed translations, original letters, and
poems to the *Monthly Magazine* from 1796 to 1800; to the
Athenaeum, a short-lived publication conducted by the Aikins
(1807–09); a life of Wesley to the *Correspondent* (1817); and for
four years (1808–11) he wrote the lengthy historical section (a full
volume) of the *Edinburgh Annual Register*. At the turn of the
century he contributed verses to the *Morning Post*; those which he
reprinted are indicated in the notes to M. H. FitzGerald's edition of

the *Poems* (1909). Certainly many of the unsigned poems in the *Morning Post* for 1798–99 are Southey's, and B. R. McElderry, Jr., (*N&Q*, Nov. 1955) and Geoffrey Carnall (*N&Q*, Feb. 1956) explore several of these possibilities, agreeing that "The Idiot"—reprinted by McElderry—is Southey's and represents a contrasting interpretation to Wordsworth's "The Idiot Boy." Half a dozen other poems plus the many translations from Spanish can also safely be attributed to Southey (cf. G. Carnall, *Robert Southey and His Age*, 1960). Southey's own poems in the *Annual Anthology*—with those of the other contributors—are identified, with the aid of Southey's annotated copies, by me in *PBSA* (1948).

Sotheby's *Catalogue of the Valuable Library of the Late Robert Southey, Esq.* (1844) provides a detailed guide to the contents of Southey's library, and my article "The Library of Robert Southey," *Studies in Honor of John C. Hodges and Alwin Thaler* (*TSL*, Special Number, 1961) surveys the formation of this library of fourteen thousand volumes and describes many of the most interesting books.

II. EDITIONS

SOUTHEY COLLECTED and published his own poems in a ten-volume edition, 1837–38, for which he wrote informative prefaces concerning their composition and first publication. This edition provides the most comprehensive and authoritative text and commentary for his poetry. After his death two slender posthumous volumes appeared: *Oliver Newman: A New-England Tale* (unfinished, 1845); *Robin Hood: A Fragment* (1847). All these volumes were reprinted in 1860 (with a memoir of Southey by H. T. Tuckerman) in a ten-volume edition—subsequently reissued in five volumes. Although several one-volume editions of Southey's poems have appeared, the most valuable one to the student is that of M. H. FitzGerald (Oxford Standard Authors, 1909), who provides many bibliographical details of first publication with pertinent quotations from both published and unpublished sources.

Since Southey's custom was to revise his poems whenever a new edition was demanded, the textual problems are often complex. *Joan of Arc*—for which the changes were most thoroughgoing—is a very different poem in its first edition of 1796 from the frequently revised poem in the collected edition of 1837–38. The student interested in the early poems of Southey must, therefore, consult the first editions.

Southey did not reprint all his poems in the collected edition; only "The Retrospect" from his first volume (*Poems*, 1795) was reprinted. Similarly, he left uncollected many others from the *Annual Anthology*, the *Morning Post*, the *Monthly Magazine*, translations from *Letters from Spain and Portugal* (1797), and many of the laureate odes. (See note on p. 745 of FitzGerald's edition of the *Poems*.) Other poems also are scattered throughout his published correspondence and in the four volumes of his *Common-Place Book* (1849–50).

The prose works of Southey have never been collected; indeed, only a few have ever been republished and edited in accordance with modern scholarly practice. Jacob Zeitlin's *Select Prose of Robert Southey* (1916) follows the suggestions of Oliver Elton in his *Survey of English Literature, 1780–1830* (1912) and includes: the description of Southey's library (*Colloquies*); scenes from the Lake District (*Espriella, Colloquies,* and *Common Place Book*); *The Doctor* (about 200 pages); the life of Bayard (*Quarterly*, 1825); the siege of Zaragoza (Zeitlin calls it his most vivid piece of narrative) and the uprising at Marvam (*Peninsular War*); the system of the Jesuits in Paraguay (*History of Brazil*); the manufacturing system (*Espriella*); and miscellaneous opinions from the *Common-Place Book*.

The *Life of Nelson*, the most frequently reprinted of his works, has been excellently edited by Geoffrey Callender (1922), with introduction, notes, and maps of the several naval battles. E. R. H. Harvey (1953) edited the *Life of Nelson*, using as his text the thirteenth edition, the last to receive attention from Southey, and prefixing the reprint with a sympathetic biographical essay and a second essay upon the biography. The biographer of Nelson, Carola Oman, has written an introduction for the Everyman edition of the *Life of Nelson* (1962). The *Life of Wesley*, including the annotations of Coleridge (first published in the third edition, 1846), has been edited by M. H. FitzGerald in two volumes (1925). The short biographies of Sir Richard Hawkins, Sir Richard Grenville, Robert Devereux, Second Earl of Essex, and Sir Walter Raleigh (*Lives of the British Admirals with an Introductory View of the Naval History of England*) were edited by David Hannay under the title

English Seamen (1895). J. S. Childers has provided the *Lives and Works of the Uneducated Poets* (1925) with a brief introduction and notes.

Canon FitzGerald has edited and abridged *The Doctor* (1930) in one volume. In this abridgment the slender narrative thread stands out more clearly than in the seven-volume original where, as the story progressed, Dr. Daniel Dove, the hero, appeared less and less frequently.

Jack Simmons' edition of Southey's *Letters from England by Don Manuel Espriella* (1951) contains an introduction praising its significant glimpses of England and English customs in 1807. The notes, although referring often to passages in Southey's other works, mainly elucidate topographical and historical points.[1]

R. Ellis Roberts has edited Byron's *Vision of Judgement* and Southey's *Vision of Judgement* (1932) with an introduction restating the familiar circumstances of the composition and publication of the two poems.

Southey's translation of *The Chronicle of the Cid* has been handsomely reprinted by the Heritage Press (1958) with an introduction by V. S. Pritchett.

Southey's letters are widely scattered in perhaps a hundred books and articles. The chief sources for his correspondence are C. C. Southey's *Life and Correspondence of Robert Southey* (6 vols., 1849–50); J. W. Warter's *A Selection from the Letters of Robert Southey* (4 vols., 1856); Edward Dowden's *The Correspondence of Robert Southey and Caroline Bowles* (1881); Kenneth Curry's *New Letters of Robert Southey* (2 vols., 1965). The text of C. C. Southey's *Life and Correspondence* is carelessly printed and transcribed with frequent editorial emendations designed to soften Southey's severe, intemperate language, especially as it related to political and religious ideas. Warter's text, although not without occasional inaccuracies, is on the whole reliable and remarkably free from textual changes. *New Letters of Robert Southey* contains about five hundred hitherto unpublished letters and a series of biographical sketches provides information about Southey's friends and principal correspondents. The annotation includes additional biographical data for the members of his circle and bibliographical details concerning several additions to the Southey canon. These letters expand considerably our knowledge of the details of Southey's career, his personal associations, the progress of his ideas,

---

[1]   An appreciative review of this edition by V. S. Pritchett (*New Statesman and Nation*, 5 April 1952) sees Southey's *Espriella* as continuing the tradition of Defoe's *Tour* and the journeys of Smollett's Humphry Clinker.

and the genesis and composition of his books and periodical essays.

J. W. Robberds' *Memoir of the Life and Writings of the Late William Taylor* (1843) contains the Southey-Taylor correspondence, important for its reflection of the wide range of intellectual and literary subjects of interest to the two authors. Joseph Cottle's *Reminiscences of Southey and Coleridge* (1847) cannot be ignored, but it must be used with the knowledge that what purports to be a single letter may very well be fabricated from several letters of varying date. Cottle was also not beyond inventing phrases and whole sentences for insertion in an otherwise correct transcript. John Forster's *Life of Walter Savage Landor* (1869) prints the bulk of the Southey-Landor correspondence. Orlo Williams' *Life of John Rickman* (1912) includes many letters of Southey to Rickman not printed by C. C. Southey or Warter, as well as many of Rickman's letters to Southey. John Dennis' *Robert Southey: The Story of His Life Written in His Letters* (1887, reprinted in Bohn's Library) presents a selection of Southey's letters so that they tell his own biography. In 1912 M. H. FitzGerald made a selection of the letters and wrote an admirable introductory essay on Southey's letters (World's Classics).[2]

2   Correspondence of secondary importance may be merely cited: *Fragmentary Remains, Literary and Scientific, of Sir Humphry Davy,* ed. John Davy (1858); *Letters from the Lake Poets . . . to Daniel Sturart* (1889); W. Knight, *Memorials of Coleorton* (1887) for letters to Sir George Beaumont; *The Autobiography . . . of Sir Egerton Brydges* (1834); *Memoirs of . . . James Montgomery* (1855); *Selections . . . of Bernard Barton* (1849); G. Greever, *A Wiltshire Parson and His Friends* (1926) for letters to W. L. Bowles; E. Betham, *A House of Letters* (1905)—and *Fraser's* (1878) for textual variants—for letters to Matilda Betham; T. Sadler, *The Diary . . . Henry Crabb Robinson* (1872); *The Life of the Reverend Joseph Blanco White,* ed. J. H. Thom (1845); E. R. Seary, "Robert Southey and Ebenezer Elliott" (*RES*, 1939); W. Partington, *The Private Letter-Books of Sir Walter Scott* (1930); C. L. Cline, "The Correspondence of Robert Southey and Isaac D'Israeli" (*RES*, 1941); W. S. Scott, "Some Southey Letters" (*Atlantic Monthly*, 1902) for letters to Mary Barker; J. de Sousa Leão, "Robert Southey" (*Revista do instituto histórico e geográfico Brasileiro*, 1943) for letters to John T. and Henry Koster; R. Baughman, "Southey the Schoolboy" (*HLQ*, 1941) for letters to Charles Collins; R. H. Cholmondeley, *The Heber Letters* (1950), A. Cabral's edition of Southey's *Journals of a Residence in Portugal 1800–1801 and a Visit to France 1838* (1960).

Individual letters of particular interest are published in *Modern Philology* (1932), to Coleridge, giving his reasons for not writing for the *Edinburgh Review;* in *Bulletin of the John Rylands Library* (1934), to Mrs. W. B. Rawson, expressing his views on the abolition of slavery.

III. BIOGRAPHIES

SOUTHEY HAS NOT been well served by his biographers. Sir Henry Taylor, the best qualified of all those who had known him personally, abandoned the idea of writing the biography because of dissension in the Southey family. In 1849–50 Cuthbert C. Southey published the *Life and Correspondence of Robert Southey*, which, with all its inaccuracies in transcription of original documents, its failure to understand Southey's complex character, and its condescending tone toward Southey's unorthodox views in religion and politics, still remains of first importance in the study of Southey since it contains documents unavailable elsewhere. J. W. Warter, Southey's son-in-law, possessed considerable scholarly ability, but in his four-volume edition of *Letters* (1856) he neglected his opportunity for showing the ramifications of Southey's personal and intellectual life in favor of the mere printing, virtually without annotation, of letters not given in C. C. Southey's *Life*.

C. T. Browne's *Life of Robert Southey* (1854) may be dismissed as a brief recapitulation of the material in the *Life and Correspondence*, although with apt quotations and a sympathetic account of Southey's interest in young men and of his loyalty to old friends.

It was not until 1879 that Edward Dowden produced (for the English Men of Letters series) the first biography based upon wide scholarship and knowledge of literature. Written with great charm and emphasizing fully as much the personal as the literary aspect of his life, the biography softens the harsh, rough sides of Southey's personality and presents him as a man supremely happy in his family, in a few old friends, his attention engrossed in books and writing. The figure that emerges from this biography is almost saintly, but the student familiar with Southey's letters, his controversial writings, and the impact which he had upon many of his contemporaries, will question this interpretation.

Dowden's account is chronological for the first thirty years of Southey's life. Thereupon the biography becomes a series of sketches of various incidents, friendships, and literary projects—many recounted with great sympathy and interesting detail; but the fre-

quent omission of dates is provoking to anyone interested in
Southey's development chronologically or in the relation of one
incident to another. Certain topics that one might expect to find
discussed are only briefly treated: little is said of the friendship with
Coleridge, although the Coleridge children receive their just due;
Southey's religious opinions are dismissed as almost impossible to
delineate accurately; we are told little of his association with
Wordsworth during the latter years of his life. Still there is much to
praise for what is included: the recognition of the importance of
Epictetus in Southey's development; the significance of Brissot; the
brief sketch of the literary group at Norwich to which William
Taylor introduced him; the picture of Greta Hall and the Lake
District; the description of his library and his enthusiasm for books;
his kindness to young authors. In his criticism of Southey's works
Dowden calls attention to the moral force of his heroes and heroines
—they are all "high-souled"; but it is to his biographies that he
accords the highest praise, although feeling that Southey does not
penetrate to the central mystery of his subjects.

In 1917, William Haller published his *Early Life of Robert
Southey,* a detailed biographical and critical work of three hundred
pages, which provides the most thoroughgoing account for this
period. Although less laudatory than Dowden, Haller presents a
portrait of Southey seen from several angles and sets him squarely
into the literary and intellectual milieu of his era. The emphasis of
Haller's study is literary, and his presentation of the relationship of
Southey's poetry to its eighteenth-century antecedents and its
intimate connection with the same movement that brought forth
Lyrical Ballads and Wordsworth's later poems is carefully detailed.
Haller's study, although confined to the first decade of Southey's
literary career, is the fullest of Southey considered as poet. Some
especially excellent parts of this study may be noted: the close
connection between the poetry of Wordsworth and Southey and the
rightness of Jeffrey's recognition that a new school had arisen; the
importance of Charles Lamb and his correspondence; the sketch of
Southey's intellectual activities (1793–1803) which embraced most
of the subjects of modern research; the explanation of Southey's
popular success with *Joan of Arc;* and finally, the account of the
quarrel with Coleridge and the breakup of pantisocracy, which
avoids censuring either but sees inevitable friction over the unequal
contributions to their joint establishment and the reluctance of
either to admit that the project was a failure. During these early
years, and in the midst of his bewildering changes of residence until

his final settlement at Keswick in 1803, Haller sees in Southey's strong desire for a home, its comforts, and the opportunity for learned leisure a compelling force that was to dictate the character of his later life.

Jack Simmons' *Southey* (1945) provides a well-written account of Southey's life that should satisfy both the general reader and the special student. Although many points are more fully treated elsewhere, Simmons has concisely presented material from widely scattered sources (much of it unpublished) and has shed new light upon many details of Southey's career. The book provides illustrations of several Southey portraits, a listing of Southey's published books, a genealogical table, and critical footnotes which furnish references not elsewhere available.

The purpose of the book has been to present Southey both as man and writer and to state Southey's side of the case when needed. Simmons has faced the unattractive side of Southey's character—the bitter, vituperative controversialist so sure of the rightness of his cause—and has been able by so doing to produce a much more lifelike portrait than Dowden's. The arrangement is chronological with the political and literary-critical sections neatly sketched in. The biography emphasizes Southey's relations with his celebrated contemporaries, the political events of the day, and the impact of his writings upon the public.

Where so much that needed to be done has been done so well, it is perhaps ungenerous to cavil, but the sketchy treatment of Southey's important friendships with Charles Danvers, Mary Barker, John May, his brother Henry Herbert, and above all Charles Wynn and Grosvenor Bedford, is certainly a blemish. As those portions of the biography descriptive of the historical and political aspects of Southey's career are excellently done, so by contrast those concerned with the literary and poetic aspects seem lacking in that sympathy and concentration one might expect in a specialized study. In the final chapter Simmons examines Southey's works, dismisses much of the poetry, but finds a good word for *Kehama*, the ballads, and the short lyrics in praise of domestic life. In his warm advocacy of Southey's prose, however, Simmons praises his plain style—at variance with the evocative, ornamental prose of his contemporaries, provides quotations from the Nelson and the *Colloquies* to illustrate his skill with narrative and description, and points out Southey's dry humor (in writing to children), his ability to draw a character, his often poetic passages (as in the final chapter of Nelson), and his mastery of narrative (especially his battle scenes) by way of denying the charge that his histories are only big, dull books.[3]

Southey's life is, however, often known only in terms of his association with his more celebrated literary contemporaries. Full-length studies of these authors are usually biased in favor of their subjects, and this bias is most clearly seen in many Coleridge biographies. Lawrence Hanson (*The Life of S. T. Coleridge: The Early Years*, 1938) is always the partisan of Coleridge: Southey receives the blame for "forcing" Coleridge's marriage to Sara Fricker, for being the first to abandon pantisocracy, and for resenting a contribution larger than Coleridge's to their joint establishment in Bristol during 1794–95. This lack of sympathy is most noticeable when reading the Southey passages consecutively and in such entries in the index as "jeers at what he thinks STC's philosophical instability." E. K. Chambers' *Coleridge* (1938), on the other hand, does not see Coleridge as entirely faultless in the quarrel over the failure of pantisocracy. Chambers' portrait of Southey, although not flattering, is not so one-sided as Hanson's. J. D. Campbell (*Coleridge*, 1894) presented a more humane and generous Southey, who is credited with selfless efforts in aid of Coleridge and Hartley during the difficult years (about 1814) of Coleridge's addiction to opium. Campbell, who made the customary charge that Southey forced an unwilling Coleridge into marriage, was answered by George Saintsbury ("Coleridge and Southey," *Collected Essays*, 1923), who maintained that Southey could not have actually forced Coleridge to return to Bristol to marry, that Southey was scarcely "meddling" since he had known Sara from childhood and had introduced the two, and that Sara had no male relatives to act for her; nor could Southey, who had not then sensed the instability of Coleridge's temperament, have foreseen the outcome of the marriage. Saintsbury further defended Southey from the charge of not writing more warmly on the occasion of Coleridge's death by pointing out that Southey was neither sentimental nor given to expressing a grief which he did not feel. Simmons in his biography quotes from an unpublished letter of 22 August 1794, showing that Southey considered Coleridge to be then engaged to Sara. Later Simmons states the case for Southey by arguing that after the failure of the marriage

---

3   Reviewers of Simmons' *Southey* were generous in their praise. Cf. Stephen Potter (*New Statesman and Nation*, 30 June 1945), Dorothy M. Stuart (*YWES*, 1945), R. W. King (*RES*, 1946), B. R. Davis (*MLN*, 1951). The praise, however, was qualified by dissatisfaction with the treatment given to Southey's religious views (King) and a desire for a fuller treatment of Southey as poet (Stuart, Davis).

Southey was censured for not having had at twenty sufficient foresight to have sought to break the engagement. "Southey's real error lay in making Coleridge in his own image, in crediting him with a rigid sense of duty and a decision of judgment equal to his own; and who will condemn him for that?" (p. 57).

H. I'A. Fausset (*Samuel Taylor Coleridge*, 1926) sees Coleridge as equally at fault with Southey in the failure of pantisocracy and interprets Coleridge's letter to Southey over that failure as necessary for Coleridge—"by attributing its nonrealization to Southey's defection, he preserved his dream and his self-approval intact" (p. 119).

E. L. Griggs ("Robert Southey's Estimate of Samuel Taylor Coleridge: A Study in Human Relations," *HLQ*, 1945), who uses the Rickman-Southey correspondence in the Huntington Library, finds Southey intolerant, bitter, meddlesome, and jealous, obstructing the moves of others to help Coleridge for the sake of advancing his own project, and keeping silent when he could have helped by speaking out. After Coleridge's death, Southey refused to cooperate with members of the Coleridge family in their efforts to write about Coleridge. Modification of this harsh view may be found in Simmons' *Southey*, where the full treatment of the Southey-Coleridge relationship is one of the strong points of the biography, and in Southey's letters to Cottle of 1836, published in Curry's *New Letters of Robert Southey*, where his difficult position with regard to the Coleridge family is made clear in the text and notes. Among Southey's services to Coleridge and his family are his efforts to secure employment for Coleridge, his encouragement of Coleridge in writing books (their joint *Omniana* is one result), his reading of proofs for the *Friend*, and, most important of all, his assumption of responsibility for the Coleridge family, whom he treated for over twenty years as members of his own household. Hartley Coleridge's tribute to Southey is one of the finest possible and shows no trace of resentment over any differences between his father and uncle: "Now if you want to make a man hated, hold him up as an Example. It is an extraordinary proof of the loveliness of Southey's character, that though his name was rife in every objurgation and every admonition I received, I never could help but love him" (Hartley Coleridge, *Letters*, 1936, ed. G. E. and E. L. Griggs).

N. C. Starr's "Coleridge's Sir Leoline" (*PMLA*, 1946) argues persuasively for Southey as the friend referred to in Christabel ("they had been friends in youth") by developing the association of Southey, Aust Cliff, and Leoline as a result of the ill-fated outing to

Tintern Abbey in the summer of 1795. Malcolm Elwin's *The First Romantics* (1948) enhances Coleridge largely at the expense of Wordsworth, and Southey consequently escapes with relatively little censure. Warren U. Ober, "Southey, Coleridge, and 'Kubla Khan'" (*JEGP*, 1959), concludes through a study of pertinent passages in Southey's *Common Place Book* and *Thalaba* that Southey provided "many of the scattered threads which were woven by Coleridge into the glowing fabric of 'Kubla Khan.'"

The pantisocratic period of Southey's life has attracted many critics. Haller gives the most satisfactory account of pantisocracy from Southey's point of view, but Edward Dowden's chapter, "Early Revolutionary Group and Antagonists," in *The French Revolution and English Literature* (1897) and Charles Cestre's *La Révolution française et les poètes anglais* (1905) are also valuable. "The Pantisocratic Phase" of H. N. Fairchild's *The Romantic Quest* (1931) emphasizes many points of similarity between Southey and Coleridge.[4]

George Whalley, "Coleridge and Southey in Bristol, 1795" (*RES*, 1950) finds confusion in the details of the collaboration during this year, but from the borrowings of the two authors from the Bristol Library he seeks "details to clarify some biographical problems and to throw light upon the poetical development of the two men." Whalley sees the crises over pantisocracy and Sara Fricker as merely the battlegrounds revealing the basic incompatibility of the two men, evidenced in Southey's "impatience of philosophy [which] became the keystone of the dyspathy which was soon to separate the two poets." At this time both were concerned with the problem of the poet—"the symbolic transmutation of experience." Whalley suggests that Southey stimulated Coleridge's interest in the poetic possibilities of travel literature and "twilight materials of nascent science," but Southey was unable to follow Coleridge, who later turned to Wordsworth—Southey's failure to appreciate the *Ancient Mariner* indicates this inability. In another article Whalley has published the most complete list of the Bristol Library borrowings of Southey and Coleridge (*Library*, 1949),

---

4 Fuller studies of pantisocracy, especially as it reflected a knowledge of America and American travel books, are by J. R. MacGillivray, "The Pantisocracy Scheme and Its Immediate Background" (*Stud. in English by Members of Univ. Coll.* [of Toronto], 1931) and Sister Eugenia Logan, "Coleridge's Scheme of Pantisocracy and American Travel Accounts" (*PMLA*, 1930). Miss M. C. Park's "Joseph Priestley and the Problem of Pantisocracy" (*Proc. of the Delaware County Inst. of Sci.*, 1947) clearly shows the connection between pantisocracy and Priestley's settlement for the friends of liberty on the Susquehanna, where the Priestleys had large tracts of land for sale.

amplifying and occasionally correcting the older article by Kaufman (*MP*, 1924).[5]

Southey's relations with his other literary contemporaries seem less complicated than those with Coleridge. R. H. Super's *Walter Savage Landor* (1954) contains the fullest account of the personal and literary ramifications of Southey's friendship with Landor. This work, often exhaustive in detail and corrective of facts in earlier studies, supplants such hitherto valuable books as E. Ehrich's *Southey und Landor* (1934) and Malcolm Elwin's *Savage Landor* (1941). John Forster's biography (1869) is less full than the above works, but it contains more extensive quotations from the Southey-Landor correspondence.

Newman I. White's *Shelley* (1940) gives an eminently fair treatment of Shelley's meeting with Southey (1811), his changed regard for Southey, and their later correspondence, and refrains from censuring either poet for what may be called mistaken interpretations of the other. W. E. Peck's *Shelley* (1927) contains a valuable interchapter on Shelley's indebtedness to Southey's poems, which at one time were his favorites. K. N. Cameron's article, "Shelley vs. Southey: New Light on an Old Quarrel" (*PMLA*, 1942), poses a special problem: Was Southey attacking Shelley in the *Quarterly?* and did Shelley have Southey in mind as the reviewer in *Adonais?* Cameron argues in the affirmative that Southey's article on "Popular Disaffection" (Jan. 1817)—which lists Shelley's pseudonymous pamphlet by the Hermit of Marlow among the pamphlets under review, although Shelley is not mentioned in the article—was based on private information that the pamphlet was by Shelley, and that he was picturing Shelley in the portrait of Pitou, a literary adventurer. The evidence, although persuasively argued, depends upon a long chain of hypotheses, one of which is the outright rejection of Southey's statement that he had never directly or indirectly referred to Shelley in his writings. The portrait of Pitou need not be that of any individual. It should be remembered that Southey's association with Shelley was quite brief and that he was never a friend, as is sometimes stated—their connection being much

---

5 Two earlier studies of this period use Bristol as their point of departure. F. E. Pierce ("The Eddy Around Bristol," *Currents and Eddies of the Romantic Movement,* 1918) has many shrewd comments about this group of young Bristolians, the only group of poets sympathetic to the French Revolution and one also interested in German-Gothic materials. The *Annual Anthology* was the last harvest of the group. A more ambitious study—Carl A. Weber's *Bristols Bedeutung für die englische Romantik und die deutsch-englischen Beziehungen* (1935)—is extremely detailed for all the minor Bristolians known to Southey during the 1790's and connects them with the strong group of dissenters in Bristol, the interest in the new poetry, and the enthusiasm for the Gothic supernatural. Weber sees in Dr. Thomas Beddoes the central figure of this Bristol group.

like that of ships that pass in the night. (On this point see Malcolm Elwin's letter in *TLS*, 27 March 1943.) R. W. King (*MLR*, 1956) traces Shelley's sentence on history—"that record of crimes and miseries"—to Southey's poem "History."

Southey's even more fleeting association with William Blake is sympathetically detailed by Geoffrey Keynes (*Blake Studies*, 1949). Southey's friendship with Wordsworth developed after his removal to Keswick. Simmons traces its beginning to 1805, when Wordsworth turned to Southey for consolation after the loss of his brother John. In 1817 Southey, when on a continental tour, acted as envoy to Caroline Wordsworth Baudouin, then recently married (K. Curry, "Southey's Visit to Caroline Wordsworth Baudouin," *PMLA*, 1944). Frederika Beatty's *William Wordsworth of Rydal Mount* (1939) gives many details of the Southeys and Wordsworths, and the indexes to the Wordsworth correspondence yield many others.

The Southey-Byron quarrel was a public one: save for one personal meeting in 1813, the two were unknown to each other. Simmons states the case succinctly and soberly, pointing out that much of Byron's rage was nurtured by false reports of what Southey had said. The complete documents are given in the Coleridge-Prothero edition of Byron (1898–1904).

IV. CRITICISM

M ANY CRITICAL essays endeavor calmly and judiciously to assess Southey's worth as man and writer, carefully weighing merits and shortcomings in the balance. These, one suspects, are little read, most readers (and many critics) deriving their views of Southey directly from his contemporary critics—Byron, Hazlitt, and Macaulay. As these writers, particularly Byron, continue to be read today, their views are the ones known. Familiarity with the criticism of Southey leads to the conclusion that Byron's highly quotable references in *English Bards* ("A bard may chaunt too often and too long"), the ironic dedication to Southey of *Don Juan*, and the witty and merciless satire of *The Vision of Judgement* have largely determined the common attitude—even to the half-acceptance of the terms *renegade* and *apostate*. This persistence of Byron's charges may be seen in Georg Brandes' *Main Currents in Nineteenth-Century Literature* (1923), where the tone of the criticism of Southey is Byron's and where much of the discussion concerns *Don Juan* and the *Vision*.

Southey has often been the target for depreciatory criticism whose purpose has been to enhance at his expense another author or group of authors. From such charges R. W. Chambers in "Ruskin (and Others) on Byron" (*Man's Unconquerable Mind*, 1939—reprinted from *English Assoc. Pamphlet, No. 62*, 1925) attempts to rescue not only Southey, whom he vigorously defends, but Coleridge and Castlereagh, by objecting to the picture of the early nineteenth century as "an age of black reaction and shameless apostasy" made blacker in order to whiten Byron and Shelley. "Now, should respect for Byron and Shelley involve our thinking of Coleridge and Southey, under the Castlereagh administration, as an 'opium-eater' and a 'renegade' under the administration of a 'jackal'?"

A third point of view is represented by those readers who approach Southey directly through his poems, his letters, and his controversial writings, and simply find him uncongenial. They are repelled by his intolerance, his self-assurance, his tendency to take himself too seriously; and his good qualities, so painstakingly brought out by Dowden or Saintsbury, by FitzGerald or Simmons, cannot counterbalance this unpleasant side of his personality and works. Such a point of view is boldly stated in the review of Simmons' biography in the *Times Literary Supplement*, 21 April 1945 ("The Industrious Poet: In Southey's Workshop"): ". . . there is something intrinsically unlikeable in the work and in its author, an imperfect sympathy. . . . His goodness, like the bulk of his poetry, lacks charm." Similarly, Miss Rose Macaulay, who describes Southey's Portuguese visit in *They Went to Portugal* (1946), finds him "a natural disapprover" and expresses constant irritation over his criticism of Portuguese customs.

Southey has not, on the other hand, failed to receive the highest praise. Landor was always generous in his admiration, and Charles Lamb cordially praised much of Southey's work. Coleridge's *Biographia Literaria*, Carlyle's *Reminiscences*, Newman's *Apologia*, Ticknor's *Journals*, Borrow's *Wild Wales*, and Thackeray's *Four Georges* contain passages of highest commendation for Southey as man and writer.

At this point, however, we might profitably consider three full-length essays which attempt a general critical evaluation. Leslie Stephen ("Southey's Letters," *Studies of a Biographer*, 1902) describes Southey as a good specimen of the author who earns his living by his pen, but who cannot be admitted to the highest group of authors. The epics reveal only too clearly the literary craftsman, but Stephen can read the ballads ("The Old Woman of Berkeley" in particular) with pleasure. In the quarrel with Macaulay over reform, Stephen thinks that Southey has posterity on his side. His literary immortality, however, is likely to rest upon the gem of *The Doctor*—The Story of the Three Bears. Stephen, in judging Southey as a man, acutely observes that his extreme self-confidence was necessary "to comfort and support him through failure and obloquy, and the protracted struggle to make both ends meet." But he lacked the philosopher's elevation and the poet's insight "to see things in their true proportions." Although Stephen praises the letters, he warns the reader that they do not yield their secrets readily; and posterity, preferring an author with fewer reticences, is alienated by his stoic reserve.

John Dennis' essay in *Studies in English Literature* (1876), like Stephen's, lays stress upon Southey as an honorable representative of literature. Dennis is unable to praise the epics, finding no passages to which the memory clings, but prefers *Roderick* and *Kehama* to the others. He commends the ballads for their treatment of melancholy subjects in comic vein. The failure of many of his works, such as the *History of Brazil*, was due to Southey's inability to judge the interests of the public. His social criticism in his essays and letters, although marred by intemperate language, was often ahead of his day. Dennis finds Southey in his personal life to be a true friend and devoted family man, who never shrank from demands placed upon him.

George Saintsbury's essay on Southey (*Essays in English Literature 1780–1860*, 2d Ser., 1895, and reprinted in his *Collected Essays and Papers*, 1923) is as laudatory as any I know. Saintsbury asserts that—in contrast to Scott—Southey has been ill-served by his biographers. Those who knew him never impugned his character; he had no humbug, but much virtue; "and a virtuous man who is not something of a humbug is apt to be a little of a Pharisee unless he is a perfect saint, which Southey, to do him justice, was not." Saintsbury praises *Roderick*, *Kehama*, and the ballads. The *Espriella Letters*, he thinks, give perhaps the best picture of England in the early nineteenth century. Saintsbury's position may best be given in a quotation:

For the man *knew* enormously; he could write admirably; it may be fairly contended that he only missed being a great poet by the constant collar work which no great poet in the world has been able to endure; he had the truest sensibility with scarcely any touch of the maudlin; the noblest sense of duty with not more than a very slight touch of spiritual pride. If he thought a little too well of himself as a poet, he was completely free alike from the morose arrogance of his friend Wordsworth and from the exuberant arrogance of his friend Landor. Only those who have worked through the enormous mass of his verse, his prose, and his letters can fully appreciate his merits; nor is it easy to conceive any scheme of collection that would be possible, or of selection that would do him justice (pp. 266–267).

If Saintsbury is the most laudatory critic, T. R. Lounsbury ("Southey as Poet and Historian," *YR*, 1915) is the most condemnatory.[6] Lounsbury finds Southey in his private life bitter and uncharitable, bigoted and confident in the absolute rightness of his own point of view. He was too much of a partisan to be a good historian, and he lacked also the requisite imagination; his notions of historical research were "elementary."

The centenary of Southey's death in 1943 brought forth no particularly notable essay. The anonymous author in the *Times Literary Supplement* (20 March 1943) suggests his theme by the subhead of his article—"Poet Who Lost His Way." The poems, despite their contriving of wonderful mysteries, have failed because he "lost his way to romance by treating his dreams as no part of it." In his proposals for reform, he survives as an advocate of a "conscientious society." John Shand (*Nineteenth Century*, 1943), after a brief survey of Southey's career, concludes that he is best in his letters. Malcolm Elwin in the *Quarterly Review* (1943) concludes that Southey suffered from too much self-control, which sapped his poetry of spontaneity and his political thought of "strict integrity." Elwin is impressed by his advocacy of political reforms, but since he was a political writer, he suffered personally because the big guns of the opposition writers were trained upon him.

Critical studies of Southey in literary histories follow with varying emphases the nineteenth-century views expressed by Stephen, Dennis, and Saintsbury. Oliver Elton (*A Survey of English Literature, 1780–1830*, 1912) feels that no picture of the poetry of the age is complete without him, emphasizing his connection with those currents that resulted in *Lyrical Ballads* and with the school of

6   Simmons calls Arthur Symons' treatment of Southey the most condemnatory judgment (*Romantic Movement in English Poetry*, 1909), but Symons does praise some aspects of Southey's life and work.

balladry of Scott, Lockhart, and the *Ingoldsby Legends*. Elton, with many another critic, commends Southey's success in the comical or terrible grotesque; in his more ambitious poems, Elton thinks that Southey lacked self-criticism and that we feel as we read that "here is a real man of letters, who has missed his subject." Elton praises Southey most highly as a biographer, although he condemns the Cromwell and Bunyan. Although Elton misses in Southey "that reaction of thought upon the subject . . . which is felt in every page of the Table Talk or of Anima Poetae," yet—"For all this, Southey, if not in any strict sense a great writer, is often, nay, is instinctively, a sound and a good one, and is repeatedly a delightful one; and he left the status of men of letters, and the tradition of their calling, higher than he found it."

S. C. Chew (*A Literary History of England*, 1948) sees in Southey an author of historical interest who often led the way for greater poets—as in his experiments in rimeless verse and in his explorations of Oriental themes. Like other critics Chew prefers those ballads which blend the humorous and the supernatural.

Ernest Bernbaum's *Guide Through the Romantic Movement* (2d ed., 1949) contains the best single chapter on Southey. The outline of his career, the leading characteristics of his most important works, together with the evaluations given them, are concisely presented. As explanation for Southey's present secondary rank among his literary contemporaries Bernbaum suggests two reasons:

> The first, and admittedly doubtful, reason is that, misled by his own estimate of the relative value of his works we have judged him too much by his poetry, and have not yet sufficiently valued his admirable works in prose. The second and less doubtful reason is that, in devoting so much of his energy to an interpretation of the past, he overlooked a principle which Scott never left out of account—namely, that those aspects of past history are most important to us which have left a permanent impress upon our Anglo-American civilization (pp. 162–163).

If critics whose approach has been primarily literary have often dismissed Southey's ideas as outmoded and even reactionary, those who approach Southey for his social ideas find his writings congenial and significant. For these purposes they turn to his correspondence, the *Espriella Letters*, the *Essays* (1832), the *Colloquies*, and the *Quarterly* articles. M. Beer in *A History of British Socialism* (1923) points out that of the three poets—Wordsworth, Coleridge, and Southey—Southey had the most anticapitalistic spirit and describes him as "one of the keenest and most one-sided critics of the industrial revolution." B. N. Schilling, *Human Dignity and the Great Victorians* (1946), observes that although Southey "has less power of thought and feeling and of abstract analysis" than Coleridge, he is equally sincere and "we welcome his greater clarity." Southey is the first of the literary humanitarians to complain of industry upon aesthetic grounds and anticipates William Morris; in his description of unsanitary conditions he anticipates Kingsley's crusade for sanitary reform; and again, like Morris, he is among the first to sympathize with those who find no joy in their labor. In his awareness of the human as well as the economic consequence of idleness, he anticipates Carlyle. Schilling in his discussion of Southey's reforms sees in emigration and education his strongest measures.

Alfred Cobban, *Edmund Burke and the Revolt Against the Eighteenth Century* (1929), is similarly impressed by Southey's answers to the questions of the day, and particularly by his awareness of the loss that comes to a nation whose chief concern is the acquisition of wealth. Cobban observes that as early as 1812 Southey had the vision of the future British Commonwealth of Nations and had abandoned completely the old Tory idea of the colonies as existing solely for the benefit of the mother country.

A. V. Dicey in his *Lectures on the Relation Between Law and Public Opinion in England During the Nineteenth Century* (1905) finds Southey an important figure—with Dr. Arnold and Carlyle—in the protest against individualism. As a preacher of Tory philanthropy, Southey protests against the cruelties of factory life and is a precursor of modern collectivism.

Crane Brinton's discussion of Southey (*Political Ideas of the English Romanticists*, 1926) comes to similar conclusions. Brinton especially admires Southey's character: "His frank acceptance of life, his dislike of systems, his common sense, always at the mercy of his enthusiasms but never the dupe of introspection, happily complement the other-worldliness of Coleridge and the self-searching intensity of Wordsworth." And his concluding remark—commenting upon a letter of Southey concerning the *Quarterly* and Spain—is that "it could have been written by no shallow man, no unsound man, no bad man, but only by a good, and perhaps a wise man."

William Haller's "Southey's Later Radicalism" (*PMLA*, 1922) ably summarizes the evidence contained in the *Essays* and *Colloquies* to represent Southey's criticism of society and his suggestions for its amelioration. Haller traces the basis of this point of view to Godwin, especially to Godwin's view that the rational being acts not according to self-interest but in the interest of society. Carlyle's praise of Southey's *Quarterly* essays—"in spite of my Radicalism I found very much in these Toryisms which was greatly according to my heart"—is cited to counterbalance that conception of Southey derived from Byron and Macaulay. An opposite point of view to Haller's is maintained by Walter Graham ("Robert Southey as Tory Reviewer," *PQ*, 1923), who asserts that "for thirty years Southey was the intolerant champion and abettor of a group of Ultra-Tories." His conclusion, then, confirms that of Macaulay's review of the *Colloquies* in the Edinburgh Review. In 1942 Martin Jarrett-Kerr, in "Southey's Colloquies" (*Nineteenth Century*), examined this work in order not only to confute Macaulay's judgment but also to challenge the Whig interpretation of history, and concluded that Southey's vision of progress is more to our taste today than that of Macaulay. Raymond Williams in *Culture and Society 1780–1950* (1958) also quotes extensively from the *Colloquies* in a ten-page discussion of Southey and Robert Owen of Lanark.[7]

The most recent book on Southey is Geoffrey Carnall's *Robert Southey and His Age: The Development of a Conservative Mind* (1960). This excellent study, based upon some unpublished material and Southey's periodical contributions, explores not only the usual background of national and international politics, but attempts also to assess the particular psychological atmosphere of the age, as it probes into Southey's underlying feelings of anxiety, depression, loneliness, and misanthropy, which he shared with many of his contemporaries. The study progresses from an examination of "The Bellicose Democrat" to "Tory," very largely through an expert use of Southey's articles in the *Annual Review*, the *Edinburgh Annual Register*, and the *Quarterly Review*. Carnall also gives us the only thorough exposition of the development of Southey's religious position, which, despite his staunch support of the Church, was never theologically orthodox. Other topics discussed are pantisocracy, missionaries, Methodists, small religious sects, the Malthusian controversy, Peterloo, *Wat Tyler*, Robert Owen, the Reform legislation, the warfare between the *Edinburgh Review* and the *Quarterly Review*. Carnall's Robert Southey and *His Age* deserves careful study and attention for any aspect of Southey's career.

The general studies and critical essays already mentioned examine the long poems of Southey either in detail (Dowden, Haller,

---

7   This interest in the social ideas of Southey may be inferred by the inclusion of three letters (out of four) of Southey to Lord Ashley on the subject of factory legislation in *English Letters of the XIX Century* (ed. James Aitken, 1946).

Simmons) or in broad critical evaluations. Minute criticisms of the individual poems are not numerous. *Joan of Arc* (1796) has received as much attention as any work of Southey, and here Haller's account is fullest. *Joan of Arc* owed its popularity and its favorable critical reception to its politics, full of sympathy for the French Revolution, and to its utilization of the contemporary interest in the religion of nature. Haller surveys these elements and the background of history used by Southey and describes the reception of the poem by the journals and by contemporary authors. H. N. Fairchild (*The Noble Savage*, 1928) considers the poem interesting for its reflection of ideas of natural religion, and Dowden (*French Revolution and English Literature*, 1897) looks at the poem for its revolutionary spirit, remarking that it is more accurate to call Southey's Joan of Arc a Mary Wollstonecraft in armor than to repeat Coleridge's phrase "a Tom Paine in petticoats." B. W. Early in an unpublished dissertation of *Joan of Arc* (Duke Univ., 1951) includes Southey's first draft of the poem (1793) and provides an elaborate collation of all the subsequent changes in the text.

Haller's discussion of the sources, style, and versification of *Thalaba* (1801) is the most thorough consideration of all the problems of this poem. Its personal revelation of Southey's own interests and its similarity of purpose to the kind of poetry Wordsworth was then writing are points especially stressed. Haller concludes that, despite Southey's pioneering use of Oriental materials in *Thalaba*, the poem remains only a tour de force since it fails to give the reader that lifelike sense of other places and times which Scott, for instance, was able to communicate. "*Thalaba* failed of its highest purpose, true, but the theme was of the noblest, the intent courageous, labor not lacking, and the performance so near to success that the reader is surprised to find the poem more beautiful than he had expected or remembered." *Thalaba* is further interesting since Jeffrey's review of the poem in the opening number of the *Edinburgh Review* (1802) began the long-continued war against the new school of poets, soon to be named the Lake Poets. Haller's study fully presents the case for Southey. W. C. Brown's "Robert Southey and English Interest in the Near East" (*ELH*, 1938) shows in greater detail than Haller that Southey was unsympathetic to Mohammedanism and the East, and that many passages are almost directly versified from the prose accounts of travelers mentioned in his notes.

To H. N. Fairchild (*The Noble Savage*, 1928), *Madoc* illustrates Southey's view of savage life, while H. G. Wright ("Three Aspects of Southey," *RES*, 1933) sees in the description of Caermadoc—the colony founded by Madoc and his sons—a remnant of the old pantisocracy, and in the account of the sea voyage a reminiscence of Southey's own rough sea passage to Spain in 1795. In my article "Southey's *Madoc:* The Manuscript of 1794" (*PQ*, 1943) I publish the first two and a half books of the first draft—all that Southey had written in 1794—and show that the poem was cut from the same cloth as *Joan of Arc,* full of revolutionary, democratic sentiment and Miltonic blank verse. Eleven years later, however, these elements had been eliminated for the first edition (1805).

Frank T. Hoadley ("The Controversy over Southey's *Wat Tyler,*" *SP*, 1941) presents chronologically the events that led to Southey's defense of himself in *A Letter to William Smith* and to his unsuccessful effort to secure an injunction against the publisher Sherwood. The numerous attacks which this act of piracy inspired in the *Morning Chronicle*, the *Examiner*, and the *Edinburgh Review* are summarized, together with quotations from the correspondence of Byron, Scott, and Wordsworth, ending with Wordsworth's comment, "Faction runs high." P. M. Zall ("Lord Eldon's Censorship," *PMLA*, 1953) places the legal decision upon Wat Tyler in its proper perspective (with similar cases involving Byron, Shelley, and others) as a reflection of the peculiar moral and legal point of view of Eldon, and suggests that these principles were adumbrations of the "moral climate that we usually identify with the Victorian era of two decades later."

"A Centenary Appreciation of Southey's Life of Wesley," (*London Quart. and Holborn Rev.*, 1943) by Samuel Davis praises Southey for presenting Wesley as a human being and not as a plaster saint, but suggests that Southey's temperamental lack of sympathy for religious enthusiasm limited the value of the book. Davis, however, calls Southey's the standard biography, despite later publications.

R. D. Havens' "Southey's *Specimens of the Later English Poets*" (*PMLA*, 1945) is a study based upon the manuscript prepared for the printer and attempts to distinguish between the contributions of Southey and his collaborator, G. C. Bedford. Havens explains the failure of the *Specimens*—Southey's least successful work—as owing to its lack of plan, to the fact that a successor to Ellis' work on the earlier poets was not needed, and to the excessive number of selections from minor poets. Havens calls it the "most extensive collection of forgotten authors to be found in any anthology of English poetry." Although Southey never came to grips with the broad fundamentals of literary criticism, he often expressed himself in quotable passages—terse epigram and literary anecdote that employed Johnsonian balance and antithesis. As a favorable example, Havens cites the notice of Ambrose Philips.

A series of notices on less significant works and bypaths of Southey's career may be briefly mentioned at this point. E. C. Knowlton in two articles on Southey's eclogues and monodramas (*PQ*, 1928, 1929) presents Southey as an innovator of literary forms who, with his dramatic and psychological interest in people, was looking forward to Tennyson's *Northern Farmer* and Browning's dramatic monologues and lyrics. E. H. W. Meyerstein in his *Life of Thomas Chatterton* (1930) gives a highly detailed account of Southey and Cottle's edition of Chatterton's *Works* (1803) undertaken for the benefit of the poet's mother and sister. To assist his friend Richard Duppa, who was writing a life of Michelangelo, Southey (who also persuaded Wordsworth to help) translated several poems of Michelangelo for his biography. An article of mine (*RES*, 1938) publishes the text of these translations, together with an account of this collaboration. Geoffrey Carnall's "Robert Southey and Quakerism" (*Friends' Quart.*, 1955) admirably surveys Southey's views toward this religious group.

An especially well-written and interesting article is H. G. Wright's "Southey's Relations with Finland and Scandinavia" (*MLR*, 1932). As a youthful poet, Southey had thought of writing a Runic poem, but it was not until the 1820's and 1830's that he continued seriously this early interest by wide reading in Scandinavian history and literature and by a study of the languages. He taught himself to read Danish, reviewed books of travel to these countries, and drew upon this reading in writing the *Lives of the British Admirals*. Indeed, he admired these peoples so much that when he thought of the troubled days in England, he even speculated upon the possibility of emigrating to Denmark or Sweden.

The laureateship of Southey is the subject of two excellent essays in book-length studies devoted to that office: by E. K. Broadus (*The Laureateship: A Study of the Office of Poet Laureate in England*, 1921) and by Kenneth Hopkins (*The Poets Laureate*, 1954). Despite the difficulties of the office—Southey had understood that task verses were not to be required—he raised it to a respectable status and resolutely expressed his own opinions in his official verses. Hopkins reprints one of the best of these official laureate odes, that upon the death of the Princess Charlotte, a poem omitted from the ten-volume edition of his poetry.

Southey's prose style received high praise from Herbert Read (*English Prose Style*, 1928, rev. 1952), who quotes approvingly from the *History of the Peninsular War* and The Story of the Three

Bears (in its entirety) as examples of narrative and fantasy. The complete story of this classic for children, "The Three Bears" (*The Doctor*, IV, 1837) — its origin and its subsequent reprintings — remains to be told. Mary R. Shamburger and V. R. Lachmann (*JAF*, 1946) suggest, after reviewing what is known of the story, that it owes something to Grimm's tale of Snow White and the Seven Dwarfs and to a Norwegian tale of a king's daughter who visits a cave inhabited by three bears. A correspondent in the *Times Literary Supplement* (23 Nov. 1951, Children's Book Section) discusses a rhymed version of the story by Eleanor Mure preserved in a manuscript dated 26 September 1831 (now in the University of Toronto Library) and sees this version as strengthening the claim for an English source of the legend. Since Southey had learned the story from his uncle William Tyler, and had told it to his own and other children (several such allusions in *New Letters of Robert Southey*), it is possible, of course, that the Mure version derives at second hand from Southey and not independently from oral tradition.

H. W. Howe published privately (1943) a charming monograph on Greta Hall, the home of "the Southeys" for forty years.

V. SPAIN AND PORTUGAL

SOUTHEY'S RELATIONS with Spain and Portugal, as traveler and writer, have been authoritatively discussed by Adolfo Cabral in *Southey e Portugal: 1774–1801* (1959) and in the introduction and notes of his edition of Southey's *Journals of a Residence in Portugal 1800–1801 and a Visit to France 1838* (1960). There is some duplication of material in these two works, but the study in Portuguese is much fuller and more detailed. *Southey e Portugal* traces everything in Southey's background and early life dealing with Portugal and its literature. Southey's first stay in Portugal (1796) and the short trip through Spain are retold largely through paraphrasing the published *Letters Written During a Short Residence in Spain and Portugal* (1797) and his correspondence, and emphasize the slightness of Southey's contact with Spain in contrast to his greater familiarity with Portugal. One section of the study compares the three editions

(1797, 1799, 1808) of the *Letters*. Southey's four articles on Spanish and Portuguese poetry in the *Monthly Magazine*—summarized and discussed in the body of the work—are reprinted. Southey's translations of various poems are likewise reprinted, together with their Portuguese originals. The account of Southey's second trip to Portugal (1800–01) is largely told through means of the new material contained in the *Journals*. Cabral concludes that of all the Anglo-Portuguese students and writers, Southey best knew and appreciated the Portuguese language. A general criticism of Cabral's study is its extreme wordiness and its overuse of paraphrase and direct quotation. In defense of so much quotation, it may be noted that the book is intended for a Portuguese audience for whom many of these books and periodicals may well be unavailable. Several unpublished bits by Southey are given: an early version of the poem on the convent of Arrabida, an unpublished birthday ode, a translation of a madrigal by Ribeiro de Macedo, and an autobiographical letter. The long lists of Southey's periodical contributions are unfortunately incomplete.

Cabral's edition of Southey's *Journals* contains explanatory footnotes—especially good, as his knowledge of his own country and its literature enables him to make clear many obscure references; maps of both the Portuguese journeys and the French trip; facsimiles of two pages of the journals and of Southey's only known letter written in Portuguese. The two journals including the footnotes comprise only 111 pages, but the volume is expanded by reprinting all Southey's letters pertaining to these journeys and, more important, by publishing twenty-two new letters (eighteen from Portugal and four from France). The list of Southey's contributions to the *Monthly* and *Critical* (but not other periodicals) are reprinted from *Southey e Portugal*.

L. Pfandl's "Southey und Spanien" (*Revue hispanique*, 1913), despite Cabral's censure for its neglect of Portugal in favor of Spain, is a three-hundred-page monograph with much valuable information. Southey's work in this field, Pfandl states, was that of a pioneer, for which he deserves all honor, but he lacked a broad view that saw the inner connections of the literary development of a nation, nor did he understand the connections of Portuguese literature with other continental literature. His ability lay rather in exploring thoroughly the problems of a particular work or author and bringing to bear upon these problems knowledge from different sources. This study devotes, in thoroughgoing Germanic fashion, fully as much space to the sources used by Southey in his works as to Southey's own treatment of these same themes. Southey's impressions of Spain and Portugal are compared with those of other eighteenth-century travelers, and his travels throughout the Peninsula are traced minutely and indicated upon an excellent map. Similarly, his connections with other Hispanophiles—Landor, Lord Holland, J. H. Frere—are thoroughly explored. Pfandl censures Southey's translation and abridgment of *Amadis of Gaul* for sacrificing the love scenes in favor of the marvelous adventures because the reader thus misses the total spirit of the romance. Pfandl sometimes finds Southey's Spanish shaky in such details as double negatives and their proper translation into English. The long discussion of Southey's *Cid* is largely devoted to the complexities of his sources. Pfandl dislikes Southey's use of Biblical English in his translation and would have welcomed some abridgment of the Cid's military campaigns. Southey's work upon *Palmerin of England*—a revision of Anthony Munday's translation—gives him an honorable place in the history of Palmerin scholarship, but Pfandl objects again to Southey's use of Biblical and chronicle English. His criticism of these translations often seems captious, and in fairness to Southey it should be emphasized that the errors in translation— both in vocabulary and in syntax—are proportionally very few, and when we consider the tremendous bulk of these romances, we can only marvel how ably the work was done. Many readers would approve of Southey's choice of an archaic English style as giving to English readers a proper sense of the antique, however much it failed to render properly the style of the original. In addition to these translations, Pfandl discusses the historical material of *Roderick*, such shorter poems as the *Pilgrim to Compostella*, and the ballads on Spanish legendary and historical themes.

Two brief studies published by the British Council give honorable mention to Southey's work in the Spanish-Portuguese field: J. C. Metford, *British Contributions to Spanish and Spanish American Studies* (1950) and W. C. Atkinson, *British Contributions to Portuguese and Brazilian Studies* (1945). Although not lengthy, these two pamphlets point up Southey's contribution in the light of contemporary interests and knowledge.

J. de Sousa Leão, "Southey and Brazil" (*MLR*, 1943), discusses Southey's interest in Brazil and Portugal, his collection of manuscripts and books concerning Brazil and South America (many of which were purchased for the British Museum), and his correspondence with John T. Koster and his son Henry Koster. The same author continued this topic in the *Revista do instituto histórico e geográfico Brasileiro* (1943), printing in full the letters to the Kosters, hitherto unpublished, and complete with Portuguese translations; that portion of the catalogue of his library devoted to Spanish and Portuguese items; and several portraits of Southey and of Greta Hall—making, all in all, a handsome and imposing article designed to introduce Southey to the Brazilians.

Rose Macaulay devotes a chapter to Southey, "A Romantic Among the Philistines," in her account of travelers to Portugal, *They Went to Portugal* (1946). Possibly Southey's only letter written in Portuguese—a letter of thanks to the bishop of Beja, 1801 — is printed by S. George West, "Robert Southey, the Rev. Herbert Hill, and the Bishop of Beja" (*Ninth Annual Report and Rev. of the Historical Assoc.* [London], Lisbon Branch, 1945), and reprinted with a facsimile of the manuscript in Cabral's two works discussed above.

E. Buceta has published from materials in the Ticknor bequest to the Boston Public Library three unpublished translations of Southey from the Spanish: two ballads, "Abenamar, Abenamar," and "The Funeral of Aliator" (*MLN*, 1919), and "The Madonna's Lullaby," by Lope de Vega (*RR*, 1922).

6

Thomas Campbell

By Hoover H. Jordan

EASTERN MICHIGAN UNIVERSITY

I. BIBLIOGRAPHIES

THOMAS CAMPBELL wrote a great deal anonymously in both prose and poetry. As a consequence, no one has attempted the laborious task of compiling a list of all his writings which would presume to be definitive, nor is there any apparent reason in our time why the task should be attempted. The compilation by R. W. King for *The Cambridge Bibliography of English Literature* is excellent and suffices for all ordinary purposes.

Additional minor items may, of course, be attributed to Campbell. Three articles have attempted such additions. In "Unacknowledged Poems by Thomas Campbell" (*MLN*, 1922) A. M. Turner suggests that Campbell wrote eight poems which appeared anonymously in the *New Monthly Magazine*. No one of these has great merit, and actually the proof of Campbell's authorship is not conclusive. In " 'Hymen's Ball': An Unpublished Poem by Thomas Campbell" (*N&Q*, 29 June 1940) Charles Duffy very reasonably suggests the addition of this light, gay piece to the Campbell bibliography and in "An Epigraph by Thomas Campbell" (*N&Q*, Jan. 1959) reprints a previously unpublished poem, addressed to Rogers.

The *CBEL* also contains a very adequate list of works about Campbell. Further items, however, can be found in the bibliographies appended to the unpublished dissertations of Albert M. [Bierstadt] Turner ("Thomas Campbell," Harvard Univ., 1920) and Charles Duffy ("Thomas Campbell: A Critical Biography," Cornell Univ., 1939). The latter contains a selected list of items on Campbell with a critical observation on the value of each.

II. EDITIONS

COMPLETE EDITIONS of Campbell's poetical works began to appear during his lifetime under his own supervision, but the first of real importance is *The Poetical Works* (1851), containing notes and an able biographical sketch by the Rev. W. A. Hill, with illustrations by J. M. W. Turner. This was the basis for the Aldine editions of 1875 and 1890, for which William Allingham wrote a biographical sketch. The most recent and most inclusive edition is the Oxford *Complete Poetical Works* (1907), edited by J. L. Robertson. None of these editions, however, are complete. As Robertson makes clear in his short but excellent introduction, a good many of Campbell's poems have been regarded by editors as unworthy of preservation; for instance, Robertson omitted "The Friars of Dijon," and on referring the curious to the *New Monthly Magazine* (1821), where it may be found, commented, "Much good may its perusal do them!" A general reader will find an adequate selection from the poems in the Golden Treasury series *Poems of Thomas Campbell* (1904), chosen by Lewis Campbell, who has written a capable introduction.

Although there is no standard edition of Campbell's prose works, the *CBEL* provides an adequate guide to the individual editions. His letters, not assembled in a single volume, can be found scattered here and there in the biographies of him, especially in William Beattie's. Walter Seton's "Three Letters of Thomas Campbell" (*The Nineteenth Century and After*, 1925) makes an interesting addition to this correspondence. The second letter of the three, about which Seton makes extensive comment, is an emphatic statement of Campbell's claims as originator of the idea which led to the establishment of the University of London.

III. BIOGRAPHIES

THERE ARE but three published biographies of Campbell. The standard among these is the *Life and Letters of Thomas Campbell* (1849), a two-volume work by Dr. William Beattie, physician in attendance on Campbell during the late years of the poet's life and one of his executors. Its thousand pages contain most of the known factual data of Campbell's life. Detailed materials which Beattie collected on Campbell's early years are especially valuable by virtue of their recording observations from those who had known Campbell and their consequent preservation of what otherwise might have lapsed with time. Though admirable in many ways, this work is not above reproach as biography. Beattie attempted to raise a noble and enduring monument to one whom he liked as a man and revered as a poet. The result is that first, by ceaseless reference to the poet's virtues and by ignoring or glossing over his faults, he loses proper perspective on Campbell as a man. Second, his attempt to include everything about Campbell produces tediousness and a clutter of trivia, as witness the minor and often querulous letters on insignificant topics. Then too the critical portions are valueless and frequently impress a modern reader as simply the curious record of a long-lost day when almost any line from Campbell's pen was treasured. Nonetheless, as J. C. Hadden comments, "As well might one expect to write a life of Johnson without the aid of Boswell as expect to tell Campbell's story without reference to Dr. Beattie."

Cyrus Redding's *Literary Reminiscences and Memoirs of Thomas Campbell* (1860) is ill-organized, occasionally too belligerent in defense of Campbell, and often too conscious of Redding's own merits, especially in the conduct of the *New Monthly Magazine*, but it is a valuable supplement to Beattie. On the decade 1820–30 it gives a more intimate picture of Campbell than Beattie does and is much more revealing on the subject of Campbell as an editor. It provides a more balanced estimate of Campbell as a man, for Redding was not lost in hero worship, and is much livelier in tone owing to its numerous anecdotes and bits of conversation which reveal a good deal about Campbell. Redding also performs a service by giving extensive quotation from and paraphrase of Campbell's lectures on poetry at the Royal Institution in 1812.

Much shorter than either of these biographies (155 pages) is J. Cuthbert Hadden's *Thomas Campbell* (1899), written for the Famous Scots series. Hadden is obviously impatient with the Beattie type of hero worship; he expresses disgust, for instance, at Beattie's preserving the wild praise of "Lochiel" by the engineer Telford: "To transcribe such stuff is really a tax on the biographer's patience." Though Hadden had access to some of Campbell's correspondence not available to the other biographers, his work is mainly a skillful condensing of Beattie and Redding, severely laying aside maudlinism, evaluating Campbell frankly as a minor poet, and yet giving a fair and balanced picture of his personality. Though apposite in many critical observations, Hadden makes no attempt to place Campbell in the main currents of English literature and so does not convey a needed critical perspective. All things considered, Hadden's biography is for usual purposes the most satisfactory of the three.

An important work on Campbell is Charles Duffy's unpublished dissertation, "Thomas Campbell: A Critical Biography" (Cornell Univ., 1939). To compare it with Hadden's is difficult owing to the different purpose of this critical biography, but Duffy has given more thoughtful attention to understanding the various activities of Campbell and, exploring more deeply, has made use of periodicals and other sources apparently not used by Hadden. The close critical treatment of Campbell's work impedes the flow of narrative but keeps a reader constantly aware of Campbell as a literary craftsman. It is regrettable that this dissertation has not been published, as it is the nearest approach to a definitive understanding of Campbell as man and poet.

Various items supplement the information found in the major biographies. Although biographical articles written during the last century range in tone from very warm eulogy to savage abuse, a large number present Campbell very favorably. "Mornings with Thomas Campbell" (*Chambers's Edinburgh Jour.*, 1845) is a pleasing and highly graphic picture of Campbell in conversation at the home of Samuel Rogers. "Literary and Familiar Reminiscences of Thomas Campbell, Esq." (*New Monthly Mag. and Humorist*, 1845), as one might expect in the columns of the journal of which he had been editor, depicts Campbell as "one of the kindest and best of men." In *Homes and Haunts of the Most Eminent British Poets* (1847), William Howitt has commended Campbell as a poet and acclaimed the "native simplicity and goodness of his heart," though privately both Mary and William Howitt were more severe on him for that coldness of temperament often observed in him and his work.

"A Graybeard's Gossip about His Literary Acquaintance" (*New Monthly Mag. and Humorist*, 1847) is a good-humored though slight article adding to the store of anecdotes about Campbell. Robert P. Gillies' *Memoirs of a Literary Veteran* (1851) describes Campbell as a genial host and also preserves several of his literary dicta. Mrs. Katherine Thomson's *Recollections of Literary Characters and Celebrated Places* (1854), which gives an especially intimate picture of the Literary Fund banquet at which Campbell was rudely coughed down when attempting to speak, contains reminiscences of Campbell worth preserving. Charles Mackay in *Forty Years' Recollections of Life, Literature, and Public Affairs* (1877) and Mary Agnew in "Lions of the Twenties" (*Temple Bar*, 1896) contribute further testimony that Campbell seemed a thoroughly delightful person to many of his acquaintance. W. Fraser Rae's "The Bard of Hope" (*Temple Bar*, 1890) is a sympathetic study of Campbell's life.

Other characterizations written during the last century are less eulogistic but generally favorable. James Grant's *Portraits of Public Characters* (1841), though not altogether accurate factually, contains a well-balanced sketch, reflecting Grant's admiration for the poet but also his cognizance of Campbell's indolence and constitutional irritability. William Jerdan's *Autobiography* (1852–53) and *Men I Have Known* (1866) should be read for their conception of Campbell as an unusual mixture of "the sterling and the absurd: the noble sentiment and the peurile conceit," but on the whole Jerdan's remarks are disappointing. He knew Campbell intimately and was therefore in a position to offer a penetrating analysis of his character; he failed to do so. "Recollections of Thomas Campbell and David M. Moir" (*The Leisure Hour*, 1878) vividly sketches Campbell presiding in the Theatre Royal, Edinburgh, at the commemoration of the fourth centenary of the invention of printing. P. W. Clayden's *Rogers and His Contemporaries* (1889) is of interest mainly for tracing the extent of Rogers' generous financial aid to Campbell.

Campbell, however, was not always so fortunate as to win the favor of those who knew him. In a letter to Harper and Brothers which forms an introduction to Beattie's biography, Washington Irving expresses his own personal dislike of Campbell for being jealous, "querulous and captious," though Irving generously welcomes the more favorable view which Beattie adopts. Carlyle, early in life an admirer of Campbell's poetry, found him "unkind looking, with a belligerent expression . . . unhappy and snappish" (*William Allingham: A Diary*, ed. H. Allingham and D. Radford, 1907) and later observed him to be "vain and dry in heart . . . his soul has got encrusted as with a case of iron; and he has betaken himself to sneering and selfishness" (*Early Letters of Thomas Carlyle*, ed. Charles Eliot Norton, 1886). H. F. Chorley, who knew him later in life, found him unendurable (*Henry Fothergill Chorley: Autobiography, Memoir, and Letters*, compiled by Henry G. Hewlett, 1873), and Charles MacFarlane was antagonized by his vanity and quarrelsomeness, especially when in his cups (*Reminiscences of a Literary Life*, 1917).

The most offensive personal abuse of Campbell is found in Maginn's "Literary Characters: The Bard of Hope" (*Fraser's Mag.*, 1830) and the anonymous "Personal Recollections of Thomas Campbell, Esq." (*Dublin Univ. Mag.*, 1845). Maginn's article, clever, pointed, scathing, jibes at his "puerile dandyism of mind" and "effeminacy of taste" and dubs him "the example and the patron of that wretched school of silk-stocking stultification . . . which must ultimately be hooted out of the world." The writer in the *Dublin University Magazine* is more virulent. He describes Campbell, especially in his old age, as "the most icy-hearted man that ever lived, wrapping himself up in selfishness" and using language consisting of "sneer, sarcasm, abuse, and contempt of everybody and everything."

The best sketches of Campbell as a magazine editor are to be found in Peter G. Patmore's *My Friends and Acquaintance* (1854) and S. C. Hall's *A Book of Memories of Great Men and Women of the Age* (1871). Patmore's remarks, which form a good general estimation of Campbell, deal in amusing and intimate fashion with the confused relations of Hazlitt, Northcote, and Campbell. Hall, a charitable man who admired both Dr. Beattie and Cyrus Redding, was antagonized by Campbell's irreverent conversation and coarse jokes, and irritated by his complete lack of business sense and of power to organize his business affairs. He concludes, "A worse editor could not have been selected."

A few more recent items of biographical interest deserve mention. James Coutts's *A History of the University of Glasgow* (1909) presents the most detailed account of Campbell as rector of the University of Glasgow, with particular examination of the bitter controversy which attended his election to a third term in 1828. Charles Duffy's "Thomas Campbell and America" (*AL*, 1942) is the most able summation of Campbell's associations with this country. It treats of his numerous family connections, his own prospects of living here, the wide popularity he enjoyed in America, and the reasons for this popularity. Duffy also engaged in an extended discussion in *Notes and Queries* (1941) concerning the date of Campbell's marriage; 10 October 1803, was finally adduced to be the most likely day.

IV. CRITICISM

T HERE IS little good modern criticism of Campbell's writings; an accurate evaluation was placed on his work long ago, and few critical problems have remained for our time. Only three studies of any size have been devoted to Campbell in this century, all doctoral dissertations: Oskar Funke's Leipzig dissertation of 1902, *Campbell als Dichter*, too superficial to be of value; A. M. Turner's "Thomas Campbell" (Harvard Univ., 1920); and Duffy's "Thomas Campbell: A Critical Biography." Turner published his main contributions as magazine articles, which are referred to below. Duffy's conclusions for the most part have not lent themselves to the piecemeal presentation of magazine articles and so must be consulted in his dissertation itself. His careful study of all critical materials on Campbell and his own critical perceptions make his analysis the most penetrating and comprehensive on Campbell's writings.

From August 1799, when the *Monthly Review* welcomed him to the company of poets, until the late years of his life, Campbell was as a general rule treated kindly by critics. As a liberal he was acclaimed by the *Edinburgh Review;* as a Scot and good friend of Sir Walter Scott, Lockhart, Wilson, and other Scotsmen he received more generous treatment from the *Quarterly* and *Blackwood's* than might otherwise have been his lot. Often this praise was extreme. In the *Edinburgh Review* (1809) Jeffrey declares *Gertrude of Wyoming to* have "a certain air of pure and tender enchantment" and in 1825 says that *Theodric* has a "fine and tender finish, both of thought and of diction . . . a chastened elegance of words and images—a mild dignity and tempered pathos in the sentiments"; in "Mr. Campbell and Mr. Crabbe" (*The Spirit of the Age*, 1825) Hazlitt says that *Gertrude of Wyoming* "appears to us like the ecstatic union of natural beauty and poetic fancy . . . we see beauty linked to beauty, like kindred flame to flame. . . . But in the centre, the inmost recesses of our poet's heart, the pearly dew of sensibility is distilled and collects, like the diamond in the mine, and the structure of his fame rests on the crystal columns of a polished imagination."

Often, however, contemporary magazine criticism was more discerning. The *Edinburgh Review* (1819), though somewhat too generous, nonetheless does offer a just estimate of the virtues and limitations of his *Specimens of the British Poets*. The *Quarterly's* review of *Gertrude of Wyoming* (1819), written by Scott, is able and just, though not distinguished; its review of *Theodric* (1825) is a stern recognition of the "bare feebleness" of this poem, a condemnation of the lesser poems published with *Theodric*, and an assertion of the growing feeling that the "character of his mind is . . . feeble and minute"; and its review of his biography of Mrs. Siddons (1834), though severe, is able and well merited. *Blackwood's Edinburgh Magazine* (1825), using the publication of *Theodric* as an excuse for a general review of Campbell's work, declares *The Pleasures of Hope* to be "feebleness strutting on stilts," *Gertrude of Wyoming* to be better, but cold, passionless, and insipid, and *Theodric* to be barren of invention and feeling—a hostile but rather penetrating analysis. *Blackwood's* had also published the previous year Maginn's devastating mockery, "A Running Commentary on the Ritter Bann. A Poem. By T. Campbell, Esq." also printed in "The Odoherty Papers," *Miscellaneous Writings of the Late Dr. Maginn*, ed. Shelton Mackenzie (1855–57). Campbell experienced no more severe abuse than this; Maginn is clever and pointed but unduly savage. The *British Critic* (1810) justly notices the feebleness of the *Annals of Great Britain;* the *Monthly Review* (1837) adequately evaluates the *Letters from the South.*

The criticism of this century has concerned more specialized aspects of Campbell's work. One group of studies investigates the influences on him. A. M. Turner's "Wordsworth's Influence on Thomas Campbell" (*PMLA*, 1923) traces Campbell's growing interest in Wordsworth, beginning about 1824, becoming more pronounced in the 1830's, and leading Campbell to a simpler style and a new treatment of nature and children. In his dissertation Duffy, though often agreeing with Turner, has properly observed that the influence has been exaggerated, that Campbell was not especially fond of Wordsworth in 1824, and that the influence was slight after 1830. In "Gertrude of Wyoming" (*JEGP*, 1921), Turner presents a better study. Here he shows that this poem engrafts a stanza form derived especially from Thomson's *The Castle of Indolence* upon a narrative modeled on *The Lay of the Last Minstrel*. He also reveals the strong marks of Chateaubriand's *Atala* in local color, mood, and wording, and of the unreal primitivism of Rousseau. On this study Duffy has built the sound analysis of *Gertrude of Wyoming* in his dissertation.

Among other studies of influence on Campbell, R. S. Forsythe's " 'Freedom's Shriek' " (*N&Q*, 9 Jan. 1926) traces the famous line from *The Pleasures of Hope*, "And Freedom shriek'd—as Kosciusko fell!" to Coleridge's sonnet on Kosciusko among the "Sonnets on Eminent Characters." In "The Wolf's Long Howl" (*MLN*, 1942) Duffy not only shows that the well-known line from *The Pleasures of Hope*, "The wolf's long howl from Oonalaska's shore," derives from "The Sentimental Sailor; or St. Preux to Eloisa," but also reveals that the later use of the same idea in *Theodric* is even closer to the original lines.

Campbell had long before been accused of borrowing. In 1825 *Blackwood's* had printed an article of dubious value berating him for plagiarizing lines from Vaughan's "The Rainbow" and for his minor poem "To the Rainbow," and two years later had printed a powerful letter accusing him of borrowing extensively and literally from Schlegel for his lectures on Greek poetry at the Royal Institution, without offering credit, and indeed of falling into various errors from following Schlegel rather than the original Greek. This matter of Campbell's indebtedness to the Germans was made the subject of an excellent article by Daniel B. Shumway, "Thomas Campbell and Germany," in the *Schelling Anniversary Papers* (1923). Shumway concludes that Campbell was little influenced by German literature, history, or philosophy. "While he was an admirer of German poetry it did not influence him in the sense in which it had influenced Scott. . . . Campbell seems to have been more interested in the authors themselves than in their works. . . . German history and German folk-lore provided him with many of the subjects of his poems, but he worked them up in a style that is distinctly English and not German."

Campbell had once been highly annoyed by the suggestion that he borrowed from Byron's "Darkness" in writing "The Last Man." In "Byron and Campbell: A Parallel" (*N&Q*, 21 Jan. 1922), Walter Graham takes issue with Campbell's contention that "The Last Man" owes nothing to Byron's poem and further maintains that "Lines on the View from St. Leonard's" derives much from *Childe Harold's Pilgrimage*, a demonstration which is not absolutely convincing.

Campbell had little influence on other writers. In "Emerson, Thomas Campbell, and Bacon's Definition of Poetry" (*ESQ*, 1959),

Kenneth W. Cameron suggests an influence on Emerson of the first lecture of Campbell's *Lectures on Poetry*, which he reprints in full from the *New Monthly Magazine and Literary Journal*. Jack Stillinger's "Whittier's Early Imitation of Thomas Campbell" (*PQ*, 1959) notes the influence of the "Exile of Erin" on Whittier's "The Exile's Departure." In "Alfred de Vigny and Thomas Campbell" (*French Quart.*, 1922), J. Ascher asserts a slight trace of the "Battle of the Baltic" in Vigny's "La Frégate la sérieuse" and a much greater influence in manner and idea of *Gertrude of Wyoming* on Vigny's *La Sauvage*. Malcolm D. McLean's "Varia: Poems to the Rainbow by Campbell and Heredia" (*HR*, 1950) clears up some confusion about a poem which José María Heredia submitted to a Mexico City newspaper, 5 September 1827. Declared by the newspaper to be original, it is actually a free translation of Campbell's "To the Rainbow," employing a better arrangement of stanzas and a more subtle rhythm, but having less compactness. That Campbell was in some measure responsible for one of Bulwer's novels is the subject of Keith Hollingsworth's "Who Suggested the Plan for Bulwer's *Paul Clifford?*" (*MLN*, 1948).

The remaining articles on Campbell which deserve notice attempt to assess the general value of his work. Several from the last century merit attention. Earliest among these is Washington Irving's introduction for the 1810 American edition of Campbell's poems, slightly revised five years later for the *Analectic Magazine*, a not especially accurate article in points of fact but a dispassionate estimation of Campbell's merits as a poet. Hazlitt's essay "On the Living Poets," in *Lectures on the English Poets*, which has especially good observations on *Gertrude of Wyoming*, is much superior to his later effusions in *The Spirit of the Age*. George Gilfillan's "Thomas Campbell" (*A Gallery of Literary Portraits*, 1845) is an unusual article in that Gilfillan was a student at the University of Glasgow during Campbell's rectorship and reflects the students' enthusiasm for their rector; Gilfillan, however, is fully aware that Campbell is not a first-rate poet. William Michael Rossetti's well-balanced essay in *Lives of Famous Poets* (1878) makes the standard judgment— that the battle odes prove Campbell to be "an authentic poet."

In our own century general articles on Campbell have mainly concerned themselves with his short poems, especially the so-called battle odes. Several of these essays pertain particularly to political considerations. In *Main Currents in Nineteenth-Century Literature* (trans. 1901) Georg Brandes portrays Campbell as a poet of liberty, interested in oppressed peoples everywhere: "He was the lover and champion of liberty, and of liberty as a divinity, not as an idol." He also finds in the lyrics "a simple, powerful, and melodious pathos which reminds us of the old Greek elegiac poets." As a Dane, however, he cannot relish the "Battle of the Baltic." The same general thesis—that Campbell espoused not just the Polish cause but the cause of the downtrodden everywhere—is the subject of Edmund Blunden's "Campbell's Political Poetry" (*English Rev.*, 1928). He observes Campbell's strangely prophetic lines about the power of Russia, which indeed hold a prophecy far more potent than Blunden could have known in the 1920's. It should be noted, however, that Charles MacFarlane in the course of his three-year friendship with Campbell remarked (*Reminiscences of a Literary Life*, 1917) that for all his enthusiasm in behalf of the Poles, Campbell was little informed about them. The same opinion is voiced by J. C. Squire ("Solomon Eagle") in *Books in General* (2d Ser., 1920).

Among the other useful essays on Campbell, perhaps the most scintillating is that by Arthur Symons in *The Romantic Movement in English Poetry* (1909). Finding that Campbell throws the "vague, rosy tinge" of unreality about his poems, he epitomizes him as the "Sir Willoughby Patterne of poets." He observes that the obvious regular rhythm which defaces some of Campbell's lyrics is the very cause of success of "Hohenlinden," where it fits perfectly. His other comments on the war odes are equally apt. In *Essays in English Literature* (1895) and *A History of English Prosody* (1906), George Saintsbury is also excellent in his remarks on the war odes. He identifies Campbell generally as an exponent of the tradition of Pope. While agreeing in this contention in *A History of English Poetry* (1895–1910), W. J. Courthope asserts that Campbell expresses a romantic feeling in classic form and that he "may justly claim to have been the first to direct the new movement [the revival of the ballad style] into popular channels." Courthope's extensive treatment of Campbell may impress some as excessively eulogistic. Lafcadio Hearn's "Note on Thomas Campbell" (*On Poets*, 1938) gives further aid toward understanding the war odes. His observations on the use of Anglo-Saxon words amid Latinisms to give strength are very pertinent. Laying aside the long poems as unworthy of study, Hearn takes as his thesis concerning Campbell, "When *he is most simple*, he is most haunting."

Although W. Macneile Dixon's *Thomas Campbell: An Oration* makes no attempt to uncover new facets of the poet's writing, it constitutes an excellent introduction to Campbell for any general student of letters and a pleasant review for more experienced scholars. Dixon presents an intelligent, sympathetic summary of the poet's character and defines his place in literature as the creator of "a handful of lyrics, a few hundred lines of verse" which any poet might claim with pride.

7

Thomas Moore

By Hoover H. Jordan
EASTERN MICHIGAN UNIVERSITY

I. BIBLIOGRAPHIES

A COMPLETE bibliography of Moore is yet to be compiled, but for ordinary purposes the list of his writings presented by R. W. King in *The Cambridge Bibliography of English Literature* is perfectly adequate. The authoritative compilation of his first editions is that by M. J. MacManus, *A Bibliographical Hand-List of the First Editions of Thomas Moore* (1934), originally issued in the *Dublin Magazine* (1933). It should be studied in conjunction with Percy H. Muir's "Thomas Moore's Irish Melodies 1808–1834" (*Colophon*, 1933), which gives an illuminating presentation of the complex problems concerning the first editions.

A number of difficulties have arisen in regard to his bibliography, attributable largely to the anonymity of much of his work. Concerning his prose writings, the following circumstances obtain at the moment. *The World of Westminster*, by "Thomas Brown the Younger," is no longer credited to him as it bears no evidence of his workmanship; in the notes to *The Harp That Once——* (1937), Howard M. Jones has stated this point clearly. There too Jones has well recounted the circumstances concerning the *Sketches of Pious Women*, which Moore suppressed. His reviews are now thought to number ten: eight are printed in the valuable *Prose and Verse, Humorous, Satirical, and Sentimental by Thomas Moore with Suppressed Passages from the Memoirs of Lord Byron* (1878), edited by R. H. Shepherd with a preface by R. H. Stoddard; a ninth is that of Charles Overton's *Ecclesia Anglicana* (*Edinburgh Rev.*, 1833); and a tenth is the review of Irish novels (*Edinburgh Rev.*, 1826), which Elisabeth Schneider convincingly ascribes to him in "Thomas Moore and the *Edinburgh Review*" (*MLN*, 1946). Her attempt to identify Moore as the author of the well-known *Edinburgh Review* critique of *Christabel* ("The Unknown Reviewer of *Christabel*: Jeffrey, Hazlitt, Tom Moore," *PMLA*, 1955) I have considered unsuccessful in my article "Thomas Moore and the Review of *Christabel*" (*MP*, 1956). Miss Schneider then replied in her second article, "Tom Moore and the *Edinburgh* Review of *Christabel*" (*PMLA*, 1962) and was in turn answered by Wilfred S. Dowden in "Thomas Moore and the Review of *Christabel*" (*MP*, 1962). Dowden offers two letters by Moore, one to Jeffrey, one to Murray, in which

Moore not only specifically denies the authorship but also attacks the review as "disgraceful both from its dulness and illiberality." Until real proof is offered to belie Moore's assertion, the controversy should cease, and the review be excluded from the Moore bibliography.

Concerning his poetry, several titles have been suggested for addition to bibliographies. W. H. Hitchcock in "Thomas Moore" (*Wiltshire Archaeological and Nat. Hist. Mag.*, 1889) presents a children's poem, written for one of Moore's daughters. In the *Bookman* [N. Y.] (1898) James C. Johnson offers "An Unpublished Poem by Thomas Moore," but though the poem may well be Moore's, the history of the manuscript as related by Johnson could not be verified by Jones. That Moore was author of *The Gypsy Prince, a Comic Opera in Two Acts* is well established; Jones's biography should again be consulted for evidence on this matter. In "Thomas Moore as the Author of *Spirit of Boccaccio's Decameron*" (*RES*, 1947), Herbert G. Wright has argued on grounds of internal and external evidence for inclusion of this item, but some doubt must yet remain concerning it.

For compilation of a list of critical writings on Moore, the most convenient sources are *The Cambridge History of English Literature*, the *CBEL*, and the notes to Jones's biography. Further items are in the bibliographies appended to Gustave Vallat's *Étude sur la vie et les œuvres de Thomas Moore* (1886) and L. A. G. Strong's *The Minstrel Boy* (1937).

II. EDITIONS

M ODERN EDITIONS of Moore's poetry are largely based upon *The Poetical Works of Thomas Moore: Collected by Himself* (1840–41), which includes his own account of his early career as verse writer to the time of producing his paraphrase of Anacreon. Additional poems will be found in Shepherd's *Prose and Verse*, mentioned above. This is a valuable work on Moore; a student should not shun it because of the somewhat tarnished reputation of its editor and the lurid, misleading title. It contains not "suppressed passages from the memoirs of Lord Byron" but rather, in Shepherd's own words in the introduction, "a selection from Moore's original notes for his Life of Byron." Convenient in one volume is the Oxford edition, *The Poetical Works of Thomas Moore* (1910), edited by A. D. Godley, whose introductory essay is unsympathetic and sometimes inaccurate. An acceptable selection from Moore's poetry is found in the Golden Treasury series *Poetry of Thomas Moore* (1903), edited by C. L. Falkiner, whose prefatory essay on Moore is admirable. Sean O'Faolain's edition of *Lyrics and Satires from Tom Moore* (1929) is a good but highly selective volume.

The lack of a complete edition of Moore's works hampers the study of his prose to the extent that some critics seem unaware that he was a prolific prose writer. In any event, it is necessary to consult separate editions of the biographies of Byron, Sheridan, and Lord Edward Fitzgerald, of the *Memoirs of Captain Rock, The Epicurean, The Travels of an Irish Gentleman in Search of a Religion,* and *The History of Ireland.* These editions are conveniently listed in the *CBEL.*

The bulk of Moore's diaries and correspondence is found in the *Memoirs, Journal, and Correspondence of Thomas Moore* (ed. Lord John Russell, 1853–56). From this work J. B. Priestley has made an admirable selection in his *Tom Moore's Diary* (1925). Other correspondence by Moore appears in numerous sources. The most extensive collection is *Notes from the Letters of Thomas Moore to His Music Publisher, James Power (The Publication of Which Was Suppressed in London) with an Introductory Letter by Thomas Crofton Croker* (1854?). The value of this volume lies first in the biographical and bibliographical information in the letters which were omitted by Russell or published by him only in part, and second in some of Croker's ill-natured but often pertinent remarks on Russell's editing and on Moore's business affairs. Unhappily, the letters are edited very badly and seldom printed in their entirety; Croker's bitterly vituperative remarks are full of exaggeration; and indeed the contents are presented in a shamefully disorganized manner.

Fourteen letters from Moore to Bowles are included in *A Wiltshire Parson and His Friends* (ed. Garland Greever, 1926) and six more in J. Charles Cox's "Some Unpublished Letters of Tom Moore's" (*Athenaeum*, 12 March 1904), which also has an accompanying letter by Rogers on Moore's financial difficulties. Other letters of interest are in R. R. Madden's *The Literary Life and Correspondence of the Countess of Blessington* (1855) and E. B. De Fonblanque's *Lives of the Lords Strangford* (1877), one of which contains Moore's request that Lord Strangford write a biographical notice of him should he the next day fall in the duel with Francis Jeffrey. Valuable for detailing some of the search by Moore for information on Byron's life and the difficulties which beset him is Bradford A. Booth's "Moore to Hobhouse: An Unpublished Letter" (*MLN*, 1940). The *Life of the Rev. George Crabbe* by his son (1834, reprinted 1932, 1948) contains a long letter from Moore to Murray full of reminiscences about Crabbe to assist the young George Crabbe in preparing the volume on his father. In J. C. Hadden's *George Thomson. The Friend of Burns: His Life and Correspondence* (1908) are letters concerned especially with Thomson's fruitless effort to get Moore to write words to three Welsh airs for Thomson's collection of Welsh songs. Other letters are in "Two Letters of Tom Moore's" (*Critic*, 1888). C. H. Hart's "Tom Moore in America" (*Collector*, 1896), the latter dealing with Moore's views on America and David B. Green's two articles, "Letters to Samuel Rogers from Tom Moore and Sydney Smith" (*N&Q*, Dec. 1955) and "Irving and Moore Again" (*N&Q*, July–Aug. 1959).

The most important addition to the Moore bibliography in recent years is Wilfred S. Dowden's *The Letters of Thomas Moore* (1964). Here is a collection of about thirteen hundred letters, many hithero unpublished, which add new dimensions to our understanding of Moore as a man and as a literary figure. For instance, one sees more clearly the daily life of Moore as an industrious writer, the routine and struggle of it, from which he departed for his occasional sorties into London social circles, so often associated with his name, that this collection restores a needed perspective on him. Dowden has performed an important service for students of Moore.

III. BIOGRAPHIES

UNQUESTIONABLY Howard M. Jones's *The Harp That Once———* is the outstanding biography of Moore. Critical objection has been offered that its attempt to supply political and other historical background is not always apposite, that its style is too lively, that it treats the historical backgrounds of literary works rather than the works themselves, and that it is too adulatory of Moore's minor writings; but, whatever the value of these objections, the volume has undeniable merit. Jones has attempted beyond any other biographer to uncover the facts of Moore's life; he has presented new items, such as those on Moore's lineage, and he has drawn the fullest picture of Moore's formative years, his duel with Jeffrey (one of the most delightful bits in the volume), the 1812–18 period, and his residence in Paris. Moreover, he demonstrates a more detailed knowledge of Moore's writings than is apparent in most of the other biographies. In this connection it must be emphasized that no one who has not thoroughly digested Moore's prose work, not only in itself but in relation to the contemporary climate of opinion, can have a measured judgment on Moore as a literary man. For instance, *The Life and Death of Lord Edward Fitzgerald* is a considerable work because of its respectable qualities as a biography, its close picture of and judgment on Irish political affairs, and the sometimes revealing passages concerning its author, who was bold enough to publish this work at such a critical juncture in English political affairs that Lord Lansdowne, Lord Holland, and others in England, and Lord Leinster and others in Ireland begged him to withhold it on account of its rebelliousness. These matters ought to be of interest to a biographer. Because of space limitations, *The Harp That Once* ——— does not enter completely into such critical questions, but beyond any other biography it delineates Moore as man, poet, and prose writer.

There are, of course, several other biographies of Moore. The earliest of these, *The Life of Thomas Moore* (1852) by James Burke, is critically worthless, representing the most adulatory hero worship, and is meager in its biographical information, attaining book length only by copious quotation from Moore's speeches and writings. Some of these quotations give it the only interest for modern students, for here are items not otherwise readily accessible, such as transcripts of the addresses by Moore and others at the public dinner accorded Moore in Dublin, 8 June 1818; of the addresses given in the autumn of 1835 at Bannow, Wexford, at the several tumultuous receptions of the poet there; and of the proceedings of the General Committee of Management of the Moore testimonial at Charlemont House, Dublin, 29 March 1852.

H. R. Montgomery's *Thomas Moore, His Life, Writings, and Contemporaries* (1860) is not all that its impressive title would lead one to believe, but it is biographically more complete than Burke, critically sounder, and all in all an adequate brief survey (208 short pages). It is superior to Andrew J. Symington's *Thomas Moore the*

Poet: His Life and Works (1880), which has perhaps less biographical information and in its excessive praise of Moore's writing is certainly less effective critically. Symington does include several of the centenary birthday odes and the address by Lord O'Hagan at the Dublin Exhibition Palace, 28 May 1879.

Gustave Vallat's *Étude sur la vie et les œuvres de Thomas Moore* (1886) is a much more considerable volume than any of its predecessors. Though Vallat passes too quickly over the late years of Moore's life, he offers more complete biographical information than the others and makes a more serious effort to indulge in useful criticism, so that the reader gets a better understanding of Moore as a literary man. Occasionally his criticism is excellent, as in his remarks on the *Odes of Anacreon*, to which he gives extended treatment. His Gallic delight in *Lalla Rookh*, *Loves of the Angels*, and *The Epicurean* will seem excessive, and some readers will be amused by his preference of Moore to Wordsworth, Coleridge, Byron, Shelley, and Keats. Vallat's subsequent volume, *Thomas Moore et son œuvre immortelle* (1895), is simply a young people's account of Moore's life and writing, which Vallat believes an illustration of the moralistic thesis, "La famille et la patrie avec Dieu."

John P. Gunning's *Moore: Poet and Patriot* (1900) is not highly successful as a biography but supplements Vallat by considering Moore from an Irishman's point of view, presenting at times very intimately the internal political circumstances of Ireland and Moore's relation to them, with particular attention to the Moore-O'Connell negotiations. Though in no sense a definitive study of the Irish political backgrounds, it does contain information and suggestions not entirely superseded. The intent of it is to show "that Moore was not only an Irishman but a patriot ever mindful of his country in her hour of tribulation," a purpose that reflects Gunning's concern over the attacks on Moore by the Irish of the Celtic school.

Stephen Gwynn's *Thomas Moore* (1905), written for the English Men of Letters series, is the culmination of these earlier studies of Moore. It treats all periods of his life with good perspective and balance, and above all brings a real sense of literary values to its critical judgments. This sanity is the more remarkable when one reflects that at the turn of the century Moore's reputation was perhaps at its ebb. This volume may safely be recommended as a reliable introduction to Moore.

Seamus MacCall's *Thomas Moore* (1935) is a very short biography for the Noted Irish Lives series. Too brief to make any real contribution to scholarship, it does provide a useful, concise summary and in the appendix a chronological list of Moore's works based on the MacManus hand list. Its thesis is that Moore was a great man "because of his remarkable plurality of talents, rather than his merits as a poet." Herbert O. Mackey's *The Life of Thomas Moore* (1951) is much too brief to perform any signal service for scholarship and is not based on original research.

L. A. G. Strong's *The Minstrel Boy: A Portrait of Tom Moore* (1937) is an able biography, chiefly distinguished by its remarks on the *Irish Melodies*. The author's sensitive and understanding perception of the close marriage of words and music produces one of the best studies of the *Melodies*. This work, however, does have some severe limitations. It adds almost nothing biographically to what Gwynn presented and is inferior on the period during which Moore was active as a prose writer, the decade 1825–35. Also it reveals no intimacy with much of Moore's work—the reviews, the *Letter to the Roman Catholics of Dublin*, the biographies of Sheridan and Fitzgerald, the *Memoirs of Captain Rock*, the *Travels of an Irish Gentleman*, and the satires. (I find no mention at all of the *Two-Penny Post Bag*.) The failure to assess these works and show how they are an integral part of Moore's productions throws the volume out of perspective and leaves some of the suggestions about Moore as a man and as a writer open to question. It is, for instance, difficult to understand from the evidence in this volume how Moore could have been taken so seriously for his learning and intellectual acumen by men of the capacity of Parr, Smith, Macaulay, Jeffrey, Russell, Holland, Lansdowne, and the others.

It may not be amiss to mention that Moore was celebrated by Theodore Burt Sayre in a lively novel entitled *Tom Moore: An Unhistorical Romance, Founded on Certain Happenings in the Life of Ireland's Greatest Poet* (1902), based on Sayre's play about Moore which opened at the Herald Square Theatre, New York, 31 August 1901, and enjoyed a long run. A reviewer in *Book News* (1902) finds the novel untrue biographically but true to Moore's spirit. The reviewer is charitable; any resemblance to Moore is coincidental.

Students of Moore may wish to examine further studies devoted to special periods in his life. A particularly vivid sketch of him as a boy, revealing his unusual precocity, is contained in J. D. Herbert's *Irish Varieties* (1836). His trip to America is commented upon in numerous works. His literary and personal relations in Philadelphia are explored in H. M. Ellis' *Joseph Dennie and His Circle* (1915), E. P. Oberholtzer's *The Literary History of Philadelphia* (1906),

H. P. Rosenbach's "Tom Moore's Cottage" (*American*, 1886), and A. H. Smyth's *The Philadelphia Magazines and Their Contributors* (1892). With surprising enthusiasm, Bermuda has celebrated him in fact and fiction. The most complete record of his sojourn there is found in J. C. L. Clark's *Tom Moore in Bermuda* (1909), but of interest also are Ella D. Kay's " 'Tom' Moore's 'Nea' " (*Bookman* [N. Y.], 1909), and Fairfax Downey's sprightly article, "Tom Moore and Bermuda" (*Bookman* [N. Y.], 1925). Terry Tucker's "Narratives of the Prize Court" (*Bermuda Historical Quart.*, 1945) contains a fictional re-creation of Moore in his official capacity in the Court of the Vice-Admiralty. B. J. Lossing's condescending "Tom Moore in America" (*Harper's*, 1877) adds a few items, especially about Moore's relations with the Merrys; George H. Smith's "Tom Moore in Canada" (*Canadian Mag.*, 1909) and Roy F. Fleming's "An Irish Poet on the Lakes" (*Inland Seas*, 1956) trace his trip from Niagara down the St. Lawrence. Perhaps also best classified among these special biographical studies is Sylva Norman's "Leigh Hunt, Moore, and Byron" (*TLS*, 2 Jan. 1953), which clarifies further Hunt's feelings toward Moore in regard to the establishment of the *Liberal*.

Moore's years at Sloperton Cottage in Wiltshire have been ably sketched. S. C. Hall's *A Book of Memories* (1871) contains an especially intimate description; further reminiscences may be found in William Winter's *Gray Days and Gold* (1891), W. H. Hitchcock's "Tom Moore" (*Wiltshire Archaeological and Nat. Hist. Mag.*, 1889), and Edmund Gosse's "Tom Moore in Wiltshire" (*Leaves and Fruit*, 1927). Rewarding too are the letter to the *Times Literary Supplement* by W. M. Parker, "Moore in Wiltshire" (16 Oct. 1937) and those commenting upon it by Ernest A. Sadler and W. Roberts (23 Oct. 1937). Two articles which deal ostensibly with Moore's religious beliefs but which, at least to this writer, are of more interest for their biographical information are Daniel Ambrose's "Thomas Moore: The Religion in Which He Died" and the sequel to it by John Canon O'Hanlon, "The Catholicity of Thomas Moore" (both, *Irish Ecclesiastical Record*, 1895).

Bessy Moore is of course important to biographical studies of her husband. Her personality and associations with her husband are well summarized in Florence MacCunn's "A Poet's Wife" (*Gentleman's Mag.*, 1907) and Maurice Hewlett's "Bessy Moore" (*In a Green Shade*, 1920). Alan L. Strout in "Tom Moore and Bessy" (*N&Q*, 31 Dec. 1938) has called attention to a dramatic story of Moore's wooing Bessy found in *Last Leaves from the Journal of Julian Charles Young* (1875). Young procured this tale from an unnamed "informant," and though the story may well be true, Young's other remarks on Moore are occasionally inaccurate.

The portrait of Moore drawn by his biographers and that presented in many works in which he figures only casually are frequently very different. Ever since the days when Hazlitt assailed him in "On the Jealousy and the Spleen of Party" (*The Plain Speaker*, 1826) and Carlyle bitingly termed him "a lascivious triviality of great name" (J. A. Froude, *Thomas Carlyle*, 1882), he has been subjected to sneers, jibes, and condescension which long ago brought from his friend Washington Irving the heartfelt cry, "He has been shamefully wronged since his death." The charges have generally accused him of subserviency ("Tommy dearly loved a lord" is the usual cliché), coxcombry, shallowness, flippancy, and immorality. Especially virulent attacks can be found in J. R. Lowell's "Rousseau and the Sentimentalists" (*Literary Essays*, 1890) and Robert Buchanan's "The Irish 'National' Poet" (*A Look Round Literature*, 1887). In the latter bitter essay, which scores Moore for frequenting the drawing rooms of London in contrast to martyrs like Emmet who were dying for Ireland, Buchanan declares, "I am sorry indeed for Ireland, if . . . she can persist in crowning as her laureate the ghost of a parvenu gentleman in tights and pumps, who spent his days and nights among the Whigs in London, whose patriotism was an amusing farce, and who, merely to make himself look interesting, pinned a shamrock to the buttonhole of his dress-coat, and warbled cheerful little dirges about the sorrows of the country he had left behind him." This sort of comment, which has been instrumental in forming the attitude of many casual critics of Moore, shows irresponsibility toward fact.

An accurate conception of Moore can be attained not only from his biographies, his own diary, and his correspondence, but from certain other essays and studies. Best known among the sketches are those by Lord John Russell as editor of the *Memoirs,* by Byron, *passim* (especially noteworthy are his remarks in *A Journal of the Conversations of Lord Byron with the Countess of Blessington,* 1834), by Leigh Hunt in *Lord Byron and Some of His Contemporaries* (1828) and his *Autobiography* (1850), and by N. P. Willis in *Pencillings by the Way* (1835). Less known but equally vivid are the remarks by "A Contemporary" [Elizabeth Rennie] in *Traits of Character* (1860), by William Gardiner in *Music and Friends* (1838–53), by James Grant in *Portraits of Public Characters* (1841; a reader should beware of occasional inaccuracy of fact in Grant's presentation), by Gerald Griffin in his brother's *The Life of*

Gerald Griffin (1843), by S. C. Hall in *A Book of Memories*, by Charles MacFarlane in *Reminiscences of a Literary Life* (1917), and by Sir Walter Scott (see especially Lockhart's *Memoirs of the Life of Sir Walter Scott*). For other evaluations of more than passing interest, one may consult Sir Jonah Barrington's *Personal Sketches of His Own Times* (1827), *The Autobiography of John Britton* (1850), A. M. Broadley's and Walter Jerrold's *The Romance of an Elderly Poet* [Crabbe] (1913), P. W. Clayden's *Rogers and His Contemporaries* (1889), Lord Cockburn's *Life of Lord Jeffrey* (1852), C. C. F. Greville's *The Greville Memoirs* (1874–87), *The Reminiscences and Recollections of Captain Gronow* (originally separate volumes but published together in 1900), *The Autobiography of William Jerdan* (1852–53), the biographies of Washington Irving by Pierre Irving and Stanley Williams and his journal edited by Stanley Williams, *Lady Morgan's Memoirs* (1862), H. C. Robinson's *The Diary, Reminiscences, and Correspondence* (1869, expanded 1927), Edith J. Morley's edition of *Henry Crabb Robinson on Books and Their Writers* (1938), C. G. Rosenberg's *You Have Heard of Them* (1854), William A. Shee's *My Contemporaries, 1830–1870* (1893), Frederick L. Jones's edition of *Mary Shelley's Journal* (1947), Julian Charles Young's *A Memoir of Charles Mayne Young . . .* (1871), the extensive review of Moore's life in the *Edinburgh Review* (1854), and "Recollections of Moore" (*Dublin Univ. Mag.*, 1852).

Three articles reproduce little-known portraits of Moore. "The Poet Moore" (*Art Jour.*, 1858) presents an engraving by W. Roffe of the Moore statue in Dublin with an accompanying description of Moore as he appeared at home with his family. *The Authors of England . . .* (1838) contains a striking profile medallion portrait engraved by Achille Collas after a bust by Kirk, and a pleasant essay on Moore by Henry F. Chorley. Booth Tarkington's "Portrait of Tom Moore by John Jackson" (*Some Old Portraits*, 1939) is a charming essay, commenting on the personal relations of Moore and Jackson and on the portrait, reproduced in the volume, a painting certainly less known to students of Moore than the oft-reprinted portraits by Lawrence and Shee.

IV. CRITICISM

To THOSE not well versed in matters pertaining to Moore, the amount of criticism devoted to him may be a surprise. Much of this is complex and varied, owing to the multiplicity of his literary talents. From these studies Moore emerges as a man of letters who commands respect, but unlike many other authors who failed to achieve greatness, he has defied easy classification; the widest differences yet remain in evaluation of his attitudes and abilities.

1. THE IRISH MELODIES

The *Irish Melodies* have occasioned the greatest amount of comment. Beyond the general intent of assessing the value of these songs, critical studies have usually concerned themselves with one of three major considerations: the origin of the airs and the variants in their musical form with particular attention to any alterations made by Moore or his arranger, Sir John Stevenson; the talent displayed by Moore in setting words to music and in catching the spirit of the music in appropriate language; and the place of the songs in the social and political movements of the time.

The first group of studies investigates a very difficult matter. Before a musical critic can know whether Moore and Stevenson altered the tempo or the melodic line of an air, he must first determine where the air originated, whether one version was accepted as standard, and what variants were known. A major study in this area is Charles V. Stanford's *The Irish Melodies of Thomas Moore: The Original Airs Restored and Arranged for the Voice* (1895). While conceding "that neither before nor since Moore's time has there been any Irish poet who so completely combined fineness of workmanship with spirit and pathos" and that "it is impossible to over-rate the value of much of Moore's work," Stanford nonetheless affirms that "there is scarcely a melody which Moore left unaltered, and, as a necessary consequence, unspoilt." Actually he enumerates about thirty-five airs which he believes Moore spoiled. That so excellent a scholar as Stanford needs a corrective can be seen by an examination of Alfred Moffat's collection of Irish airs, *The Minstrelsy of Ireland* (1897), which shows Stanford frequently in error, often in his most serious attacks on Moore. Moffat says, for instance, "In 'restoring' Moore's song ["Fairest— Put on Awhile"] to what he considers the correct version of 'Cummilium,' Professor Stanford has made a singular mistake; he has stripped the song of its Irish melody to deck it out anew in an English garb"; and of another song, "An examination of . . . [the setting] with the older printed forms proves that it is not only good, but that Professor Stanford's statement in his edition of Moore's *Melodies* 'restored,' 'there is scarcely a passage right in Moore's version,' is entirely without foundation." Whatever else these divisions of opinion teach, they indicate the folly of dogmatism. A further large repository of information and an additional corrective to opinion is "The Bunting Collection of Irish Folk Music and Songs," edited by D. J. O'Sullivan for the *Journal of the Irish Folk Song Society* (1926–32). George Petrie, who contributed several airs for use in the *Melodies*, comments on his relations with Edward Bunting and Moore in the introduction to *The Complete Collection of Irish Music* (ed. C. V. Stanford, 1905).

Whereas the above research belongs properly to musicians and musical historians, a second group of studies—on the setting of words to music—though best understood by musicians, cannot be neglected by anyone concerned with Moore as poet. The demands of the song, the relation of musical notes to meter and to vowel and consonant combinations and accents, the mood and meaning of the words as an expression of the musical notation, all are matters to be examined and understood. But many literary critics not only have made no effort to understand the *Irish Melodies* as musical compositions but have waved aside the whole consideration as irrelevant. Though it is conceded that Moore thoroughly understood the art of setting words to music, these critics have frequently sneered at such skill or even thought it an undesirable attribute for a poet to possess. As to whether Moore caught the spirit of the music, opinion is divided. In *A Treasury of Irish Poetry in the English Tongue* (ed. Stopford A. Brooke and T. W. H. Rolleston, 1900) Brooke makes one of the most violent attacks on Moore by asserting, "How he could wed some of the spiritual Irish music to the bacchanalian words with which he degrades its Elfin mysticism, I have never been able to understand." He decides that the excellence of Moore's lyrics results from the poet's being lifted by the inspiration of the music in a way no true poet would find necessary, and he arrives at the unique conclusion that Moore deserves at least "the praise of originality," for "his poetry is no more English than Irish," he stems from no "poetical ancestors" in England, and has not influenced "any of the

English poets that followed him." This dubious conclusion should be considered in the light of the observation by James Travis in "Moore's Irish Melodies" (*Cath W*, 1944) that the elements of sentimentality, decorum, and conventional eighteenth-century poetic diction in the lyrics are an English inheritance by Moore and constitute the major flaws in the lyrics, and that "the greatest things in the Irish Melodies are rhythm and melody of a Gaelic flavor, and thought and emotion of a Gaelic kind."

In *The Romantic Movement in English Poetry* (1909) Arthur Symons has expressed general agreement with Brooke. He assails Moore violently for rendering trivial everything in the songs, for failing to gain any of the dignity of song or passion, for degrading the drinking songs until "only the lees are left," and for sacrificing "the accent of the sense to the accent of the rhythm"; he refuses to admit that Moore wrote even one "good poem." Though few will approve the bitterness of this essay, its contentions merit attention. The comments by Symons, Buchanan, and Brooke represent the most severe abuse of the *Irish Melodies*.

While not enthusiastic about the *Irish Melodies*, W. B. Yeats in *A Book of Irish Verse Selected from Modern Writers* (1895) more nearly approaches orthodox criticism by finding in select poems like "At the mid hour of night" such a "delicate beauty in the meaning and in the wavering or steady rhythm that one knows not where to find their like in literature." Padraic Colum, in "On Rereading Thomas Moore" (*Cweal*, 1930), a review of O'Faolain's *Lyrics and Satires from Thomas Moore*, expands this theme well, though embracing in his critical favor a much wider group of lyrics than Yeats would permit himself. Reviewing the biographies of Jones and Strong in "The Irish Melodist" (*Cweal*, 1937), Colum advances his views further in defending Moore against the charge of being too much "a rococo decorator" and offers some interesting observations on Moore's use of proper names such as Mononia. Brendan P. O. Hehir in "Moore's 'The Song of Fionnuala' " (*Expl*, 1957), shows how the title lyric is enhanced by a close reading for ambivalence and symbolic pattern.

L. A. G. Strong's able remarks on this subject in his biography of Moore have already been mentioned; J. A. Robinson's "Dear Harp of My Country" (*Étude*, 1942) follows the same course of criticism and leans heavily on Strong for illustration. The consideration of how Moore produced unusual metrical rhythms is also briefly treated by George Saintsbury in *A History of English Prosody* (1906). In *The Celtic Song Book* (1928) Alfred P. Graves observes, "Moore was before his time in recognizing the artistic value of brevity in the modern song and ballad. . . . But he most asserts his mastery in songcraft by the apparent ease with which he handles the most intricate musical measures, and mates the striking notes of each tune to the words most adapted to them both in sound and sense; to say nothing of the art with which he almost Italianizes English speech by a melodious sequence of varying vowel and alliterative consonants which almost sing themselves."

The most extensive treatment of this subject is that which I have attempted in "Thomas Moore: Artistry in the Song Lyric" (*SEL*, 1962). This analysis contemplates the requisites of a song musically and verbally, and the resultant demands upon the poet if he is to achieve a perfect organic unity of notes and syllables. It treats various songs of Moore in detail to show the craftsmanship that eludes the attention of critics who know only the words. The intention behind this article is not simply to show that Moore is a genuine artist in the song lyric, but to stimulate others to a more penetrating criticism of this medium than is usually presented by literary critics.

Perhaps the most enthusiastic defender of Moore in our century is Michael Monahan. In *Nova Hibernia* (1914) he offers effusive praise of the "finished" workmanship of the lyrics and takes direct issue with Stopford Brooke. In "Thomas Moore" (*Cath W*, 1924) he insists upon the artistic excellence of the lyrics and condemns Stephen Gwynn for not valuing Moore highly enough. Monahan was convinced that Moore gave expression to the true Irish spirit; the same conviction is defended by T. L. Blayney in his dissertation, *Thomas Moore, Ein irischer Dichter* (1906).

The third sort of study of the *Irish Melodies* concerns the general literary and historical importance of the lyrics, especially for Ireland. In "Thomas Moore" (*Dial*, 1921) Raymond Mortimer, taking his cue from Hazlitt's famous phrase about Moore's converting the wild harp of Erin into a musical snuffbox, reasons that by appealing to the higher social classes, the *Melodies* voiced an ineffective boudoir sentimentality and failed to arouse the mob, which he believes to be the highest service they could have performed. He also argues, not very convincingly, that Moore finally had to turn to prose to give adequate expression to his patriotic fervor.

Mortimer speaks well for those of his conviction, but he seems to express a judgment of the minority. Moore's contemporaries in Ireland were especially prone to feel that he had made a profound impression on the Irish people. Daniel O'Connell declared that "any tribute his countrymen could pay him would but feebly discharge the debt of gratitude Ireland owes him." Thomas Mooney in *A History of Ireland* (1845) asserts that the *Melodies* "worked miracles in the national sentiment, which, indeed, they may be said to have created. Their melody and their passion awoke the soul of Ireland from the torpor of slavery." The *Dublin Review* (1841) spoke directly to Mortimer's thesis by denying that boudoir sentimentality pervaded the songs and fitted them only for higher circles of English society: "Let him [the reader of the *Melodies*] not be led to suppose that the sphere of their greatest popularity was the saloon and the drawing-room. We know that among the peasantry, the 'hewers of wood and drawers of water,' the notes of his patriotic songs were raised." As a consequence, "It was among the people of Ireland, who were in reality their own emancipators, that the songs of their own bard helped to kindle the flame that afterwards blazed forth."

Later critics have often agreed with this thesis. In the chapter on "The Poetry of Irish Opposition and Revolt" in *Main Currents in Nineteenth-Century Literature* (trans. 1901–05), Georg Brandes gives extended treatment to the *Melodies*, observing "when Moore's *Irish Melodies* appeared, it was as if the grief and wrath of a whole nation had suddenly found expression." He stresses also the relation of such writing to the romantic movement as a whole with attention to Moore's contributions to poetry by his choice of subject, his language, and his metrics. Alois Stockmann's *Thomas Moore, der irische Freiheitssänger* (1910) reaches similar conclusions and also comments upon the importance of these songs in arousing strong sympathy for Ireland among other nations. Thierry's letter to Moore on the *Melodies* (*Memoirs*, VII, 251), commenting on them as "non seulement le cri de douleur d'Irlande, mais encore le chant de tristesse de tous les peuples opprimés," states this sympathy in the widest sense; Allen B. Thomas' *Moore en France* (1911) traces the influence of Moore on French writers and composers. Moore's success in winning sympathy for Ireland among the English public is explored in several of the foregoing works and in such articles as Robert M. Sillard's "Thomas Moore" (*Cath W*, 1904) and Elbridge Colby's "The Singer of Irish Melodies" (*American Catholic Quart. Rev.*, 1918). An inclusive treatment of the importance of the *Irish Melodies* is W. F. Trench's *Tom Moore* (1934), an admirable little volume which can be recommended as a summary of critical opinions for the casual reader and as a stimulant for the specialist in Moore.

2. OTHER POEMS AND "THE EPICUREAN"

For discriminating critics *Lalla Rookh* never has stood in the first rank of literary excellence. The question has simply been, how much excellence does it have? Powerful early criticism can be seen in

Carlyle's letter to Robert Mitchell, 25 May 1818 (*Early Letters of Thomas Carlyle*, ed. C. E. Norton, 1886) and in two of Hazlitt's essays, the scintillating "On the Living Poets" (*Lectures on the English Poets*, 1818) and the embittered "Mr. T. Moore—Mr. Leigh Hunt" (*The Spirit of the Age*, 1825). More favorable judgment is expressed in several biographies of Moore, notably Vallat's, and in such essays as those by Edmund Gosse on Moore for *The English Poets* (ed. T. H. Ward, 1880–81), George Saintsbury in *Essays in Literature, 1780–1860* (1890), Louis Cazamian in *A History of English Literature* (1924), and Alois Stockmann (above). The common agreement of these writers is that *Lalla Rookh* has, in Cazamian's phrase, "the easy, varied happiness of an astonishing prosodic virtuosity." Moore's use of the heroic couplet is noted in W. C. Brown's *The Triumph of Form* (1948). In "Paradise and the Peri" in the *Ninth Year Book of the Bibliophile Society* (1910), W. P. Trent reports the result of his close study of the manuscript revisions of this portion of *Lalla Rookh*. The final version is a "smoother and more satisfying piece of craftsmanship," it has greater metrical variety, and it seems the work of "a man of letters of remarkable skill rather than a heaven-born poet." The identification of Erin and Iran in *Lalla Rookh* is studied by W. F. Trench in *Tom Moore*, and its relations to Goethe are the subject of John Hennig's "Goethe and 'Lalla Rookh' " (*MLR*, 1953), which observes Goethe's esteem for Moore, enumerates well the materials discussing the Goethe-Moore association, and notes a possible influence of Moore on Goethe.

A useful summary of information concerning Moore's Eastern tales with liberal quotation from contemporary reviews is found in W. C. Brown's "Thomas Moore and English Interest in the East" (*SP*, 1937). A wider picture, placing *Lalla Rookh* in the general vogue of Eastern tales, is drawn by Agnes Repplier in her delightful essay, "When Lalla Rookh Was Young" (*Atlantic Monthly*, 1907). Robert Birley's *Sunk Without Trace: Some Forgotten Masterpieces Reconsidered* (1962), the Clark Lectures for 1960–61, presents some intelligent talk about *Lalla Rookh* and the Oriental vogue, and though its lightly pejorative tone is often well merited by the quality of this poem, one cannot help wondering if Moore is quite so unknown and forgotten as Birley assumes.

Other Eastern tales by Moore often share in the comments offered on *Lalla Rookh* but are seldom mentioned by themselves in any extended way. But as Jones comments, "If the world lost little by ignoring *The Epicurean*, critics of Moore have erred greatly by not giving serious consideration to this religious romance," a remark illustrated by the fact that in the heated discussions of the orthodoxy of Moore's Catholicism this work is seldom mentioned. The classic statement on *The Epicurean* is the scathing denunciation of its weaknesses by Thomas Love Peacock (see the edition of his works by H. F. B. Brett-Smith and C. E. Jones, 1924–34). The fragmentary poetical version of the work, entitled *Alciphron,* is the subject of a notice by E. A. Poe in "Moore's 'Alciphron' with Some Remarks on James Rodman Drake."

Defying regular classification but perhaps appropriately mentioned here with other works on Moore's poetry is Richard Bohndorf's *Das persönliche Geschlecht unpersönlicher Substantiva bei Thomas Moore* (1913). This dissertation, of interest to linguists, shows how Moore was following a tradition in gender usage in English dating from the Renaissance and also following the usage in Greek, Latin, and French: "[daβ] Moore nicht allein Dichter, sondern auch Gelehrter war."

Moore's verse satire has usually excited favorable comment. A good summation of its contents and characteristics may be found in H. O. Brogan's "Thomas Moore, Irish Satirist and Keeper of the English Conscience" (*PQ,* 1945) or in my dissertation on Moore (Cornell Univ., 1937). In the "Preface and Critical List of Authors" (*Select British Poets*) Hazlitt declared, "Thomas Moore is the greatest wit now living. His light, ironical pieces are unrivalled for point and facility of execution." This thesis Hazlitt explores at length in a review of "The Fudge Family in Paris" (*Political Essays*), and it is approved by L. H. Vincent in "A Regency Satirist" (*Dandies and Men of Letters,* 1913) and by Richard Garnett in *Essays of an Ex-Librarian* (1901). These critics question the effectiveness of the satires: Though the display is brilliant, does it reach its mark? No one has a well-documented answer despite strong expression of opinion. To arrive at a reasonable conjecture, a student must read widely in the diaries, letters, and reviews of the time for reactions to Moore's shafts. Tory publications of course are valuable in this regard, as, for instance, *The Croker Papers: The Correspondence and Diaries of . . . John Wilson Croker* (ed. L. J. Jennings, 1884), which details the Prince Regent's violent hatred of the *Two-Penny Post Bag;* or the *Quarterly Review* (1853), which declares of the satires, "There never was a bitterer or sourer specimen of concentrated malignity." It would appear that at least occasionally Moore drew blood.

Another topic of discussion concerning the satires has been the astuteness of Moore's political doctrines. In "Moore's Satirical Verse" (*QQ,* 1905) W. F. P. Stockley, after a well-informed review of the historical circumstances surrounding the satires, argues that Moore's political position, like that of O'Connell, Wilberforce, Macaulay, Sydney Smith, and Whigs generally, was a superficial liberalism not thought through to ultimate conclusions. This doctrine he advances further in "Moore and Ireland" (*Essays in Irish Biography*, 1933), by arguing not just from the satires but from Moore's work generally that his patriotism was weak and that he believed ultimately "the better England . . . will prevail" to effect the improvement of conditions in Ireland, a position which Stockley finds unacceptable. W. F. Trench in *Tom Moore* takes direct exception to Stockley and credits Moore with greater realistic insight. Moore's attitude toward the Holy Alliance is happily presented by John Hennig in "Thomas Moore and the Holy Alliance" (*Irish Monthly*, 1946), which depicts the irony of Moore's being considered "something like the poet laureate of the Prussian Court" even as he was launching his verse satires against this very court.

In *Rhymes on the Road* Moore commented scathingly upon the morality of Rousseau and Madame de Warens. He drew some envenomed replies, notably by J. R. Lowell in "Rousseau and the Sentimentalists" and Hazlitt in "On the Jealousy and the Spleen of Party" (*The Plain Speaker*). Though the latter tirade is almost always on Moore bibliographical lists as an important essay, the inaccuracies and the curious logic occasioned by the violence of the onslaught render it Hazlitt's poorest critical essay on Moore. In it Hazlitt attacks Moore and Hobhouse especially, but also Burke, Pitt, Malthus, Ricardo, Wordsworth, Coleridge, Southey, Hook, Jerdan, *Blackwood's*, the *Edinburgh*, the *Westminster*, the Tories, the "painted booths of Whig Aristocracy," and "the sordid styes of Reform." P. G. Patmore in *My Friends and Acquaintance* (1854) remarks that Moore's attack on Rousseau drove Hazlitt " 'all but mad'; and he never after lost an opportunity, public or private, of venting his indignation against the perpetrator of it."

On the whole, Moore had greater success than many of his contemporaries in escaping charges of plagiarism. After his death, however, a tempest in a teapot was raised by an anonymous writer ("Is Moore the Thief?" *Irish Monthly*, 1878) who asked if Moore had not taken his *Sacred Song* "This world is all a fleeting show" from the "Soupir vers le ciel" of Jean Reboul, the baker-poet of Nîmes. The question was answered by "M" in " Thomas Moore or Jean Reboul" (*Irish Monthly*, 1878) and by William Bates in "Moore and Reboul" (*N&Q*, 23 March 1878), who showed that

Reboul probably took his poem from Madame Belloc's French translation of the Moore poem.

Among notices of single works by Moore, worthy of mention are: L. S. Converse's "Thomas Moore's 'Canadian Boat-Song'" (*Literary World*, 1884) ; D. Turner's "Dead Man's Island and the Ghost Ship" (*Mag. of American History*, 1890), which concerns the ballad "Written on Passing Deadman's Island"; and the admirable review of "M. P.; or, The Blue Stocking" by Leigh Hunt (see *Leigh Hunt's Dramatic Criticism, 1808–1831*, ed. L. H. Houtchens and C. W. Houtchens, 1949).

3. PROSE WORKS

Moore's biography of Byron has occasioned more comment than any of his other prose works. As is so often true of Moore's writings, critics simply do not agree in their evaluations of this biography. Competent scholars range from sneers to encomiums in their judgments. The point of general agreement is that this biography provides a basis for subsequent studies that cannot be ignored. Though a frequent modern charge is that Moore was not brave enough to tell all, the contemporary charge was more often that he told too much and allowed too many of Byron's letters and other documents to be published; opinion divided as to whether he glorified Byron or vilified him. Lady Byron and her advocates believed she was traduced and Byron sanctified; Whittier represents the other extreme: "We would not for our right hand read this book before a sister. . . . Moore has exposed the dark errors and moral corruption of his friend, with the most unscrupulous fidelity. We are sorry for it—it was an unkind deed" (E. H. Cady and H. H. Clark, *Whittier on Writers and Writing*, 1950) ; J. C. Collins represents the middle ground: "On a general review of these poems it is impossible not to be struck, as in the case of the letters, with the admirable judgement which Moore displayed both in what he published and in what he suppressed" (*Studies in Poetry and Criticism*, 1905). A much-needed study of Moore's complex problems in writing the biography is offered by Doris Langley Moore, *The Late Lord Byron* (1961). It is a tawdry story; bristling hostility by Lady Byron, Mrs. Leigh, Hobhouse, and others, which placed the biographer in a nearly untenable position, gives rise to wonder that he ever found the courage and skill to surmount such obstacles. Doris Moore's easy assumptions about Moore's character are sometimes open to question, and, helpful though she is, future investigations may throw much more light on this dark matter. The nineteenth-century reception of the biography is well reviewed in *The Harp That Once————*.

Apart from the biographies of Moore there has been little criticism of many of the prose works, but a few items need to be mentioned. The *Memoirs of Captain Rock* created a great stir on publication; the generally favorable reception by the press is typified by Sidney Smith's article on it in the *Edinburgh Review* (1825), and the most violent denunciation of it by the Rev. Mortimer O'Sullivan's *Captain Rock Detected* (1824). The *Memoirs of the Life of the Right Honourable Richard Brinsley Sheridan* is evaluated in modern biographies of Sheridan; the comments in *The Croker Papers* (above) are also of especial interest. On *The Life and Death of Lord Edward Fitzgerald*, Southey's long article for the *Quarterly Review* (1832) is of value; it reflects Tory alarm at the incendiary nature of the work and in depicting well a Tory's attitude toward Moore as liberal, Irishman, and Catholic, reads oddly alongside Stockley's remarks in *Essays in Irish Biography*. The most succinct evaluation of Moore's lamentable *History of Ireland* is to be found in the quietly judicious comments by Eugene O'Curry in *Lectures on the Manuscript Materials of Ancient Irish History* (1861). Of interest in connection with Moore's biographical sketch of Sallust is J. Homer Caskey's "The First Edition of Arthur Murphy's *Sallust*" (*PQ*, 1934).

The Travels of an Irish Gentleman in Search of a Religion has touched off more discussion than any of Moore's prose works except the biography of Byron, for it is the focal point of arguments concerning Moore's religious beliefs. On the basis of this work and other contributory sources, Daniel Ambrose (above), John O'Hanlon (above), N. Walsh ("A Reminiscence of the Poet Moore," *Irish Monthly*, 1904), and others around the turn of the century argued the sincerity of Moore's belief as a Catholic. Their declarations impelled Stockley to write his long and closely reasoned article, "The Religion of Thomas Moore" (*Essays in Irish Biography*). He maintains that Moore was merely "a representative Catholic" (i.e., one who does not have a deep, heartfelt devotion) and a "brilliant amateur theologian": "Facts show that he was a good-hearted and probably well-meaning man; that he was of that early nineteenth century superficial school of Liberalism; that he had its illogical terror of dogmatic theology, while accepting Theism; that in Moore there was also emotional piety, acute artistic sensibility, and a refusal, or an incapacity, to push theological premises to personally logical conclusions." Those who do not hold the "dogmatic theology" of Stockley may, however, use the rich materials of the article to arrive at conclusions different from the author's. Stockley's thesis is supported by "John Eglinton" (William K. Magee) in *Anglo-Irish Essays* (1917), though his argument is relatively thin, and by Alois Stockmann (above). The converse argument is presented by John Hennig ("Thomas Moore as Theologian," *Irish Monthly*, 1947), who argues that Moore won his way to a genuine belief, and by Beda Herbert ("Thomas Moore, Apologist," *Irish Monthly*, 1952), who asserts a certain parallelism of Moore and Newman. Actually, despite all the generalizations about *The Travels of an Irish Gentleman*, its real deficiences and excellences have never been set forth in scholarly detail.

4. MISCELLANEOUS STUDIES

Critics have often compared Moore with other writers. In his own day many variations were played on the theme that Scott walks the earth, Byron plunges into the abysses, and Moore soars into the heavens. Comparisons of Moore and Byron abound. Perhaps the most successful early effort is Hazlitt's "Byron and Moore." Of a number of German works on the topic, the best are Oscar Thiergen's *Byrons und Moores orientalische Gedichte* (1880), which explores some likenesses of rime and meter, and an identity of thought; and the more inclusive study by Edgar Dawson, *Byron und Moore* (1902), which details the evidence of Moore's influence on the *Hours of Idleness* and *Hebrew Melodies*. The most complete work to date on this theme is my study "Byron and Moore" (*MLQ*, 1948). W. Pierson's *The Epic Poems of Walter Scott Compared with the Like Poetry of Thomas Moore* (1863) does about all that can be done with such a topic, but the land is not arable. In "Tom Moore and John Keats" (*Athenaeum*, 3 Sept. 1898) Robert Bridges attempts to show the influence of *Endymion* on *The Epicurean*, but the demonstration is not highly convincing and evoked a letter in the *London Mercury* (1922) by Gardner Teall reviewing what is known of the Keats-Moore relationship.

Moore's strong influence on Poe has been carefully surveyed. Killis Campbell's *The Poems of Edgar Allan Poe* (1917) and "Poe's Reading" (*Univ. of Texas Stud. in English*, 1925) are the fundamental studies in this area. My article "Poe's Debt to Thomas Moore" (*PMLA*, 1948) makes a considerable addition to Campbell, and is in turn supplemented by T. O. Mabbott's "Poe's 'The Sleeper' Again" (*AL*, 1949).

A further influence of Moore upon an American is noted in

R. H. Morrison's "An Apparent Influence of Thomas Moore on Longfellow" (*PQ*, 1956). Thomas A. Kirby's "Irving and Moore: A Note on Anglo-American Relations" (*MLN*, 1947) proves a useful comment on these two friends to supplement the observations made by Irving's biographers. Donal O'Sullivan in "Charles Dickens and Thomas Moore" (*Studies*, 1948) produces a surprising set of quotations from the Dickens novels to demonstrate that Moore was Dickens' favorite poet.

Moore's importance in France has been the subject of very able treatment. Fernand Baldensperger's "Thomas Moore et Alfred de Vigny" (*MLR*, 1906) is a very careful observation of Moore's influence on Vigny, especially from 1820 to 1823: "Vigny . . . trouvait us coloriste à sa guise dans le poète des *Amour des anges.*" Allen B. Thomas' *Moore en France* (1911) is perhaps the definitive treatment of this topic; it observes Moore's rise to greatest fame in the 1820's and decline thereafter, his acclaim by Vigny, Stendhal, Berlioz, Lamartine, Gautier, and others, the translations made of his work, and the sort of writing by Moore which made the greatest appeal in France.

Erwin G. Gudde's "Traces of English Influences in Freiligrath's Political and Social Lyrics" (*JEGP*, 1921) asserts, "There are more echoes of Thomas Moore in Freiligrath's political lyrics than of any other British poet. The way the Irish bard conceived and treated political ideas could not fail to touch a responsive chord in Freiligrath." Studies of Moore's influence on German writers, other than Goethe, are wanting.

If scholars of the future continue to devote attention to lesser literary figures, they will find that the work of Moore can be subjected to much more serious consideration than it has hitherto received. In the past there has been too much expression of wild opinion and too little cautious examination of large bodies of fact, excusable in part by the specialized knowledge demanded for competent judgment of his work. Far less excusable, however, are the sneers which have frequently marred comment on him, even in our time. Moore is not a great man of letters, but he is an able one who merits the respectful and sympathetic reading necessary to produce informed and objective conclusions.

8

Walter Savage Landor

By R. H. Super

UNIVERSITY OF MICHIGAN

I. BIBLIOGRAPHIES

L ANDOR'S FRIEND and biographer, John Forster, bequeathed many of Landor's own copies of his works, as well as manuscripts and letters (chiefly those addressed *to* Landor), to the South Kensington (now Victoria and Albert) Museum; the published catalogue of his collection (printed books, 1888; manuscripts, etc., 1893) is still an important tool of Landor bibliography. C. G. Crump's bibliographical studies in preparation for his edition of Landor (1891–93) are to be found in several appendices to that edition; he confined his attention to Landor's books, and made no search of the periodicals for Landor's contributions. So much Landoriana was sold in the Browning Collections that the catalogue of that sale (Sotheby, 1–8 May 1913) is also of great importance, though the cataloguer made some strange blunders. (The item [No. 851] described as a proof copy of Landor's 1795 volume, e.g., turns out to be *Simonidea* [1806], revised and bound up with manuscripts of many new poems for the 1831 volume.)

The dominant figure in Landor bibliography, however, as in all Landor studies from 1888 to 1936, was an enthusiastic amateur named Stephen Wheeler, who, in addition to the books to be mentioned in this chapter, contributed upward of seventy items on Landor, some important, some mere trifles, to the London periodicals during that period. His first attempt at a bibliography of Landor was appended to his edition of *Letters and Other Unpublished Writings of Landor* (1897), which attracted the attention of Landor's grandnephews, F. G. R. Duke and R. E. H. Duke, both of whom thereafter gave Wheeler considerable assistance. Through the Bibliographical Society Wheeler met Thomas J. Wise, already a collector of Landor, and the first fruit of their collaboration was *A Bibliography of the Writings in Prose and Verse of Walter Savage Landor* (1919), the Landor student's most valuable tool and a singularly useful one. Here are listed Landor's separately published works, with full descriptions and (usually) tables of contents; Landor's contributions to periodicals and his letters and other writings published posthumously in books and journals; the collected editions of Landor's works; and (a less important section) books about Landor. In 1928, with Wheeler's help, Wise printed a catalogue of his own collection of Landor, *A Landor Library*, which, though it necessarily omits the few Landor editions he did not own, adds several items discovered after the publication of the *Bibliography*, and includes (as the *Bibliography* does not) descriptions of manuscript material. Nearly all the collection described in this volume is now in the British Museum.

Students will have no difficulty discerning the value of the Wise and Wheeler *Bibliography*; it will not be invidious to warn them against some of its failings. The greatest of these is a superstitious regard for "firsts." Though such books as the second English and the Latin editions of *Gebir*, the second edition of *Imaginary Conversations*, and the *Hellenics* of 1859 are as important to the Landor student as the first editions of these works, they are given only cursory treatment, under descriptions of the first editions (so that the 1859 *Hellenics* must be sought under 1847), and tables of contents of some of the books are distorted by listing only those writings which appeared in them for the first time. Second, though the order of describing first editions is chronological by year, little attempt is made to date the books more exactly, and when (as in 1836) Landor produced several books in one year, these are likely to be listed in the wrong order. Third, the compilers were content with examining only one or two copies of each book, and made misleading statements about the rarity of volumes without exhaustive search (Wise's complete copy of the *Letters to Lord Liverpool* is twice described as "presumably unique," though the New York Public Library has owned a copy since 1899; the British Museum copy of *Poche osservazioni* is not unique: there is one at Harvard). Fourth, the collector's zeal has led to the listing of one work, *The Dun Cow* (1808), which was probably not Landor's, and another, *Solon and Pisistratus*, which was not a separate publication but an offprint from a periodical.[1] Fifth, there is a surprisingly high rate of error in the minutiae of transcription. Finally, the obviously great industry with which Wheeler searched the nineteenth-century periodicals has obscured the fact that the search is not yet complete: by no means have all Landor's contributions yet been uncovered.

In *The Publication of Landor's Works* (1954) I supplement the Wise and Wheeler *Bibliography* by tracing, so far as I am able, the history of each of Landor's books from the writing of the manuscript to its public appearance. Here is an account of the difficulties in publication which so greatly affected Landor's literary career and which among other things caused the dates of composi-

---

1   Similarly, the *Poemata Latina* which occasionally appears on the market is an offprint from a periodical.

tion of some of Landor's works to be appreciably earlier than their dates of publication. This monograph shared something of their fate: despite the date on the title page, it was set in type as early as 1949 and is therefore not fully cognizant of research done later than that year. Its first chapter, "The Publication of Landor's Early Works," appeared in *PMLA* (1948). Specific problems of Landor bibliography are taken up in John Carter's *Binding Variants in English Publishing 1820–1900* and *More Binding Variants* (1932 and 1938), R. C. Bald's "Landor's *Sponsalia Polyxenae*" (*Library*, 1949), Simon Nowell-Smith's "*Gebir: A Poem*. 1798" (*Library*, 1962), Ann Lohrli's "The First Publication of Landor's 'Diana de Poictiers' "—anonymously in *Household Words* for 19 June 1858, and Landor was paid two guineas for it—(*N&Q*, Jan. 1963), my Introduction to Landor's *To the Burgesses of Warwick* (1949) and my articles "The Authorship of *Guy's Porridge Pot* and *The Dun Cow*" (*Library*, 1950), "Notes on Some Obscure Landor Editions" (*PBSA*, 1952), "Landor's Unrecorded Contributions to Periodicals" (*N&Q*, 8 Nov. 1952), and "Landor's American Publications" (*MLQ*, 1953). My conclusion respecting the authorship of *Guy's Porridge Pot* and *The Dun Cow* (that Robert Eyres Landor did write the former, Walter Savage Landor probably did not write the latter) has been disputed on both points. Roman Czerwinski, "Robert Landor and *Guy's Porridge Pot*" (*Library*, 1961) believes "there is good reason to doubt whether Robert Eyres Landor wrote *Guy's Porridge Pot*" (a mock-heroic attack on Dr. Parr, published anonymously in 1808 and 1809), but he misses the force of my evidence and takes refuge in rhetoric: "Why should he decide to [complete writing the poem] after seven years? Why is there no further reference in the known letters either before or after this one [from Rome in 1816]?" The questions can be answered: (1) By 1816 Parr was becoming actively engaged on behalf of the Princess of Wales, Caroline of Brunswick, and Robert Landor was soon to be equally active against her; and (2) no letters whatsoever of Robert Landor survive so early as the date of the *Pot*'s publication, nor do any survive for the first four years after his return to England in 1816, the time when he said he would "finish" the *Pot* (a task he did not actually perform). That there should be minor inconsistencies of opinion between an anonymous pamphlet of 1809 and anonymous political letters to the press in 1820 hardly constitutes serious evidence against common authorship. Malcolm Elwin in his *Landor: A Replevin* finds me obtuse in taking seriously rather than ironically *The Dun Cow*'s praise of a Warwick physician Walter Landor scorned, and seeks to reclaim the poem for Walter. For obtuseness there is no cure; nevertheless there is nothing to link the *Cow* with Landor except an attribution in the very inaccurate catalogue of Dr. Parr's library published after Parr's death.

Another bibliographical debate was set off by W. D. Paden's "Twenty New Poems Attributed to Tennyson, Praed, and Landor" (*VS*, 1961), in which he claims for Landor the anonymous poem "The Descent of the Naiad," published in 1828. There is no ground for the attribution.[2]

Marjorie Karlson describes the interesting items of Yale University's Walter Savage Landor collection in the *Yale University Library Gazette* (1952), and R. G. Lyde indicates the scope of Lt. Col. J. W. N. Landor's gift to the British Museum of more than forty volumes that once belonged to Walter Savage Landor, and descended from him to his granddaughter (*BMQ*, 1960). Useful hand lists of writings about Landor are available to the student in *The Cambridge Bibliography of English Literature* (1940; Supplement 1957) and Elwin's *Landor* (1958). The latter, in his "List of Landor's Publications," does not distinguish between books and pamphlets actually known to exist and works for which there may be some evidence but of which there is no modern record. My section on Landor in the forthcoming *New CBEL* is not so much a revision of the old as an entirely fresh compilation.

II. EDITIONS

1. LITERARY WORKS

AT THE AGE of seventy-one, Landor published a collected edition of his English writings in two large volumes, closely printed in double columns (1846; reprinted 1853, 1868, 1895). Seven years later, he gathered the prose and verse he had published or composed in the interim, under the title *Last Fruit off an Old Tree* (1853). These volumes generally (but not quite always) represent

2   Most bibliographers who recorded Paden's articles missed both my long caveat (*VS*, 1961) and Paden's unabashed announcement that one of the poems he had attributed to Tennyson was in fact by R. H. Horne (*VS*, 1963). It is easier to make an error than to correct one, and an irresponsible attribution is one of the hardest errors to correct.

his final revisions of the writings included in them. They omit many of his ephemeral contributions to periodicals on affairs of the day and some other writings he apparently did not wish to preserve, notably *A Satire on Satirists, Terry Hogan*, "High and Low Life in Italy," and a good many early poems. Landor continued to publish for another ten years after *Last Fruit*; his final book appeared in 1863, the year before his death.

In the publication of both these collected editions, Landor was assisted by John Forster, to whom he assigned his copyright. Forster in 1876 (the year of his own death) published *The Works and Life of Walter Savage Landor* in eight volumes, of which the first was the *Life*. He included nearly everything in the volumes of 1846 and 1853 (occasionally with differences that suggest subsequent revisions by Landor), but only a selection of what Landor published during his last decade. Early works which Landor himself omitted in 1846 were likewise omitted by Forster. He retained Landor's own simple classifications of his poems, but grouped the *Imaginary Conversations* under the headings of "Greek," "Roman," "Dialogues of Sovereigns and Statesmen," "Dialogues of Literary Men," "Dialogues of Famous Women," and "Miscellaneous." He made no attempt to collate editions or record variants, and did not annotate.

The first scholarly edition was that by C. G. Crump (*Imaginary Conversations*, 6 vols., 1891; *Poems, Dialogues in Verse and Epigrams*, 2 vols., 1892; *Longer Prose Works*, 2 vols., 1892–93). Crump added a few *Imaginary Conversations* that Forster had overlooked, omitted some minor prose pieces, and gave merely a selection from Landor's verse, though he added some early poems that Forster had not printed. He recorded the more important variants in the texts of the prose works, provided occasional (but useful) annotations, and indexed prose and poetry carefully (the prose by subjects as well as by proper names). His edition of Landor's prose is still the most satisfactory one, whatever its defects, though for many of Landor's writings it is necessary to seek elsewhere.

In 1927 Chapman & Hall began the publication of *The Complete Works of Walter Savage Landor*, edited by T. Earle Welby. Twelve volumes of prose were published by 1931; at least one other apparently was planned, but Welby's death brought the work to a halt. The edition was completed in 1933–36 with four volumes of poetry under the editorship of Stephen Wheeler. The whole was expensive and impressively produced, but the editorship of the prose works is in every respect unsatisfactory. The reader will find in

Welby six *Imaginary Conversations* that were not in Crump's edition
(one of them, "John Dryden and Henry Purcell," is not Landor's at
all) ; the original "Dedications" to Landor's first five books of
Imaginary Conversations (curiously divided between Vols. IX and X,
and improperly called "Suppressed Dedications") ; "High and Low
Life in Italy"; and a volume (XII) of "Miscellaneous Papers" and
pamphlets, most of which are not to be found in Crump. Except for
these items, students would do well not to use the Welby edition.

Its principal claims are completeness (patently false, as a
quick comparison of its contents with the Wise and Wheeler
Bibliography will show) and careful collation of texts and record
of variants. Let it be confessed at the outset that some of Landor's
Imaginary Conversations underwent such extensive revision as to
make editing very difficult indeed. But it must also be said that
Welby hardly made the attempt. His records of variants are so
frequently erroneous as to make them altogether worthless, and
the student who wants to be sure at what date Landor made a
given statement must simply go to the original editions, fortunately not excessively rare. "From explanatory and appreciative
annotation," Welby tells us, he has "for the most part abstained"
on the ground that "Landor is not the reading of ignorant,
indolent, unsensitive persons." His is the only important edition of
Landor's prose since 1846 that lacks an index. His arrangement
can be bewildering, especially when he puts into an "appendix"
in the middle of Volume IX some of the longer variant readings of
Conversations printed in Volumes I, III, IV, and VI. And he has
unwisely classified the *Imaginary Conversations* by the nationality
of the speakers and arranged them in the order in which they
might be supposed to occur historically.

In fact, the only order which has Landor's sanction is also the
one which is most useful to students—the order, roughly, in
which the *Conversations* were composed. It is true that at various
times in his life, Landor toyed with the notion of publishing
separately those *Conversations* which had female speakers and
those on Italian subjects; he actually did publish *Imaginary
Conversations of Greeks and Romans* (1853). Nevertheless, his
collected edition of 1846 printed the *Conversations* without
classification, generally in the order of their first appearance, and
those gathered in *Last Fruit* (1853) were similarly unclassified.
The author himself is the only continuous element in the *Conversations*, and their only valid sequence is in reference to his own life.
Since Pericles and Sophocles discuss the quarrels of Walter Savage
Landor with members of the British *Corps Diplomatique*, they

should be allowed to do so in reasonable proximity to Peter Leopold and President du Paty, who concern themselves with the same debate. The *Conversations* are not moments of history, they are Landor's rambling reflections on a variety of topics.

When we turn to the edition of the poetry by Wheeler (issued also separately in three volumes, 1937), the story is quite different. The work is a final monument to Wheeler's loving industry: its claims to completeness and to textual accuracy are valid; it is well indexed and usefully annotated.[3] In one respect, his zeal has run away with him: he has certainly overclassified the poems, and in doing so has gone counter both to Landor's practice and to good sense. Once again, a prevailingly chronological arrangement within a few large classes would give a clearer picture of Landor's writing at any one time. The twenty-five poems from *Simonidea* (1806), to take a single example, are scattered in seven places, not always intelligibly, and a system that puts three of Landor's translations from his *Idyllia Heroica* among the "Heroic Poems" and seven others among the "Hellenics" can hardly be said to be useful. Wheeler's pudicity forbade him to print *Terry Hogan* and an (in my opinion) erroneous belief in Landor's authorship made him include *The Dun Cow*.

A selection of Landor's articles in the press (chiefly the *Examiner*) makes up the latter half of Wheeler's *Letters of Landor, Private and Public* (1899). His edition of Landor's *Charles James Fox: A Commentary on His Life and Character* (1907) is the only available printing of this lively political document which Landor composed late in 1811. M. F. Ashley-Montagu has published from Landor's manuscript four new "Imaginary Conversations" (*Nineteenth Century and After*, 1930, 1931), and several other "waifs" (*RES*, 1932; *Nineteenth Century*, 1939).

Landor's very considerable writings in Latin have not been reprinted; most of them are available in the collected edition which Landor published in 1847, *Poemata et Inscriptiones*. Of his two principal pamphlets in Italian, *Savonarola e il priore di San Marco* (1860) and *Poche osservazioni* (1821), he himself translated one (a translation printed in the Welby edition) and Felice Elkin translated the other as an appendix to *Walter Savage Landor's Studies of Italian Life and Literature* (1934). The original Italian editions are uncommon.

Those who incline to lament Landor's unpopularity will note with pleasure that the first years after the Second World War saw

---

3   The notes in Sidney Colvin's *Selections from Landor* (1882) also retain their usefulness.

no less than three volumes of selections from his work published in England and a fourth in Florence; three were devoted to his verse and the other was divided equally between poetry and prose: *Landor, Poetry and Prose*, edited by E. K. Chambers (1946), *The Shorter Poems of Walter Savage Landor*, edited by J. B. Sidgwick (1946), *The Sculptured Garland*, edited by Richard Buxton (1948), and *W. Savage Landor: Brevities / Epigrammi*, edited by A. Obertello (1946). Much more significant than these is the large selection of Landor's poems made by Geoffrey Grigson in the centenary year of Landor's death (1864). Here is a return to good sense in the preservation (for the most part) of the order of composition or first publication. None of the dramas are included (though many of the shorter dramatic scenes are here), and none of the longer heroic narratives except *Gebir*. About half the volume is drawn from poems later than the 1846 *Works*. Textual variants are not listed; there are very few notes; and no uniform policy is enforced with respect to the adoption of an earlier or later version. Nevertheless, this volume will very fittingly represent Landor the poet for all readers except the specialist who has the patience to wrestle with Wheeler's edition. The brief Preface was published earlier in *The Listener* (30 May 1963).

2. LETTERS

Landor took little pains in the writing of his personal letters and once remarked that they would be the ruin of any publisher who undertook to collect and publish them. No attempt has ever been made to do so, except in small segments, so that very many letters remain unpublished and those that have been printed have appeared under a wide variety of auspices and conditions. One can only describe the principal published collections of Landor correspondence and point out where a few other odd letters may be found in print.

John Forster's *Walter Savage Landor: A Biography* (1869) printed large excerpts from three important groups of Landor's letters: those to Southey, those to the Landor family (his mother, brothers, and sisters), and those to Forster himself. The letters were dissected to suit the biographer's needs, they were sometimes loosely or wrongly dated, and Forster took unwarrantable liberties with their texts. The originals of the letters to Southey disappeared after Forster used them; those to the Landors were returned to the family (where they remained until 1944) and were used by both Elwin and me in our biographies of Landor;[4] and many of those to Forster, long supposed to have been destroyed, were found in a London bookshop by J. Lee Harlan, Jr., and have recently been deposited by him in the Huntington Library. Still others to Forster are in the Library of the University of Chicago. Aurelia Brooks Harlan has announced her intention of editing all these letters to Forster; such an edition will be a valuable and revealing check upon his reliability as a biographer.

During Landor's lifetime, a few of his letters to Dr. Parr were published in Volume VIII of John Johnstone's edition of *The Works of Samuel Parr* (1828), and a large number of those to Lady Blessington in R. R. Madden's *The Literary Life and Correspondence of the Countess of Blessington* (1855). Two editions of the latter were published in London in the same year; of these the second is far the better. The American edition is printed from the first English edition. Madden's slovenly editing is superseded in large part by Alfred Morrison's *The Blessington Papers* (1895), apparently a painstaking and accurate transcription of the text, though Morrison did not own, and therefore did not print, quite all the letters that appeared in Madden. It should be noted that when the dates of letters in this edition are placed in parentheses, they are usually taken from the postmarks, and the postmarks frequently indicate the date of arrival in London, rather than the date of posting. Other letters from Landor to Lady Blessington were published by W. R. Nicoll and T. J. Wise, *Literary Anecdotes of the Nineteenth Century*, Volume I (1895), one by A. H. Mason, "Landor and Lady Blessington" (*Howard Coll. Stud.*, 1929), and yet another by T. B. Brumbaugh, "A Landor Letter" (*N&Q*, Jan. 1963).

Some of Landor's letters to Crabb Robinson appeared in Thomas Sadler's *Diary, Reminiscences, and Correspondence of Henry Crabb Robinson*, of which the best edition is the third, in two volumes (1872).[5] Stephen Wheeler's *Letters and Other Unpublished Writings of Landor* (1897) contains in fact only a few of Landor's letters, principally to Arthur de Noé Walker; it is an unreliable book in every respect and except for these few letters has been superseded by Wheeler's later work. The first part of his *Letters of Walter Savage Landor, Private and Public* (1899) is a

---

4 A large proportion of these were sold at Sotheby's on 2 June 1959 and 3–4 December 1962.
5 See also the list of Landor's letters to Robinson in Appendix VIII of *Henry Crabb Robinson on Books and Their Writers*, ed. E. J. Morley (1938).

selection of letters to Rose, Lady Graves-Sawle and her mother, Mrs. Sophia Paynter (Rose Aylmer's half sister); they have been too carefully pruned to be satisfactory, but the annotation has been industrious and the collection is useful. G. S. Layard's *Mrs. Lynn Linton* (1901) contains a number of letters from Landor to Mrs. Linton; these are augmented by others printed in my article "Landor's 'Dear Daughter,' Eliza Lynn Linton" (*PMLA*, 1944).

Landor's letters to Browning were published in the *Baylor University Browning Interests*, Fifth Series (1932), altogether without editorial supervision and indeed even without proofreading. The same collection was the basis of H. C. Minchin's *Walter Savage Landor: Last Days, Letters and Conversations* (1934), where the transcriptions are somewhat better but the dating is so often erroneous as to make the volume unreliable.[6] Other friends of Landor's final years in Florence have written about him and printed some of his letters: Kate Field, "Last Days of Walter Savage Landor" (*Atlantic Monthly*, 1866) and the Marchesa Peruzzi de' Medici, "Walter Savage Landor" (*Cornhill*, 1915). I have edited an especially interesting series of seven letters to Wordsworth from the years 1820–28 (*MP*, 1957); Wordsworth's side of the correspondence will be found in *Letters of William and Dorothy Wordsworth* (ed. Ernest de Selincourt, 1939). Wordsworth's admiration of Landor's English poetry is largely responsible for Landor's return to the use of his native tongue for verse writing. The same article prints a short note Landor wrote to Coleridge in 1808.

Mary Boyle and G. P. R. James were well-known friends of Landor whose names today will hardly be recognized. James Russell Lowell supplied an interesting prefatory note for Landor's letters to Mary Boyle when they were published in the *Century* (1888); they are pleasant reading but have little literary interest and are for the most part undated. The originals are now in the Ashley Library, British Museum. Jay B. Hubbell edited eleven letters from Landor to James in the *Virginia Magazine of History and Biography* (1943).

T. A. Trollope published Landor's letters to his wife Theodosia and to her father, Joseph Garrow (*Lippincott's Mag.*, 1874, and Trollope, *What I Remember*, 1887–89). An interesting collection of early letters from Landor to his school and university friend Walter Birch was published by E. H. R. Tatham in "Some Unpublished Letters of W. S. Landor" (*Fortnightly Rev.*, 1910);[7] there are

---

6 Minchin printed eight new letters from the Baylor Collection and omitted three that appeared in the *Baylor University Browning Interests*. He censored a few passages on personal matters.
7 Most of these were sold at Sotheby's on 2 June 1959.

a few inaccuracies and omissions, and these letters are to be supplemented by what Forster's biography prints of the same correspondence. Brief excerpts from letters to James Fitzgerald, now housed in Wellington, New Zealand, appeared in the *Turnbull Library Record* (1940), and a long letter to an unnamed correspondent with anecdotes about Byron appeared in the *Cornhill* (1926). A few letters from Landor to Leigh Hunt have appeared in various places: *The Correspondence of Leigh Hunt* (ed. Thornton Hunt, 1862); L. A. Brewer's *My Leigh Hunt Library: The Holograph Letters* (1938); Karl G. Pfeiffer's "Landor's Critique of *The Cenci*" (*SP*, 1942; see also 1943). Three of Landor's are among the *Letters to William Allingham* (1911), and there are others in T. W. Reid's *Life, Letters and Friendships of R. M. Milnes* (1890) and in *Bryan Waller Procter, An Autobiographical Fragment* (ed. C. Patmore, 1877).

Letters from Landor to his publishers are to be found in Edmund Blunden's *Keats's Publisher: A Memoir of John Taylor* (1936) and S. Wheeler's "Landor and His Publishers" (*TLS*, 19 Jan. 1922); in John Drinkwater's *A Book for Bookmen* (1926: letters to James or John Nichol, now in the Huntington Lib.); and in G. J. Holyoake's *Sixty Years of an Agitator's Life* (1892) and M. Q. Holyoake's "The Last Writings of Landor" (*Gentleman's Mag.*, 1899). Letters to the famous printer Bodoni and his widow were published by A. Boselli in *Aurea Parma* (1913).

Still other Landor letters may be found in *Notes and Queries* (4 Sept. 1869, 1 April 1871, 15 April 1882, 5 March 1949); Mrs. Julian Marshall, *Life and Letters of Mary Wollstonecraft Shelley* (1889); Sir Charles Gavan Duffy, *Thomas Davis: The Memoirs of an Irish Patriot* (1890); *Spectator* (20 June 1891); T. J. Powys, *Poems* (1891); Mrs. Andrew Crosse, *Red-Letter Days of My Life* (1892); W. J. Linton, *Memories* (1895); Margaret Oliphant, *Annals of a Publishing House* (1897); *Athenaeum* (31 Aug. 1901); Walter Jerrold, *Douglas Jerrold, Dramatist and Wit* (1914); Sidney Colvin, *John Keats* (1917); Harold W. Thompson, *A Scottish Man of Feeling* (1931); *The Keats Circle* (ed. H. E. Rollins, 1948); and Thomas B. Brumbaugh, "On Collecting Landor" (*EUQ*, 1956).

III. BIOGRAPHIES

D URING HIS LIFETIME, Landor supplied autobiographical information to various inquirers like S. C. Hall (*The Book of Gems*,
3d Ser., 1838, and *Book of Memories*, 1871), R. H. Horne (*New
Spirit of the Age*, 1844), and William Howitt (*Homes and Haunts
of the Most Eminent British Poets*, 1847; with corrections by Landor, 1857). A few months after Landor's death Edward Spender, son
of his physician at Bath, published a long article, "The Life and
Opinions of Walter Savage Landor" (*London Quart. Rev.*, 1865), for
which he obtained the assistance of Landor's brother Robert.
Robert Landor was not entirely content with the article. I describe
his marginal comments, made for Forster's benefit, in "Forster as
Landor's Literary Executor" (*MLN*, 1937) and "An Unknown
Child of Landor's" (*MLN*, 1938).

John Forster accepted from Landor the task of writing his
biography, to which end Landor gave him all the correspondence
he had preserved except from his very latest years, and the Landor
family and other friends supplied what materials they could.
These materials proved unwieldy, and Forster was plagued by
illness and the call of other business, so that the task he had
undertaken with the best of good will became very distasteful. His
Walter Savage Landor (2 vols., 1869; Boston ed., 1869, in one
vol.) is bulky and rather oppressive to read. Long arid stretches
are devoted to mere summaries of Landor's writings; much of the
rest was composed by pasting clippings from Landor's letters to
sheets of paper and sending them to the printer. Forster also was
not much concerned with exactness: he pronounced pontifically
upon matters of which he knew nothing, and altered and garbled
letters with inexplicable willfulness. It is a curious sidelight on
him that although he knew Landor well, his book contains very
little personal reminiscence. He was furthermore unquestionably
embarrassed by the necessity of dealing with Landor's separation
from his wife while Mrs. Landor was still living and with the
Yescombe-Landor libel suit while the Yescombes were still in close
touch with their solicitors, and he was hampered generally by the
necessity of keeping all Landor's friends and surviving relations
content. His book is a storehouse of source materials for Landor

biography (unfortunately not reliably transmitted), but not at all a satisfactory account of Landor's life, and the principal task of Landor's subsequent biographers has been breaking down Forster's dominance in the field. Forster pruned his biography into one volume for his edition of Landor's *Works and Life* in 1876, and this one-volume edition was reprinted in 1895. Students will naturally use the 1869 edition, but since some factual corrections were made in 1876, they must constantly check with that also.

Faced with the impossible task of crowding Landor's long career into about 225 pages for the English Men of Letters series, Sidney Colvin produced a thoroughly readable biographical and critical essay (1881). He necessarily depended heavily on Forster, but also made use of various published reminiscences of Landor which had appeared in the interim, and had access to some original sources (such as Landor's letters to Francis Hare) which no one else has been able to use. There are nevertheless glaring inaccuracies in the biographical account.

Though other admirers of Landor from time to time have planned to write his biography, no one did so until Malcolm Elwin published his *Savage Landor* in 1941. He was able to refer to nearly complete copies of Landor's correspondence with his family (which no one since Forster had used), and discovered in Landor's letters to an Abergavenny attorney a hitherto unknown source of information about his attempt to establish himself as a landed proprietor at Llanthony. In addition, Elwin had the benefit of the scholarship, reminiscences, and other material on Landor printed in the seventy-odd years since Forster wrote. Nevertheless, his was a wartime book; he was unable to make extensive researches into unpublished materials abroad, or even in the United Kingdom, and the volume itself had to find a publisher in the United States and got only a limited distribution in England.

The front-page article in the *Times Literary Supplement* for 27 May 1955 and Elwin's letter to the same journal a week later suggest the differences between his theory of biography and mine in *Walter Savage Landor: A Biography* (1954). The latter work, less than half the size of Forster's unabridged life, combines the findings of earlier scholars with a great deal of fresh research to give the most complete and the only thoroughly documented account of Landor's life. Relying firmly on the evidence and declining to speculate where the evidence was lacking, I have nevertheless tried to give an understandable, well-proportioned portrait. Though there are no long passages of literary criticism, critical remarks are not lacking; it is to be hoped that readers of

Landor who turn to this book will find much to help their understanding of his writings, and much especially to dispel the quaint notion that the events of Landor's life have little to do with his works. The five-page bibliography must be supplemented by reference to the notes for titles of books, articles, and manuscripts less frequently drawn upon in the text. The indexes are uncommonly complete.

Elwin had already resolved upon an extensive revision of his biography when mine appeared, "a massive work in the manner fashionable among modern American scholars, enumerating every detail that [Super] has been able to discover about Landor in almost half a lifetime's research, with one-fifth of its 654 pages devoted to source references." The appearance of my book was indeed doubly fortunate, for my ungenerous treatment of Landor —"readers must wonder why [Super] persevered so long in studying a subject with whom he felt so little sympathy"—made a new biography immediately imperative, and my researches, to which Elwin makes generous acknowledgment, made it possible. (How little one knows the impression one makes; I had remarked in my preface: "Despite the impartiality I have attempted to maintain throughout the book, its very existence may be taken as evidence of my own admiration and affection for its subject. It will have failed of one of its purposes if it does not convey to the reader some part of the charm and generosity that all Landor's friends loved in him and some sense of the literary achievement which his contemporaries valued so highly.") And therefore he called his revised biography *Landor: a Replevin* (1958), "because it is an attempt to recover Landor's character from misrepresentation and his work from neglect."[8] The new biography is basically the former one, expanded by about one fourth to include more description of Landor's writings and to give greater order to the account of Landor's latter years in Bath. Revisions of the earlier text have uniformly improved it, most notably by removing some of the eccentricities of its author and by tempering the former positiveness about some of the speculations for which there is no clear evidence; the book is knowledgeable and readable. Elwin's long familiarity with the literary history of the period has enabled him to correct or amplify some of my statements (perhaps not quite so many as his footnote references to me indicate), but it is fair to say that the quantity of new

---

8   A replevin is the restoration to the former possessor of property or money taken from him in a legal dispute over ownership, pending settlement of the dispute; it was by a writ of replevin that Landor's Llanthony tenant Charles Betham was able to avoid paying his rents and drove Landor to bankruptcy and exile.

research in his book is small. It has a fine index and is generous with portraits; it is not documented, and despite the increased space given to Landor's works, it hardly deals with them critically; it is frankly partisan: the author is much at the reader's shoulder telling him what to think, generalizing about his characters. If one excludes the documentation from my biography, the two books are about the same length.

A few shorter items of biographical research have been published since the first edition of Elwin's book appeared: E. K. Chambers, "Some Notes on Walter Savage Landor" (*RES*, 1944), not quite trustworthy speculations about Landor's early life in Wales and the West of England; Giuliana Artom, "Landor and Dickens" (*TLS*, 28 Dec. 1951), about Landor's quarrel with his Fiesolan neighbor, Joseph Antoir, which set the pattern for Boythorn's difficulties with Dedlock; and the following articles by me: "Extraordinary Action for Libel: Yescombe *v.* Landor" (*PMLA*, 1941, with an "Addendum" by Robert F. Metzdorf) ; "When Landor Left Home" (*MLQ*, 1945), on his separation from his wife in 1835; introduction to the Luttrell Society reprint of Landor's *To the Burgesses of Warwick* (1949) ; "Landor's Lodgings in Bath" (*TLS*, 25 July 1952), touching also upon his friendship with Dickens ; and "None Was Worth My Strife" (*PBSA*, 1953), records of Landor in the archives of the Tuscan police. Elwin's "Landor and Alfieri" (*TLS*, 26 Feb. 1944) corrects the date of Landor's meeting with Alfieri from the winter of 1794–95 to the summer of 1791, but in *Landor: a Replevin* he finds this probably too early a date for Landor's Italian study in London and concludes that Landor did not in fact meet Alfieri as he later claimed to have done. Giuliana Artom Treves' *Anglo-Fiorentini di cento anni fa* (1953; English trans., *The Golden Ring*, 1956) contains a lively chapter on Landor in Florence that makes some use of researches into the archives.[9]

An aspect of Landor's biography that has attracted some attention is his relation to his contemporaries in English literature. The most interesting of these special studies is Emil Erich's dissertation, *Southey und Landor* (1934). Erich's investigation takes him from an account of their personal relations into an examination of Landor's literary criticism (since Southey is an interlocutor in four of Landor's most important critical *Conversations*) and of the religious and political views of the two men, based chiefly on their correspondence. For Southey's letters he has gone to the manuscripts in the Victoria and Albert Museum. Both

---

9   Dale R. Mitchell's colossal unpublished dissertation, "A Record of British Authors in Italy during the Years 1814–1825" (Cornell Univ., 1930), contains nothing about Landor which the student will not already know.

men show up well in the light of their friendship, which is far less paradoxical than flippant commentators have inclined to make it, and Erich writes with sympathy and a common sense from which there is only an occasional lapse, as when he views Landor's Llanthony venture as a kind of practical pantisocracy, or when, more regrettably, he rejoices to find in modern fascism the fulfillment of Landor's political ideals. Less successful, because more ambitious and superficial, is Gustav F. Beckh's youthfully enthusiastic dissertation, *Walter Savage Landor und die englische Literatur von 1798–1836* (1911). After a chapter on Landor's personal relations with his literary contemporaries, he examines the use of the Roderick–Count Julian story by Byron, Scott, Southey, and Landor, then makes a hasty comparison between the Grecian *Imaginary Conversations* and other contemporary writing, with respect to style as well as political, philosophical, and aesthetic ideas. His approach in the latter chapters is critical rather than biographical or historical. My article "Landor and the 'Satanic School' " (*SP*, 1945) is a detailed account of Landor's part in the Southey-Byron controversy; my note under the heading "Landor on a Waterloo Poem" (*N&Q*, 6 Aug. 1949) discusses Landor's slight acquaintance with Tennyson, and my "A Grain of Truth about . . . Landor and Swinburne" (*MLN*, 1952) expresses the view that, in the absence of confirming evidence, the story of Landor's gift of a "Correggio" to the young Swinburne was a fiction of Edmund Gosse's; more recently Lowell Kerr has published (*TLS*, 31 July 1959, and *Manuscripts*, 1964) a letter of Swinburne's dated 27 April 1869 which does in fact allude to that gift, and so my inference stands corrected. My article "Landor's Letters to Wordsworth and Coleridge" has already been described.

IV. HISTORICAL AND CRITICAL STUDIES

STUDIES OF INDIVIDUAL WORKS AND GROUPS OF WORKS

1. Pierre Vitoux's *L'Œuvre de Walter Savage Landor* (1964), a very long study of Landor's literary works, is a joy to read. In dealing with Landor's poetry, Vitoux finds that a generally chrono-

logical arrangement provides a satisfactory organization; he discusses the prose writings topically. He is well informed in the classics and has done a good deal of research into Landor's literary background, so that everything he touches he illuminates. When he deals with the prose, he is able to give form and structure to Landor's ideas; he is nearly the first critic to have done so. He has a higher regard for the prose than the poetry, and devotes a mere eight pages to the epigrams, which many modern writers regard as Landor's greatest accomplishment: but the epigrams are easier to enjoy than to discuss and his restraint here is probably the right choice. He writes with a delightful urbanity. G. Rostrevor Hamilton's *Walter Savage Landor* (1960) is an agreeable brief introduction to the man and his work, marred by inaccuracies in matters of fact.

Two earlier critical surveys of the whole of Landor's work have little to offer to students. Edward W. Evans' university prize essay, *Walter Savage Landor, a Critical Study* (1892), is pleasantly written to bring out Landor's quality as primarily a "literary" man, a stylist with a high ideal of authorship and aesthetics, whose bent was toward a practical epicureanism and who had no insight into speculative or transcendental matters. Helene Richter's "Walter Savage Landor" (*Anglia*, 1926 and 1927) is a laborious and wearisome analysis of Landor's writings, one after another.

By no means has all modern criticism of Landor been favorable. Elwin's vigorous championship of his hero merely drew from F. R. Leavis the comment: "In a world where there is more literature worth attention than anyone can hope to find time for, it seems worse than pointless to keep up the pretence that Landor is, or should be, current classic, yielding to the elect an elevated delight" ("Landor and the Seasoned Epicure," *Scrutiny*, 1942). Donald Davie, after a close study of Landor's diction and poetic structure ("The Shorter Poems of Walter Savage Landor," *Essays in Criticism*, 1951, and "Landor as Poet," *Shenandoah*, 1953; the former reprinted in Davie's *Purity of Diction in English Verse*, 1952), finds in Landor a "bewildering insecurity of *tone*" and a childish simplicity in the much-admired pastorals. Much of the fault lies with Landor's stubborn refusal to acknowledge the temper of his age in writing a kind of poetry that requires greater awareness of tradition than his audience could have. Davie's essays are thoughtful and stimulating, but clearly with a poet as prolific as Landor, it makes some difference where one looks. My centenary essay, "The Fire of Life" (*Cambridge Rev.*, 16 Jan. 1965), suggests some directions in which Landor may be revalued and points out the fallacy of the proposition that the life of the man was singularly divorced from his writings.

2. Landor's earliest poems, and especially *Gebir*, have attracted greater attention from scholars than any other part of his writing. Since Wheeler's edition has made available many poems that formerly were nearly inaccessible, most of the earlier studies have lost some of their usefulness.

In his preface to *Gebir*, Landor acknowledged debt to "The History of Charoba" appended to Clara Reeve's *Progress of Romance* (1785); scholars have traced the story much further back. Robert Schlaak, *Entstehungs- u. Textgeschichte von Landors "Gebir"* (1909) compares Reeve's "History" with the story of Charoba and Gebir in Pierre Vattier's *L'Egypte de Murtadi* (1666). Stanley T. Willams, in "The Sources of Landor's *Gebir*" (*MLN*, 1921) and "The Story of Gebir" (*PMLA*, 1921), attempts to determine whether Clara Reeve used Vattier's book in French or in its English translation by John Davies of Kidwelly (1672). After comparison of her version with the latter, he asserts that "it is evident that Miss Reeve depended in no way upon Davies' translation." He appears to have reached his conclusion without examining Vattier, for Davies' is a very close translation and Williams' arguments would be equally valid against her use of the French. The matter is doubtful, but Davies was probably her source. Stephen Wheeler, in "Landor's Gebir" (*Bookman* [London], 1924), identifies the figure of Gebir in Arabic legend. F. M. Mahmoud, "The Arabian Original of Landor's *Gebir* (1798)" (*Cai SE*, 1960), merely summarizes the versions of Vattier and Davies. Like Williams in *PMLA*, Martha Pike Conant in *The Oriental Tale in England in the Eighteenth Century* (1908) compares Landor's treatment of the Gebir story with Clara Reeve's, but students now can easily make the comparison for themselves, since Reeve's *Progress of Romance* has been reprinted by the Facsimile Text Society (1930).

Schlaak's analysis of *Gebir* is competent and useful; William Bradley's *Early Poems of Walter Savage Landor* (1914) is even more valuable in putting *Gebir* into the context of Landor's other early writings. He, like Schlaak, rightly believes that the fragmentary "Phocaeans," though published later, was composed before *Gebir*, and he points out the moral influence of Landor's love for Nancy Jones and the literary influence of his study of Milton on Landor's poetic growth. He does not, however, pretend that *Gebir* is in any sense "Miltonic"; R. D. Havens in *The Influence of Milton on English Poetry* (1922) finds that "As Southey's blank verse ought not to be Miltonic but is, so Landor's ought to be but is not. . . . What may at first seem to be Miltonic in *Gebir* will usually prove to be classic" (and classic of the Hellenistic period). Bradley's monograph is useful also for its explication of the knotty "Phocaeans." My unpublished Oxford dissertation, "The English Poetry of Walter Savage Landor before 1812" (1937), is a more detailed analysis of Landor's sources and a study of the composition and the reception of Landor's early works; I demonstrate among other things that the customary statement that these were ignored by reviewers is quite erroneous.

I. A. Richards used fifteen lines from *Gebir* (III, 4–18) in an experiment concerned with the problem of poetic communication (*Criterion*, 1933). After studying analyses of the passage by a large number of British and American students of English literature, none of whom recognized the author, he concludes that "judgment seemingly about a poem is chiefly about its reader," though he insists that there *are* tests of the correctness of an interpretation, which are "its internal coherence and its coherence with all else [history, literary tradition, etc.] that is relevant." Neither his own "paraphrase exposition" of the lines, nor that offered by Charles Mauron in the same journal three months later, meets either of these tests satisfactorily: both treat the lines out of context, unaware that they introduce a visit to the underworld, and both miss the topographical significance of "Avon," in that Landor, like Shakespeare, was born on its banks. Richards' article has been reprinted in his *Speculative Instruments* (1955).

Lawrence S. Wright's "Eighteenth-Century Replies to Pope's Eloisa" (*SP*, 1934) is a very interesting bibliographical and critical study that throws significant light on one of the poems in Landor's first published volume.

The well-known epigram on Rose Aylmer is the subject of two short notes, an explication by me (*Expl*, 1945) and a suggestion by V. Scholderer that the poem contains significant echoes of some sentimental stanzas which had recently been published beneath the frontispiece of a book of songs (*TLS*, 16 March 1922). With respect to the sources of the poem, George Saintsbury remarked in his *History of English Prosody* that the epigram was "almost a mosaic, not merely of thought, but of solid phrase taken from this and that poet, even such an unlikely one as Beattie."

3.   Charles M. Hudson, Jr., in an unpublished dissertation, "The Roderick Legend in English Romantic Literature: Scott, Landor, and Southey" (Yale Univ., 1943), has presented a workmanlike and interesting account of the old Spanish legend which caught the attention of three English poets at the time of the Peninsular War:

he investigates the sources of the story and discusses its treatment by the three (Landor's of course is his drama, *Count Julian*). An earlier dissertation on the same subject, Erich Schwichtenberg's *Southeys "Roderick, the Last of the Goths" und Landors "Count Julian," mit einer Darstellung des Verhältnisses beider Dichter zu einander* (1906) is superficial and of no scholarly value.

4. Despite the general belief that the *Imaginary Conversations* are the heart of Landor's literary production, they have been in themselves the subject of remarkably little scholarly attention, though many a critical essay has been written about them. Hermann M. Flasdieck, in a forty-page article, "Walter Savage Landor und seine 'Imaginary Conversations'" (*Englische Studien*, 1924), surveys with lively intelligence some of the problems presented by the *Conversations;* no student of Landor can afford to overlook this essay. He bases himself firmly (and correctly) on the view that the *Conversations* are neither historic nor (for the most part) dramatic, but a species of informal essay which is dominated throughout by the personality of the author. The student will find in Flasdieck stimulating remarks on Landor's intellectual bias, his Hellenism, his religion, his politics, his literary criticism, his use of the dialogue form, and his style.

Another valuable study of the *Conversations* is an unpublished dissertation by Doris E. Peterson, "Landor's Treatment of His Source Materials in the 'Imaginary Conversations Greek and Roman'" (Univ. of Minnesota, 1942). Though distressingly wordy and repetitious, hers is precisely the sort of close study of a limited subject from which Landor scholarship can profit most. From an analysis of the sources of each Conversation she moves to a discussion of their treatment, and throws valuable light on Flasdieck's central proposition that in the *Conversations* the personality of Landor is more significant than the reconstruction of history. She greatly prefers the dramatic *Conversations* (and chief among them "Tiberius and Vipsania"), in which Landor's strength, tenderness, and power of intense realization are most strikingly called forth, and she becomes plainly annoyed with some aspects of Landor's writing, such as his treatment of women. As she remarks about one of the discursive dialogues ("Lucian and Timotheus"), two features of Landor's method emerge from a study of his source materials: first, the way in which, building upon the known opinions of a historical speaker, he engrafts upon them his own view and by shifts in emphasis and subtle changes in tone completely alters the effect of the original; and second, the refining and softening process that all his sympathetically presented characters undergo. Only one small part of Miss Peterson's dissertation has seen print, "A Note on a Probable Source of Landor's *Metellus and Marius*" (*SP*, 1942), in which she points out an interesting parallel between certain details in the Conversation and in a little-known drama by Cervantes, *Numantia,* first published in 1784. Her suggestion that Landor knew the play from seeing it presented in Spain in 1808 encounters a stumbling block in Landor's hopelessly inadequate knowledge of Spanish, but is not central to her argument. J. W. Warren, "Walter Savage Landor's Views of English Life and Literature," a University of Tennessee dissertation (1961) that calls itself "a critical study of his English *Imaginary Conversations*" (i.e., those so classified in the Welby edition, Vols. IV–VI), is little more than a summary of what Landor says.

Elizabeth Merrill's dissertation, *The Dialogue in English Literature* (1911), devotes eight pages to some critical remarks on the *Imaginary Conversations* (in her opinion, Landor lacked deep artistic sincerity and sustained power of thought; "he never conquered and mastered life itself, and therefore could not master it in literature"), but does nothing to show how Landor's use of the dialogue form compares with that of other writers. Guy Bayley Dolson, in a note, "Southey and Landor and the 'Consolation of Philosophy' of Boethius" (*American Jour. of Philology,* 1922), asserts what has long been well known, that Landor was moved to write the *Imaginary Conversations* by the news that Southey was writing some *Colloquies* on the model of Boethius; there is no attempt to consider the claims of either Boethius or Plato as Landor's model, and the problem is left just where it was. Valéry Larbaud, "Identification d'un personnage des Conversations Imaginaires" (*Revue germanique,* 1913), identifies "Salomon the Florentine Jew" who converses with Alfieri as a poet of the late eighteenth and early nineteenth century known as Salomone Fiorentino. A modest article by A. C. Keys, "Landor's Marginalia to the *Dictionnaire Philosophique* [of Voltaire]" (*AUMLA,* 1956), gives a glimpse into Landor's workshop as he jotted opinions of French literature that found their way into the Conversation between "The Abbé Delille and Walter Landor."

5. The *Pentameron* is of course the keystone of any examination of Landor's literary relations with Italy, though other *Imaginary Conversations* and several of his dramas are also significant. Johannes Auer's University of Münster dissertation, *Walter Savage Landor in seinen Beziehungen zu den Dichtern des Trecento: Dante, Boccaccio, Petrarca* (1903), consists almost entirely of summary

and quotation of Landor's opinions of the three writers; its value comes only from an occasional bit of historical information and its few pages of evaluation of Landor's remarks. Auer finds, for example, that in his criticism of Dante Landor lacked the good will a critic must bear toward his subject, as well as the historical sense of Dante's relation to the medieval world and a sympathy for his religious conception. Far more illuminating is Elbert N. S. Thompson's two-page note, "Dante and Landor" (*MLN*, 1905), which indicates that Landor altogether failed to understand Dante's central conception of divine justice. "To Landor the *Comedy* in its entirety appeared as a vast, formless structure reared on no sound foundation. . . . The strongest indication [of his failure to appreciate the work] is that the great scenes of the poem apparently left slight impression upon him." Nevertheless, Thompson points out quite rightly that these shortcomings were characteristic of Dante criticism in Landor's time. Felice Elkin's University of Pennsylvania dissertation, *Walter Savage Landor's Studies of Italian Life and Literature* (1934), is far too ambitious in its scope: it includes Landor's opinions of Italy, her people, her art, her history, her politics, her religion, and her literature, and is for the most part a series of quotations and summaries of what Landor wrote. There are many inaccuracies and there is no real grasp of Italian matters, though students may find some useful information in the pages on the *Pentameron* (160–181). Paget Toynbee's anthology of English authors' remarks about Dante, *Dante in English Literature* (1909), contains more than thirty pages of quotations from the whole range of Landor's works, Latin as well as English. Werner P. Friederich's *Dante's Fame Abroad, 1350–1850* (1950) places Landor's judgments in their historical context. The scope of C. P. Brand's very useful *Italy and the English Romantics* (1957) does not permit any extended treatment of Landor, who is mentioned in passing from time to time.

Guido Fornelli's *W. S. Landor e l'Italia* (1930), despite its title, is a comprehensive essay on Landor's life and work; it may have served a purpose in introducing Landor to a modern Italian audience but it has no scholarly pretensions. Lilian Whiting's *The Florence of Landor* (1905) is a formless ramble through Forentine history and Tuscan landscape, richly endowed with sentimentality but not with information about Landor; it contains some interesting photographs of his Fiesolan villa, and the most hideous portrait ever made of him.[10]

---

10   Other photographs of the Villa Landor may be found in the biography of one of its later owners, H. S. White's *Willard Fiske* (1925).

6. The dramas and dramatic scenes on Italian history have not been made the subject of separate study; they are touched upon by both Auer and Elkin. Roderick Marshall's *Italy in English Literature, 1775–1815* (1934), though its period is too early for detailed consideration of Landor's work, gives something of the background of the English interest in the story of Giovanna of Naples and tells the history of Ferrante and Giulio, on whom Landor once wrote a play of which he preserved only two scenes. Eino Railo, in *The Haunted Castle* (1927), traces the character of Fra Rupert, who dominates Landor's Giovanna trilogy, to the villainous monks of Mrs. Radcliffe and M. G. Lewis, just as he finds that Landor's character of Count Julian "belongs to the family of vengeful Gothic barons." Georg Herzfeld, in an article entitled "Fouqué und Landor: Ein merkwürdiges literarisches Motiv" (*Archiv*, 1926), notes that Fouqué, in one of his "Romantic Idylls," uses the motif of a noble lady's suckling a famished soldier and probably got it from Sismondi, just as Landor got the same episode for his *Siege of Ancona*. Guido Fornelli, *L'Italia nel drama inglese dell' ottocento* (1931), gives selections from Landor's Italian dramas, with inconsequential introductory remarks.

7. The "Hellenics" have received little treatment by themselves (but see the discussion of Landor's classicism, below). Lucetta J. Teagarden, "The Myth of the Hamadryad and Its Continuity" (*Studies in English*, Department of English, University of Texas, 1945–46), devotes about a quarter of its fourteen pages to Landor; the study is superficial but illuminating in the absence of better. Horst Oppel, "W. S. Landors 'Iphigeneia' " (*NS*, 1955) is a perceptive brief analysis of Landor's fifty-eight-line poem, somewhat pretentiously embedded in a discussion that aims to prove Landor's depth and complexity, which makes him, with Keats, the most "modern" of the romantics, satisfying the rigorous criteria of both the humanist critics and the new critics. Professor Oppel must look at Davie's essays.

8. Landor's lyric poetry is the subject of a University of Paris dissertation by Augustus H. Mason, *Walter Savage Landor, poète lyrique* (1924). This work is an attempt to see the ideal man behind the paradoxes of his life and character by studying the qualities that reveal themselves in his lyric poems, on the principle that "the personality of the poet interests us much more than the subject of the poetry itself." If Mason's enthusiasm leads him to the view of many recent critics that "the lyric poetry of Landor will be the immortal branch of his work," the book nevertheless contains neither critical illumination nor fruitful

research. For the most part, despite his professions, the ideas Landor expresses in verse turn out to be Mason's real concern, the poems themselves nothing. Mary Ellen Rickey's good critical analysis of the epigram "Mild is the parting year" (*Expl*, 1954) finds as the only interpretative crux the word "spray," which she rightly understands as a spray of flowers, not the ocean spray. Laurence Perrine's article, "Landor and Immortality" (*VP*, 1964) discusses how Landor in his poetry views the immortality of the soul. Landor clearly was not much interested in the subject, and since neither the prose nor the letters are brought into evidence, the article is not very satisfying.

9. Despite Landor's own view of the importance of his Latin poetry, the longest modern study of this subject is ten pages in Leicester Bradner's *Musae Anglicanae* (1940), pages which Bradner characterizes as "merely a preliminary attack on the problem." "Until the Latin poems have been studied by scholars from various points of view no satisfactory critical essay upon them can be written," he continues. In his opinion, "Only in the field of the epigram did Landor achieve real distinction in Latin verse. . . . In the short poem of personal feeling, be it on love, old age, or death, his work challenges comparison with the best." Certainly a careful study of Landor's Latin writings would be one of the most fruitful undertakings upon which the Landor student could embark.[11]

GENERAL PROBLEMS

1. Landor's classicism has inevitably seemed like a rich subject for discussion, but it has proved by no means an easy one. Frederick E. Pierce, "The Hellenic Current in English Nineteenth Century Poetry" (*JEGP*, 1917), finds in the "Hellenics" the noblest expression of "the growing tendency toward Attic dignity freed from excess of romantic atmosphere." In an article that is much too neatly divided into chronological periods, he discovers that "before 1830 [the Greek tradition] was mainly romantic. Between 1830 and 1860 it wavers between romanticism and the more restrained and reflective classicism, the latter finally winning a temporary triumph in the work of Landor and Arnold." Landor "ignores the lofty but somewhat threadbare themes of a too well-known past, and deals in characters and stories that are new." Moreover, "unlike most of his fellow Hellenists . . . he made no compromise with the sham medievalism of the roman-

---

11 A detailed and scholarly review of Landor's *Idyllia Heroica Decem* in Valpy's *Classical Jour.* (1822, 1823, 1824) still has value.

tics." Ruth Ingersoll Goldmark's *Studies in the Influence of the Classics on English Literature* (1918) are sections of an uncompleted dissertation, published posthumously. Though her chapter on "The Influence of Greek Literature on Walter Savage Landor" makes good use of the curriculum at Rugby while Landor was a student there, it is for the most part a pastiche of quotations from Landor himself and from other writers upon Landor, with no critical orientation other than a slight sentimentality. Elizabeth Nitchie's article, "The Classicism of Walter Savage Landor" (*CJ*, 1918), attempts to reconcile the romantic and classical elements in Landor and to show how he differs from his contemporaries in his use of classical material. The scope of her article is far greater than she can profitably comprehend in so few pages; the consequence is a series of broad statements not all of which would be borne out by an attentive reading of Landor's works. She has some valuable remarks on the Latinisms of his English style and the merits of his Latin style. The pages on Landor in Miss Nitchie's *Vergil and the English Poets* (1919) discuss the limitations of Landor's criticisms of Vergil (which dwell too much on minutiae and are blind to the real significance of Vergil's poetic achievement), then point out the Vergilian influence on *Gebir* and the Latin *Gebirus*.

For Miss Nitchie, though Landor sometimes spoiled a classical dialogue by introducing allusions to the politics of his own day, his chief merit was imbuing his characters with a reality and self-sufficiency, independent of our modern world, that no other English poet has succeeded in producing. Douglas Bush, on the other hand, in *Mythology and the Romantic Tradition in English Poetry* (1937), has as a principal thesis "that mythological poetry is alive when myths are re-created, when they carry modern implications, and that mythological poetry in which myths are merely re-told is, if not dead, at least of a very inferior order." "The author of *Crysaor* had a message, the author of the *Hellenics* has none," and therefore Landor "lapsed from a major into a minor poet when he gave up the philosophic for the decorative." Landor's style is rather Hellenistic and Ovidian than Hellenic, and in his prose especially, "with some qualifications, Landor was a man of enormous and delicate literary sensibility, a unique craftsman in words, who had little or nothing to say. . . . This lack of a philosophic center, of philosophic depth, is very manifest in Landor's literary criticisms." Stephen A. Larrabee, in *English Bards and Grecian Marbles* (1943), disagrees. "The sculpture of the Greeks was not only the favorite art of Landor but it was also a major source of his inspiration. . . . Landor felt also that in the poetry of his maturity, such as the series of splendid idylls, the *Hellenics*, he had achieved a beauty akin to that of the Grecian artists." Nevertheless, "devoted as he was to the Greeks, Landor did not forget that he lived in another age. . . . Landor was a 'Greek' . . . not only because he often concerned himself with Grecian subject matter, mythology, history, and art, but also because he tried to make great art out of the thoughts, aspirations, and beliefs of Englishmen in the very same way in which he conceived the Greeks as having worked. . . . He always returned from the Ancients to his own age. . . . Like other 'romantic' writers, Landor felt that he must deal with matters of interest to his contemporaries." It will be seen that neither Bush nor Larrabee has said the last word on the problem of Landor's classicism, but the very difficulties they encounter are illuminating and their books stimulating and profitable.

Leonard B. Beach, "Hellenism and the Modern Spirit" (*Books Abroad*, 1946), bases his brief discussion principally on Landor's opinions of Aeschylus and alludes to the Landorian re-creation of the Agamemnon-Orestes story. Ann Gossman's "Landor and the 'Higher Fountains' " (*CJ*, 1955) is an excellent study of classical parallels and classical tones in Landor's writings on fame, death, and love, in his epigrams—abusive and otherwise—and in his Hellenics. David M. Robinson supplements this article with a few notes on Landor's admiration of Aeschylus, Sappho, and Pindar ("Landor's Knowledge of the Classics," *CJ*, 1955).

It must be added that Ernest de Selincourt's essay, "Classicism and Romanticism in the Poetry of Walter Savage Landor" (*Vorträge der Bibliothek Warburg 1930/31*, 1932), is scarcely concerned with the problem implied in his title (unless perhaps to deny that it has meaning), but is a most engaging appreciation that does for Landor's poetry what the essay "Landor's Prose," in the same author's *Wordsworthian and Other Studies* (1947), does for the *Imaginary Conversations*. The student will want to return again and again to these two essays for insight and refreshment.

2.   The admirers of Landor's "classicism" have always found the strong political bent of his writings difficult to tolerate and usually conceive of it as a blemish. In Landor's opinion, however, the political doctrines were the very core of his writing, and no impartial reader can fail to take them into account. As early as 1911 Beckh asserted that, from *Gebir* through the *Imaginary Conversations*, the problem of Tyranny versus Freedom directly or indirectly controlled Landor's choice of material. In his discussion of the *Conversations* in 1924, Flasdieck remarked that the

essential heart of the dialogues was political in character: even those which introduce statesmen of the past almost always have an eye to the present. Two years later Helene Richter devoted some thirteen pages (the most satisfactory part of her series of articles) to Landor's political thinking. In 1937 George J. Becker submitted a dissertation at the University of Washington, "The Political Idealism of Walter Savage Landor" (unpublished), in which he surveyed Landor's stand on political questions throughout a long life and explained the issues as they have been viewed by more modern historians. Insofar as he dealt with Landor's contributions to the periodical press, he was limited to those articles which had been reprinted; since he did not have access to the journals themselves, he did not always see the context. Nevertheless, his is a valuable pioneering study. His article, "Landor's Political Purpose" (*SP*, 1938), insists that we can understand Landor's work only when we recognize that his dominant concern from start to finish was politics. "Once we make this approach, a considerable order and coherence appear at once in a body of writing which has often been condemned as a meaningless and capricious jumble." Whether in fact a political orientation will disclose such coherence, and, still more, whether most readers will take pleasure in such a revaluation of the *Imaginary Conversations* as Becker proposes, are open to doubt, but one dares not blind himself to Landor's political beliefs, and Becker's emphasis is a necessary one.

Too often Landor is viewed by himself, as if he stood alone without reference to others of his generation. The real value of quite a different approach is seen in Harry W. Rudman's *Italian Nationalism and English Letters* (1940), in which, though Landor is by no means the central figure, the student will discover much that was previously unknown about Landor's political activities and will see how they were related to what other Englishmen were doing at the same time. On the other hand, the few pages on Landor in Edward Dowden's *The French Revolution and English Literature* (1897) appear to be derived largely from Colvin's short biography of Landor and are hardly illuminating. Carl H. Edgren's unpublished dissertation, "The Concept of the Political Leader in the Romantic Period" (Northwestern Univ., 1951), devotes eight pages (154–161) to the formative influence of Alfieri upon Landor's political thought. He quotes passages from the treatise *Della Tirannide* (1800) that might almost have been written by Landor himself.

Partly political, partly biographical is a pleasant and suggestive essay by Maurice J. Craig, "Landor and Ireland" (*Dublin Mag.*, 1943), which despite its brevity covers a great deal of ground and unobtrusively brings home the very great importance of the Irish and their country to Landor's life and thought.

3. If politics seem close to the heart of Landor's work, literary criticism occupies nearly as great a space, and perhaps has greater importance for the modern reader. The trap into which most writers on Landor as critic have heretofore fallen is that of merely culling Landor's critical remarks wherever they can find them, and then trying to put them into some sort of order. This was the failing of the discussions of the *Pentameron* mentioned above; it is even more seriously the failing of an unpublished dissertation by Helen Bigham Browne, "Walter Savage Landor as a Literary Critic" (Cornell Univ., 1939), an inconsequential compendium of Landor's remarks on literary men, arranged by nationality and date (Donne among the minor eighteenth-century writers). The most effective compilation of this sort was made more than a hundred years ago by Edward Quillinan in his "Imaginary Conversation, between Mr. Walter Savage Landor and the Editor of *Blackwood's Magazine*" (*Blackwood's*, 1843), which still provides a witty warning against taking Landor's remarks out of context. Thus far the only scholarly discussion of Landor's criticism which has any value is Stanley T. Williams' "Walter Savage Landor as a Critic of Literature" (*PMLA*, 1923), in which he remarks, "If we examine the *Conversations* minutely (which it has been my misfortune to do) we encounter everywhere brilliant epigrams on literature," but "as a critic of literature Walter Savage Landor had ideals but few principles. . . . He was not interested in the relations of things, but rather in the things themselves. . . . As a critic he never saw literature in perspective . . . but as something directly before him,—foreshortened. Thus he judged Pindar and Wordsworth each *per se;* one would think he was a contemporary of both. In all his criticisms we cannot find [a method or] a body of guiding principles. Personal ideals are the determinants." Moreover, his critical writings are weighed down with mere verbal criticism (Landor incidentally explicitly justified this practice) : "It is hardly critical analysis. It is rather the examination of a text. Whenever Landor abandons his broad, general preferences he is apt to fall into a bog of annotation." Williams' note, "Landor's Criticism in Poetry" (*MLN*, 1925), deals with Landor's poems about books and writers and may be said to have been supplanted by the subject index in Wheeler's edition of the *Poetical Works*. There is still the greatest need for a study of Landor as critic which

will be fully cognizant of the dates and circumstances of his utterances and will concern itself not merely with what he said, but with why he said it.

Much of Landor's literary criticism was based on his annotation of the books he was reading, and marginalia in his handwriting are occasionally to be discovered in volumes he once owned. Such marginalia have been the subject of several brief articles: G. E. Wall, "Stray Words from Walter Savage Landor [on Aubrey de Vere]" (*Critic* [N.Y.], 1901); S. Wheeler, "From Landor's Library" (*Spectator*, 24 March 1923), on Grote's *History*, Shelley's *Essays*, Defoe's *Works*, etc.; T. O. Mabbott, "Landor on Chatterton and Wordsworth" (*N&Q*, 9 March 1929), and P. M. Zall, "Landor's Marginalia on a Volume of Cowper's Poems [1819]" (*BNYPL*, 1960). Comments on Voltaire are described in the article by A. C. Keys mentioned above.

4. For all the willingness of critics great and small to speak of Landor's "style," that style has not been made the subject of detailed study. George Saintsbury, in his *History of English Prosody* (1910), rightly makes the point that Landor's superb epigrams "derive sometimes the greater part, and almost always something, of their admitted charm from the fingering of the measure," though he finds Landor's longer poems (in respect to their form) too much like very perfect school exercises. His study of Landor's prose is more detailed, in *A History of English Prose Rhythm* (1912). "It is quite clear," he concludes, "that [Landor] is aiming at—and, in scattered observations through various mouthpieces, defining as much as it was his nature to define—a sort of prose 'Grand Style,' which was to unite magnificence with a certain simplicity, severity with a not more than appropriate opulence." Perhaps this is also the point at which to note that Landor as spelling reformer receives some attention (along with his close friend Julius Hare), but not very seriously, in T. R. Lounsbury, *English Spelling and Spelling Reform* (1909). One of the most valuable chapters in Vitoux's book (mentioned above) is his discussion of Landor's prose style.

5. Following the trend of a number of studies of literary reputations, Karl G. Pfeiffer wrote a dissertation (unpublished), "Periodical Criticism of Walter Savage Landor by His English and American Contemporaries" (Univ. of North Carolina, 1939), in which he discussed the reception of each of Landor's books, then viewed the same material in terms of the opinions about Landor held over a period of years by each critical journal. This latter arrangement is likely to suppose too much integrity in a magazine

or review, and indeed Pfeiffer pays less attention than he might
have done to the authorship of the articles he cites (which is
frequently discoverable, even when the article is anonymous). If
most of the reviews seem worthless in themselves and perhaps no
real index of Landor's impact on his contemporaries, the fault is
not that of the author of the thesis, whose work was exceedingly
conscientious. A brief appendix to his study is to be found in the
two pages on Landor in Luise Sigmann's *Die englische Literatur von
1800–1850 im Urteil der zeitgenössischen deutschen Kritik* (1918;
Vol. LV of *AF*), where five reviews of Landor's books in the German
periodical press are cited.

.Another aspect of Landor's reputation is that discussed in the
essay "Landor and His Contemporaries" in Stanley T. Williams'
Studies in Victorian Literature (1923), a witty survey of the high
praises of Landor sung by the literary greats who knew him. "It is
difficult to state in a few words the exact character of Landor's
influence among his contemporaries," Williams concludes. "It was
exerted upon a few through his poetry, and upon many more
through his personality. Certainly its essence lay in his austere
idealism. In an age in which poets were introspective, Landor was
objective. . . . Landor never relinquished the ideal that poetry
should be restrained, intellectual, and architectonic." "Palgrave's
Marginalia on Landor's Works" has been published by R. J. Owens
(*N&Q*, June 1961).

W. B. D. Henderson's *Swinburne and Landor* (1918) takes by
no means a narrow view of its subject: it is a book about the
formative influences upon Swinburne's poetry, and is both a
sensitive and an illuminating study of his work. If the emphasis
upon Landor among these influences is perhaps too great, it hardly
exceeds what Swinburne himself repeatedly said about the debt.
Landor's work takes on a new and somewhat strange light when
viewed through the eyes of Swinburne and a Swinburnian, but it
is a welcome relief to be entirely freed of the critical clichés
about Landor, and the lover of his work will hesitate long before
he ventures to alter the proportions of this evaluation. The student
will nevertheless be wise to read S. C. Chew's review of the book
(*MLN*, 1919).

Since Browning said "that he owed more as a writer to
Landor than to any contemporary" (as Mrs. Browning reported),
Boyd Litzinger's note, "The Prior's Niece in 'Fra Lippo Lippi' "
(*N&Q*, Sept. 1961), pointing out that the suggestion for the prior's
niece comes from Landor's Imaginary Conversation, "Fra Filippo
Lippi and Pope Eugenius the Fourth," is more suggestive than its

limited scope might indicate. In fact, a good deal of Browning's skill in handling the Italian scene for literary purposes was learned from Landor.

In the earlier edition of this essay, I concluded: "The reader of this survey may have noticed how great a proportion of the research on Landor has taken the form of doctoral dissertations; he may have remarked also how seldom the author of such a dissertation is ever heard from again in the field of Landor scholarship. Though this circumstance may be due partly to a feeling among American scholars that Landor is not 'important' it is principally, no doubt, a natural consequence of the significance attached to the doctoral degree in American and German universities. Since there is every reason to suppose that Landor will continue to provide his share of thesis topics, it may not be amiss to observe that by far the most profitable dissertations have been those which made a close study of a very limited body of his work. Indeed, in view of the inadequacy of all editions of Landor's prose, one can hardly imagine a more useful undertaking than the editing, with annotation and introduction, of segments of the *Imaginary Conversations;* it is many years since W. Hale White's note, 'The Editing of a Classic' (*Athenaeum,* 22 Dec. 1900), indicated the sort of thing that is needed, and no one has yet undertaken any part of the work. Similarly, there has been no satisfactory study of the 'Hellenics.' The broader problems—Landor as literary critic, Landor's Hellenism, Landor's political views— have not yet received their final treatment; they require a breadth of knowledge which a doctoral candidate cannot be expected to have. Yet such broad studies must rest on the sort of foundation which the doctoral dissertation can well provide for them, if its scope is properly limited." Since that time, one very significant study of Landor has appeared, Vitoux' excellent book. For the rest, the picture remains much as it was.[12]

12 Perhaps in consequence of my earlier suggestion, however, two doctoral candidates are at work on the *Imaginary Conversations:* Mrs. LaVonne Prasher, at Northwestern University, is editing the first eleven of them (as they appeared in 1846), with a careful collation not only of printed texts but of surviving manuscripts as well, and with thoroughgoing explanatory annotation; and Charles Proudfit has begun an annotated edition of the first volume of the Second Series (1829) at the University of Michigan. Both have discovered that Landor depended far more on written sources than has generally been supposed.

9

Leigh Hunt

By Carolyn W. Houtchens

AND

Lawrence H. Houtchens
MIAMI UNIVERSITY

I. BIBLIOGRAPHIES

T HE MOST COMPREHENSIVE bibliography of works by and relating
to Leigh Hunt is the one appended by Louis Landré to his two-
volume *Leigh Hunt (1784–1859)* : *Contribution à l'histoire du romantisme anglais* (1935–36). In extensiveness it supersedes any other
Hunt bibliography, although it needs correction for certain omissions
and minor inaccuracies. George L. Marsh (*MP*, 1937) and William
S. Ward (*The Criticism of Poetry in British Periodicals, 1798–1820,*
Duke Univ. dissertation, 1943; microcards, Univ. of Kentucky,
1955) between them mention thirty-five periodical articles on
Hunt which are not in Landré. Additional items can also be found
in other sources. Nonetheless, Landré's bibliography is an indispensable tool for advanced research.

For a less overwhelming introduction to Hunt, one should
begin with Ernest Bernbaum's good selective and critical bibliography in the Hunt chapter of his *Guide Through the Romantic
Movement* (2d ed., 1949). The selective bibliography in G. B.
Woods's *English Poetry and Prose of the Romantic Movement*
(1950) should be avoided as an initial approach to Hunt because
it is carelessly revised from the 1916 edition and omits some
major items. The critical bibliography of the *Guide* can be
supplemented by that of Edmund C. Blunden in *The Cambridge
Bibliography of English Literature* (1941; supplement, 1957),
and Ian Jack in the *Oxford History of English Literature,* x, *1815–
1832* (1963). These are the most thorough of the recent bibliographies in the field aside from Landré's. Blunden has also a useful list
of works by and about Hunt in his biography (*Leigh Hunt and His
Circle,* 1930), as well as a good, very brief bibliography at the end
of his Hunt article in *Chambers's Encyclopaedia* (1950). This last, in
fact, is the only general encyclopedia article which makes any
pretense at an up-to-date Hunt bibliography.

Several bibliographies are available in special fields. H. S.
Milford in his *Poetical Works of Leigh Hunt* (1922) has an
excellent one of the poetry, with a few minor errors, but it is not

entirely complete; its omissions are supplied by Landré. Luther A. Brewer's *My Leigh Hunt Library: The First Editions* (1932) is a detailed description of the first editions (sometimes second and third) in his famous Hunt collection, with frequently an account of events connected with the publication and a brief comment on Hunt items not in the collection; the book also includes fifteen portraits of Hunt. Clyde C. Walton, curator of rare books at the University of Iowa Library, which contains the Brewer Collection, has made a helpful report of some rare Hunt editions in "Leigh Hunt: The Spirit of an Age" (*Amateur Book Collector*, 1952). With Brewer may be used the much shorter bibliography of Alexander Mitchell (*Bookman's Jour.*, 1927, and 1930–31), which details certain editions of Hunt; although frequent good critical appraisals are inserted, the Mitchell bibliography has more value for the collector than for the average student. In an article reproducing Hunt's marginal notes on a work by Sismondi, W. J. Burke includes a long checklist of books annotated by Hunt and located in the United States ("Leigh Hunt's Marginalia," *BNYPL*, 1933).

Among the older bibliographies, Alexander Ireland's *List of the Writings of William Hazlitt and Leigh Hunt* (1868), although not always reliable for bibliographical details, has an interesting compilation of the judgments of Hunt's contemporaries in a section entitled "Opinions of Leigh Hunt's Character, Genius, and Writing." The favorable tone of these "Opinions" evoked a bitter tirade from John Stores Smith, former partner in *Leigh Hunt's Journal*, and an unpublished defense by Thornton Hunt (G. D. Stout, "A Posthumous Attack on and Defense of Leigh Hunt," *TLS*, 30 Aug. 1923).

Even the best of the Hunt bibliographies, however, needs to be brought up to date. For more recent publications one should consult the annual bibliographies published by the Modern Humanities Research Association and especially those in the *Philological Quarterly* (preceded by *ELH*, 1937–50), *Modern Philology*, and the *Keats-Shelley Journal*, beginning in 1952.

II. EDITIONS

A DECIDED inconvenience in working with Leigh Hunt is the absence of a well-developed, scholarly edition of his letters and publications. A complete edition, requiring fifty or sixty volumes, would no doubt be too expensive to be feasible; nor is it really desirable, for much of Hunt's journalistic writing was done under pressure, and certainly not all of it merits republication. Aside from the unauthorized four-volume set published in the United States in 1856, the only approach to a full edition of Hunt is the seven-volume one without introduction or editorial notes, issued by Smith, Elder and Company (1870–72) and containing the *Table-Talk, A Jar of Honey, Men, Women and Books, Wit and Humour, The Town, Imagination and Fancy,* and the *Autobiography.* Research on Hunt involves gathering individual volumes and trying to locate copies of the newspapers and magazines to which he contributed, many of them difficult of access.

Fortunately most of the poems have been united in an excellent edition. Prior to 1922, the best that one had to work with was the selected edition prepared by Hunt just before his death and edited in 1860 by his son; this was a very imperfect representation. Late in 1922, H. S. Milford published his carefully edited, almost complete collection of Hunt's poetry (postdated 1923), the only regrettable omission being the *Amyntas.*

Several useful volumes of the essays are available. Edmund Ollier's selections from the *Indicator—A Tale for a Chimney Corner, and Other Essays* (1869) —includes a good introduction. *A Day by the Fire; and Other Papers, Hitherto Uncollected* (1870), with a prefatory note by J. E. B[abson], derives from half a dozen of the journals. Also prefaced by Babson is a series from the *Examiner—*Hunt's *Wishing-Cap Papers* (1873). One of the best collections, drawn primarily from the *Indicator, Companion,* and *Seer,* is the annotated edition of Arthur Symons, whose introduction contains some excellent criticism (*The Essays of Leigh Hunt,* 1887; enlarged, 1903). Charles Kent's selection, taken from a wide range of sources, is more representative of Hunt as an essayist, although the biographical introduction is not very discriminating in its critical remarks (*Leigh Hunt as Poet and Essayist,* 1889). Other helpful

259

collections are two by R. Brimley Johnson (1891 and 1906) and those of J. H. Lobban (1909), Edward Storer (1911), and Hannaford Bennett (1924). The Everyman edition (1929, reprinted 1947) is one of the best in the sense that it includes a broad selection with a good, short appraisal by J. B. Priestley and is readily obtainable; like most of the preceding collections, unfortunately, it is not annotated. Recently we have edited an extended volume of previously unreprinted essays by Hunt, predominantly literary criticism, with notes and with an introductory essay in evaluation by Clarence D. Thorpe (*Leigh Hunt's Literary Criticism*, 1956).

For many years Hunt's theatrical criticism was known almost entirely by means of extracts from the *Critical Essays* . . . and the *Tatler*, edited by William Archer and R. W. Lowe, with notes and an often-quoted introduction (*Dramatic Essays. Leigh Hunt*, 1894). In 1949, this was supplemented by *Leigh Hunt's Dramatic Criticism, 1808–1831*, an annotated edition of uncollected reviews from the *Examiner* and *Tatler*, with the essay on masks (ed. L. H. and C. W. Houtchens).

A few editors have been attracted to Hunt's journals. *Lord Byron, Leigh Hunt and the "Liberal"* (ed. Leslie P. Pickering, 1925) begins with a brief history of the collaboration and then reproduces "such poems and essays as are necessary to give the reader an idea of its style." R. B. Johnson's title *Prefaces by Leigh Hunt Mainly to His Periodicals* (1927) is misleading, as the book includes more than Hunt's preliminary addresses to his readers; the introduction is a sound statement of Hunt's contribution to journalism. *Shelley—Leigh Hunt: How Friendship Made History* (1928, enlarged 1929), also edited by Johnson, assembles from the *Examiner* Hunt's reviews of, and selections from, the poems of Shelley, the 1832 preface to the *Masque of Anarchy*, a long series of Political Examiners, and some correspondence; Johnson's introduction and interwoven commentary and notes succeed in clarifying the sympathy of emotion and thought found in the two writers. The first half of Edmund Blunden's *Leigh Hunt's "Examiner" Examined* (1928) sketches in lively fashion the history of the paper for the years when Hunt was associated with it, but the thirteen articles of his that follow are almost wholly literary in character. *Leigh Hunt's Political and Occasional Essays* (ed. L. H. and C. W. Houtchens, 1962, with an introduction by Carl R. Woodring) is an annotated volume of uncollected articles, many of which appeared in the *Examiner* and the rest in other periodicals. One small pamphlet merits notice: *Leigh Hunt's "Rules for*

Newspaper Editors" (1930), taken from the *Examiner* with a short introduction by R. H. B[ath], is a good example of the author's irony.

Among the noteworthy editions of individual works by Hunt are those of the *Autobiography*, considered by some as the author's most secure claim to an enduring reputation. Roger Ingpen's two-volume set (1903) has been surpassed in its notes by Morpurgo's scholarly edition; however, it is helpful for the inclusion of Thornton Hunt's introduction, the "Testimonia" of famous contemporaries, "An Attempt of the Author to Estimate His Own Character," and miscellaneous information in the appendices. Edmund Blunden's edition (1928), unannotated, is now useful primarily for its index, its reprint of Thornton's introduction, and its short commentary detailing Hunt's surprising omissions. J. E. Morpurgo (1948) furnishes an excellent critical apparatus for the *Autobiography;* his careful notes, table of sources, and evaluation of Hunt—not as a man of letters but as a journalist with few rivals—make this edition the most desirable.

An Answer to the Question "What Is Poetry?" annotated by Albert S. Cook (1893), has long been a standard text; although there is no introductory essay, Cook has appended the chief passages from Jean Paul Richter, Coleridge, and Wordsworth which establish the derivation of Hunt's conception of imagination and fancy. Two books on the streets of London, each with brief notes and an appreciative introduction, have been edited by Austin Dobson—*The Old Court Suburb* (1902) and *The Town* (1907), the former with delightful illustrations. *Imagination and Fancy* (1907) should be mentioned for its fine preliminary essay by Edmund Gosse. *Leigh Hunt's "The Months"* (1929), edited by R. H. B[ath] with a preface by R. B. Johnson, is a valuable reprint of a small volume reissued only once (1897) since 1821, and previously difficult to acquire in any form. The best that can be said of *Men, Women and Books* (ed. L. Stanley Jast, 1943) in the Live Books Resurrected series is that it makes available a volume not formerly easy to obtain. David R. Cheney has published with a good introduction (1964) Hunt's unfinished manuscript of the first of his *Musical Evenings*.

The most annoying gap in Hunt publications is a scholarly edition of his letters. The two volumes of correspondence (1862) which his son Thornton tried to adapt to a narrative of Hunt's life leave much to be desired. Hundreds of letters are omitted, partly because they could not be located or gave a less favorable impression of Hunt. There are none, for instance, to Keats, Byron,

Lamb, Hazlitt, Carlyle, and Dickens. Often the letters are incomplete; John Forster advised, incidentally, that those to Bessey Kent be partially suppressed. Not all were accurately copied. Browning, angry at the inclusion—without permission—of a letter from him and his wife, asserted that "the whole [letter is] improved by such a series of blunders in the copying . . . that the result is unintelligible beyond even *my* unintelligibility."

The contributions of Luther A. Brewer materially rectified the situation. His slender annual books as a rule included some Hunt correspondence—for example, *Around the Library Table* (1920), *Leigh Hunt's Letter on Hogg's Life of Shelley with Other Papers* (1927), *Joys and Sorrows of a Book Collector* (1928), and *Some Letters from My Leigh Hunt Portfolios, with Brief Comment* (1929). The culmination was two handsome volumes entitled *My Leigh Hunt Library*. Of these, *The First Editions* (1932) reprinted, according to the introduction, all the letters of Hunt at that time in Brewer's possession. The second, *The Holograph Letters* (1938), was devoted exclusively to correspondence, with explanatory comment; unfortunately more letters were reserved for a third volume, left in galleys at the time of Brewer's death, but never published. A collected edition of Hunt's letters would need to reprint those published by Brewer, rearranging them chronologically with scholarly annotation. The entire Brewer Hunt Collection of 3,570 pieces, including 1,578 manuscript letters, is at the University of Iowa; the library filing cards for the collection, available in many union card catalogues, partially indicate the content of the letters.

Aside from the preceding, Hunt's letters are scattered through a considerable range of publications. Books and articles by and about his extensive circle of acquaintance frequently contain one or two pieces of correspondence, and to list every source would be space-consuming. S. R. Townshend Mayer, who acquired many letters from Thornton Hunt, reproduced a number (from and to Hunt) in a series of articles: "Leigh Hunt and B. R. Haydon," "Leigh Hunt and Dr. Southwood Smith," "Leigh Hunt and Charles Ollier" (*St. James's Mag. and United Empire Rev.*, 1874–75), and "Leigh Hunt and Lord Brougham with Original Letters" (*Temple Bar*, 1876). *Recollections of Writers* (1878), by Charles and Mary Cowden Clarke, has a lengthy chapter on "Leigh Hunt and His Letters"; others are quoted in the latter's articles on Hunt in the *Century Magazine* (1882).

Hunt's correspondence with Byron and Carlyle, omitted from the 1862 edition, appears in the following: *The Works of Lord*

Byron: Letters and Journals (ed. R. E. Prothero, 1898) ; Payson Gates, "A Leigh Hunt–Byron Letter" (*KSJ*, 1953) ; and Charles Richard Sanders' "The Correspondence and Friendship of Thomas Carlyle and Leigh Hunt" (*BJRL*, 1963). It may be helpful to add that many letters *to* Hunt, not in the 1862 edition, are included in *The Complete Works of Percy Bysshe Shelley* (ed. R. Ingpen and W. E. Peck, 1927 ff.), *The Letters of Mary W. Shelley* (ed. F. L. Jones, 1946), and *The Letters of Charles Dickens* (Nonesuch edition, ed. W. Dexter, 1938).

A number of other publications may be cited: "Six Letters of Leigh Hunt Addressed to W. W. Story, 1850–1856," *Bulletin and Review of the Keats-Shelley Memorial, Rome* (1913) ; Thomas J. Wise's catalogue of *The Ashley Library* (1922 ff.) ; *Letters to Leigh Hunt from His Son Vincent with Some Replies* (ed. A. N. L. Munby, 1934) ; *The Athenians* (ed. W. S. Scott, 1943) ; *The Keats Circle: Letters and Papers, 1816–1878* (ed. H. E. Rollins, 1948) ; David E. Kaser, "Two New Leigh Hunt Letters" (*N&Q*, March 1955) ; and *Shelley and His Circle, 1773–1822* (ed. K. N. Cameron, 1961). David Bonnell Green has a succession of articles involving Hunt letters: "The First Publication of Leigh Hunt's 'Love Letters Made of Flowers' " (*PBSA*, 1958) ; "Some New Leigh Hunt Letters" (*N&Q*, Aug. 1958) ; "The Publication of Leigh Hunt's *Imagination and Fancy*" (*SB*, 1959) ; and "Leigh Hunt's Hand in Samuel Carter Hall's *Book of Gems*" (*KSJ*, 1959). William H. Marshall has reprinted several from the Pierpont Morgan Library: "Leigh Hunt on Walt Whitman: A New Letter" (*N&Q*, Sept. 1957), and "Three New Leigh Hunt Letters" (*KSJ*, 1960).

Manuscript letters of Hunt are widely disseminated, from those in the Brewer Collection at Iowa, the New York Public Library, the Carl H. Pforzheimer Collection and Harvard University Library to others in the Forster Collection at the Victoria and Albert Museum, the British Museum, and the Ireland Collection at the Manchester Public Reference Library—not to name them all. The need for a well-edited, reasonably extensive edition of the correspondence is obvious.

III. BIOGRAPHIES

WHEN THE Milford edition of Hunt's poetry was published in November 1922, Edmund Gosse, reviewing it for the London *Times*, commented on the persistent effect of Dickens' caricature on subsequent interpretations of Hunt; his "faults as a writer and a man are almost proverbial," asserted Gosse, "his merits rarely mentioned" (*More Books on the Table*, 1923). A few biographical articles, published near this time, opposed the usual current of opinion. Brewer in one of his small Christmas books, *Stevenson's Perfect Virtues as Exemplified by Leigh Hunt* (1922), illustrated from Hunt's writing as well as from the opinions of his contemporaries how well Hunt had possessed the "perfect virtues" of gentleness and cheerfulness. In 1925, George Dumas Stout specifically attacked the portrait of Skimpole as an unjust representation of Hunt in a well-documented article on "Leigh Hunt's Money Troubles: Some New Light" (*Washington Univ. Stud.*); and the following year, Maurice Buxton Forman produced evidence from "Some Unfamiliar Apologists" (*London Mercury*, 1926) for a fairer delineation of Hunt than the character suggested by Skimpole.

The Milford edition brought about a revived interest in Hunt —an interest steadily encouraged in this country by Brewer, and more generally by the selections from Hunt published by Pickering, Brimley Johnson, and Blunden, as described in the preceding section. A major factor, however, in restoring Hunt to his proper place in literary history was Blunden's *Leigh Hunt, a Biography* (1930; N. Y. edition, *Leigh Hunt and His Circle*), the best biography of Hunt in English. The earlier lives written by Cosmo Monkhouse (1893) and R. Brimley Johnson (1896) had relied very largely on the *Autobiography* and *Correspondence*; although both books are interesting for their authors' critical views of Hunt's writing, they are now quite superseded as biographies. Blunden, by contrast, drew on many fresh sources of information; and unlike his two predecessors, whose work had been affected by the distorted proportioning of the *Autobiography*, Blunden produced the first well-balanced life of Hunt, with a good development of

Hunt's experiences after 1825. The American title of the book is significant, because Hunt—radical journalist, theatrical critic, and man of letters—had a gift for friendship; and, although he himself was not a writer of the first rank, in the course of almost sixty years he knew well or was at least acquainted with almost every man of letters of consequence in his day. Blunden's biography leaves the reader feeling that he too is intimately acquainted with Shelley, Keats, Hazlitt, and the rest of Hunt's circle. For the general reader, the book is delightful, with its many poetic touches. Although Blunden explains in his preface that he has "preferred not to interrupt the reader . . . with a researcher's specifications, and bristling references," the scholar finds himself annoyed by the lack of documentation and by the author's occasional inaccuracies and flights of fancy. Benjamin West, for example, is said to have married Mrs. Isaac Hunt's sister (not her aunt, as specifically stated in the *Autobiography* and elsewhere), both young women having previously been in love with Isaac. When the two families temporarily live together in London, Blunden is struck by the possible drama of the situation. Among Leigh Hunt's brothers and sisters, Blunden names "Horatio, who presumably (his name almost proves it) is the one who ran away to sea and was not heard of again." This was Isaac; Hunt had no brother Horatio. On the basis of manuscripts in American collections, Stephen F. Fogle gives by far the best account of Isaac in "Leigh Hunt's Lost Brother and the American Legacy" (*KSJ*, 1959). Blunden perpetuates the mistake of assigning Hunt a place in Hazlitt's essay "Of Persons One Would Wish to Have Seen," although P. P. Howe had already called attention to the error (*Life of William Hazlitt*, 1922), and was to do so more fully in his edition of Hazlitt. Richard D. Altick (*N&Q*, 7 Oct. 1944) carefully examines the evidence for dating the first meeting of Keats and Hunt, concludes that it cannot be established more specifically than sometime between 9 October and 1 December 1816, and describes Blunden's version of the first meeting as a "pleasant fancy, but . . . nothing more"; Hyder E. Rollins (*The Keats Circle*, 1, 4–6) sets the date at soon after 9 October. Other deficiencies of Blunden's biography have been pointed out by George L. Marsh (*MP*, 1931) and George D. Stout (*MLN*, 1932), but to dwell on the weaknesses of the book might overemphasize their importance. Blunden's vivid narrative of Hunt's life is the fullest account that we have in English and has substantially contributed to the reevaluation of Hunt as a literary figure. Yet Blunden's failure to make more than superficial use of the great Brewer Collection, as well as of other American collections, leaves us still without a definitive English biography.

For the advanced student, the most scholarly account of Hunt is Louis Landré's monumental *Leigh Hunt* (*1784–1859*): *Contribution à l'histoire du romantisme anglais* (1935–36), of which the first volume is devoted to biography and the second to Hunt's work. Unlike Blunden, Landré has studiously investigated the Brewer Collection, and drawing on that as well as on other new sources of information, he has made a painstaking, almost exhaustive study of Hunt which ought to be made accessible in translation. With a wealth of material at his command, Landré does not suppress unfavorable evidence; he has no tendency to see Hunt through rose-colored glasses as Blunden sometimes does. The result is a sympathetic, but sane and well-balanced presentation of Hunt as man and writer. In the biography, Landré has fulfilled his three expressed objectives: "retracer l'évolution psychologique de Hunt," "le replacer dans son milieu et dans son époque," and finally "indiquer la genèse de ses œuvres principales." Landré enriches his volume with the first full use of the Brewer manuscript letters, and throws new light on Hunt's personal life. He interweaves the most comprehensive account of how Hunt was received by the contemporary reviewers, as, for example, in the discussion of the "Cockney School" which, after a full coverage of the *Quarterly* and *Blackwood's*, proceeds to the lesser journals. For its careful recording of the vicissitudes and struggles of Hunt's life, his personal relationships with an astonishingly wide range of the eminent and the less distinguished writers of the first half of the nineteenth century, Landré's biography is an excellent source of reference and a landmark in Hunt scholarship.

Aside from these two biographies, numerous short articles relating to Hunt, as well as longer works—primarily concerned with Hunt's friends and acquaintances—provide information about specific phases of his life. The best concise account in English of the Cockney School as a whole is Frederick E. Pierce's "The Eddy around Leigh Hunt" (*Currents and Eddies in the English Romantic Generation*, 1918). Hunt's share in the invective is amplified in Paul Mowbray Wheeler's "The Great Quarterlies of the Early Nineteenth Century and Leigh Hunt" (*SAQ*, 1930), which also carefully judges the validity of the charges made against him as a poet. Two short but enlightening articles on the subject are G. D. Stout's "The Cockney School" (*TLS*, 7 Feb. 1929), which points out the alterations made in the second edition of *Blackwood's Magazine* for October 1817, and the first part of A. L. Strout's "Hunt, Hazlitt, and *Maga*" (*ELH*, 1937), an amusing report of "The Lighter Side of 'Cockney'-Killing." Supplementary details are found in letters quoted from the *Blackwood* Papers by A. L. Strout (*SN*, 1953–54).

Before turning to the research which illuminates Hunt in relation to certain of his friends, several other biographical articles should be mentioned. Monica C. Grobel's "Leigh Hunt and 'The Town'" (*MLR*, 1931) is a careful reconstruction of Hunt's early dealings with Charles Knight and the Society for the Diffusion of Useful Knowledge, from whose manuscript papers and letters this article has been derived. In "Leigh Hunt—American" (*Univ. of California Essays in Crit.*, 1934), Myron Brightfield predicts that when the term "American" has been conclusively defined, it will apply to Leigh Hunt, for "Hunt's system of thought was un-English." Hunt might not have appreciated this conclusion. As Lewis Leary points out, Hunt reciprocated the admiration of Bryant, Emerson, and Lowell, but he did not think highly of Americans in general. Leary's "Leigh Hunt in Philadelphia: An American Literary Incident of 1803" (*PMHB*, 1946) discloses how Philadelphia claimed Hunt for her own after the third edition of *Juvenilia* and how "Samuel Saunter" in the *Portfolio* urged the publication of an American edition, which later proved a failure; "Leigh Hunt returned little of the admiration Philadelphia offered, but never was quite able to shower on him." In "Leigh Hunt and His Pennsylvania Editor" (*PMHB*, 1957), David Kaser traces the relationship between Hunt and Samuel Adams Lee, showing that Hunt believed himself defrauded. Of more general interest is J. P. Brawner's "Leigh Hunt and His Wife Marianne" (*W. Virginia Univ. Stud.*, 1937), a well-argued objection to the severe estimates of Marianne's character in Blunden's biography and in a number of its reviews. Brawner substantially proves that mitigating circumstances show her character in a better light and that her alleged obliquities were not a demoralizing influence on her husband's career. Notably, he defends her against the charge that she was for many years a confirmed alcoholic.

Among the publications that concern Shelley, Barnette Miller's *Leigh Hunt's Relations with Byron, Shelley, and Keats* (1910) is based on out-of-date sources, and has been shown by both Walter Graham and Landré to contain numerous inaccuracies and misstatements. In "Shelley's Debt to Leigh Hunt and the *Examiner*" (*PMLA*, 1925), Graham protests that no adequate study had been made of Hunt's service to Shelley, and he traces the Shelley criticism from 1816 to 1822 to establish that no other contemporary critic approached Hunt as an apologist of Shelley's poetry. The most thorough history of the intimacy between Hunt and Shelley is interwoven in detail through Newman Ivey White's two-volume *Shelley* (1940), although White errs in describing Hunt as the probable author of a description of Shelley which was written by Julian Harcourt (*Literary and Pictorial Repository*, 1838). Kenneth N. Cameron has also pointed out (*KSJ*, 1954) that White's account of the cremation in Italy is "taken uncritically from Trelawny's *Recollections*" and is inaccurate. Since Hunt is inextricably involved in any account of Shelley's drowning and the harrowing days thereafter, and since most descriptions depend to varying degrees on Trelawny, Leslie Marchand's precise comparison of Trelawny's ten narratives of the death of Shelley should be consulted (*KSMB*, 1952). Even Hunt's version in the *Autobiography*, based partly on a Trelawny manuscript, is not wholly correct. Blunden's biography of Shelley (1946), drawing on an unusual source, introduces a long paragraph from *Sir Ralph Esher* by Hunt and applies it to Shelley as descriptive of him on Hunt's arrival in Italy, but the book as a whole is quite inferior to White on the Hunt-Shelley relationship. A short article by Henry Tyler, "Hunt and Shelley" (*TLS*, 8 Nov. 1947), clarifies the fate of Hunt's manuscript essay on Shelley, submitted in 1825 to the *Westminster Review*. More important is Sylva Norman's scholarly *Flight of the Skylark: The Development of Shelley's Reputation* (1954), which elucidates the relationship between Mary Shelley and Hunt from 1822 on, and the influence of Hunt on Shelley's posthumous reputation, especially in his contribution to the "Shelley legend" through *Lord Byron and Some of His Contemporaries* (1828).

Regarding Keats and Hunt, a number of studies are important. Hyder E. Rollins has a valuable summation of their friendship in the section preliminary to the first volume of *The Keats Circle: Letters and Papers, 1816–1878* (1948). In particular, he assigns to Hunt the authorship of the second life of Keats, written in 1828 for Gorton's *General Biographical Dictionary*—"an altogether remarkable biographical and critical sketch that forever established Keats in such works of reference." Rollins believes that in composition it probably antedated Hunt's chapter on Keats in *Lord Byron*. J. R. McGillivray's essay "On the Development of Keats' Reputation," introductory to his *Keats: A Bibliography and Reference Guide* (1949), gives an excellent analysis of the decisive influence of

Hunt on Keats's reputation, with especial attention to the attacks made on Keats as a member of the Cockney School. This account of their relationship is more inclusive than that in Blunden's *Leigh Hunt* and more unfavorable to Hunt; McGillivray theorizes that Shelley's distorted view of the violent effect of the *Quarterly Review* on Keats may be attributed to a lost letter from Hunt to Shelley, and he particularizes the reasons for dissatisfaction with the material on Keats in Hunt's *Lord Byron*. Furthermore, Robert Gittings has presented new evidence concerning Hunt. In his scholarly *John Keat: The Living Year, 21 September 1818 to 21 September 1819* (1954), he traces "the germ of much of the thought and expression" of Keats's poems "Fancy" and "Bards of Passion" to Hunt's *Literary Pocket-Book* for 1819; and he deduces an indirect influence of the same book on the "Eve of St. Agnes." The definitive biography of Keats by Walter Jackson Bate (1963) is very thorough in covering Hunt and surprisingly favorable to him. The influence of Hunt on Keats's early poetry, for example, was not a real misfortune, according to Bate, but a definite benefit. Moreover, Keats's versification is "one of the most graphic examples in literary history of a pupil's imitating not what the master actually did so much as what the master intended to do." Because of the association of Keats and Fanny Brawne, her biography by Joanna Richardson (1952) should be noted for its references to her attitude toward Hunt.

On Hunt's relationship with Byron, the most extensive source of information is Leslie Marchand's *Byron: A Biography* (1957). Marchand's account is detailed and factual in its judgment. The short analysis by Nettie S. Tillett of the collaboration on the *Liberal*, concluding with Hunt's unfortunate *Lord Byron* (" 'The Unholy Alliance of Pisa'—A Literary Episode," *SAQ*, 1929) is now superseded by William H. Marshall's scholarly history, *Byron, Shelley, Hunt and The Liberal* (1960). Iris Origo's *The Last Attachment* (1949), derived partly from Teresa Guiccioli's *Vie de Lord Byron*, her unpublished account of his life in Italy, and from their correspondence, shows Hunt in the light of a "malicious British observer," disliked—and Mrs. Hunt too—by Teresa, whose wrath at Hunt's *Lord Byron* found expression in an unpublished letter to John Murray, Jr., when she first read the book in 1858.

As to certain of his other friendships, the best single study of Hunt and Lamb is Nettie S. Tillett's "Elia and 'The Indicator' " (*SAQ*, 1934). A most thorough and scholarly account of Hazlitt's relationship with Hunt is in Herschel Baker's *William Hazlitt* (1962). Richard W. Armour's *Barry Cornwall: A Biography of*

Bryan Waller Procter (1935) furnishes more detailed information about Procter's association with Hunt than either Blunden, who is sketchy on the point, or Landré, who gives just the essentials. Of the friendship between Hunt and Barnes—the most enduring of all the latter's personal relationships—Derek Hudson in *Thomas Barnes of* THE TIMES (1943) develops an extended account and discloses proof of a revived correspondence in later years. Hunt's intimacy with the Clarkes and their circle is fully revealed by Richard D. Altick's *The Cowden Clarkes* (1948), which combines delightful reading with sound scholarship. For the Howitts, concerning whom Blunden and Landré are almost silent, and with whom Hunt was on close terms, primarily in the late 1840's, the best source of information is Carl R. Woodring's *Victorian Samplers: William and Mary Howitt* (1952). In "Skimpole Once More" (*NCF*, 1952) Stephen F. Fogle clearly integrates the material pertinent to Dickens' intentional caricature of Hunt in *Bleak House,* and gives the best summary of the incident so far, examining the interpretations of the Dickens biographers; but Fogle goes beyond such earlier discussions as Brewer's *Leigh Hunt and Charles Dickens: The Skimpole Caricature* (1930) in his well-reasoned explanation that Dickens' act was probably motivated by his offense at Hunt's *Autobiography.* With this article should be read the one by George D. Stout on "Leigh Hunt's Money Troubles: Some New Light" (above) and K. J. Fielding's "Skimpole and Leigh Hunt Again" (*N&Q,* April 1955). Edgar F. Shannon's *Tennyson and the Reviewers* (1952) identifies Hunt as the author of an extensive article on Tennyson in the *Church of England Quarterly Review* (1842) and suggests its possible influence on Tennyson's adoption of the mock-heroic treatment in *The Princess;* Shannon intimates that Tennyson's decision not to reprint "Love and Sorrow" may have been affected by Hunt's remark in an earlier review, and he corrects a misstatement that Hunt's name was one of four submitted by the prime minister to be considered for poet laureate. About the friendship of Hunt and Lewes, neither Blunden nor Landré has much to say, although Landré is the more informative. Alice R. Kaminsky's "George Henry Lewes: A Victorian Literary Critic" (New York Univ. dissertation, 1952) identifies Lewes' authorship of two articles on Hunt, notes the important influence of Hunt and his circle in encouraging Lewes' intellectual growth, summarizes his opinions of Hunt, and observes the contrasts in their theories of poetry. The scattered entries in Landré on Hunt's relationship with Macaulay are supplemented by R. C. Beatty's report of the most derogatory comments on Hunt in Macaulay's *Journal* during 1850–57 (*Lord Macaulay*, 1938).

No discussion would be complete without some attention to the way Hunt's life and character appeared to himself and his contemporaries. Of all the accounts of Hunt's life, the most vivid—and in some ways the most unsatisfying—is his *Autobiography* (1850, revised 1859), which concentrates on the first forty-one years of his life, and spends only four out of twenty-six chapters on the concluding thirty-four years when he had contact with many well-known Victorians. The explanation of Hunt's organization and of his curious omissions is primarily his habit of reprinting earlier works with some editing but a minimum of new material. In addition, Hunt may have preferred the years which in his old age he himself liked best to recall, the years before the death of Shelley; indeed, "Memoirs" might have been a more exact title. With some of his journalistic writings, Hunt incorporates into his *Autobiography* much of *Lord Byron and Some of His Contemporaries* (1828), the animosity toward Byron now charitably tempered. The extent to which the earlier book is used verbatim is shown in the parallel tables in Morpurgo's edition. Shelley emerges as a kind of central hero, just as Byron emerged as the chief villain in the earlier work. Hunt is annoyingly indifferent to dates, documentation, and general orderliness, directing his autobiography, as Blunden points out, "in a kind of a lyrical bliss." The introduction which Thornton Hunt wrote for the revised edition of the *Autobiography* partially explains some of his father's omissions: burdened with extreme conscientiousness, Leigh Hunt constantly questioned his right here to discuss other people, and as a result introduced them into his *Autobiography* in inverse proportion to his intimacy with them; "those with whom he held intercourse chiefly in literary matters or in society," explains Thornton, are freely mentioned, but "those whose intercourse powerfully affected his own life" are treated sparingly. (This might apologize for the slighting of John Forster, but it does not harmonize with the focusing on Shelley.) There is, for example, almost nothing about Hunt's marriage or about his sister-in-law Bessy Kent, his letters to whom arouse speculation; his financial difficulties are not well explained, and his dispute with his brother John over the proprietorship of the *Examiner* in 1825 is barely alluded to; more disappointingly, there is nothing about his personal contacts with his neighbors the Carlyles, although Carlyle's character and writing are estimated; and

Macaulay, Tennyson, and the Brownings are omitted. Thornton Hunt observes in the same introduction that the *Autobiography* is "less a relation of the events which happened to the writer, than of their impression on himself, and the feelings which they excited, or the ideas which they prompted." Within the foregoing limitations, the *Autobiography* is a revealing self-portrait, valuable as well for its picture of Hunt's friends as for the light it throws on life in his day.

Stephen F. Fogle has published significant new material in *Leigh Hunt's Autobiography: The Earliest Sketches* (Univ. of Florida Monographs, 1959). In an introduction to the manuscript pages which Hunt apparently discarded from *Lord Byron and Some of His Contemporaries*, Fogle theorizes that the proportioning and emphasis of the *Autobiography* resulted from Hunt's being under pressure to fulfill a contract, and from his hopeful attempt to show himself qualified for the poet laureateship. Hunt's efforts to gain the laureateship are fully described by Fogle in an earlier article (*SP*, 1958).

Thornton Hunt has left us two sympathetic portraits of his father which should be read in combination. "A Man of Letters of the Last Generation" (*Cornhill Mag.*, 1860) sketches the events of Leigh Hunt's life and evaluates his writing; Hunt viewed reality through the medium of books, his son concludes, and "failed in practical life, because he was not guided in it by literature." The other more important portrait, in the introduction to the revised *Autobiography* published the preceding year, analyzes the character of Leigh Hunt, objecting to his self-description in a suppressed fragment which had been intended to appear in *Lord Byron*. "An Attempt of the Author to Estimate His Own Character" (later published by J. D. Campbell, *Athenaeum*, 25 March 1893) had depreciated the writer's physical courage, attributed to him something of the doubting vacillation of Hamlet, and deplored the difficulties of earning a living; "I think also," Hunt had added, "that the world would have been losers in a very large way . . . . if certain men of a lively and improvident genius—humanists, of the most persuasive order, had not sometimes left themselves under the necessity of being assisted in a smaller way." Thornton Hunt responds that his father's notion of personal timidity was a hallucination—with examples to prove it; that his so-called "improvidence" was due to disappointment in his professional work, an inability to understand figures, and a readiness to self-sacrifice; and that his lack of final confidence in his own judgments derived from a mastering trait of ultraconscientiousness. He was a "Hamlet buckling himself to hard work," a man who "never swerved from what he believed to be the truth." To know Leigh Hunt as he was, was to love him. Thornton's conclusion outlines the points frequently stressed in Hunt criticism: "To promote the happiness of his kind, to minister to the more educated appreciation of order and beauty, to open more widely the door of the library, and more widely the window of the library looking out upon nature,—these were the purposes that guided his studies and animated his labour to the very last."

To these articles of Thornton Hunt's may be added his brief biographical links in the *Correspondence*, which he edited in 1862, and also the passage from his unpublished *Proserpina*, in which he describes his father and some of his circle. The latter is appended, with indentifications, to Blunden's *Leigh Hunt*. The need for a fuller account of Thornton Hunt, incidentally, has been supplied by Blunden's essay, "Leigh Hunt's Eldest Son" (*EDH*, 1942).

Although not in any sense biographies, the brief accounts of Hunt's daily life and the judgments of Hunt's character which have come down to us from his famous contemporaries are a vital part of his biographical materials. The tribute to him in Shelley's letter to Maria Gisborne (1820) and in the dedication of *The Cenci*, Lamb's letter to Southey in the *London Magazine* (1823) describing Hunt as a matchless fireside companion, Hazlitt's impressions of Hunt as a conversationalist ("On the Conversation of Authors" and "On People with One Idea") and his fine characterization of him in the *Spirit of the Age*, Carlyle's graphic picture of Hunt's household in 1834, Hawthorne's account of his visit to the aging Hunt, Dickens' celebrated denial of an intentional caricature in Skimpole with his expression of regard and Macaulay's rejoinder in his *Journal*, Mary Cowden Clarke's warm remembrances in her article on Hunt in the *Century Magazine* (1882)—these and many more are reported in Landré. Haydon's *Diary*, recently edited by Willard B. Pope (1960–63), contains many passages about Hunt, including information not in Landré.

One of the best of the nineteenth-century biographical sketches—best in the sense that it is well written and does not depend almost exclusively on the *Autobiography*—is Edmund Ollier's introduction to his edition of *A Tale for a Chimney Corner, and Other Essays* (1869). Ollier does of course make use of the *Autobiography*, but he draws also on his personal intimacy with Hunt, whom he had known as long as he could remember knowing anyone, and he ranks the evenings spent in Hunt's companionship as among his most cherished recollections. The emphasis of the introduction is on criticism, but in outlining the events of Hunt's life Ollier protests against the "species of cant" about Hunt's "gentleness" in which some writers indulged, delineates his character without sentimental adulation, and includes personal memories of his appearance, home, and conversation.

Charles Kent's long biographical introduction to his edition, *Leigh Hunt as Poet and Essayist* (1889), is primarily a good digest of the *Autobiography*, interspersed with what is sometimes undiscriminating praise of Hunt's virtues as a writer. The chief value of this sketch is in the section after 1846, where Kent draws on his personal reminiscences of Hunt in his last years.

Alexander Ireland's article on Hunt in the *Dictionary of National Biography* (1891) is a factual account primarily of Hunt's publications; but like the biographies of Monkhouse and Brimley Johnson it has many omissions, now supplied by more recent scholarship, and cannot be recommended highly as a source of biographical information.

Louis Landré's appraisal of Hunt's character one hundred years after his death is a well-balanced evaluation of Hunt's weaknesses and strengths of personality (*KSMB*, 1959).

IV. CRITICISM

1. GENERAL STUDIES

THE ONLY GENERAL study of Hunt's work that is really comprehensive, in fact almost exhaustive in scope, is the second volume of Landré (1936, above). To the modern reader who inclines to think of Hunt primarily as an essayist, Landré's volume may seem curiously proportioned. Almost one fourth of the text is given to the poetry, whereas the chapter on essays, including the *Autobiography*, is next to the shortest in the book, even shorter than the one on Hunt's religious and political ideas. Obviously, Landré has concentrated on neglected areas in order to provide new information about Hunt.

On the apparent, and logical, assumption that a basic knowledge of Hunt's liberal and critical attitudes of mind is essential to an enlightened understanding of his plays, prose fiction, and essays, virtually the first half of the book is given to a carefully detailed history of his liberalism in religion and politics, and then, more important, to his work as a critic. Landré justifies the emphasis on Hunt's religious ideas by pointing out that all of his work is colored by his lifelong concern with the problem of religion, by his sentimental idealism. Although more has been written about Hunt's political activity, aside from G. D. Stout's fine monograph on *The Political History of Leigh Hunt's Examiner* (1949), until recently much of it has been superficial, and Landré has provided the only full analysis of Hunt's political ideas.

The section on Hunt as a critic of drama, art, and literature supersedes any other general treatment of this subject. Instead of depending primarily on the selections in Archer and Lowe as commentators have been apt to do, Landré has turned to the original files of eight newspapers and periodicals to which Hunt contributed, including the London *True Sun* (unavailable in the United States). He substantiates that Hunt has an important rank in dramatic criticism, not as a great theoretician, but as an inaugurator of a type of review that is still current and as an arbiter of the theater who, in the course of almost thirty years, judged with penetration, spontaneity, and absolute independence. The considerably briefer account of Hunt as a critic of architecture, sculpture, and especially painting and music draws likewise on a wider range of sources than is elsewhere considered. Having explained the reasons for Hunt's principal tendencies up to 1821, Landré progresses to the development of Hunt's theory of poetry, concluding that his studies were more than mere borrowings from Wordsworth, Coleridge, and Hazlitt; often the formulas of the two latter simply confirmed or clarified earlier ideas of Hunt's. Passing to the more important topic of his criticism of individual authors, Landré systematically covers what Hunt had to say about each, from Chaucer to the Victorians, from ancient classical writers to those of nineteenth-century France. This survey derives not only from readily accessible sources of information but also from the *True Sun* and marginalia in Hunt's personal copies located in scattered collections. Landré's appraisal is sympathetic but also discerning and well balanced. Hunt's aptitude for feeling the literary qualities of authors yet poorly known, Landré attributes partly to his great reading, his sense of nuance resulting from the meticulous care he gave to his first criticisms, his gift of sympathy, perhaps to the fact that he lacked profound originality and sought in others the qualities he himself wished to possess. In his type of explanatory criticism, according to Landré, Hunt deserves a high rank for his judgment of English writers. The long section on Italian literature clarifies how Hunt's criticism for almost fifty years helped to propagate British interest in Petrarch, Ariosto, and others, his originality lying in the fact that he addressed the general public of the reviews which was only beginning to be interested in foreign literature.

Evaluating the poetry as estimable among that of the second-rate writers, Landré shows that Hunt, a demi-Romantic among the second-generation romantic poets and later a demi-Victorian, illustrates the transition from one period to another better than do the great geniuses. Landré takes issue with Hunt's opinion of his *Juvenilia* as "all but absolutely worthless"; observes how Hunt rejected the contemporary tendency to make Italian translations more elegant than faithful, and affirms that the short personal poems reveal not the temperament of a true lyric poet, but a sincere, essentially good and affectionate soul singing the joys of his everyday life with vivacity, picturesqueness, and grace. Landré praises certain features of the *Rimini*, but his detailed analysis is mostly unfavorable. This chapter gives the whole picture of Hunt's many years as a poet instead of concentrating on *Rimini* and the handful of short poems usually reprinted in modern anthologies. The evolution of Hunt's style and versification is clearly traced.

The discussion of Hunt's plays and his novel is short. After considering all of Hunt's attempts at drama, whether in printed or manuscript form, Landré defines him as not truly a man of the theater. *Sir Ralph Esher*, summarized in great detail and its sources described, is shown to suffer from a loose style and to be influenced by being written at the same time as *Christianism*; its chief interest lies in its evocation of a long, moving period of English history.

Hunt, the essayist, is presented under three major topics: imagination and fancy, his painting of the exterior world (nature, English customs, portraits and short tales, quarters of London), and the "moi" in his essays (covering sentiments and personal preoccupations, and autobiographical writing). This cross section of ideas is more revealing, less cumbersome and repetitious than a straight chronological account of his works would have been, although chronology is maintained wherever possible. Landré's method facilitates a detailed analysis of many more selections than are discussed in comparable studies of Hunt's essays. The absence of a definition of terms, however, makes one question why *One Hundred Romances of Real Life* as well as numerous short tales such as "Jack Abbott's Breakfast," "Ver-Vert," and "The Bull-Fight" are in this chapter. They belong with *Sir Ralph Esher*, perhaps in a section on narrative technique. The *Autobiography* is included, plausibly, on the strength that much of it derives from *Lord Byron and Some of His Contemporaries*, in itself a collection of essays, and represents the culmination of Hunt's writing about himself. The value of the chapter lies not so much in the newness of its general conclusions as in its comprehensiveness.

More recently, Landré has published a good concise commentary on Hunt's contribution to English romanticism (*KSJ*, 1959).

Of the short general studies, the outstanding one limited to critical appraisal is by Clarence D. Thorpe: "Leigh Hunt as Man of Letters: An Essay in Evaluation," written for *Leigh Hunt's Literary Criticism* (ed. L. H. and C. W. Houtchens, 1956). After considering Hunt's literary reputation in the past and noting its present insecurity, Thorpe examines the position of Hunt as a poet and literary man in general. He tentatively suggests that when and if Hunt's works outside the field of original poetry are read as they deserve to be, and their value is recognized, it is possible that Hunt as critic, journalist, translator, anthologist, and educator in literature "will be seen as one of the half-dozen greater literary men of his time." The long, solidly developed analysis that follows is offered as only a "partial justification" of the idea, but succeeds in becoming a convincing argument. Thorpe makes a close, retrospective analysis of Hunt's literary principles. In the past, critics who wished to praise him have followed the example of Amy Lowell in pointing out that he knew instinctively what was good in literature, that he possessed a remarkably authentic intuition where critical accuracy was concerned. Thorpe does not minimize any of these conclusions about Hunt's intuition, but he goes further in insisting that Hunt arrived at his judgments by the systematic application of sound principles of criticism.

Ernest Bernbaum's chapter on Hunt in his *Guide Through the Romantic Movement* (2d ed., 1949) is excellent. The purpose here is different from that of the preceding essay, and in order to give a well-rounded view of the essential facts about Hunt as a man and writer, Bernbaum necessarily includes biographical material. There is less development of criticism, but the vital points of Hunt's contribution to the romantic movement are emphasized, and the general conclusions are essentially in agreement with those of Landré. This is the most scholarly, concise discussion of Hunt.

A much briefer but very fair appraisal of Hunt's achievements in literature can be found in Kenneth N. Cameron's *Shelley and His Circle, 1773–1822* (1961).

The work of three earlier critics should be mentioned. George Saintsbury's article on Hunt in *Essays in English Literature, 1780–1860* (1890) is a vigorous and penetrating judgment of him as a poet, literary critic, and miscellanist—"a man of letters, of talent almost touching genius, who seldom writes a dozen consecutive good pages." Hunt comes off best as a literary critic whom Saintsbury ranks with Coleridge, Lamb, and Hazlitt, "his defects as compared with them being in each case made up by compensatory, or more than compensatory merits." Although Saintsbury indicates Hunt's good attributes, his general conclusion is lukewarm—that Hunt at his best seldom or never stimulates admiration but merely a mild pleasure, yet he "wrote not a little that was good literature." His briefer discussion in *The Cambridge History of English Literature* (1916), said to have started Hunt's fame on an upward path (*TLS*, 26 July 1928), is little changed in attitude. Saintsbury regrets the failure to recognize adequately the historical interest of Hunt, praises a few poems—a view only slightly modified in 1923 by Milford's edition (*A Last Vintage*, 1950), and finds a "considerable bulk . . . of good and pleasant matter" in the prose, though perhaps "nothing quite so good as the few best things of his verse."

R. Brimley Johnson devotes over half of his *Leigh Hunt* (1896) to separate chapters on the literary work. That on journalism is mostly factual with little critical comment, and quite inadequate on the *Examiner* and Hunt's theatrical criticism. Although the poetry is evaluated more fully than by Saintsbury and certain of the short poems are praised more highly, essentially the two critics agree that Hunt was not in the highest sense a poet. The chapter on Hunt's criticism is superficial, while that on his work as a miscellanist is useful for the content of his essays rather than for any extended judgment of them. Oliver Elton includes a good short criticism of the poetry in his *Survey of English Literature, 1780–1830* (1912), but his discussion of the prose is too brief.

2. POETRY

On the basis of the fullest examination any scholar has made of the magazine reviews of Hunt's poetry in the British Isles through 1820, William S. Ward concludes that approximately 48% were favorable, 32% unfavorable, 17% mixed, and 2% uncertain (*The Criticism of Poetry in British Periodicals, 1798–1820* [above], a valuable analysis of critical opinion in the romantic period, derived from a study of 831 magazines). Considering that the great part of Hunt's poetry was written before his departure for Italy, these reviews indicate a higher degree of approval than Hunt later maintained. Except for a number of short poems, some translations, and scattered passages, Hunt has never been universally admired as a poet. The glowing esteem in the joint essay of Elizabeth Barrett and R. H. Horne (*A New Spirit of the Age*, 1844) is not typical of the period; perhaps such a remark as "the tragic power of the 'Story of Rimini' has scarcely been exceeded by any English poet, alive or dead . . ." may explain Miss Barrett's protest that Horne's friendship for Hunt affected his judgment. More representative is the tempered admiration of S. Adams Lee, who reports that Hunt has been accepted as a true poet, though not a great one, and acknowledges certain deficiencies of the verse while praising its "beauties"; surprisingly, he regards the *Feast of the Poets* as "one of the raciest and most sparkling specimens of good-humoured satire in the English language . . . as brilliant with delightful fancies as a morning meadow with dew-drops" (introd., *The Poetical Works of Leigh Hunt*, 1857). Two years later, in one of the articles occasioned by Hunt's death, the *Athenaeum* (3 Sept. 1859) speaks of the difficulty of ranking Hunt as a poet; his great fault lay in his "excessive effort to express very nice distinctions of feeling," and, while some of his shorter verse is praiseworthy, his poetry as a whole is little quoted; yet many poets themselves turn with profit to it, especially the *Rimini* and the Italian translations. Hunt's friend, Edmund Ollier, truthfully predicted in 1869 that although Hunt had undoubtedly written some beautiful poetry, he would be known to posterity less for his verse than for his essays and criticism. By 1883, Hunt's reputation, in the eyes of T. Hall Caine, had degenerated still further: "Hunt as a poet may be said to be the apostle of those who perceive nothing poetic that is not petty"; he "chirps of hawthorn and lilacs." Caine's title is apt: *Cobwebs of Criticism* . . . . R. B. Johnson, who edited the poems and prefaces in 1891, speaks more highly of Hunt's accomplishments, although he finds in the verse the same faults as in the prose, such as the slightness of treatment, frequent triviality of subject, and pet ideas sometimes allowed to run to seed. He concedes that the miscellaneous essays have always been the most popular of Hunt's writings. By 1897, William Andrews, in editing *The Months*, remarked that Hunt who had once been placed on a level with Keats was now little known as a poet.

One of the best criticisms of Hunt's poetry, published before Milford's edition but according with most opinion today, is Arthur Symons' in *The Romantic Movement in English Poetry* (1909). He finds that Hunt's verse was more important historically than actually, that although he helped to emancipate both speech and meter, he fell into a "tone of chatty colloquialism . . . from which, however, the vulgar idioms are not excluded." He "acquired a certain lightness and deftness which is occasionally almost wholly successful," but marred almost the whole of his work by the "ignoble quality of jauntiness." The *Legend of Florence* "has his ripest feeling and his most chastened style," catching and momentarily reviving the gentle Elizabethan manner. Hunt achieved many brilliant Italian translations, showed a special talent for brief narrative poems, and succeeded well in certain sonnets, such as the one on the Nile, but the puzzle is why Hunt, who was really poetically minded and knew so much about all forms of verse, "was never quite safe when he wrote in metre."

To Hunt's dexterity in meter, however, George Saintsbury pays a remarkable tribute: Hunt is "one of those very distinctly second-, if not third-rate poets, who deserve almost the first place in a history of prosody." After lauding the metrics of certain poems, Saintsbury questions where you will find such a diversity of skills in an earlier writer. "Leigh Hunt is beginning the nineteenth-century *karole* of eclectic and varied versifying" (*A History of English Prosody*, 1910). An article by C. W. Parks, "Leigh Hunt as a Timid Prophet of *Vers Libre*" (*Nation* [N. Y.], 5 July 1917), maintains that Hunt "blunderingly discovered" free verse, a "poetic genre which he might have publicized to great advantage" had he possessed the "instinct for modern advertising." Hunt's own opinion is best expressed in his statement that "poetry, without the fit sculpture of verse, is no more to be called poetry than beauty conceived is beauty accomplished."

The numerous reviews of Milford's edition, although they praised certain previously little-known poems such as "The Nymphs," revealed little change in the general estimate of Hunt. Maurice Hewlett (*Sat. Rev.*, 9 Dec. 1922) averred that he "wrote exceedingly good prose, and might have written as good verse if he had written less of it. As it was, he stands below Tom Moore, except as a doggerelist, and there, as they say, he beats the band." Edmund Gosse (*More Books on the Table*, 1923) found in Hunt "a buoyant irrepressible gaiety rarely paralleled on the melancholy steps of Helicon," but regretted his laxity of judgment as well as his want of taste, sufficient toughness of intellect and imagination in its highest sense. He quotes Hunt's own remark made in 1831: "To move a tear with a verse is the highest poetical triumph I can boast of."

Three special studies are valuable. Paul M. Wheeler in "The Great Quarterlies of the Early Nineteenth Century and Leigh

Hunt" (*SAQ*, 1930) summarizes the charges against Hunt's poetry and assesses their validity. Douglas Bush analyzes Hunt's treatment of mythology in relation to the romantic movement (*Mythology and the Romantic Tradition in English Poetry*, 1937). *Rimini*, he states, "did more than any other single work to create the convention which Hunt himself, Keats, and others more or less followed in their mythological verse"; and "no critic of his time set forth with such full intuitive sympathy the esthetic and spiritual values which the romantic poets had re-discovered in myth." The late Clarence De Witt Thorpe has a very fine extended discussion of *The Nymphs* (*KSMB*, 1959), which he intended to be part of a longer work on Hunt as a poet.

3. HUNT'S CRITICISM

The most often-quoted discussion of Hunt's theatrical criticism is William Archer's introduction to the *Dramatic Essays* (1894), which he edited with R. W. Lowe. This, however, gives only a partial view of Hunt's work, is not always reliable (see Landré), and has been completely superseded by Landré's comprehensive history. "Leigh Hunt's Dramatic Criticism" by C. M. Bowen (*Chambers's Jour.*, 1927) contributes little except some marginal comments showing how an apparent contemporary disagreed with Hunt's opinions. A. C. Ward (*Specimens of English Dramatic Criticism, XVII–XX Centuries*, 1945), who indicates knowledge only of Hunt's earliest reviews, has high praise for his work and places him above Hazlitt as a theatrical critic. Donald J. Rulfs ("The Romantic Writers and Edmund Kean," *MLQ*, 1950) depends on Archer and Lowe and misses the greater part of what Hunt wrote about the actor. Jeffrey Fleece's dissertation, "Leigh Hunt's Theatrical Criticism" (State Univ. of Iowa, 1952), on the other hand, is a broad study useful to the student who cannot read French, but unfortunately marred at times by careless scholarship. From one chapter Fleece has derived his article, "Leigh Hunt's Shakespearean Criticism" (*Essays in Honor of Walter Clyde Curry*, 1955), a good analysis of the theatrical reviews. With this should be compared "Leigh Hunt's Shakespeare: A 'Romantic' Concept" by G. D. Stout (*Studies in Memory of Frank Martindale Webster*, 1951), a scholarly article, the material for which is drawn partially from Hunt's dramatic criticism, but mostly from his other writings; Stout makes clear how "the pattern of critical ideas that we think of as characteristically 'romantic' " is found in Hunt's criticism of Shakespeare. J. C. Trewin has a brief appreciation of "Leigh Hunt as a Dramatic Critic" (*KSMB*, 1959).

More thorough and scholarly are E. D. Mackerness' "Leigh Hunt's Musical Journalism" (*Monthly Musical Record*, 1956) and David I. Jones's "Hazlitt and Leigh Hunt at the Opera House" (*Symposium*, 1962), with its comparison of the two reviewers, particularly concerning Mozart.

It is as a literary critic, however, that Hunt has received his chief recognition. Elizabeth Barrett Browning called him the "most delightful and genial of poetic critics," although she did not always agree with his opinions; Ruskin recommended that *Imagination and Fancy*, "Hunt's admirable piece of criticism," be read with care; Amy Lowell, as she could never forget, first learned what poetry was from *Imagination and Fancy*—"There is no better text-book for the appreciation of poetry than that volume" (*John Keats*, 1925); and Edwin Markham asserted:

> I have been a reader of him for forty years, and I think he has done more than anyone else to teach me what poetry is in her high immortal moments. His *A Jar of Honey From Mount Hybla* was one of my early joys; and this was followed by *Men, Women and Books*. I must confess that my chief indebtedness to Hunt is for the suggestiveness of his poetry criticisms; and his *Imagination and Fancy* is the volume most crammed with criticism of this order. To a poetry lover, this volume is worth its weight in gold.
>
> (Letter, n.d., quoted in Vincent Starrett,
> *A Student of Catalogues*, 1921)

At the time of Hunt's death, the *Athenaeum* (3 Sept. 1859) affirmed that "his most solid claim to a place in our standard English literature" is as a critic. Edmund Ollier, in one of the best prefatory essays to an edition of Hunt, asserted that his criticism "may never have reached the majestic and sonorous heights of Hazlitt's masterpieces; it had less of eloquence and force; but it was more reliable and more even. . . . No doubt, sympathy was a chief element; but not more so than judgment. Leigh Hunt has never had justice done him for the excellent sense and sanity of his mind." In comparison with Coleridge, Hazlitt, and Lamb, "Hunt seemed always to preserve the balance of his faculties" (*A Tale for a Chimney Corner, and Other Essays*, 1869). James Russell Lowell, who at one time thought Hunt's "feminine temperament gave him acute perceptions at the expense of judgment" ("Chaucer," *Literary Essays*, 1870), later termed him "a critic whose subtlety of discrimination and whose soundness of judgment, supported as it was on a broad base of truly liberal scholarship, have hardly yet won fitting appreciation" ("Fielding," *Literary and Political Addresses*, 1883).

The best short evaluations of Hunt as a literary critic are by George Saintsbury and Edmund Gosse. Of the two, Saintsbury covers a slightly broader field, but centers his remarks on *Imagination and Fancy*. Hunt, in his opinion, was perhaps more catholic in his tastes regarding English literature than any preceding critic, and "has left a very large range of critical performance, which is very rarely without taste, acuteness, and felicity of expression." Yet he was overshadowed by Coleridge, Lamb, and Hazlitt. Unfortunately Hunt combines an "abundance in quantity with a certain want of distinction in quality"; except in such rare lapses, however, as in his Dante criticism, his judgment is trustworthy. In *Imagination and Fancy*, Hunt "brings out, often as no one had ever done before, that sheer poetical quality of Dryden to which the critics of 1800–1830 had been as a rule unjust." His appreciation of Spenser is one of our very best. Although Ben Jonson "made him uncomfortable" and he is "almost at his worst on Beaumont and Fletcher," he "is sounder than some greater ones on Ford and Massinger," and the "first to discover the greatness of the tragic part of Middleton's *Changeling*." With Coleridge, Keats, and Shelley, Hunt is at his best; "in truth, nine-tenths of his criticism is admirable, and most admirably suited to instruct and encourage the average man" (*A History of Criticism*, 1904).

Edmund Gosse, concentrating on *Imagination and Fancy* in an introduction to that book (1907), believes that Hunt's essay on poetry is closely analogous to Hazlitt's "On Poetry in General," Hazlitt being "the more robust and more widely equipped" critic, and Hunt "the sweeter and the more delicate." *Imagination and Fancy*, Gosse points out, "legitimatized in popular form, the theories and experience of the finest spirits who had flourished in this country during the previous half-century." It became the last word of the propaganda for freedom in poetic art begun with the *Lyrical Ballads*. In contrast to Hazlitt, Hunt discusses Shelley and Keats at length and awards Coleridge his first full justice; while Hunt and Hazlitt are alike in their fundamental criticism of Spenser, Hunt exaggerates the "sweetness and softness" of the *Faerie Queene* and Hazlitt tries to make it "seem more rugged and robust than it really is"—yet "no one has appreciated the exact and limited charm of Spenser so exultantly as Leigh Hunt."

Several studies relate to particular aspects of Hunt's criticism. Alba H. Warren devotes the sixth chapter of his *English Poetic Theory, 1825–1865* (1950) to a fine analysis of Hunt's theories, particularly as expressed in "An Answer to the Question 'What Is Poetry?'" Of less importance to Hunt, but nonetheless enlightening, are the scattered passages in M. H. Abrams' *The Mirror and the Lamp* (1953), showing Hunt in relation to romantic theory and the critical tradition. Also Stuart Tave's *The Amiable Humorist* (1960) makes numerous references to Hunt's contribution to the comic theory and criticism of the early nineteenth century. Although Hunt did not write a formal essay on *The Rambler*, his opinions of Dr. Johnson and primarily of that periodical have been assembled by W. W. Pratt in an account of the marginalia in Hunt's own copy ("Leigh Hunt and *The Rambler*," *Univ. of Texas Stud. in English*, 1938). In a much briefer article, Frank H. Ristine reports on Hunt's critical interest in Horace as revealed in the copious marginalia of an edition Hunt owned ("Leigh Hunt's *Horace*," *MLN*, 1951). Stephen A. Larrabee, who has studied the relationship between sculpture and poetry in the romantic period, points out that Hunt sometimes stated his "criticism of poetry and drama, both ancient and modern, in the language of the sculptor's art" (*English Bards and Grecian Marbles*, 1943); he traces Hunt's allusions to statuary in his prose and poetry. George D. Stout has an excellent study, "Leigh Hunt on Wordsworth and Coleridge" (*KSJ*, 1957), in which are evaluated Hunt's various judgments of the two writers.

Hunt as a critic and translator of Italian literature has attracted more attention. Henry A. Beers (*A History of English Romanticism in the Nineteenth Century*, 1901) includes a few pages in which he says the usual things about Hunt and Italian literature, but, unlike most writers, praises his Dante essay as "a fine piece of critical work," although noting that Hunt's nature was antipathetic to the individual Dante and Dante's theological thought. R. W. King, in a three-part study of "Italian Influence on English Scholarship and Literature During the 'Romantic Revival'" (*MLR*, 1925, 1926) concludes with four paragraphs on Hunt, comparing his contribution to the Italian revival with that of his contemporaries. Erika Fischer's *Leigh Hunt und die italienische Literatur* (1936) is a solid and careful examination of Hunt's criticism of the great poets and his translations, by a scholar who is herself a native Italian. Essentially the same ground, although in less detail, is covered by Landré, whose book appeared in the same year. The best English discussion of Hunt's treatment of Dante is by W. P. Friederich in his book *Dante's Fame Abroad, 1350–1850* (1950). Herbert G. Wright, covering Hunt's interest in Boccaccio, finds that Hunt "occupies a remarkable position among English writers after the Jacobean age" in his knowledge of not merely the *Decameron*, but other works by Boccaccio (*Boccaccio in England from Chaucer to Tennyson*, 1957).

4. ESSAYS

No monograph has been devoted exclusively to Hunt's essays, but they are studied in detail in Landré's second volume. Hunt's reputation as an essayist has declined since the decade following his death. Although certain of his contemporaries indulged in eulogy, the nineteenth-century critics inclined to judge his essays with more discrimination and with the recognition that with all his fine qualities he was probably not one of the very best. Hazlitt, writing "On the Prose-Style of Poets," attributed to Hunt's familiar and miscellaneous papers "all the ease, grace, and point of the best style of Essay-writing"—but with modifications: "Perhaps there is too much the appearance of relaxation and trifling . . . a caprice, a levity, and a disposition to innovate in words and ideas. Still the genuine master-spirit of the prose-writer is there." Although the *Examiner* predicted (3 Sept. 1859) that as an essayist Hunt would never be forgotten, Samuel C. Chew defined his position less glowingly: "Most of his essays and miscellaneous prose writings have proved ephemeral; they were good journalism in their day but are of little moment in ours. He could handle acceptably, and occasionally adorn, any subject that occurred to his quick and facile fancy" (*A Literary History of England*, ed. A. C. Baugh, Vol. IV, 1948).

One of the most substantial periodical articles on Hunt, almost certainly by Gerald Massey (*North British Rev.*, 1860), begins with a long defense intended to offset, for a new generation of readers, the prejudicial effect of earlier unjust criticism. The latter part is mostly extended admiration of Hunt as a prose writer. The essays in the *Indicator*, *Companion*, and *Seer* are said to "contain the best and fullest expression of his genius" and "place their author in the first rank of English Essayists; the equal companion of Addison and Steele." Edmund Ollier, in his primarily biographical introduction to *A Tale for a Chimney Corner, and Other Essays* (1869), is more restrained and discriminating in his judgments, but regards his selections from the *Indicator* as "among the most admirable essays in the English language."

Arthur Symons has one of the best criticisms in an edition of Hunt's essays and more clearly foreshadows later opinion (introd., *Essays by Leigh Hunt*, 1887). Although he believes that Hunt "has left us little, perhaps nothing, of a secured immortality," the appraisal that follows is discerning, impartial, and appreciative.

The few pages of criticism included in Edward Storer's introduction (*Leigh Hunt: Poetry and Prose*, 1911) define Hunt as a man of talent who combines "the nimble, fanciful, suggestive artist" and "the weeping willow of sentimentality." He is very effective in essays of pure literature, especially those that are almost metaphysical; but he is often irritatingly cheerful, impertinently optimistic. J. B. Priestley's introduction to the Everyman edition (1929) is a fine short criticism which develops the thesis that although Hunt was certainly not of the first rank as an essayist, pure and simple, yet "as a miscellaneous writer, talking in print on an extraordinary variety of subjects . . . he has few serious rivals."

Two studies of the familiar essay compare the work of Hunt, Hazlitt, and Lamb. Marie H. Law's book *The English Familiar Essay in the Nineteenth Century* (1934) is a sound analysis that concentrates on Hunt's mature work. An excellent supplement is Melvin R. Watson's discussion of Hunt in *Magazine Serials and the Essay Tradition, 1746–1820* (1956), concluding that in "his own writing before 1820, Hunt did little to foreshadow the familiar essay."

5. JOURNALS

In his *Masters of English Journalism* (1911), T. H. S. Escott has a good survey of Hunt's career, concluding that his "special newspaper mission was to adapt to nineteenth-century journalism . . . the essay which Addison and Steele had introduced." Arthur Aspinall's "The Social Status of Journalists at the Beginning of the Nineteenth Century" (*RES*, 1945) furnishes a helpful background for several studies relating to the *Examiner*. Although Aspinall covers Hunt only incidentally, he gives a well-documented explanation for the low repute in which journalism was held as late as the 1820's, and attributes to Hunt a distinguished service in redeeming the newspaper profession from "charges of licentiousness, dishonesty, lack of principle, and vulgarity." The first half of *Leigh Hunt's "Examiner" Examined*, by Blunden (1928), is a colorful, abbreviated report of the newspaper for each year of Hunt's association with it, but the book as a whole primarily stresses the contribution of the *Examiner* to literary history. Benvenuto Cellini's "Leigh Hunt e 'The Examiner' (1808–1812)" in *Studi sul romanticismo inglese* (1932) attempts to fill the gap left by the foregoing work and briefly studies the Political Examiners to the time of Hunt's imprisonment. In an article more limited in scope, Michael Roberts analyzes "Leigh Hunt's Place in the Reform Movement, 1808–1810"

(*RES*, 1935) and emphasizes the significance of Hunt's "Reform-
ist's Answer to the Article Entitled 'State of Parties' . . . ," the
most interesting selection ever published in the *Examiner*, Roberts
believes, so far as the historian is concerned, and also proof of
Hunt's constructive thinking in politics. A much more valuable
publication, however, devoted exclusively to this newspaper, is
George D. Stout's scholarly monograph, *The Political History of
Leigh Hunt's Examiner, Together with an Account of "The Book"*
(Washington Univ. Stud., 1949). As Stout explains in his preface,
Blunden's *Leigh Hunt* deals with the subject in only the sketchiest
fashion, and although Landré "devotes forty pages to 'Leigh Hunt
et la politique,' as well as some ninety to the events of Hunt's life
during the years 1808–21," Landré's method of treatment is analytical whereas Stout's is biographical and historical. With competent
documentation, Stout recounts the subject matter of the Political
Examiners and the establishment of a policy—not a real political
creed—appropriates five chapters to the subject of libel suits, and
clarifies the decline of the *Examiner* in the early 1820's. A short
supplement to this monograph is Carl R. Woodring's "The Hunt
Trials" (*KSMB*, 1959), concluding that for "those who wish all the
unsavory details, much exploration remains possible." Woodring's
long introductory essay, "Leigh Hunt as Political Essayist" (*Leigh
Hunt's Political and Occasional Essays*, ed. L. H. and C. W.
Houtchens, 1962), is an important study, broader in scope than
Stout's, and primarily "historical rather than appreciative or
exegetic." It is the best discussion of the subject. In a more
restricted field, Ahmad Hasan Qureshi covers in some detail Hunt's
view of Napolean ("The Attitude of Some English Liberals Toward
Napoleon as Reflected in the *Edinburgh Review* and Leigh Hunt's
Examiner," Univ. of Illinois dissertation, 1959). To these might be
added a section in David Erdman's *Blake: Prophet Against Empire*
(1954), which explains on political grounds the early quarrel
between the *Examiner* and William Blake, although Robert Hunt
rather than Leigh was primarily involved.

A few publications relate to other journals conducted by Hunt.
"Leigh Hunt and the *Plain Dealer*" (*MLN*, 1927) by G. D. Stout
covers the brief editorship of Hunt and his probable contributions,
pointing out that the newspaper was a very mediocre one and Hunt's
articles sound weary. Launcelot Cross (Frank Carr) in his *Characteristics of Leigh Hunt, as Exhibited in That Typical Literary
Periodical, "Leigh Hunt's London Journal"* (1834–1835), published
in 1878, has much good factual information if one can disregard
such occasional remarks as "every page is pervaded with an odour of

homely sanctity, as of hidden violets." More recently, Edmund Blunden has studied this periodical in relation to Shelley, Keats, Wordsworth, and other writers (*Eibungaku Kenkyu,* 1952). Hunt's two years with the *Monthly Repository* receive very cursory treatment in Blunden's biography, but full development in Landré. A good English supplement to the former is the discussion in Francis E. Mineka's *The Dissidence of Dissent* (1944), the conclusion being that under Hunt the periodical lacked character, but was pleasant and sometimes amusing. Mineka and Landré, incidentally, disagree regarding Hunt's authorship of three articles, although both have apparently made their identifications from the same book in the Brewer Collection.

10

Thomas De Quincey

By John E. Jordan
UNIVERSITY OF CALIFORNIA

I. BIBLIOGRAPHIES

D E QUINCEY PRESENTS a special problem to the bibliographer: he himself had no record of his scattered and usually unsigned periodical writings and was not always wise enough a father to recognize his own children. In assembling his *Selections* he sometimes depended upon the American edition, which had been constructed partly by stylistic identification; he left out many essays—as would be expected in "Selections"—and he or his publisher even included one article which subsequently proved not to be his. There is not, therefore, and probably never will be, an exhaustive bibliography of his writings. The earliest listing is in W. T. Lowndes's *The Bibliographer's Manual of English Literature* as revised by H. G. Bohn in 1861, which gives the contents of De Quincey's collected edition, part of that of the American edition, and an incomplete record of contributions to the *London Magazine, Blackwood's Magazine,* and *Tait's Magazine.* One of the essays here attributed to De Quincey, "Traits and Tendencies of German Literature," is, however, by J. S. Blackie. In an appendix to *The Collected Writings of Thomas De Quincey,* David Masson provides a useful chronological register of De Quincey's writings as printed in that edition and adds a list of items not included.

The most elaborate attempt to record all of De Quincey's known works is *Thomas De Quincey: A Bibliography Based upon the De Quincey Collection in the Moss Side Library* (1908), by J. A. Green, who lists periodical publications chronologically with an occasional note as to source, and describes the various editions. W. E. A. Axon adds thirty-four items positively and several others conjecturally in "The Canon of De Quincey's Writings, with References to His Unidentified Articles" (*Transactions of the Royal Society of Literature of the United Kingdom,* 1914).

Green's *Bibliography* is likewise the most elaborate listing of materials about De Quincey. Among its 796 entries are even scrapbooks of De Quinceyana and records of his portraits and statues. It is, nevertheless, neither entirely reliable nor exhaustive; it omits some significant biographical sources and some American periodical articles, and many of its entries are of little significance — mere mentions of De Quincey. Valuable as a supplement to Green on nineteenth-century essays is the full bibliography in Lane Cooper's *The Prose Poetry of Thomas De Quincey* (1902). Of most general use is the rich but selective listing of Horace A. Eaton in *The Cambridge Bibliography of English Literature* (1941) and the critical bibliography of Ernest Bernbaum in *Guide Through the Romantic Movement* (2d ed., 1949). There are, of course, convenient lists in anthologies and biographies; those in G. B. Woods's *English Poetry and Prose of the Romantic Movement* (rev. ed., 1950) and H. A. Eaton's *De Quincey: A Biography* (1936) are particularly full. S. K. Proctor's *Thomas De Quincey's Theory of Literature* (1943) has both a substantial bibliography and an appendix by C. D. Thorpe on contemporary De Quincey scholarship. Modern scholarship is also summarized by Anne Agnes O'Rourke in "A Critical Survey of Recent Writings About Thomas De Quincey" (University of Illinois M.A. thesis, 1945). Specialized studies contain interesting limited bibliographies or add titles of tangential application: Ernst T. Sehrt, *Geschichtliches und religiöses Denken bei Thomas De Quincey* (1936), lists German material; Gertrud Meyer, *Das Verhältnis Thomas de Quinceys zur Nationalökonomie* (1927), adds works in economics; and Paul Guerrier, *Étude médico-psychologique sur Thomas De Quincey* (1907), is excellent for French translations of De Quincey's work and nineteenth-century studies of opium. A *Loci Critici* tabulating De Quincey's chief critical utterances may be found in my study *Thomas De Quincey, Literary Critic* (1952).

Although many of the precious papers with which De Quincey "snowed" himself into one lodging after another have come to light, there is no listing of his manuscripts. Green is particularly skimpy in this field, and the only modern efforts are by Claude E. Jones ("Some De Quincey Manuscripts," *ELH*, 1941), and Richard H. Byrns ("Some Unpublished Works of De Quincey," *PMLA*, 1956), which between them describe eighteen items. His "neat, bright little handwriting, sometimes dimmed by haste and exhaustion" can be seen reproduced in T. J. Brown, "English Literary Autographs XXXIV: Thomas De Quincey, 1785–1859" (*BC*, 1960).

II. EDITIONS

"Sir, the thing is absolutely, insuperably and forever impossible," said De Quincey to suggestions that he collect his own works (*Eclectic Mag.*, 1850). The manifold difficulties were, however, partly surmounted for him by the ingenuity of the American firm of Ticknor and Fields, which published a twenty-four-volume edition (1851–59). This edition is particularly useful because it is for the most part printed from the original periodical text of De Quincey's papers and therefore provides an easy means of studying his revisions. Although it is not complete and lacks editorial notes and index, it was for years the best collection available. Encouraged by the American trailblazing, De Quincey allowed himself to be persuaded by the Edinburgh publisher, James Hogg (not, as is sometimes asserted, the Ettrick Shepherd), to undertake his own collected edition, so that by the time twelve volumes had appeared in Boston one was published in Edinburgh, the first volume of *Selections Grave and Gay, from Writings Published and Unpublished* (1853–60). This edition ran to fourteen volumes, the last appearing posthumously, and seems to have been concocted partly on the basis of availability—those papers for which the American edition had provided him a text and those which by De Quincey's famous "sortilege" came to the surface of his bathtub file—and partly on the basis of variety and readability in each volume. De Quincey took his editorial task seriously and revised his essays painstakingly, sometimes cutting out passages which were offensive to his friends or toning down polemical statements, sometimes elaborating details and adding footnotes to footnotes, sometimes making the most minute stylistic changes in recognition of "the duty that forever calls to the stern valuation of words." More organic changes came in the earlier volumes, particularly in the *Autobiographic Sketches*, which were drastically rewritten, and *Confessions of an English Opium-Eater*, which was tripled in length. W. E. A. Axon's "Some De Quincey Proof Sheets" (*Scottish Rev.*, 26 Nov. 1908) shows that he often sent to press corrected pages from the American edition.

These different versions afford interesting opportunities to examine De Quincey's method of composition, opportunities only touched upon in the preface to Richard Garnett's edition of the *Con-*

fessions (1885) and Edward Dowden's "How De Quincey Worked" (*Sat. Rev.*, 23 Feb. 1895). Ian Jack ("De Quincey Revises His *Confessions*," *PMLA*, 1957) makes a careful analysis of the differences between the 1821 and 1856 versions, noting the later insistence on the medical value of opium, new importance assigned to dreams, expanded treatment of early life, and generally more involved and artificial style. Comparing the holograph manuscript in the National Library of Scotland, the *Blackwood's* version, the 1854 revision, and a fragment published in *Posthumous Works*, Richard H. Byrns considers "De Quincey's Revisions in the 'Dream Fugue'" (*PMLA*, 1962) and finds that the changes tend to "intensify the emotional quality of the passage" and "increase the undulating movement of the prose."

After De Quincey's death there was manifested surprising interest in the small man who had flitted about Edinburgh by night and was so little known that visitors were sometimes assured that he was dead. Three more somewhat expanded Edinburgh editions were called for: 1862–63, seventeen volumes; 1871, sixteen volumes; 1878, sixteen volumes. The American edition, already twice reprinted, was reissued in eleven volumes as the "Riverside Edition" (1877), with notes and a general index. This so-called "Popular Edition" has been several times reprinted. In 1889–90 appeared the fourteen-volume Edinburgh *Collected Writings, New and Enlarged Edition,* by David Masson, with critical introductions to each volume, notes, index, and considerable new material. Contemporary reception was mixed: a reviewer in the *Saturday Review* (8 Feb. 1890) rightly called the edition "exceeding ugly" and, along with J. Dennis in the *Spectator* (24 May 1890), objected to Masson's heavy-handed editorial practices of ignoring De Quincey's classifications and sometimes even splitting up an article and printing it in two pieces. Masson, however, usually informs the reader of these manipulations and does bring some order out of the chaotic heterogeneity of De Quincey's output; although we could wish his notes were more frequent and his impulse to tidy up a little restrained, he has the merit of being a sympathetic editor. In "The Nature and Origin of Modifications in the Text of De Quincey's Writings Published in Collective Editions" (Univ. of Florida dissertation, 1956), Phares Leroy Mixon provides an indispensable "Table of Variants," comparing Masson's text with that of the original periodical publication, indicating the line of textual descent, and calculating a "revision coefficient" to measure the extent of De Quincey's revisions. Mixon finds over seven thousand variants, most of them De Quincey's changes, but many the result of textual corruption, in which each edition had a share—

including Masson's. Nevertheless, Masson's work has been several times reprinted, and has become the standard edition by default of any better.

Before Masson's edition was complete, James Hogg brought out *The Uncollected Writings* (2 vols., 1890), containing some of De Quincey's most interesting essays and stories. Aside from a slight preface the editorial apparatus of these volumes is negligible, and many of the papers were subsequently published by Masson; yet the work went to a second edition. In 1891–93 appeared the last substantial addition to De Quincey's work: *The Posthumous Works, Edited from the Original MSS, with Introduction and Notes*, by A. H. Japp, in two volumes. This work draws upon the papers in the hands of De Quincey's daughters and incorporates the "Two Newly Discovered Papers" and "Further Newly Discovered Papers" printed in the *New Review* (1890 and 1891). Although it is possible to understand the *Athenaeum* reviewer (23 Dec. 1893) who expostulated that only two essays in the whole two volumes were worth printing, the work is valuable to De Quincey scholars because it includes some interesting criticism, some probably early articles, the fragments of the "Suspiria de Profundis," and—under the title of "Brevia"—a revealing section of scattered comments and reflections, many of them religious. The editing is slight and probably unreliable.

Despite the editorial hazards of identifying De Quincey's unsigned essays, subsequent scholarship has so far challenged only two of the papers published as his in these early editions. "Traditions of the Rabbins" was proved George Croly's in time to be omitted from the standard edition, and the translation, with a critical note, of Tieck's "The Love Charm" has more recently become suspect. Although De Quincey could not remember doing this translation and did not print it in his *Selections*, Hogg included it in *Uncollected Writings* and Masson in his edition, on authority of Charles Knight, who first published it in *Knight's Quarterly Magazine (Passages of a Working Life*, 1864–65). In "Is Thomas De Quincey Author of 'The Love Charm'?" (*MLN*, 1937), H. K. Galinsky makes a persuasive case that the author is really Julius Hare.

Neither any one of these editions of De Quincey's works nor even the combination of collected editions and *Uncollected Writings* and *Posthumous Works* is complete. Nor are all of his writings yet readily available: some more or less ephemeral essays still may be found only in their original journals, and a few manuscript materials remain unpublished. Many supplementary publications, however, have appeared. A. H. Japp's "Some Unconscious Confessions of De Quincey" (*Gentleman's Mag.*, 1886) added a valuable series of "extracts" from De Quincey manuscripts, and Charles Pollitt's *De Quincey's Editorship of the Westmorland Gazette, July, 1818 to November, 1819* (1890) made available samples of De Quincey's earliest periodical writings. Pollitt tried to refute Japp's pronouncement that De Quincey was "not born for a successful newspaper editor" by seventy pages of excerpts in a matrix of comment. W. E. A. Axon in *Transactions of the Royal Society of Literature* (1914) printed parts of an essay on Hannah More, and in the same year the *Independent* published a long-hoarded manuscript, "Lessons of the French Revolution," which the editors dated about 1848, but which was probably written about 1831. Since this essay is more favorable to France than usual with "John Bull" De Quincey, it should be more generally known. The same is true of the seven fragments published under the title "De Quincey on French Drama" in *More Books* (1939), although these jerky and incomplete paragraphs are perhaps more interesting for an indication of how De Quincey worked than for their content. "Close Comments upon a Straggling Speech," discovered by Axon and long thought to exist in a unique copy at Tullie House, Carlisle, was lately reprinted by John Edwin Wells from another copy which came into his hands ("Wordsworth and De Quincey in Westmorland Politics, 1818," *PMLA*, 1940). This essay, written in 1818 by De Quincey as his contribution to the efforts of the Lowther interest to keep Henry Brougham from capturing one of their seats in Parliament, is significant both as an example of De Quincey's Tory thinking and as the production which probably got him the appointment as editor of the *Westmorland Gazette* that began his career as a journalist. *Dr. Johnson and Lord Chesterfield*, privately printed in New York in 1945, is a perverse defense of Chesterfield in the affair of Johnson's famous letter. It is not quite, as the title page says, "printed now for the first time," for Japp gives a version in "Unconscious Confessions."

One of the richest of the subsequent additions to the body of De Quincey's writings is his youthful diary, which was beautifully published both in facsimile and in transcript, with full notes, by Horace A. Eaton (*A Diary of Thomas De Quincey, 1803, 1927*). This *Diary* preserves revealing records of De Quincey's reading and whoring, and the first draft of the all-important introductory letter to Wordsworth. A significant recent addition is De Quincey's translation of approximately the first three chapters of Ludvig Holberg's satirical voyage, *Niels Klim*, which was discovered in the

Sir George Grey papers in the Auckland Public Library and admirably edited, with an introduction and notes on the translation, by S. Musgrove (*Auckland Univ. Coll. Bull.*, 1953). Musgrove suggests plausibly that De Quincey made a lively adaptation of Baggesen's Danish translation of the Latin original, probably between 1822 and 1827 as an intended contribution for R. P. Gillies' *Foreign Quarterly Review.*

Perhaps the greatest gap in De Quincey scholarship is an edition of his letters. W. H. Bonner's *De Quincey at Work: As Seen in One Hundred and Thirty New and Newly Edited Letters* (1936) is an admirable collection of correspondence—much of it by De Quincey's daughters—which is especially welcome for the light it casts upon De Quincey's painful editing of the *Selections* and his family life of the last years; but it makes no pretense of being more than a special group of letters. Similarly, my *De Quincey to Wordsworth: A Biography of a Relationship, with the Letters of Thomas De Quincey to the Wordsworth Family* (1962) prints only sixty letters to the Wordsworths from 1803 to 1848. De Quincey was not a voluminous letter writer—he hated to write and he had to do enough of it to scrape out a living—but several hundred of his letters are known to be extant. Most of them are to his editors and his family, concerned largely with his writing plans, financial difficulties, and physical ailments, and chiefly of biographical interest. Many have not yet been printed, most notably the Tait correspondence, and others have appeared piecemeal, in biographies and the following less obvious places: Mary Gordon, *Christopher North* (1862); Charles Knight, *Passages of a Working Life during Half a Century* (1864–65); Rosamond and Florence Davenport-Hill, *The Recorder of Birmingham, A Memoir of Matthew Davenport Hill* (1878); A. H. Japp, "Early Intercourse of the Wordsworths and De Quincey" (*Century Mag.*, 1891); Alice A. Clowes, *Charles Knight: A Sketch* (1892); Mrs. J. T. Fields, *A Shelf of Old Books* (1894); G. B. Hill, *Talks about Autographs* (1896); M. O. W. Oliphant, *Annals of a Publishing House* (1897–98); *Manchester Guardian* (30 Oct. 1906); W. E. A. Axon, "De Quincey and T. F. Dibdin" (*Library*, 1907) and "Thomas De Quincey" (*Bookman* [London], 1907); Lady E. Priestly, *The Story of a Lifetime* (1908); E. H. Fairbrother, "Lieutenant Horatio De Quincey" (*N&Q*, 9 Oct. 1915); Mary L. Armitt, *Rydal* (1916); W. Forbes Gray, "De Quincey as Lady Nairne's Tenant" (*Chambers's Jour.*, 1926); E. H. Moore, "Some Unpublished Letters of Thomas De Quincey" (*RES*, 1933); Coleman O. Parsons, "The Woes of Thomas De Quincey" *RES*, 1934); H. A. Eaton, "The Letters of De Quincey to Words-

worth, 1803–1807" (*ELH*, 1936); H. McCusker, "De Quincey and
the Landlord" (*More Books*, 1939); J. E. Wells, "Wordsworth and
De Quincey in Westmorland Politics, 1818" (*PMLA*, 1940); L. N.
Broughton, "Wordsworth and De Quincey in Westmorland Politics,
1818: Addendum" (*PMLA*, 1941); Wallace Brockway and Bart K.
Winer, *A Second Treasury of the World's Great Letters* (1941);
Evelyn Grantham, "De Quincey to His Publisher" (*More Books*,
1945); David Bonnell Green, "A Thomas De Quincey Letter"
(*N&Q*, 1958). Interesting evidence of the way in which De Quincey
drew upon material of his letters for subsequent essays is suggested
in Georges le Breton's long review of several De Quincey items under
the title "De Quincey et Wordsworth" (*MdF*, 1964).

Selections of De Quincey's works are legion; to list them all
would be tedious and not very profitable. Among the selectors the
prevalent contention—and it is a tenable one—is that no writer
profits more from judicious selection than the harried and sometimes
potboiling De Quincey. The precedent for culling was established by
Beauties, Selected from the Writings of Thomas De Quincey (1862),
which was several times reprinted. Another version is the Modern
Library *Selected Writings of Thomas De Quincey* (1937), edited by
Philip Van Doren Stern, a convenient collection of De Quincey's best
works marred for all but the casual reader by the editor's compul-
sion "to excise many irrelevant passages." A welcome volume is
Edward Sackville-West's *Recollections of the Lake Poets* (1948),
for it restores some—not all—of the interesting passages which De
Quincey cut from his revised version and which have not been
available in reprints. In *Reminiscences of the English Lake Poets*
(1961) I give the text of the final version, but supply in the notes all
significant material omitted in revision. At the end of the nineteenth
and beginning of the twentieth centuries many volumes of De
Quincey selections were published as textbooks, usually featuring
"Joan of Arc" and "The English Mail Coach," and offering slight
biographical and critical introductions and notes. Such a one was
edited as late as 1938 by A. A. Purcell. Among the selections with
more specific aims are Thomas Burke's *The Ecstasies of Thomas De
Quincey* (1928), which limits itself to "those papers in which he
realized poetic ideas in a prose invested with the pomp and colour of
the symphonic orchestra"; *Ann: A Memory* (1908), a collection of
De Quincey's comments on Ann of Oxford Street; Fred N. Scott's
Essays on Style, Rhetoric, and Language (1893); and Louis J.
Bragman's compilation of "The Medical Wisdom of De Quincey"
(*Annals of Medical History*, 1928). Helen Darbishire's *De Quin-*

cey's Literary Criticism (1909) is a handy selection which, however, gives a somewhat limited picture of his critical activity.

Except for the *Confessions*, there are few significant editions of individual works. De Quincey published only three other books: a very free "translation" of a German novel, *Walladmor* (1825); a novel, *Klosterheim* (1832); and *The Logic of Political Economy* (1844). None has been thought worthy of a separate scholarly edition, although *Klosterheim* was edited with an introduction by Shelton Mackenzie in 1855, and J. R. Ballantyne published in 1854 *Chapters on Political Economy* "adapted from . . . Mr. De Quincey's Essay." Among separate appearances of his articles the many late nineteenth-century editions for school use of "Revolt of the Tartars" are noteworthy. This popular piece has also been edited more recently by Edward Shanks (1948) and drawn upon for a novel by W. L. River (*The Torguts*, 1939). In 1893 W. D. Armes issued a critical edition of *Theory of Greek Tragedy*. Rather curiously, the erudite *Toilette of the Hebrew Lady* was edited in a cheap reprint by E. V. Mitchell in 1926. Another unusual reprint is the pleasant little book issued in 1945 by the Colt Press in their California Classics series, *California and the Gold Mania*, illustrated by sketches from *Punch*.

Confessions of an English Opium-Eater has been published in everything from "Little Blue Books" to fine press editions and has been translated into many languages, including French, German, Italian, Dutch, Spanish, and Russian. In De Quincey's lifetime the original two short installments in the *London Magazine* were six times printed in book form in England and four times in America. After 1856 the much longer revised version generally supplanted the original short form, which the author rightly suspected to be more effective than "the present full-blown development," especially "as a book to *impress*." The original version has, however, been reprinted, most notably in the editions of Richard Garnett (1885), George Saintsbury (1928), Edward Sackville-West (1950), and Malcolm Elwin (1956). Garnett not only supplied notes, largely drawn from the later version, but printed Richard Woodhouse's interesting "Notes of Conversations with Thomas De Quincey" and an excerpt from De Musset's additions in his translation of the *Confessions*. Saintsbury contributed a vigorous critical introduction and, by printing *Confessions of an English Opium-Eater Together with Their Sequels*, conveniently brought together most of De Quincey's "impassioned prose," though on the dubious ground of thereby separating out the Opium-Eater. Elwin claims to offer "the first complete and satisfactory presentation of the *Confessions* and its sequels," because he publishes not only both the 1821 and 1856 texts of the *Confessions* but also the original *Blackwood's* version of the *Suspiria* instead of the commonly reprinted remnants after De Quincey had plundered *Suspiria* for his *Autobiographic Sketches*. The addition of notes, a chronology, a bibliography, illustrations, and a slightly revised reprint of Elwin's 1935 life, make this a welcome and useful volume.

III. BIOGRAPHIES

T HREE YEARS after De Quincey's death John Wilson's daughter declared: "If this singular man's life were written truthfully, no one would believe it, so strange the tale would seem"; three generations later Philip Stern remarked, "As a subject for biography he is difficult beyond all reason." De Quincey's biographers agree at least that he is strange, interesting, and—for all the apparent openness of his autobiographical writing—finally elusive. There have been, however, various efforts to write his life more or less truthfully, and a considerable body of material has come to light.

1. CONTEMPORARY WITNESSES

It has been noted with regret that De Quincey left chatty, revealing papers on Wordsworth, Coleridge, Southey, Lamb, and Hazlitt, but that none of them returned the favor. De Quincey had, nonetheless, his minor Boswells, although with one or two exceptions they wrote after his death and most often about his later years. A handy gathering of many of these commentaries is *De Quincey and His Friends: Personal Recollections, Souvenirs, and Anecdotes* edited by James Hogg, 1895. Here the student may find the best source of information about De Quincey's London years, Richard Woodhouse's "Notes of Conversations with Thomas De Quincey." Woodhouse is obviously a favorable witness, but his materials have a convincingly De Quinceyan flavor. Here are also the official records of De Quincey's Oxford career from Dr. Cotton, the Provost of

Worcester, and Colin Rae-Brown's "Recollections of the Glasgow Period," somewhat curtailed from their original appearance in the *Universal Review* (1889). And here too are many recollections from the last days at Lasswade: James Hogg's illuminating trivia, "Days and Nights with Thomas De Quincey"; J. R. Findlay's sympathetic "Personal Recollections of Thomas De Quincey"; Francis Jacox's valuable record of conversations, "Recollections"; "A Daughter's Memories," Mrs. Baird-Smith's defensive remarks which are largely responsible for the long-lived legend that De Quincey's debts were "mainly the figments of his own imagination"; and interesting anecdotal excerpts from James Payn's *Some Literary Recollections* (1884) and J. G. Bertram's *Some Memories of Books, Authors and Events* (1893). Hogg also includes that much reprinted and perhaps most influential of the early portraits, John Hill Burton's kindly caricature of "Thomas Papaverius," and draws upon Thomas Hood's *Literary Reminiscences* (1861), R. P. Gilles' *Memoirs of a Literary Veteran* (1851), Carlyle's *Reminiscences* (1881), Charles Knight's *Passages of a Working Life* (1864–65), and Mary Gordon's *Christopher North* (1862). Hogg's excerpts, however, are not entirely to be trusted—he often omits interesting things, and especially some of Carlyle's derogatory comments.[1]

Hogg's book is, however, the record of "friends." The only important favorable contemporary reports missing from his anthology are the brief but impressive tributes to De Quincey's shaping influence left by Dr. Robertson (James Brown, *Life of William B. Robertson, D.D.*, 1888) and Matthew Hill (R. and F. Davenport-Hill, *Memoir of Matthew Davenport Hill*, 1878), Mrs. J. T. Fields's account of her husband's experiences as publisher and friend to the Opium-Eater (*A Shelf of Old Books*, 1894), George Gilfillan's overwritten sketches in *Galleries of Literary Portraits* (1856), Emerson's impressions of a "gentle old man" (*Journals*, ed. E. W. Emerson and W. E. Forbes, 1912), and the "Reminiscences" of the elder Hogg printed by A. H. Japp in *Thomas De Quincey: His Life and Writings* (1877). This picture needs to be rounded by reference to the irate remarks of Harriet Martineau in her *Biographical Sketches* (1869), or the sour version of the London days given by B. W. Procter (Barry Cornwall) in *Autobiographical Fragment and Biographical Notes* (1877), or the amusing account of De Quincey's going to sleep during one of Emerson's lectures told by

---

1 Carlyle's opinions of De Quincey, sometimes acid, were on the whole kindly. See also *Early Letters*, ed. C. E. Norton (1886); *Letters, 1826–36*, ed. Norton (1889); *New Letters*, ed. A. Carlyle (1904); *Letters . . . to John Stuart Mill, John Sterling, and Robert Browning*, ed. Carlyle (1923); and J. A. Froude, *Life* (1884).

P. Landreth in "Emerson's Meeting with De Quincey" (*Blackwood's Mag.*, 1894). For a really hostile and perverse contemporary report one should turn to Charles MacFarlane's *Reminiscences of a Literary Life* (1917). Another source of the more sensational view of De Quincey is Charles Mackay's pompous and unconvincing portrait in *Forty Years' Recollections of Life, Literature, and Public Affairs* (1877). Crabb Robinson's opinion of De Quincey as a personality also appears much more unfavorable in Edith J. Morley's *Henry Crabb Robinson on Books and Their Writers* (1938) than in Thomas Sadler's edition of the *Diary, Reminiscences, and Correspondence* (1869).

One of the most valuable of the contemporary records is the complete story of De Quincey's £300 loan to Coleridge, found in Joseph Cottle's *Early Recollections* (1837). Some useful firsthand material—along with some stuffy moralizing—may be found in the Chetham Society publication of *The Admission Register of the Manchester School*, Volume II, edited by J. F. Smith (1868) ; a young editor's view of De Quincey in G. E. Troup's *Life of George Troup Journalist* (1881) ; and a charming picture of the Opium-Eater by another editor in Christopher North's (John Wilson's) *Noctes Ambrosianae* (*Blackwood's*, 1823–30). Wilson is certainly caricaturing his silver-tongued friend, but there is much that rings true in the portrait.[2]

Eighteen years passed after De Quincey's death in 1859 before a full-length biography appeared. In the interim there were, of course, short sketches in periodicals and introductions, most of them obviously uninformed and some incredibly erroneous. They naturally leaned heavily on De Quincey's autobiographical writings and took a "child is father of the man" point of view. Most important of the magazine lives are the "Life and Writings of Thomas De Quincey" by H. W. S., which appeared in two installments in *Fraser's Magazine* (1860–61), and T. E. Kebbel's "brief memoir" in the *Quarterly Review* (1861). Shelton Mackenzie's "Biographical Notice" prefaced to his edition of *Klosterheim* (1855) is brief but balanced, and Francis Espinasse's long chapter in *Lancashire Worthies* (1877) is perhaps as good a life as could have been written without access to manuscript material. Among these one finds already the differences of opinion about De Quincey's birthplace which, along with the question of whether he or his mother added the

2   See also the pungent letters by De Quincey's daughter Emily, some of which are printed by H. S. Salt ("The Depreciation of De Quincey," *National Rev.*, 1928) and C. A. Scott ("De Quincey and Lamb," *TLS*, 24 Jan. 1935), and the reminiscences—largely about the daughters—of Mrs. E. M. Sellar (*Recollections and Impressions*, 1907).

"De" to the family name, loom significantly in the early biographies. On the authority of W. E. A. Axon and considerable correspondence in the *Manchester Guardian* and *Manchester City News* in the last two decades of the nineteenth century, it seems likely that he was born in the Manchester house later known as Prince's Tavern, although Greenhays has often been claimed as his birthplace. The "De," made a matter of scorn by many Victorian commentators who were ready to cite Thackeray's "snobs," seems to have been added by De Quincey's mother; the most authoritative discussion of the question is by H. A. Eaton in his edition of De Quincey's *Diary*.

2. FULL-LENGTH LIVES

Full-length biographies of De Quincey are few and literally far between: there are only three which accurately can be called full-length, or, if we interpret the term generously, only six; and these fall into two widely separated periods. Two of these works, appearing in the generation of his death, are earnest and proper Victorian portraits; the other four, coming out in a cluster more than fifty years later, range from imaginative re-creations to scholarly portrayals. All of these lives are essentially sympathetic. De Quincey, so vulnerable to caricature and moral censure, has been fortunate in his biographers.[2a]

Dominant in the first period of De Quincey biography was A. H. Japp who, under the pseudonym of H. A. Page, published in 1877 the first substantial life, *Thomas De Quincey: His Life and Writings*, in two volumes. Japp was neither a good writer nor an unimpeachable scholar; the book is chaotic, awkward, and wrong in a number of factual details. He had access to a rich body of material but he was unable and unwilling to use it. Since he was working closely with De Quincey's daughters and trying to produce an "official" life, his work is as much an apology as a biography. He gives the impression, for instance, that De Quincey left the editorship of the *Westmorland Gazette* only because he wanted to make more money elsewhere, and he gives no hint of any prenuptial relations with Margaret Simpson. Although Japp's introduction sets forth the paradox which crops up throughout De Quincey scholarship, that he was a logician as well as a dreamer, the biographer makes no effort to develop the relation thematically. Indeed, in the welter of facts and quotations, no idea emerges as perceptive as the statement by J. R. Findlay, made the same year in the *Encyclopae-*

2a   Since this chapter was written another substantial work has appeared, Françoise Moreux, *Thomas De Quincey, La Vie—L'Homme—L'Œuvre*, 1964.

dia Britannica, that the clues to De Quincey's character are in his own description of himself as "framed for love" and a "eudaemonist." But Japp's book is not mere whitewash and part of the reason for the confusion of the text is its richness in incorporated material. Japp quotes liberally from contemporaries and from fragments of De Quincey's manuscripts; he draws continually, if selectively and unreliably, on De Quincey's letters; and he frequently cites and quotes large chunks of periodical articles, either to lean on them or to refute them angrily. His two long chapters called "Criticisms and Characteristics" survey De Quincey's personality, traits, and beliefs in a way that is sometimes superficial, but occasionally acute and generally helpful. In 1890 Japp brought out a new one-volume edition "thoroughly revised, and rearranged, with additional matter," which is somewhat more readable at the cost of leaving out much of the quoted material. There are especially numerous omissions and substitutions among the letters of the last decade and there is a chapter of "New Reminiscences." Whatever its faults, Japp's *Life* was for sixty years the standard biography and the fountainhead of other studies. David Masson's *De Quincey*, which appeared in 1881 in the English Men of Letters series, is frankly based on Japp and does a good job of reducing his garrulity to readability. Masson intends to present facts—or so many as he thinks proper—and he does not burden himself with much interpretation or analysis. The result is a simple, rather shallow, Victorian document—at one point he dismisses De Quincey's use of opium as a "disagreeable subject." Other treatments dependent upon Japp are the densely factual life by Leslie Stephen in the *Dictionary of National Biography* (1888) and Peter Anton's largely biographical *England's Essayists: Addison, Bacon, De Quincey, Lamb* (1883), interesting for its argument that De Quincey completely lacked moral indignation.

Nor is this all of Japp's services to De Quincey biography. One of the inevitable questions is, how much can De Quincey's autobiographical writings be trusted? Skepticism goes back to James Montgomery's essay in the *Sheffield Iris* in 1821, which wondered whether "this character be real or imaginary," and which elicited an assurance from the Opium-Eater that the record contained nothing *but* the truth if not the whole truth. But reviewers continued to be dubious and to remark unkindly that the earls and ladies with whom De Quincey claimed to have associated in his youth had strangely faded out of his life. Finally the family decided that something should be done about it and turned over to Japp documents calculated to scotch the heresy. Japp accordingly published in 1891 two volumes of *De Quincey Memorials*, in which he singled out one of the milder critics, George Saintsbury, who had expressed himself "rather sceptical" in an essay reprinted in *Essays in English Literature, 1780–1860* (1890). The *Memorials* is a collection of letters, most of them to De Quincey from members of his family, but including some from the Marquis of Sligo, Coleridge, the Wordsworths, Hannah More, and John Wilson. Despite Joseph Bain's attempt, also in 1890, to deflate De Quincey's claims to noble ancestors ("De Quincey and His Supposed Descent from the Earls of Winchester," *Genealogist*, 1890), contemporary commentators accepted *Memorials* as vindication of De Quincey's veracity. So in large measure they are, but as E. L. Griggs points out in "Coleridge, De Quincey, and Nineteenth-Century Editing" (*MLN*, 1932), Japp was not above introducing subtle changes in the text of a letter to make De Quincey look better. The collection also shows his mother as more admirable than she is painted by her son and many of his enthusiasts; devoted, generous, anxious, yet distant and dogmatic, she gets some of her due in the ironic article by D. Hussey, "The Trials of a Great Man's Mother" (*Living Age*, 1920). And a document which Japp did not publish, De Quincey's 1803 *Diary*, turned up later to complicate the picture still further. Could the boy who went through the harrowing experiences of the *Confessions* have so completely avoided reference to them as De Quincey does in his diary written immediately afterward? Despite the defense of *Memorials*, then, it must be admitted that De Quincey's autobiography, though essentially true, is selective and interpretative; Eaton has well said that in it he "is honest as artist rather than as man."

Japp's influence lasted even into the second period of De Quincey biography and provided the materials for a very different book, Malcolm Elwin's *De Quincey* (1935, reprinted with minor revisions in *Confessions* [1956]). Elwin's is a short, vivid, readable book which dispenses with most of the paraphernalia of scholarship. His premise is that the trouble with the former biographers has been "insufficient imagination"; exercising his own, he writes vigorously and positively, recognizing few alternatives and remaining untroubled by the doubts which vex some scholars. His thesis is that De Quincey was "consciously a dual personality," submitting to being thought queer and impractical so that he might inwardly lead the intellectual life. A claim that De Quincey was "no ineffectual eccentric" is valid, and refreshing after such treatments as Thomas Burke's "De Quincey, the Goblin" (*Nineteenth Century*, 1928), which asserted that he spent all his life furtively hiding from a traumatic experience he had in London. But Elwin would appear to be on more dubious ground when he pronounces De Quincey's life a success because "at the expense of health and comfort, he achieved the cultivation of a perfect human intellect," a contention as extreme in its way as that of H. S. Salt who, in "De Quincey the Defaulter" (*Sat. Rev.*, 30 May 1908), repeats the Victorian commonplace that De Quincey failed because he lacked "moral ballast"—he "should have done more."

In 1936 the reign of Victorianism and Japp came decisively to an end, although the suspicion of whitewash lingered on. In that year appeared two biographies of enduring value which curiously complement each other: Edward Sackville-West's *A Flame in Sunlight* (published in America as *Thomas De Quincey: His Life and Work*) and Horace A. Eaton's *Thomas De Quincey: A Biography*. Eaton has produced a scholarly, substantial book; Sackville-West an interpretative, speculative, critical one.

Eaton's work is nearly, if not quite, exhaustive. It presents most of the facts that are now available and usually lets them speak for themselves; when the facts fail, Eaton says refreshingly, "I do not know," or, "There is no answer," and is not above admitting: "It is all very confusing." Eaton supplants Japp as the storehouse of De Quincey information. His painstaking investigations have turned up much new information, most substantially in the areas of De Quincey's efforts to get Wordsworth's *Convention of Cintra* through the press, his relations with Blackwood, and his debts. He forever explodes the theory that De Quincey flitted about conspiratorially because of imaginative fears conjured up by his furtive and secretive personality, explodes it with legal documents to prove the deadly seriousness of creditors. Although he does not indulge in much interpretation, he does make cogent brief analyses, so that there emerges a picture, on the whole favorable, of a self-contained, strong-willed, naïve personality, the protagonist in a lifelong tragedy. His "Epilogue" is as authoritative a short sketch of De Quincey's character as is to be had. Only one factual slip is important enough to call to the reader's attention: heading No. 9 in De Quincey's essay on "The Constituents of Happiness" is surely "contemplation" and not "contempt."[3]

The title of Sackville-West's book—*A Flame in Sunlight*—and such chapter headings as "The Dark Idol" reveal an approach quite different from Eaton's. Sackville-West's study is neither so rich nor so reliable in details, although he has done independent research and

---

[3] This emendation was first suggested by a writer in the *London Quarterly Review* (1877), was made by Japp in the appendix to *Memorials,* and is urged by Sackville-West.

adds some new material, especially letters from the Wordsworth Collection. His purpose, however, is interpretation—to try to find a unity in De Quincey's life and his works. More than any other biography, his book is the saga of the Opium-Eater, and its vivid picture of the depressing yet stoically victorious life is valuable and unforgettable. Perhaps inevitably his thesis that De Quincey's life is dominated by four opium crises leads to a certain simplification of the story. He sees the 1821–22 crisis as marking a sudden end to De Quincey's youth, an immediate drop into middle age indicated by the abrupt loss of his fiery enthusiasm, his jauntiness and ardor. Yet in 1829 De Quincey was ebulliently inviting Charles Knight to come share his "glorious Eldorado" at The Nab. Similarly, Sackville-West is perhaps too facile in calling De Quincey a complete Tory to whom freedom "meant very little" because he submitted to his private disciplines. As Sackville-West points out in another passage, one would be impercipient to view De Quincey's life as only a flight from authority and convention; still it was in some ways a rebellion; and despite his generally conservative attitude he favored educational reform and abolition of corporal punishment; despite his distaste for the French, he had some good things to say about the French Revolution.

Sackville-West uses cautiously and sensibly some of the techniques of psychoanalysis, and can find significance in such a detail as the fourteen-year-old De Quincey's signing himself "Tabitha" in a letter to his sister. His most original suggestion concerns the letter containing £40 which was misdelivered to De Quincey at Manchester Grammar School and which he says he gave to a strange woman in Chester to return to the post office. Doubting this curious story, Sackville-West plausibly supposes that De Quincey delayed in returning the letter to the authorities in Manchester until he felt that he could not do so without being liable to questions, became terrified, and fled—probably destroying the letter. Such insights, always presented tentatively, and carefully documented, are the chief contributions of this book as biography; it has even greater merits as criticism.

Most recent and most charming of the biographies is *De Quincey: A Portrait* (1940), by John Calvin Metcalf. It is obviously a labor of love, avowedly written with no "thought of making a contribution to knowledge" and published without documentation. Although generally accurate, it was completed before the appearance of the work of Eaton and Sackville-West and does not incorporate the latest material. Metcalf has indeed painted a portrait, on the whole a flattering one with insufficient detail in the background. His "Epilogue" is an excellent summary of De Quincey's personality and powers, and his swift, imaginative, and metaphorical style makes this pleasantest of "lives" a good introduction for the general reader.

If another biographer should arise to produce the great critical biography which is still lacking, he will be indebted to the careful articles of Kenneth Forward: " 'Libellous Attack' on De Quincey" (*PMLA*, 1937) and "De Quincey's 'Cessio Bonorum' " (*PMLA*, 1939). Forward painstakingly investigates the facts of the attack on De Quincey in the *John Bull Magazine*, identifying the attacker as William Maginn, and fully reveals the circumstances of De Quincey's bankruptcy in 1833. The latter article is particularly interesting because it proves that he was actually once imprisoned for debt and shows that he listed among his assets £708 15s. owed him by Coleridge—the original loan of 300 guineas (probably a mistake for pounds) plus 5% interest.

3. SPECIAL BIOGRAPHICAL STUDIES

The only facets of De Quincey's biography which have been subject to any specialized study are his use of opium and his relations with his contemporaries, particularly Wordsworth. None of De Quincey's serious biographers paints him as a "damaged soul" and several protest against that view, which appears in such popular, anecdotal, and sensational treatments as Joseph J. Reilly's "The Vagaries of De Quincey" (*Cath W*, 1937), and is sometimes implied by association with Poe, Baudelaire, and Proust, as in Eve Paul-Margueritte's derivative and unreliable article in *Revue bleue* (1937). The taint of *maudite* hangs over him, however, so that there has been great interest in the role of opium in his life and in his state of health.

Two medical men are disposed to take De Quincey at his word that opium was necessary to relieve physical suffering and may even have saved his life, though for different reasons. Dr. W. C. B. Eatwell's "Medical View," which Japp prints as an appendix to his *Life*, diagnoses De Quincey's ailment as "severe nervous irritation or gastrodynia" caused by experiences and diet as a youth. Dr. George M. Gould's *Biographic Clinics: The Origin of the Ill-Health of De Quincey, Carlyle, Darwin, Huxley and Browning* (1903) dismisses this theory as not worthy of refutation. He argues rather that De Quincey was suffering from "reflex ocular neurosis" caused by the strain of accommodating divergent eyes. He bases his conclusion on the Archer portrait, apparently unaware of corroborating evidence in Gilfillan's report of something like an occasional squint. To the lay reader his case seems plausible but perhaps overpleaded.

The weightiest of the studies which fully accept De Quincey's opium eating and see him as a "prophète impénitent des paradis artificiels" is *Poètes et névrosés*, by Arvède Barine (pseudonym for Cécile Vincens), 1898. Here De Quincey is compared to morphinomaniacs as reported in medical studies, and is declared to demonstrate the language of "pécheurs endurcis," to equivocate, to suffer from paralysis of the will, to have become a vandal of books, and to show the inertia and change of mood characteristic of morphinomania. All of this may be true, but Miss Barine does not inspire confidence by asserting that De Quincey had daytime hallucinations and that if they are not in the *Confessions* it is because part of the manuscript has been destroyed. And she does not seriously consider whether opium was the sole, or indeed the principal, cause of the phenomena she observes. Later investigators are more suspicious of the importance to be accorded opium. There had always been a recognition that, as G. P. Lathrop put it in a discerning essay, De Quincey had a "morbid tendency in the brain" ("Some Aspects of De Quincey," *Atlantic Monthly*, 1877) ; and Arthur Compton-Rickett went so far as to say that he "never grew up" (*Personal Forces in Modern Literature*, 1906), and even that there was a "strain of insanity about him" (*The Vagabond in Literature*, 1906). It remained, however, for Paul Guerrier (*Étude médico-psychologique sur Thomas De Quincey*, 1907) and Augustin Cabanès (*Grands névropathes*, 1935) to develop this thesis. Guerrier does not insist that De Quincey was insane, but he does point to nervous disorders in his family and urges that the Opium-Eater was really a neurotic to the point of hypochondria and hysteria. Arguing that he did not show the physical degeneration or the loss of memory inevitable with such a consumption of opium as he claims, Guerrier concludes that De Quincey exaggerated his use of the drug, partly out of autosuggestion. There is much that is plausible in this study and its hereditary approach is useful, but later investigations have shown some of the phenomena here blamed on neuroses to have solid bases in fact. The obsession of pursuit, for instance, proved traceable to very real bailiffs, and the morbid reaction to the death of Catherine Wordsworth has been persuasively identified as poliomyelitis by Cecilia H. Hendricks ("Thomas De Quincey, Symptomatologist," *PMLA*, 1945). Furthermore, the assertion that De Quincey "probably took little" laudanum goes against too much contemporary evidence, although possibly, as W. R. Bett suggests (*The Infirmities of Genius*, 1952), his claims to have taken more than 320 grains of

opium daily were an "exaggeration prompted by the very drug by
which he had become enslaved."

A full study of De Quincey's place in the Lake circle or the
Edinburgh circle has yet to appear. Maria Cramer's *Thomas De
Quincey und John Wilson (Christopher North), ihre literarischen
und persönlichen Beziehungen* (1929), is a routine and superficial
work which concludes that the two men were drawn together by the
attraction of opposites and influenced each other little. It does not
explore the puzzling implication of Woodhouse's *Conversations* and
an 1821 letter of De Quincey's published by Evelyn Grantham ("De
Quincey to His Publisher," *More Books*, 1945), that for some reason
a rift developed between the two friends.

More has been written about De Quincey in the Lake District.
Mary L. Armitt (*Rydal*, 1916) contributes some local information
and with the help of letters discovered at Rydal Hall, gives the first
full account of De Quincey's "purchase" of his father-in-law's estate,
The Nab. Miss Armitt's record is of continued value because the
letters are not elsewhere printed, but her interpretation of De
Quincey's motives—as Eaton points out—is unnecessarily harsh.
Scholarly interest, however, has centered around the De Quincey–
Wordsworth relationship. Japp, aiming to soft-pedal the strained
conditions of later days, emphasized "Early Intercourse of the
Wordsworths and De Quincey" (*Century Mag.*, 1891). The best
concise report of the early intercourse is Horace A. Eaton's essay,
"The Letters of De Quincey to Wordsworth, 1803–1807" (*ELH*,
1936). In his chapter on De Quincey in *Wordsworth and His Circle*
(1907), David W. Rannie presents a helpful picture of the relationship but is superficial in not sensing the strain over *The Convention
of Cintra*. An elaborate account of De Quincey's struggles to get
that work published is given in John Edwin Wells's "The Story of
Wordsworth's 'Cintra'" (*SP*, 1921). Here, and in a cogent defense
in the *Times Literary Supplement* (3 Nov. 1932), Wells refutes the
charges of Southey and Coleridge that De Quincey insisted on
inserting eccentric punctuation and was to blame for holding up the
piece until its audience was gone. Wells also notes the remarkable
closeness with which De Quincey's essays follow the A text of *The
Prelude* ("De Quincey and *The Prelude* in 1839," *PQ*, 1941) and
describes the partial reconciliation of the two writers in "Wordsworth and De Quincey in Westmorland Politics, 1818" *PMLA*,
1940). The fruit of this association was De Quincey's editorship of
the *Westmorland Gazette*, and Wordsworth's willingness to help is
shown by Alan Strout's tabulation of the poems Wordsworth sent to
the *Gazette* ("De Quincey and Wordsworth," *N&Q*, 11 June
1938).

The crux of the relationship between the two men is the explanation of De Quincey's disillusionment which allowed him to write the appreciative but not respectful biographical sketches that contemporaries deplored and posterity applauds. Japp blames Wordsworth's reaction to De Quincey's belated marriage to the daughter of a local farmer. Rannie wonders if De Quincey were not merely too ingenious and bookish to appreciate the naked-souled Wordsworth. De Quincey himself blamed a misunderstanding with his housekeeper. Others have suggested opium, alcohol, the *Cintra* misunderstandings, De Quincey's acute sensitivity, and various combinations. Perhaps the most perceptive explanation is Sackville-West's in the introduction to his edition of *Recollections of the Lake Poets* (1948), in which he adds the suggestion that Wordsworth had become a "father figure." Ralph H. Wolfe prefers the figure suggested by the title of his 1960 Indiana University dissertation, "Priest and Prophet: Thomas De Quincey and William Wordsworth in Their Personal and Literary Relationships." Treating personal and literary associations separately in chronological development, he presents a sensitive analysis, sympathetic to De Quincey, and somewhat limited by dependence upon published materials. Wolfe also points out a possible example of the poet's accepting the advice of the younger man for "Ode. Intimations of Immortality" ("De Quincey, Wordsworth, and *Hamlet*," *N&Q*, Jan. 1961). In *De Quincey to Wordsworth: A Biography of a Relationship* (1962), I have tried to survey the whole connection, from the embarrassingly idolizing approach of the youthful would-be-poet to the clay-foot pecking of the disillusioned essayist.

IV. CRITICISM

THE *Christian Examiner* critic who compared De Quincey to the Leaning Tower of Pisa and asked who would wish either straight ("De Quincey," 1863) was in the solid tradition of De Quinceyans. With some outstanding exceptions, they have usually seen his faults only to palliate them or even call them assets. This defensive attitude is frequent throughout the nineteenth-century reviews, most of which are chiefly of antiquarian interest, but several of which are worth going back to for the vitality of their response. The pleasantly sympathetic article by "Monkshood" ("Thomas De Quincey," *Bentley's Miscellany*, 1855) provides a useful summary of what according to the contemporary mind were the faults needing defense. A convenient example of the most favorable Victorian point of view is the critical section at the end of Masson's *De Quincey* (1881). Masson, as usual, praises nearly everything, but not indiscriminately.

There is yet only one primarily critical general work on De Quincey, H. S. Salt's short monograph, *De Quincey* (1904). Salt's thesis that the clue to De Quincey's writings lies in the "dawning sense of the infinite," that he is "one of the great mystics of literature," is not so distorting as such a one-sided emphasis might be, because the critic also recognizes the analytic and playful aspects of De Quincey. His comments on specific works, however, are often shallow and his whole attitude uncritically admiring. Correspondingly unsympathetic is the essay by Caleb T. Winchester (*A Group of English Essayists*, 1910), who reduces all De Quincey's work to "talk put into print" and quite inaccurately damns him for never really composing anything. For a balanced short criticism the reader can still do no better than Oliver Elton's chapter "Thomas De Quincey" in *A Survey of English Literature, 1780–1880* (1920). Elton makes a rare attempt to find four phases in De Quincey's productive period, and although his categories obviously overlap, the effort is much preferable to the oft-repeated half-truth that De Quincey showed no development. He well recognizes De Quincey's contribution to both the literature of knowledge and the "dream-territory of art," though he perhaps gives opium too much credit for the latter.

The short critiques in handbooks and literary histories suffer inevitably from compression and oversimplification—the great variety of De Quincey will not submit itself to a brief scope. Among the best of these is the judicious treatment by Samuel C. Chew (*A Literary History of England*, ed. A. C. Baugh, Vol. IV, 1948). Louis Cazamian's sketch in *A History of English Literature* (1927) is a distorted picture of De Quincey as a morbid, repressed romantic. More valid is Ernest Bernbaum's view of him as an idealistic, transcendental romantic who consistently placed the highest value on things of the spirit (*Guide through the Romantic Movement*, 1949). Joseph Warren Beach's description of De Quincey as "interior decorator for the spirit of mercantile England" is somewhat harsh (*A History of English Literature*, 1950). Mario Praz's chapter on De Quincey in *The Hero in Eclipse* (1956) also emphasizes the essentially Victorian character of his work, pointing especially to the moral tone of his criticism, and to his delight in drawing "lively *genre* pictures in the purest bourgeois taste." In a long chapter on De Quincey in *The Disappearance of God* (1963), J. Hillis Miller suggests provocatively that De Quincey's critical thought, political theory, vision of history, and style all stem from his "attempt to create, in language, a human equivalent of God's mode of existence," an ultimately futile effort to find perfect continuity, to fill space and time in a musical dream construction of simultaneity and omnipresence.

Certainly the fullest and most generally perceptive of the criticisms of De Quincey is that of Sackville-West in *A Flame in Sunlight*. In two substantial chapters called "Critical Retrospect," as well as elsewhere throughout the book, Sackville-West offers acute, vivid comment. He sees De Quincey as a sophisticated, conscious artist, who usually controlled his medium, and was concerned with style mightily, with the verities of life constantly, and with form scarcely at all. Although he finds no important development in De Quincey—and there is none in the *volte-face* sense in which he uses the term—he does recognize two periods and sees in the latter a preponderance of pedantry, digression, prolixity, and facetiousness. Readers may think he values *Klosterheim* and the narratives too highly, or wonder what he can mean by calling "illfounded" De Quincey's valid and pioneering charges of Coleridge's plagiarism from the German. Readers will, however, recognize the poetic sensitivity he brings to the poetry which he finds pre-eminent in De Quincey.

Despite their agreement in a generally favorable climate of opinion, De Quincey's critics are at odds on many points. Their differences are well illustrated by the gamut of reaction to his humor. To most of his Victorian critics he was "essentially a humorist": the *New Monthly Magazine* published in 1852 a paper on "The Humour of Thomas De Quincey," claiming him "one of the wittiest of humorists and most humorous of wits"; E. B. Chancellor, in his generally admiring essay in *Literary Types* (1895), compared him favorably with Swift; and H. M. Alden in an incredibly overblown article (*Atlantic Monthly*, 1863) allowed him sufficient humor "to have endowed a dozen Aristophaneses." But from the beginning there had been Gilfillan's complaint of "elephantine humour," and as taste changed, more and more critics felt that De Quincey's jocosities were thin, vulgar, clumsy, tasteless. Instead of comparing him with Swift, they argued that he had no real sense of irony. Eaton has found that his horseplay lacks the depth, universality, and seriousness of true humor; and M. R. Ridley, in his excellent little introductory sketch to *De Quincey Selections* (1927), has gone so far as to call his humorous efforts "almost uniformly deplorable." But Francis Thompson, in a sensitive essay reprinted by Ridley, pointed out that De Quincey gave us the first example of "the topsy-turvydom which we associate with the name of Gilbert," and Sackville-West rightly sees some connection with Lewis Carroll and Edward Lear. Ralph H. Wolfe cites an example of De Quincey's love of "pure nonsense" in "De Quincey Quotes Himself" (*N&Q*, March 1960). Critics have most often come to blows, however, over two more significant questions: the distinctive character of De Quincey's poetic prose and the importance of his role as a thinker.

1. PROSE STYLE

Much has been written on the subject of De Quincey's prose style, but it remains elusive. Somehow none of the sober attempts to analyze it seem as rewarding as do such suggestive remarks as G. W. Stonier's figure of De Quincey's blowing "huge iridescent bubbles" which either hang gracefully or burst devastatingly (*New States-man and Nation*, 17 April 1948). It may be, as Leslie Stephen declared in perhaps the most influential single critique of De Quincey (*Hours in a Library*, 1874), difficult or impossible and even super-fluous to define the peculiar flavor of his style. H. P. Robinson ("De Quincey and the 'Grand Style,'" *Academy*, 17 Feb. 1906) facilely found his claim to fame in the "splendour of his diction"; M. B. Anderson ("The Style of De Quincey," *Dial*, 1891) contradictorily and more perceptively discovered it in his "sentence-architecture." De Quincey's own designation, "impassioned prose," has not proved helpful; for, as many critics from Stephen down have pointed out, there is not much of what is normally called passion in his work. The most discerning short discussion of this question is a *Times Literary Supplement* lead article ("Impassioned Prose," 16 Sept. 1926), which notes that the best passages are not lyrical outbursts but composed descriptions of states of mind.

First of the serious attempts to analyze De Quincey's style is William Minto's discussion in his *Manual of English Prose* (1872). He investigates the varied sources of De Quincey's figures, points to "explicitness of connection" as the chief characteristic of his paragraphing, and shows how his elaborate syntax sometimes be-comes unwieldy, yet helps to produce his "punctilious exactness." Finding "elaborate stateliness" his predominant characteristic, Minto ranks De Quincey with Milton as a master of stately cadence and sublimity: Milton is sweeter and more varied, De Quincey more magnificent. His description of De Quincey's vocabulary as predominantly Latinate needs qualification from the study of Albert S. Cook, who analyzed about 10,000 words and found them 41.13% native English ("Native and Foreign Words in De Quincey," *MLN*, 1886). And even Cook's study would not have satisfied De Quincey, who insisted on the value of both main stocks of words and argued that the sinews of connection were Anglo-Saxon—the very words which Cook eliminated from his count.

As yet the only substantial published attempt to concentrate on De Quincey's style is Lane Cooper's *The Prose Poetry of Thomas De Quincey* (1902). Cooper sets out to study just that particular kind of prose which De Quincey called "impassioned," and which Cooper equates with the Literature of Power and finds better designated as ornate prose affecting "sensibilities." He becomes rather too sure of his touchstone for this kind of prose, undertaking to distinguish it in a sentence or even a clause. This style, largely written after 1844, is marked by the outer characteristic of a high proportion of semivowels, dashes, exclamation points, and short sentences, and by the more significant inner characteristics of subjectivism and a distinctive vocabulary which shows limited cycles of association. His analysis of this vocabulary and of De Quincey's imagery is helpful, but one feels continually that too small a body of De Quincey's work is drawn upon. Cooper's narrow specialization does not account adequately for what Elton calls the "endless variety" of De Quincey's prose (*A Survey of English Literature, 1780–1880*, 1920). Elton's excellent brief treatment finds the key in "verbal balance" and illustrates by diagraming sentences. Elton also compares De Quincey's style to Landor's, as does George Saintsbury in the slight essay (*Cambridge History of English Literature*) which repeats his favorite epithet for De Quincey's prose: "rigmarole." Earlier critics were more apt to contrast De Quincey with Carlyle and Macaulay.

Valuable as it is, Cooper's work has little to say about two of the most significant aspects of De Quincey's style: its relation to music and its relation to poetry. Although Cooper does comment on the musical quality of De Quincey's prose, he curiously says that the "first appeal is to the eye," and his treatment of "Dream Fugue" indicates that he does not recognize the degree to which music molded the style. The first appreciation of the true fugal quality of this piece came from Lucile P. Leonard ("De Quincey's Dream-Fugue," *Poet Lore*, 1917), but her impressionistic remarks have been superseded by the detailed and valuable analysis of Calvin S. Brown, Jr. ("The Musical Structure of De Quincey's *Dream-Fugue*," *Musical*

Quart., 1938). The larger matter of the necessary role of music in De Quincey's life has been treated by Horace A. Eaton ("De Quincey's Love of Music," *JEGP*, 1914). An interesting psychological explanation of the musical effect in his prose may be found in Virginia Woolf's *The Common Reader* (2d Ser., 1935).

Cooper never comes to grips with the question of the validity of such a "bastard product"—Winchester's phrase—as prose-poetry, a question which does not bother a modern critic like Sackville-West but which has exercised many commentators, like the *Dublin University Magazine* (1854) writer who declared that "mode of warbling in prose" to be "utterly execrable." Masson tries valiantly to justify the hybrid on theoretical grounds in *Essays, Biographical and Critical* (1856), as does W. J. Dawson in *The Makers of Modern Prose* (1899). There has been, however, no adequate study of the rhythms of this poetic prose. George Saintsbury, who thinks that only about five percent of De Quincey's prose is rhythmical, does little more than scan a few passages subjectively and point to the skillful avoidance of blank verse as an example of his principle of the utmost variety with the least disturbance (*A History of English Prose Rhythm*, 1912). A. C. Clark (*Prose Rhythm in English*, 1913) and J. Shelly ("Rhythmical Prose in Latin and English," *Church Quart. Rev.*, 1912) only suggest De Quincey's use of the Latin *cursus*. Oliver Elton ("English Prose Numbers," *A Sheaf of Papers*, 1922) makes an interesting comparison with Gibbon, showing De Quincey to use shorter feet and many more monosyllables, but his count is based on too small a sample to be very significant. John H. Scott (*Rhythmic Prose*, 1925) finds in De Quincey several illustrations of his quadral theory, and William M. Patterson (*The Rhythm of Prose*, 1916) records drumbeat rhythm tests on one of De Quincey's sentences in competition with sentences from Newman and Pater: De Quincey won. The variety and subtlety of De Quincey's rhythms in "The English Mail-Coach" is clearly demonstrated by Shozo Kobayashi's study *Rhythm in the Prose of Thomas De Quincey* (1956). Kobayashi conveniently brings together comments on De Quincey's prose style and scans all of "Dream-Fugue" and other selected sentences, carefully tabulating the pattern of rising, falling, waved, and level accents and analyzing the cadences; but he makes no effort to relate rhythm to meaning or to generalize about De Quincey's technique. Richard H. Byrns's dissertation "An Analytical Study of the Prose Style of Thomas De Quincey" (Edinburgh Univ., 1955) has not yet been published, but he has presented some insights from it in the article on the "Dream Fugue" already mentioned and in "A Note on De Quincey's 'The Vision of Sudden

Death' " (N&Q, May 1962), which prints unpublished notes from the holograph manuscript, showing De Quincey's concern with his prose style.

Some of the commentators on De Quincey's poetic prose need to lend an ear, however, to Arthur Symons, whose generally unreliable "A Word on De Quincey" (*Studies in Prose and Verse*, 1904) makes the good point that much of it is not poetry but rhetoric, oratory. Even more debunking is the discussion by Violet Paget ("Vernon Lee") in *The Handling of Words* (1923), which—although admitting the result is sometimes matchless grandeur—complains of "lack of movement," "redundancy of auxiliaries," "senseless, flurried changing of point of view," "vulgarity," and "slang." The ubiquitousness and the American source of much of this sometimes tasteless slang are well described by Robert E. Hollinger ("De Quincey's Use of Americanisms," *AS*, 1948).

Cooper did, however, come to grips with another problem of De Quincey scholarship, and was one of the first to do so: the influence of opium on his writing. From the beginning there was the tendency to recognize the drug as both the key to "many of the discrepancies of his genius" (G. Cheever, *Christian Examiner*, 1863) and the "magician" responsible for his gorgeous dreams (G. S. Phillips, *North American Rev.*, 1859). Like Ripley Hitchcock in his short essay, *Thomas De Quincey: A Study* (1899), Cooper attacked the notion that the dream visions were poured from a laudanum decanter, and the course of scholarship has gradually vindicated him. Alfred R. Lindesmith (*Opiate Addiction*, 1947) asserts, "The notion that narcotics produce hallucinations or dreams is completely false." And Elisabeth Schneider's studies ("The 'Dream' of *Kubla Khan*," *PMLA*, 1945; *Coleridge, Opium and* KUBLA KHAN, 1953) conclude that no evidence warrants the beliefs that opium of itself either produces or imparts any special character to kaleidoscopic imagery, visions, or dreams, although dreams may be indirectly caused by some of the concomitants of addiction such as withdrawal cycles. She points out as more significant the convergence of De Quincey's native dreaming tendency and the literary vogue of the Gothic which exploited visions.

The idea that opium played some vital part in De Quincey's writing is, nevertheless, frequently expressed. Helene Richter's routine essay (*Englische Studien*, 1924) admits that De Quincey's dreaming proclivity was innate, but thinks opium "macht seine Traumkraft schöpferisch," and M. H. Abrams finds a characteristic opium imagery in his work (*The Milk of Paradise*, 1934). Other commentators, dubious about the positive effects of opium on De

Quincey's prose, are nonetheless sure of its negative effects. H. M. Paull, pointing out that De Quincey often did not follow his own advice on brevity, directness, and footnote control, suggests that opium weakness made him unable to correct the faults he saw ("De Quincey—and Style," *Fortnightly Rev.*, 1922). Long before, John Wilson had remarked that De Quincey's writing was powerful only when he was free of opium (Viscount Cranbrook, "Christopher North," *National Rev.*, 1884), and Cesare Lombroso argued that the drug devastated his strong intellect (*Genio e degenerazione*, 1907).

Scientific consideration of other influences on De Quincey's style connected with his opium addiction begins with Wilhelm Stekel (*Die Träume der Dichter*, 1912), who argues that De Quincey became an opium eater out of emotional need and that both the opium and the dreams were products of his neurotic personality. This interesting Freudian interpretation finds in the dreams the characteristic helplessness of a little child and sees Ann as a mother symbol. Jeannette Marks raises another pertinent argument by emphasizing (*Genius and Disaster: Studies in Drugs and Genius*, 1925) what Roger Dupouy had already pointed out (*Les opiomanes*, 1912), that De Quincey usually took his opium in the form of laudanum, a tincture of alcohol, and that at his peak consumption he was taking the equivalent of a quart of whiskey daily. She urges, therefore, that in his works one sees not the characteristic opium traits of recessiveness, femininity, inhibited sexuality, secretiveness, pathological imagination, and broken structure, but the alcoholic traits of egotism, sexuality, pessimism, sensual imagery, and exaggerated but clear structure. Unfortunately for her thesis, she offers little proof beyond a statement that De Quincey was not secretive but boastful, and a case might be made that he indeed displayed some of the traits she associates with opium. C. E. Terry and Mildred Pellens (*The Opium Problem*, 1928) also argue that De Quincey's use of laudanum was really a case of "mixed intoxication" and find in his boastful style "the psychologic picture of the alcoholic with his very common megalomania," but they limit their evidence to one half-facetious passage and take no cognizance of De Quincey's own discussions of the differences between the effects of alcohol and those of opium.

Recent commentators have been disposed to find a significant aspect of De Quincey's writing not so much the opium as the "tormented spirit" of the opium eater (Fernando Alegría, "Los Sueños de Thomas De Quincey," *ND*, 1955). Henry Amer ("Les

Confessions de Thomas de Quincey," *NRF*, Oct. 1962) and J.-J. Mayoux ("De Quincey et le sens du temps," *Let N*, Jan. 1960) both suggest a masochistic streak in De Quincey, and Mayoux makes an interesting analysis of his tendency to manipulate time so as to maintain simultaneously a Godlike immediate perception of the totality, and a shudderingly human suspense at the ticking moments. De Quincey's verbose and digressive style is explained by Aurelio Zanco in his essay "Temi e Psicologia di T. De Quincey" (*RLMC*, 1956) as the result of insecurity and even sadism, a defense mechanism to ward off the unbearable reality.

2. DE QUINCEY AS A THINKER

If Edith J. Morley is right in saying of De Quincey, "It is improbable that he will ever again come to be ranked among the greatest of prose-writers" (*MLN*, 1937), the reason is not merely that modern tastes prefer simpler styles and find him somewhat grandiloquent, but principally that in perspective the substance of much of his work seems thin. Many of his writings are concerned with personalia and trivia; others belong to his category of the Literature of Knowledge and have been superseded by later investigations—though many can never be supplanted because De Quincey's amber could preserve colonies of maggotty facts.

Message-hunting Victorians were apt to be violent on this question of his substance: one analysis sees De Quincey as almost a monster because "his finest productions teach nothing" (*London Quart. Rev.*, 1857), another finds in him no sense of duty and fears he is "little better than an artist" (*British Quart. Rev.*, 1863), and one obituary announces the close of an "almost profitless career" (*Athenaeum*, 17 Dec. 1859). On the other hand, comments on his essential humanity are frequent, and his friends find positive value in his "hopeful spirit," his "innate nobility of thought," and his "sincere religious feeling" (*London Quart. Rev.*, 1877; *North British Rev.*, 1863; *North American Rev.*, 1852). And certain it is that De Quincey felt a deep responsibility to teach and did in fact contribute to the sum of human experience. Modern commentators might not agree with the reviewer who called De Quincey's opium struggles "his contribution to the great story of mankind" (*Blackwood's*, 1877), or with Paul Bourget that the Opium-Eater's intuitions are valuable because all the problems of destiny are enveloped in the problem of intoxication (*Études et portraits*, 1889). Most of them, however, would count W. E. Henley's often-quoted epithet, "Thomas De Sawdust," as slander and, though granting that De Quincey can be dull and is sometimes thin, hold that he is never dry or empty of human values.

Many of De Quincey's early critics exclaimed over his intellectual capacity, and some even insisted that he had "performed intellectual service for the age" (Peter Bayne, *Essays in Biography and Criticism*, 1857–58) and "made real additions to the existing stock of thought" (*Fraser's*, 1860–61). It is true that De Quincey was prone to set himself up as an authority and purveyor of light, and that to his periodical audiences he was in effect original and informative. But his harried and bookless circumstances during most of his productive period were not conducive to scholarship; he was a journalist and a popularizer, and later commentators have found it easy to prove him wrong and derivative in many things. *Notes and Queries* bristles with corrections of his quotations or facts, and Leslie Stephen—temperamentally incapable of sympathetic appreciation of De Quincey—venomously points out logical flaws and blatant prejudices (*Hours in a Library*, 1874). Most comprehensive of these exposés is the valuable but carping series of notes by V. R., "De Quincey: Some Objections and Corrections" (*N&Q*, 17 June, 1, 15 July, 9 Sept. 1939; 21 Sept., 14, 21 Dec. 1940), which call De Quincey's famous memory a "forgettery" and reveal many of his prejudices and inaccuracies. The best summary of De Quincey's pretensions as a thinker is Renè Wellek's excellent article, "De Quincey's Status in the History of Ideas" (*PQ*, 1944), which finds little system or originality in the scattered writings and sees De Quincey as a curious mixture of eighteenth-century rationalist, Christian pietist, and conservative romantic. De Quincey's participation in the romantic sense of eternity is well described by Georges Poulet, who points out that in De Quincey—and in Baudelaire, who was influenced by him—the mysterious feeling for simultaneity in time receives its most modern and most natural expression ("Timelessness and Romanticism," *JHI*, 1954).

Those areas in which De Quincey or his commentators have claimed significant contributions are philosophy, economics, history, biography, importation of German thought, and literary criticism. No one since Samuel Davey (*Darwin, Carlyle, and Dickens*, 1876) has taken very seriously De Quincey's philosophical pretensions. The fullest discussion of his knowledge of philosophy, by S. K. Proctor (*Thomas De Quincey's Theory of Literature*, 1943), is perhaps too sanguine on De Quincey's understanding of Kant; Wellek (*Immanuel Kant in England, 1798–1838*, 1931) and James Hutchison Stirling (*Jerrold, Tennyson and Macaulay with Other Critical*

Essays, 1868) doubt if he could have really understood the German, since he considered him a destructive force and paid most attention to his peripheral works.

The paradox of a great authority on economic theory who didn't know how to negotiate a draft has amused many commentators on De Quincey, but his considerable writings on economics have been given little serious attention. John Stuart Mill (*Principles of Political Economy*, 1848) praised his discussion of value but found fault with his doctrine of use, and Shadworth H. Hodgson, in partisan fashion, tried to show that Mill was wrong (*Outcast Essays and Verse Translations*, 1881). The fullest study, Gertrud Meyer's *Das Verhältnis Thomas de Quinceys zur Nationalökonomie* (1927), concludes that although De Quincey perhaps extended the theory of value, his chief merit lies in his skill in popularizing and clarifying Ricardo.

According to De Quincey's own classification of historical writing into narrative, scenical and philosophical, he was primarily —as Sackville-West points out—a scenical historian who took the broad view. That this view could sometimes be prejudiced is shown by Frank R. Gay in "De Quincey as a Student of Greek, and a Writer on Greek Literature and History" (M.A. thesis, Univ. of Chicago, 1917), although Gay's conclusion that it is very doubtful whether De Quincey possessed any real classical scholarship is valid only in the narrowest sense of the term and takes no cognizance of the anti-Hellenic movement of which he was perhaps England's most fervent member. That De Quincey's historical thought is of considerable interest is excellently proved by Ernst Theodor Sehrt (*Geschichtliches und religiöses Denken bei Thomas De Quincey*, 1936). Sehrt sees De Quincey at the same time a pure conservative and a believer in progress, in both his political and his religious thinking. As a staunch Tory and a good Church of England man, he viewed the English as the chosen people and every effort at constitutional reform as *hybris* against God and against history; yet under the influence of Kant and Hegel as well as Burke, he saw a historical determinism as God's plan. Thus his historical view was genetic, teleological, and progressive. This explanation of De Quincey's nationalism, conservatism, defense of colonialism and war, and even his attitude toward the Gothic novel in relation to his religious convictions is perhaps too ready to give a wholeness to his disparate and opportunist works, but it is nonetheless welcome. A much slighter account of this religious history from the point of view of contemporary readers may be found in C. M. Ingleby's *Essays* (1888). Only two of De Quincey's historical writings have received any individual attention. "Joan of Arc" has naturally attracted French complaint: G. de Contades ("La Jeanne d'Arc de Thomas de Quincey," *RDM*, 1893) praises the apocalyptic visions but is disgusted by the pamphleteering and the strained humor. Surveying the whole Pucelle record, Eduard von Jan (*Das literarische Bild der Jeanne D'Arc*, 1928) says that De Quincey added the concept of Joan as the advocate and redeemer of fallen sinners. Joseph A. Sandhaas ("De Quincey's *Revolt of the Tartars* Seen in the Light of Chinese, French, German and English Source Material," Boston Univ. dissertation, 1946) constructs a mighty engine to prove that De Quincey is "quite undependable" as a historian because, led by prejudice against the Russians and a love of the sensational, he played fast and loose with his sources. This study supersedes the skimpy discussions of De Quincey's sources in Masson's and C. S. Baldwin's editions of the *Revolt* and the "Historical Note" appended to W. L. River's *The Torguts*, and is welcome for bringing together and translating inaccessible material; it is disappointing, however, in that it makes no real attempt to analyze the artistic effects of De Quincey's "deviations" from his sources.

So much of De Quincey's work is biographical that James C. Johnston (*Biography: The Literature of Personality*, 1927) thinks that he should be regarded primarily as a biographer; yet little attention has been paid to this aspect of his writing. "The Last New Life of Shakespeare" (*Fraser's*, 1841) finds De Quincey's essay in the *Encyclopaedia Britannica* admirable, ingenious, and shaky in its facts. Modern critics have usually praised the life of Bentley and been amused by the vivid if prejudiced picture of Parr, but have been more interested in the revealing sketches of his contemporaries, whom De Quincey seemed to see with the sharp eye of an observant child.

Neither has De Quincey's autobiographical writing received the attention it deserves. In his slight sketch (*Literary Celebrities of the English Lake District*, 1905), Frederick Sessions rated the autobiography first; some earlier critics, however, thought De Quincey revealed too much and forfeited "the respect of his reader" (*Westminster Rev.*, 1854), and some later critics accuse him of perplexing, disappointing, and ultimately evading us, concealing with the air of revealing (Peter Quennell, "Books in General," *New Statesman and Nation*, 11 Nov. 1950). More perceptively, Virginia Woolf points out that for all his diffuseness and aloofness, De Quincey had the secret of two levels of existence, and that he could analyze the mysterious and solemn moments of slow time with a skill which Scott, Austen, and Byron did not possess (*The Common Reader*, 2d Ser.,

1935). Arguing that De Quincey's autobiographical writings are "pieces of introspective analysis that in some ways anticipate modern psychology by almost a century," Brooks Wright attempts to show that De Quincey used myths as projections of family relationships and parables of his inner state ("The Cave of Trophonius: Myth and Reality in De Quincey," *NCF*, 1954). The essay builds a great deal upon slight classical references and, in declaring that "the stuff of De Quincey's phantasies" is "guilty love" of a sister who died when he was six and "guilty hate" of a brother who died when he was about twelve, appears to ignore much of the reality of his life.

Since De Quincey followed up the success of *Confessions* by publishing in the *London Magazine* translations, adaptations, and discussions of German literature, and then went on to provide some of the same fare for *Blackwood's*, scholarly argument has arisen over the importance of his role as an importer of German literature and ideas. In his circle he had some reputation as a German authority, but Carlyle's louder and steadier voice soon drowned him out in the public ear, so that Walter Y. Durand has argued that Carlyle's significance as a translator and critic is considerably greater than De Quincey's, much of whose work was wiredrawn hack writing ("De Quincey and Carlyle in Their Relation to the Germans," *PMLA*, 1907). Most of the general discussions of German literature in England appear also to consider De Quincey's influence as slight.[4] The extent of this general neglect of De Quincey's significance as a propagator of German thought is disapprovingly shown by C. D. Thorpe, who points out that some studies simply ignore him (appendix to S. K. Proctor, *Thomas De Quincey's Theory of Literature*, 1943).

The two chief studies of De Quincey's relation to German literature are at daggers' points. William A. Dunn's *Thomas De Quincey's Relation to German Literature and Philosophy* (1900) is essentially unsympathetic. He objects that De Quincey sees German works exclusively from an English point of view; that he is capricious, unreliable, and prejudiced; and that the best that can be said for his services to German literature is that he stimulated interest and curiosity. Although inclined to see nothing but the holes in the cheese, the study is valuable for its collection of De Quincey's

4 Wilhelm Todt, *Lessing in England, 1767–1850* (1912); Emma G. Jaeck, *Madame De Staël and the Spread of German Literature* (1915): V. A. Stockley, *German Literature as Known in England, 1750–1830* (1929); Frederic Ewen, *The Prestige of Schiller in England, 1788–1859* (1932); Ernst Margraf, *Einfluss der deutschen Litteratur auf die englische* (1901); and Emil Koeppel, *Deutsche Strömungen in der englischen Literatur* (1910).

comments on German writers, and especially for the interesting index to his reading afforded by an appended list of references to German scholarship. Vehemently presented as a corrective to Dunn's pessimistic view is the overoptimistic analysis of Erhart H. Essig, "Thomas De Quincey and Robert Pearse Gillies as Champions of German Literature and Thought" (Northwestern Univ. dissertation, 1951). Essig emphasizes the points made by an early reviewer (*London Quart. Rev.*, 1877) that De Quincey preceded Carlyle, that he was a pioneer and a popularizer. This thesis allows him to play down the superficialities and omissions in De Quincey's treatment. Since he does not write from quite such a Germanophile position as Dunn, he can demonstrate that some of De Quincey's unfavorable judgments are plausible and have often been vindicated by subsequent literary historians. One of the most valuable aspects of his work, however, is his analysis of De Quincey's practice as a translator. The very bulk of these translations—excellent of Lessing and Richter—and the constant and interesting way in which De Quincey wrote from and about the Germans, suggest that his part in introducing them to nineteenth-century England must have been appreciable.

In a series of essays appearing in various places over the last ten years, Peter Michelsen has contributed some helpful analyses of De Quincey's treatment of German writers. The point of view which underlies these studies is that De Quincey's judgments stem from subjective bases and tell more about himself than the Germans: he is more successful where he has some sympathy—with Jean Paul and to a lesser degree with Lessing and Schiller—least so with Goethe and Kant, yet he "folgt Kant, soweit man das zu jener Zeit von einem in ganz anderer geistiger Tradition Aufgewachsenen erwarten konnte" ("Der Träumer und die Ratio: Zu Leben und Werk Thomas De Quinceys," *Deutsche Universitäts-Zeitung*, 20 Dec. 1954; "Thomas De Quincey und Schiller," *German Life and Letters*, 1956; "Thomas De Quincey und Goethe," *Euphorion*, 1956; "Thomas De Quinceys Lessing-Bild," *Monatshefte*, 1958; "Thomas De Quincey und die Kantische Philosophie," *RLC*, 1959; "Thomas De Quincey und Jean Paul," *JEGP*, 1962).

Controversy has also played around the subject of De Quincey as a critic. Henry Tuckerman (*Christian Examiner*, 1863) chose as the one word for De Quincey's mind "appreciative," and Francis Thompson thought he was the first to practice the mode of criticism known as "appreciation"; yet V. R. accused him of enjoying the pleasure of disparagement (*N&Q*, 9 Sept. 1939). Some commentators, like Eaton and Saintsbury, have considered him a preceptist;

others, like Sackville-West and Miss Darbishire, have labeled him a romantic. Some, like Kebbel (*QR*, 1861) thought him a "critic of uncommon delicacy"; others, like Dunn, not essentially a critic at all. Gilfillan remarked on the narrowness, Minto the comprehensiveness of his critical view.

Among the early comments on De Quincey the critic, those of Minto (*Manual of English Prose*, 1872) and Japp (appendix to *Memorials*, 1891) are noteworthy defenses. The first balanced judgment is Saintsbury's (*A History of Criticism and Literary Taste in Europe*, 1904). Although Saintsbury puts too much emphasis on the preceptist element in De Quincey's criticism, his description of him as eminently suggestive and eminently unsafe has not been modified by subsequent scholarship, which has developed along two lines: that which emphasizes De Quincey's comments upon the theory of literature and that which investigates his specific critical judgments. Helen Darbishire, in the introduction to her volume of selections (*De Quincey's Literary Criticism*, 1909), argues that he excels in the theoretical sphere. She sees him as a romantic critic, strongly influenced by Wordsworth's valuation of the emotions, by what she considers his mysticism, by his love of symbolism, and by his use of opium. She values most highly his conception of the inseparableness of form and substance and his sense of literary productions as living organisms. Her essay is stimulating and perceptive, but needs qualification; she does not take sufficient cognizance of the facts that these ideas are neither original with De Quincey nor consistently and simply held by him.

A full and careful analysis of De Quincey's literary theory is S. K. Proctor's *Thomas De Quincey's Theory of Literature* (1943), which analyzes De Quincey's philosophical background, his general aesthetic, and his concepts of style, of rhetoric, and of literature as power. Proctor's thorough explication of De Quincey's original definition of rhetoric as mind-play supersedes the salmagundi treatment of Hoyt H. Hudson ("De Quincey on Rhetoric and Public Speaking," *Studies in Rhetoric and Public Speaking*, 1925) except that Hudson has an interesting section on De Quincey's rhetorical practice. The thesis of Proctor's study is that De Quincey was both an intellectual and a mystic and that his work is marked by a fundamental and unconscious dichotomy which made him alternately think of the purpose of art as pleasure or as power, and which made him view style as sometimes of intrinsic value, sometimes only ministerial. Valuable and painstaking as this work is, it suffers somewhat from a tendency to claim too great originality for De Quincey's thought, and from a readiness to discard an idea as

unrepresentative or develop what appear to be the possible exten-
sions of his thought. Throughout there is the inclination to take too
seriously and demand too much unity and consistency in the
scattered journalistic products of many different impulses. His
discussion of De Quincey's theory of the relation of the artist to his
work needs to be qualified by A. E. Powell's interesting chapter in
The Romantic Theory of Poetry (1926). Although De Quincey is
probably not the expressionist *manqué* she would make him, he did
sometimes treat art as expression. In "On De Quincey's Theory of
Literary Power" (*UTQ*, 1957) and his University of Toronto
dissertation, "De Quincey's Theory of Literature of Power,"
1957–58, John W. Bilsland argues that the basis of De Quincey's
famous conception of the literature of power is a pattern of
disturbing childhood experiences marked by powerful stimuli, emotion, revelation, and permanent aftereffects – the harmonizing counterpart of which he found, without the attendant pain, in music and
his early reading.

De Quincey's theory of Poetic Diction has been discussed by
Alexander Brede, who finds that he thought all the resources of
language were open to poetry ("Theories of Poetic Diction . . . ,"
Michigan Academy of Science, Arts and Letters, 1931). In a more
intensive study I have suggested that De Quincey moved from an
early admiration of Wordsworth's view to a position akin to
Coleridge's, believing that the language of poetry was privileged, not
prescriptive, but emphasizing the innately appropriate word ("De
Quincey on Wordsworth's Theory of Diction," *PMLA*, 1953).

J. H. Fowler reintroduced the other line of investigation, De
Quincey as a practicing critic, by vehemently denouncing the
theoretical distinction between the Literature of Knowledge and the
Literature of Power, and instead listing as his special services to
English literature the criticism of Shakespeare, the recognition of
Wordsworth and Landor, and the perceptive appreciation of Milton
(*De Quincey as Literary Critic, English Assoc. Pamphlet*, 1922). De
Quincey's criticism of Wordsworth has been unfavorably reviewed by
David W. Rannie (*Wordsworth and His Circle*, 1907), and the
famous "Knocking at the Gate in *Macbeth*" essay discussed by
Augustus Ralli (*A History of Shakespearian Criticism*, 1932), who
praised it shortsightedly as emotional rather than intellectual
criticism. I have tried to show the intellectual element underlying
this and other dramatic criticism and to suggest that De Quincey
took a more consistently theatrical view of Shakespeare than his
principal critical contemporaries ("De Quincey's Dramaturgic Criticism," *ELH*, 1951). On the other hand, Geoffrey Carnall has called

attention to the "emphatically nineteenth-century" character of the "Knocking" essay because of its concern with the "tiger spirit" expressed by Wordsworth, Blake, Southey, and Shelley—with a "clash of forces, not of men" ("De Quincey on the Knocking at the Gate," *REL*, 1961). The use in *Othello* and *Oedipus* of De Quincey's device of "Königsmord in Parenthese" is the subject of Klaus Ulrich Leistikow's "Zu einem Gedanken De Quinceys" (*Antaios*, 1959), published with a translation into German of De Quincey's essay. Another treatment of De Quincey's criticism in a special area is Charles I. Patterson's "The Romantic Critics' Conception of the Novel: Hazlitt, Coleridge, and De Quincey" (microfilmed doctoral dissertation, Univ. of Illinois, 1950).[5] Patterson obviously has difficulty fitting De Quincey into his thesis that the romantic critics had greater respect for the novel than has been generally recognized, for De Quincey had a poor opinion of the genre. But he does good service in showing that De Quincey's love of the Gothic novel has been overemphasized and has not been adequately related to his concept of the dark sublime, his sense of the problem of sin, and his placing the novel in the Literature of Power, albeit of a low order. This is substantially the contribution of Patterson's essay, "De Quincey's Conception of the Novel" (*PMLA*, 1955). The fullest discussion of De Quincey as a practicing critic is my study *Thomas De Quincey, Literary Critic* (1952), which analyzes his critical method. I contend that the logician and the dreamer cooperate in De Quincey the critic, to build a logical superstructure upon a basically affective criticism. Seeking to objectify and communicate the effect he feels, De Quincey sometimes explores the historical cause in the characteristic difference of the age, sometimes seeks the personal factor in the author's ruling passion, and sometimes analyzes the demands of the genre.

Recently Clifford Leech has noted some relations of De Quincey to the New Critics and defended his "seminal property" ("De Quincey as Literary Critic," *REL*, 1961). In his chapter on De Quincey in the forthcoming third volume of *A History of Modern Criticism* (1955–   ), René Wellek presents an informed and judicious summary showing De Quincey to belong "to the empirical psychological tradition of the British, and to the emotional trend, descending from Dennis through Hartley to Wordsworth."

---

5   Among master's theses in this area are: Mayoux, "De Quincey's Moral and Literary Criticism" (Univ. of Paris, 1922); Mary E. Pierce, "The Contributions of Hazlitt and De Quincey to Shakespeare Criticism" (Univ. of Illinois, 1930); and Eunice H. Helmkamp, "De Quincey's Attitude toward Life and Literature as Revealed in His Opinions of His Contemporaries" (Univ. of Illinois, 1942).

3. SOURCES, INFLUENCE, AND REPUTATION

Although there is a general assumption among commentators that De Quincey drew upon the prose stylists of the seventeenth century, particularly Sir Thomas Browne, no one has investigated the matter or paid much attention to his sources at all. The frequent suggestion that he owed something to Jean Paul Richter has been studied by Dr. Friedrich Christoph (*Über den Einfluss Jean Paul Friedrich Richters auf Thomas De Quincey*, 1898–99). Christoph shows many similarities and some differences between the two writers, but is too ready to assume that the German was the Englishman's model. Some of the elements De Quincey allegedly got from Jean Paul could have come from a number of sources; although he was probably influenced by Richter, whom he obviously loved, the significant thing is that the two men were kindred spirits—De Quincey dreamed rich dreams long before he could read German. The only other studies having anything to do with De Quincey's sources are some explorations into the materials and impulses of his papers on murder. W. E. A. Axon prints an interesting letter which seems to be the "germ" of "Murder Considered as One of the Fine Arts" (*Bookman* [London], 1907) and recounts the career of "De Quincey's Highwayman" (*Echoes of Old Lancashire*, 1899). The newspaper version of the Marr murder is given by Thomas Burke ("The Obsequies of Mr. Williams: New Light on De Quincey's Famous Tale of Murder," *Bookman* [N. Y.], 1928), and the source of a murder story in De Quincey's essay on Kant has been found in the *Westmorland Gazette* by Robert H. Super ("De Quincey and a Murderer's Conscience," *TLS*, 5 Dec. 1936).

Numerous suggestions have been made concerning De Quincey's literary influence. J. H. Ingram thinks Poe learned much from the *Confessions* (*International Rev.*, 1877); Thomas Bayne sees a relationship between Charlotte Brontë's *Villette* and "Our Ladies of Sorrow," ("De Quincey and Charlotte Brontë," *N&Q*, 9 Sept. 1893); and Richard Garnett believes Dickens profited from reading the Opium-Eater (*Confessions*, 1885). De Quincey's impact on the development of the English essay seems to Hugh Walker (*The English Essay and Essayists*, 1915) such that without him Stevenson and Ruskin could not have written as they did, and the aestheticism of "On Murder Considered as One of the Fine Arts" suggests to Klaus Mann ("Thomas De Quincey," *Sammlung*, 1934) general parallels to the work of Oscar Wilde. Widening the circle, J. K. Bostock points out that Shaw takes the same view of Joan of Arc

as De Quincey ("Johanna d'Arc als Nationalistin und Protes-
tantin," *Englische Studien*, 1928); E. J. Simmons finds direct
influence of the *Confessions* on Gogol's *The Nevsky Prospect*
("Gogol and English Literature," *MLR*, 1931); and Rudolf Kass-
ner compares Anne with Sonja and suggests that Dostoyevsky was
influenced by De Quincey ("Thomas De Quincey," *Corona*, 1939).
Frederick S. Rockwell persuasively conjectures that "Mail Coach"
and *Suspiria* may have "generated the transmuting of *The Whale*
into *Moby-Dick*" by providing the concept of a dark, self-torment-
ing nature, suggestions in the use of symbolism, and even some
details of the final scene ("De Quincey and the Ending of 'Moby-
Dick,' " *NCF*, 1954). D. H. Lawrence's use in several stories and
novels of the device of the "Knocking on the Gate in *Macbeth*" is the
subject of Philip Appleman's "D. H. Lawrence and the Intrusive
Knock" (*MFS*, 1957–58), and Ann Gossman points out Robert
Louis Stevenson's employment of the same stratagem in his short
story "Markheim" ("On the Knocking at the Gate in 'Markheim,' "
NCF, 1962). Most of these studies make no serious effort to claim
direct influence.

Serious and heated claims have been made, however, that De
Quincey exercised significant influence over French literature—an
ironic turn of affairs, in view of his usual disparagement of the
shallow French. Many of his works have been translated into French,
beginning with Alfred de Musset's *L'anglais mangeur d'opium*
(1828), a Gallicized adaptation which has De Quincey find Anne of
Oxford Street at a ball and involves him in a duel with her lover.
Charles Baudelaire also translated and analyzed parts of the
Confessions and *Suspiria* in *Les paradis artificiels* (1860).[6] The
relation of these two authors to De Quincey is sketchily studied by
Paul Peltier, who finds parallels in *La confession d'un enfant du
siècle, Rolla,* and *Poète déchu,* which make him agree with Musset's
editor, Arthur Heulhard, that De Quincey's *Confessions* were of
capital importance in Musset's life ("Musset et Baudelaire à propos
des confessions d'un mangeur d'opium," *MdF*, 1918). As Paul F.
Jamieson has shown ("Musset, de Quincey, and Piranesi," *MLN*,
1956), the French writer in his story "La Mouche" plagiarized from
the *Confessions* a passage on Piranesi. The best analysis of Baude-

---

6   Other translations include V. Descreux, *Confessions d'un mangeur d'opium*
(1890); André Fontainas, *Essai sur l'assassinat considéré comme un des beaux-arts*
(1901); Albert Savine, *Souvenirs autobiographiques d'un mangeur d'opium* (1903);
M. de Contades, *Jeanne d'Arc* (1909); Pierre Leyris, "Des coups frappés à la
porte dans *Macbeth*" (*NRF*, 1933); Armel Guerne, "Rêve-fugue sur le thème de la
mort soudaine" (*MdF*, 1951); Pierre Schneider, "La nonne militaire d'Espagne,"
Les lettres nouvelles (1953); and Pierre Leyris, *Confessions d'un Opiomane
anglais* (1962) and *De l'Assassinat considéré comme un des Beaux Arts* (1963).

laire's version—preferable to Robert Vivier's *L'originalité de Charles Baudelaire* (1926)—is G. T. Clapton's *Baudelaire et De Quincey* (1931), which painstakingly compares Baudelaire with the original, finding some mistranslations, more reorganization and compression. R. Lalou points out that a passage which Baudelaire did not translate is the source of his "Le Thyrse" ("De Thomas De Quincey à Baudelaire," *Revue germanique*, 1923).

Other specific works which perhaps can be traced to De Quincey are cited by Randolph Hughes ("Vers la contrée du rêve: Balzac, Gautier et Baudelaire, disciples de Quincey [sic]," *MdF*, 1939). Hughes sees De Quincey's imprint on Balzac's *Peau de chagrin*, *Opium*, and *Massimilla doni*, and argues that Balzac's work became more imaginative after he read De Quincey. He finds in Gautier profound analogies to De Quincey's dream world, insists that many of Baudelaire's works, such as "Sur le Tasse en prison," "Le Poison," and "Rêve parisien," show that his imagination was oriented by De Quincey, and concludes that the Englishman was more important to the development of French literature than to that of his own country. Georges-Albert Astre had already pointed out Balzac's debt to De Quincey ("H. de Balzac et 'L'anglais mangeur d'opium,'" *RLC*, 1935) and argued that Balzac associated De Quincey with Swedenborg and valued him for his visions and symbols. Answering Hughes, he repeats his belief that De Quincey was for Baudelaire a symbolic transcription of his own inner drama (*MdF*, 1939). In a perceptive but one-sided article, "Thomas de Quincey, mystique et symboliste" (*La revue hebdomadaire*, 23 Oct. 1937), Astre pushes his thesis that the secret of De Quincey's influence in France was that he was a symbolist before the letter who had to dream to comprehend and who, like Proust, spent his life transposing into spiritual and mystical terms a reality which opened to him once and never returned. Still another name is added by Jules Castier, who thinks De Quincey possibly influenced Flaubert (*MdF*, 1939). But almost all of these claims suppose that knowledge of De Quincey came through Musset's translation, and Jacques Crépet objects that Musset's early work, signed only with his initials, went completely unnoticed (*MdF*, 1939, 1940). An answer by Hughes (*MdF*, 1940), as well as evidence presented earlier by Astre, suggests that Crépet's assertion is too strong, and that, principally through Musset, De Quincey indeed exercised some influence in France. J.-G. Prod'homme makes a persuasive case that the scenario of Berlioz' *Fantastique* came partly from Musset's *Mangeur d'opium* ("Berlioz, Musset, and Thomas De Quincey," *Musical Quart.*, 1946). The recent discovery of Mallarmé's unpublished manuscript, "Beaut's de l'anglais," reveals that he considered De Quincey "un des plus magnifiques prosateurs qui aient écrit dans aucune langue" (Henri Mondor, "Quincey, Dickens, Poe, Ruskin . . . parmi bien d'autres: Comme les voyait Mallarmé," *FL*, 18 Nov. 1961).

No one has studied the curious phenomenon of De Quincey's reputation. George Saintsbury (*Cambridge History of English Literature*) points to the "almost unique" popularity of his works for a generation after his death. Yet most of the commentators writing in this period, although often admiring De Quincey and prophesying great fame for him ultimately, regret that he has not yet been recognized and predict that he will never be really popular. L. W. Spring, for example, amusingly presents arguments that De Quincey is the greatest English writer of the past seventy-five years, but does not pretend that this judgment is at all general (*Continental Monthly*, 1864). When at the end of the century what Saintsbury calls "something of a reaction" set in, critics deplored and sought to explain the reasons for De Quincey's depreciation: Abraham Stansfield, *Essays and Sketches* (1897); H. S. Salt, "The Depreciation of De Quincey" (*National Rev.*, 1928); and J. B. Jarvis, "The Neglect Shown to De Quincey" (*Month*, 1906). Among more plausible reasons advanced are moral censure of the Opium-Eater and changing tastes.

Although, as Frank Swinnerton pointed out ("Thomas De Quincey: Forgotten Highbrow," *Sat. Rev.*, 17 Sept. 1960), the hundredth anniversary of De Quincey's death passed almost unnoticed, the amount of scholarship on him in the last thirty-odd years suggests that his reputation is secure. Not only are his best works, to use Sackville-West's words, built from "durable material—that of poetry—which confers a universality of emotional appeal," but, as Dan Jacobson suggested in one of the articles which did take cognizance of the centenary ("I Was Sacrificed," *Spectator*, 18 Dec. 1959), De Quincey's argument for the importance of individual acts is especially pertinent for our time.

11

Thomas Carlyle

By Carlisle Moore
UNIVERSITY OF OREGON

OFTEN REGARDED as the most Victorian of Victorians, Thomas Carlyle was first of all a romantic. Coeval with Keats, he developed his full literary powers later than any of the other romantics, but wrote some of his most original and durable works, *Sartor Resartus* and the early essays, before 1832, and went on through an active career of nearly threescore years to outlive such great Victorians as Macaulay, Thackeray, Dickens, Mill, and George Eliot. His literary longevity has created taxonomic difficulties for more than one critic. Norman Foerster observes that "it seems necessary to keep the first half of him with the Romantics, as Professor Bernbaum has done in his *Guide Through the Romantic Movement*, or else to regard him as a Victorian misfit" (*The Reinterpretation of Victorian Literature*, ed. J. E. Baker, 1950). Carlyle is so complex and refractory a figure that he can be fitted neatly into neither of these categories (themselves refractory), yet he undoubtedly belongs in both. With the romantics he shared a temperamental aversion to eighteenth-century rationalism, and felt their exhilarating hope that French revolutionary ideals might fill that vacuum and create a new and better order. Like them he sought to read new truths symbolically in the profound mysteries of nature and of man's spirit, and he regarded poetry as the highest expression of those truths.

Yet because his proclivities were mainly religious and philosophical rather than aesthetic, he consorts strangely with his English contemporaries, with most of whose writings he was unsympathetic. Only in Germany could he find the metaphysic and morality that were needed to reinforce and develop the latent powers of his mind, and the tendency of German philosophy, as he read it, was to lead him directly to the Victorians. During the 1830's and early 1840's he spoke as one of them, pronouncing with effective moral earnestness and humor his views on the need for social reform and wise leadership based on his spiritual conception of society. At length he proved a misfit after all, one who took the wrong road, who, though still a potent force, turned his face obstinately against the triumphant progress of democracy and science. Even before mid-century the paradox of Carlyle's influence and reputation began to show itself : he was distrusted by those who acknowledged his power, and feared by those who also admired him. Arnold's description of him as a "moral desperado" is better known than Meredith's more favorable "heaver of rocks." Though recognized as a prophet and literary genius, he began to realize that what he taught was either misunderstood or ignored, and when his voice grew more strident he was further misunderstood. The truths which history and the German romantics had taught him, moreover, history itself now seemed to be repudiating. England's shameful policy of *laissez faire* and compromise was not visibly leading to her decline as a nation and world power. The revolution did not take place. Basil Willey remarks (*Nineteenth Century Studies,* 1949) that Carlyle's life shows what happens to a romantic when he survives into the latter days of the nineteenth century. His message "was essentially that of the great Romantic poets and thinkers applied to the condition of England in the days of Chartism and the dismal science." Much of that message was never received, but it nevertheless gave a powerful stimulus to a whole succession of younger generations.

It is for this reason that the present chapter undertakes the whole of Carlyle's work rather than only the earlier part of it. At a time when lines of demarcation between literary and historical periods are being blotted out and when the romantic sensibility, instead of disappearing in 1832, is being traced throughout the century and into our own time, it seems fitting to conclude this volume with a figure who serves not only to bridge but, in many ways, to unite the two periods and to illustrate the persistence of romantic ideas and attitudes. Although he fell from high favor into severe disapproval and neglect after his death, he and his writings now seem to be attracting a more objective, as well as a more literary, consideration.

I. BIBLIOGRAPHIES

IN 1928 the large body of Carlyle's work and the critical as well as uncritical commentary on it were brought together in Isaac W. Dyer's *A Bibliography of Thomas Carlyle's Writings and Ana.* Still the mother lode of Carlyle research, it gives the first and later editions of all the works great and small, with liberal annotation; it lists translations of his work into other languages, his many contributions to periodicals, and his published and unpublished correspondence so far as it was then known. The largest section, of *Ana*, is an exhaustive list of critical books and articles, memoirs, and even works containing only scattered references to Carlyle. Finally, there is an iconography by J. A. S. Barrett, "Principal Portraits, Statues, Busts, and Photographs of Thomas Carlyle," and a Commentary on these by James L. Caw. Accurate except for minor errors and omissions, all but complete to 1927, and well indexed, it is still the indispensable basis for Carlyle studies. Unfortunately it is rare, only six hundred copies having been printed.

Several bibliographies before Dyer's may be mentioned: R. H. Shepherd's *Bibliography of Carlyle* (1881); that by John P. Anderson appended to Richard Garnett's *Life of Thomas Carlyle* (1887); W. C. Lane's *The Carlyle Collection. A Catalogue of Books on Oliver Cromwell and Frederick the Great Bequeathed by Thomas Carlyle to Harvard College Library* (1888); and M. E. Wead's *A Catalogue of the Samuel A. Jones Collection* (1919).

An excellent bibliography *in petto* is to be found in *CBEL*, Volume III (1940) and Volume V (1955), and a good selective bibliography may be expected in the forthcoming *Oxford History of English Literature, Volume XI: The Mid-Nineteenth Century*, by Geoffrey Tillotson. For completer reference these may be supplemented by the annual bibliographies in *PMLA* (1921–   ; until 1956 this includes work by American scholars only) and *MHRA* (1921–   ); the annual "Victorian Bibliography" published in *MP* (1933–57) and *VS* (1958–   ); and the two volumes collecting some of these, *Bibliographies of Studies in Victorian Literature . . . 1932–1944* (1945), ed. W. D. Templeman, and *Bibliographies of Studies in Victorian Literature . . . 1945–1954* (1956), ed. Austin Wright. *Victorian Newsletter* includes a current Victorian bibliography in each issue. The bibliographies in *Modern Philology, Victorian Studies*, and *Victorian Newsletter* are annotated.

One might say that Carlyle's bibliographical problems have been among the least of his troubles. Most of them relate to the identification of newly discovered or doubtful works. In her *Rebellious Fraser's* (1934) Miriam M. H. Thrall gives a list of Carlyle's contributions to *Fraser's* in which she adds to Dyer's list a review of Cunningham's *Life of Burns*, April 1834, and another review, apparently written in collaboration with Heraud, of Cunningham's *Maid of Elvar*, July 1832. A more tentative ascription to Carlyle, also showing signs of collaboration with Heraud, is a letter on "The

Doctrine of St. Simon," July 1832. Three more articles, listed in Dyer, and earlier claimed as the work of Carlyle on stylistic grounds by J. A. S. Barrett (*TLS*, 20 January 1927), she finds are largely the work of Heraud and Maginn: "The Last of the Supernaturalists," March 1830 (an excellent essay on Blake), "Fashionable Novels: The Dominie's Legacy," April 1830, and "Bulwer's Novels; and Remarks on Novel Writings," June 1830. Examining the last two of these by external evidence, Hill Shine (*MLN*, 1936) concurs. It is perfectly possible that there are other unidentified articles by Carlyle hidden in the periodicals, but according to Walter E. Houghton, editor of the forthcoming and extremely important *Wellesley Index of Victorian Periodicals: 1824–1900*, nothing new has so far been found. G. B. Tennyson, in "Unnoted Encyclopaedia Articles by Carlyle" (*MLN*, 1963), gives firm evidence for the addition of two encyclopedia articles, on "Persia" and "Quakers," to the accepted canon of eighteen which Carlyle wrote in 1820–23 for David Brewster's *Edinburgh Encyclopaedia*. In "Carlyle's Poetry to 1840: A Checklist . . ." (*VP*, 1963), the same scholar brings together all the known poems by Carlyle (excluding his translations of German poetry), gives six previously unpublished poems from manuscripts at Yale, and makes a new attribution. Coleman O. Parsons, in "Carlyle's Gropings About Montrose" (*Englische Studien*, 1937), has published, with an introduction and notes, a manuscript fragment preserved at the National Library of Scotland containing Carlyle's abortive investigation in 1839 of James Gordon, First Marquis of Montrose. Hill Shine (*VN*, 1958) gives a short but valuable guide to the present location and extent of Carlyle manuscripts. The greater part of them have been published, but not all have been published adequately. Of those that were sold at auction in 1932 at Sotheby's, some still cannot be traced. A few are unavailable.

II. EDITIONS

FROM 1839 Carlyle published collections of his essays—the Miscellanies—and from 1857, collected editions of his works, notably the Library Edition of 1869 and the People's Edition of 1872, both containing his own summaries and indexes. Today the Centenary Edition, edited by H. D. Traill, published in thirty volumes by Chapman and Hall (1896–99), is standard. An additional, supplementary volume, edited by Alexander Carlyle, contains the *Historical Sketches* (1898). H. D. Traill's astringent introductions present Carlyle as he was most widely regarded at the end of the century, "neither political prophet nor ethical doctor, but simply a great master of literature who lives for posterity by the art which he despised." Yet the edition, though it contains all the major works and incorporates much hitherto uncollected material (an early story, some translations from the German, a number of the *Edinburgh Encyclopaedia* articles), cannot be called either complete or definitive. It is not a critical text; the notes and indexes are still Carlyle's, and a number of minor but significant writings were not included. Some of these are to be found in the following volumes: *Last Words of T. C. on Trades-Unions, Promoterism and the Signs of the Times* (1882) ; *Rescued Essays*, ed. Percy Newberry (1892) ; *Last Words of Thomas Carlyle* (1892), containing *Wotton Reinfred*, "Excursion (Futile Enough) to Paris," and some letters to Varnhagen Von Ense; *Montaigne and Other Essays, Chiefly Biographical*, ed. S. R. Crockett (1897) ; and *Collectanea . . . 1821–1855*, ed. Samuel A. Jones (1903), containing among other things Carlyle's first two literary reviews written in 1821.

At his death Carlyle left an enormous body of unpublished manuscript material, some of it in the form of journals and diaries, some of works left unfinished. One of the most important of these, and the most portentous because its publication by J. A. Froude did such hurt to his reputation in the very year of his death, was the *Reminiscences* (2 vols., 1881), containing Carlyle's recollections of Jane, set down soon after her death in 1866, and of his father (in part written earlier, in 1832), of Edward Irving, Lord Jeffrey, Southey, Wordsworth, and "Christopher North." By thus airing his master's private grief, Froude stood guilty of disloyalty, and, worse, he was accused of gross inaccuracy in transcribing the manuscripts. They were later retranscribed and republished (2 vols., 1887) by Charles Eliot Norton with a condemnatory preface and with corrections which, as Waldo Dunn has demonstrated, were not so extensive or serious as Norton claimed. Also edited by Norton were the *Two Note Books of Thomas Carlyle from 23rd March 1822 to 10th May 1832* (1898) which furnish, along with the letters, an invaluable record of his early intellectual and emotional development. Corrections and emendations to Norton's editorial work were amiably supplied by J. A. S. Barrett (*N&Q*, 10 March 1934). Carlyle's narratives of three trips have been published: "Reminiscences of My Irish Journey in 1849" (*Century Magazine;* also in book form, both 1882) ; "A Three-Days Tour to the Netherlands," ed. Alexander Carlyle (*Cornhill,* 1922) ; and *Journey to Germany, Autumn 1858,* ed. with introduction and notes by R. A. E. Brooks (1940). Finally, two fragmentary works have recently been made available: Hill Shine's excellently documented edition of *Carlyle's Unfinished History of German Literature* (1951), written in 1830, and Marjorie P. King's "Illudo Chartis" (*MLR,* 1954), an embryonic version of *Sartor Resartus* written, she estimates, in 1825 or 1826. It is the merest sketch of the early years of a Scottish hero, Stephen Corry, born in Duckdubs, the son of a mason, who grows up in southern Scotland and is off to the University of Edinburgh when the manuscript ends.

Several of Carlyle's finished works have received excellent editorial treatment. The first, and still valuable, scholarly edition of *Sartor Resartus* is that of Archibald MacMechan (1896). Mac-Mechan did pioneer research into the teeming allusions of the work, provided an introduction which contains an analysis of Carlyle's style, background, and personality, a discussion of his sources, and added a full index. J. A. S. Barrett's edition of *Sartor* (1897), done independently of MacMechan's, is notable for its early attempt to relate Carlyle's ideas to those of Hume, Kant, and Goethe. Barrett also pointed to the influence of *Reinecke Fuchs* on Carlyle's abiding conception of the dual nature of man: half beast and half god, both descendental and transcendental, as evident in both the name and nature of Diogenes Teufelsdroeckh.

All subsequent editions of *Sartor,* like those of P. C. Parr (1913), Clark S. Northup (1921), and C. F. Harrold (1937), were indebted to MacMechan. Parr's and Northup's, though excellent, contain some errors and are limited in their usefulness. Harrold's is by all odds the best, containing a wealth of footnotes which at once illuminate the text and direct the student to further study. An annotated bibliography describes earlier editions and evaluates biographical and critical works bearing on *Sartor,* and lists Carlyle's German sources. Appended material includes the familiar "Testimonies of Authors," Sterling's criticism of *Sartor* in 1835, and a list of parallelisms between *Sartor* and *Wotton Reinfred* expanded from that in Dyer's *Bibliography.* The introduction, presenting the work as a highly artistic expression of profound thought, explores most of its principal aspects: its milieu, its genesis and structure, the Calvinist and German subpatterns, Carlyle's ethical and social doctrines, the dynamic world which it poetically evokes, and, finally, the characteristics of style, imagery, symbolism, and humor which give the work its special literary and Carlylean impress. Since Carlyle's death *Sartor* has gone into many translations, most recently into Japanese (1963).

The *French Revolution*, twice edited, by C. R. L. Fletcher (3 vols., 1902) and J. Holland Rose (3 vols., 1902), with introductions and notes, stands in need of more exact and more objective treatment. The first of these, especially, suffers from the bias of its editor, who fails to incorporate some of Carlyle's own corrections, for example, the statement that Frederick the Great was the only king ever to attempt suicide, which Carlyle later (1868) corrected in a footnote. The French translation (1912) has a valuable introduction by F. V. A. Aulard on Carlyle as a historian.

Carlyle published only one of the four series of lectures which he delivered, with increasing success, from 1837 to 1840. The fourth, *On Heroes, Hero-Worship, and the Heroic in History*, is to be found in Volume V of the Centenary Edition of his works, but a scholarly edition was produced soon after by Archibald MacMechan (1901), based upon the text of the People's Edition, with collation of the first three English editions of 1841, 1842, and 1846, the last having received Carlyle's most careful revision and the People's Edition having contracted a number of errors. The introduction includes summary accounts of Carlyle's other lecture series and discussions of the ideas, style, and influence of *On Heroes*. Liberal notes explain the allusions, and there is an index to these and the introduction as well as Carlyle's index to the lectures.

The *Lectures on the History of Literature*, delivered in 1838, were not published as Carlyle gave them but were written out from notes taken by a young man in the audience named T. Chisholm Anstey who, departing for India, seems to have carried one copy with him and left another, or others, with friends in England, so that there appeared in 1892 two books based on Anstey's transcriptions, one edited by R. P. Karkaria, published in Bombay, the other edited by J. Rea Greene, published in London. Neither of these can be called an "edition"; neither is in Carlyle's style, as a comparison with Leigh Hunt's reports of the lectures in the *Examiner* shows. One must nevertheless be grateful to Anstey, for Hunt's reports are brief. Of the other two lecture-series, that on German Literature delivered in 1837, and that on Revolutions in Modern Europe delivered in 1839, we know very little beyond a few reports and what can be gleaned from contemporary memoirs and correspondence.

Of the many editions of *Past and Present*, the best to date is that by A. M. D. Hughes (1918). This contains ample notes,

Carlyle's summary and index to the text, and an index to notes and introduction which is both a survey of the social and political conditions in the early 1840's and a sketching of Carlyle's thought from his early sympathy with the Radicals to his later position, when, however, he was no Tory but demanded a new radicalism to cure Britain's ills. Richard D. Altick's recently published Riverside Edition of *Past and Present* (1965) has a good introduction and notes.

It is all but impossible to produce a representative selection of Carlyle's writings, as much because of the diversity of his thought and expression as because of their development through many different stages. More than with most authors, his works suffer out of context. A. M. D. Hughes, in his slender volume, *Thomas Carlyle, Selections* (1957), has chosen relatively short passages from the principal works to illustrate Carlyle's descriptive and narrative skill, and his poetic style. Perhaps to bolster these passages, in their isolation, he has prefaced them with "Appreciations" of Carlyle by such contemporaries or near contemporaries as Edward Caird, Mazzini, Arnold, and Saintsbury. Julian Symons' *Carlyle, Selected Works, Reminiscences, and Letters* (1956) offers a longer and wider variety of selections, but represents Carlyle less as an artist than as a social thinker whom one may admire if one makes the proper reservations. G. M. Trevelyan, in his *Carlyle, An Anthology* (1953), gives us the Carlyle he loves, the early Carlyle, poetic historian and superb portrait painter. This is perhaps the place to mention the excellently chosen and edited selection of Carlyle's works in C. F. Harrold and W. D. Templeman's *English Prose of the Victorian Period* (1938), with its scholarly introductions, notes, and bibliography, still the best student's introduction to the study of Carlyle.

Needless to say, passages from the works were often gathered into sentimental posies. A few choice examples may be cited: *Polonius: A Collection of Wise Saws and Modern Instances* (1852); *Treasure Bits* (1898); *Philosophic Nuggets* (1899); *Carlyle Year-Book; Selections from Thomas Carlyle for Every Day in the Year* (1900); *Beautiful Thoughts* (1900). Carlyle authorized several collections, however: *Passages Selected from the Writings of Thomas Carlyle* (1855), *Prophecy for 1855. Selected from Carlyle's "Latter-Day Pamphlets"* (1855), and *Essays in Mosaic* (1875), all edited by Thomas Ballantyne; *The Carlyle Anthology* (1876), ed. Edward Barrett; and the *Carlyle Birthday-Book* [1879], ed. C. N. Williamson.

Like many of his contemporaries, Carlyle was an inveterate letter writer. Little went on in his mind and life but found its way into his correspondence. From his college years, friends had recognized his mastery of the craft, and Henry James *fils* ranked him "among the very first of all letter-writers." Thus the vast and impressive corpus of his letters has a double value, literary and biographical. Most of them seem to have been preserved carefully by their recipients, and volume by volume, in article after article, they have found their way into print. J. A. Froude incorporated many of them, of course, into his four-volume *Life of Carlyle* (1882–84), but it was given to C. E. Norton to edit, in quick succession, *The Correspondence of Thomas Carlyle and Ralph Waldo Emerson, 1834–1872* (1883), *Early Letters . . . 1814–1826* (2 vols., 1886), *Correspondence Between Goethe and Carlyle* (1887), and *Letters of Thomas Carlyle and Jane Welsh* (2 vols., 1909), "Thomas Carlyle and Thomas Spedding" (*Cornhill*, 1921), and *Letters of Carlyle to John Stuart Mill, John Sterling, and Robert Browning* (1923). Among recent editions may be mentioned *The Letters of Thomas Carlyle to William Graham* (1950), ed. John Graham, Jr., and *Thomas Carlyle: Letters to His Wife* (1953), ed. Trudy Bliss. More recently, Edwin W. Marrs, Jr., in "Discovery of Some New Carlyle Letters" (*Thoth*, 1962), has announced the existence of 245 letters written by Carlyle, mostly to his brother Alexander in Ontario, Canada, and mostly new, some of them having been published earlier by Norton.

Much more Carlyle correspondence than this has been published. The loci are legion. They need not be indicated here, however, even if it were practical, because all known, extant letters by Carlyle and by his wife, published and unpublished, are soon to appear in a single edition, under the editorship of Charles Richard Sanders, of Duke University, who with the help of his associate editor, John Butt, of the University of Edinburgh, has for years been locating and gathering together all the available correspondence. In "Carlyle's Letters" (*BJRL*, 1955) Sanders listed the libraries and private collections where the largest holdings exist in manuscript, and several groups of them have been described in his "Carlyle's Letters to Ruskin: A Finding List with Some Unpublished Letters and Comments" (*BJRL*, 1958) and "Some Lost and Unpublished Carlyle-Browning Correspondence" (*JEGP*, 1963). The Haddington Edition, as it may be called, is to contain some nine thousand letters in about thirty-five volumes, with two or three additional volumes for the index. Since many of these have never been published, and since Carlyle addressed himself to so many eminent persons, the edition is bound to invigorate and enrich the study not only of Carlyle but of broader areas too, by bringing together a mass of materials formerly difficult or impossible to obtain. It should be the greatest single reservoir of information about Carlyle and about the literary and cultural life of nineteenth-century England. The first volumes are to be published in 1966, the hundredth anniversary of the death of Jane Welsh Carlyle. One section of Sanders' general introduction has appeared: "Carlyle as Editor and Critic of Literary Letters" (*EUQ*, 1964).

Despite its immense importance, the Haddington Edition will not render useless all the previous editions of the letters, many of which contain special editorial value. Individual groups remain to be studied, their significance explored. Sanders has written a number of interesting articles in which he uses Carlyle's correspondence with various acquaintances as the basis and running record of the dramatic interplay of personalities and ideas, for example, his "Carlyle and Tennyson" (*PMLA*, 1961) and "The Correspondence and Friendship of Thomas Carlyle and Leigh Hunt" (*BJRL*, 1963). Joseph Slater has just published the definitive edition of *The Correspondence of Emerson and Carlyle* (1964) with an extensive critical introduction.

It must also be said that despite all efforts to make this a complete and definitive edition of the letters, it is still possible, and still to be hoped, that other letters will be found, letters known to have been written but thus far undiscoverable.

III. BIOGRAPHIES

CARLYLE'S LONG LIFE has been told and mistold many times. It was not a particularly dramatic life, but he dramatized every stage of it in an almost Byronic way, putting himself intensely into all his works, and ensuring the importance of biography to the study of all he wrote. His rugged Scottish background, his struggles at the university, his "conversion," his courtship of Jane, his six-year retirement at Craigenputtoch, and his descent upon London to reform and prophesy—all gave him the character and appeal of a Hebrew prophet, so that many a biography of him reads almost like a saint's legend.

But some do not. The deplorable Carlyle-Froude controversy which arose after his death set a mark on Carlyle biography which has hardly disappeared to this day. Because of the violent, and it now appears unwarranted, objections that were hurled at Froude for his publication of the *Reminiscences* (1881) and of his *Life of Carlyle* (1882–84), biographers have felt bound to take sides, so that impartial lives of Carlyle are rare and some are mere polemic or panegyric. His teachings and pronouncements have sometimes produced the same partisan tendency, and critical examinations of his ideas have not infrequently been based on an indictment of certain aspects of his private life and character. More of this later.

So prolonged was the period of Carlyle's old age that when he died no fewer than five book-length biographies were ready for publication—not to mention the pious obits and a quantity of articles. Innocent as yet of Froude's awful revelations, these reverently recounted the life and career of the Sage of Chelsea, quoting liberally from his conversation and writings and interlacing these with anecdotes, and frequently quoting valuable correspondence or reprinting early, uncollected works. W. H. Wylie, in *Thomas Carlyle* (1881), first identifies the poem "Drumwhirn Bridge" as Carlyle's. Richard Herne Shepherd's *Memoirs of the Life and Writings of Thomas Carlyle* (2 vols., 1881) contains personal recollections and the first publication in book form of a number of fugitive pieces. Though frankly a memoir, it is more accurate than either Wylie's or H. J. Nicoll's *Thomas Carlyle* (1881), the errata in both of which Shepherd listed at length in his *Bibliography of Thomas Carlyle* (1881). Moncure D. Conway's *Thomas Carlyle* (1881), like Shepherd's work, shows intimate acquaintance with Carlyle, contributes a number of Carlyle's early letters, and, as in his *Autobiography* (2 vols., 1904), pictures Carlyle as fundamentally cheerful and generous.

It is perhaps a sign of his affinity with Dr. Johnson that Carlyle had so many Boswellian memoirists. Their importance to the scholar lies not so much in their recording of Carlyle's teacup crashing remarks as in what they reveal sometimes about the complex and often contradictory character of his mind and temperament. One of the best of these is David Masson, whose *Carlyle Personally and in His Writings* (1885) gives an affectionate but penetrating picture of the man, and records the effect produced on him by some of Carlyle's writings when they appeared. Masson also wrote chapters on Carlyle's early years in *Edinburgh Sketches and Memories* (1892), and in *Memories of London in the Forties* (1908) described Carlyle's kindly and generous manner and his daily life, particularly while he was at work on *Cromwell.* The following memoirs may be listed as containing valuable materials, although, as with the work of Wylie, Nicoll, and Conway, they should always be checked for accuracy: Andrew J. Symington's *Some Personal Reminiscences of Carlyle* (1886), David S. Meldrum's "Carlyle and Kirkcaldy" (*Scots Magazine*, 1891), Sir Charles Gavan Duffy's *Conversations with Carlyle* (1892), John Tyndall's "Personal Recollections of Carlyle" (*Fortnightly*, 1890), Francis Espinasse's *Literary Recollections and Sketches* (1893), and William Allingham's *A Diary* (1907). For firsthand description of the young Carlyle one should consult Emerson's *English Traits* (1856) and *Journals* (1914), George Gilfillan's *A Gallery of Literary Portraits* (1845) and *The History of a Man* (1856), Henry Crabb Robinson's *Diary, Reminiscences and Correspondence* (1869), E. J. Morley's "Carlyle, in the Diary, Reminiscences, and Correspondence of Henry Crabb Robinson" (*London Mercury*, 1922), and Thomas Murray's *Autobiographical Notes* (1911).

In compass and quality J. A. Froude's *Life of Carlyle* surpasses all of the above. Froude met Carlyle in 1849 and became a close friend. His work was based on intimate acquaintance also with many of Carlyle's friends who had known him earlier, and upon the mass of private papers which Carlyle turned over to him for the express purpose of enabling him to write the kind of biography Carlyle wanted. The work was written under considerable stress, and Carlyle's hand was often difficult to decipher. It is true that Froude's accuracy in transcribing these papers leaves something to be desired, but the errors, like those in his edition of the *Reminiscences*, are less fatal (one might say) than was claimed by C. E. Norton who, as Hyder E. Rollins has shown in his "Charles Eliot Norton and Froude" (*JEGP*, 1958), harbored a strong emotional dislike of Froude. Rollins also shows that Waldo H. Dunn, in his *Froude and Carlyle* (1930), makes some errors himself in his effort to clear Froude against his attackers. It is not necessary to agree with Dunn that Froude's work ranks with Boswell's *Johnson* to claim for it the first place among biographies of Carlyle, both as a work of literature and as an accurate portrait of the man. Froude's achievement is the more remarkable when one considers that he was so close to his subject, and a Carlylean; not only did he see Carlyle largely and objectively, but he drew Carlyle's defects and weaknesses along with his virtues. Dunn is correct in saying that it was Froude's attackers, not Froude, who misrepresented Carlyle.

It will be wise to say as little as possible here about the abominable Carlyle-Froude controversy. The curious student is

directed to Dyer's *Bibliography* (pp. 347–348) and to the works by
Dunn and Rollins mentioned above.

Briefly, the bones of contention were three: the integrity and
accuracy of Froude's use of the Carlyle papers, Carlyle's allegedly
cruel treatment of Jane, and the question of his sexual impotence.
Dunn effectively clears Froude on the first two counts, and agrees
with Froude that Carlyle's impotence was a proved fact and the
cause of much marital unhappiness. The matter is largely extrane-
ous and irrelevant. Yet it may be asked whether the evidence which
Dunn adduces in both his *Carlyle and Froude* and his recent *James
Anthony Froude* (2 vols., 1961–63) is conclusive. In her "Jane
Welsh Carlyle" (*QR*, 1955) Marian Lockhead suggests that it may
rather have been sexual awkwardness induced by lifelong puritan
repression which allowed for some, but not normal, sexual relations.
In any event we have no really satisfactory proof on either side, and
the claims of impotence are somewhat difficult to credit in the face of
his manly life and work and of the total absence, even in his private
writings, of any expression of inadequacy as a husband or embar-
rassment at the thought or mention of children. The dramatic
evidence supplied by Frank Harris in his "Talks with Carlyle"
(*English Review*, 1911) was effectively put out of court by Alexander Carlyle in "Frank Harris and His (Imaginary) Talks with Carlyle" (*English Review*, 1911). The whole subject is intelligently re-
assessed by Edward Sharples in "Carlyle and His Readers: The
Froude Controversy Once Again" (Univ. of Rochester dissertation,
1964).

David Alec Wilson intended his six-volume *Life of Thomas
Carlyle* (1923–34) to be a massive antidote and corrective to
Froude, whom he makes out to be both a villain and a fool whose
work is not only valueless but pernicious. The picture offered of
Carlyle is a hero worshiper's image of the Hero as Man of Letters
who can do no wrong. One cannot but be grateful to Wilson for
amassing so much interesting and detailed information, often from
the remotest sources, about Carlyle's daily life, his opinions, and his
innumerable friends and acquaintances. Yet our gratitude is curbed
both by Wilson's failure to attempt any unified picture of his subject
and by the spirit in which the whole is written, by his unmitigated
scorn of all who ever disagreed with Carlyle and by his uncritical
praise of all his hero ever did or thought. In a judicious and
scholarly assessment of the first five volumes (the sixth was completed after Wilson's death by D. W. MacArthur) Waldo Dunn
offers convincing evidence to prove that "Froude's methods are

remarkably accurate in comparison with those of Wilson" (*SR*, 1932). Numerous passages from Carlyle's works and letters are misquoted, often so as to alter the sense; uncorroborated assertions or statements supported only by anonymous evidence abound; and, in order to aggrandize Carlyle, he seriously misrepresented Jane, as well as others like Geraldine Jewsbury and Frederick Martin. These are serious defects, yet it remains, as George Saintsbury described it, a "remarkable thesaurus, which, though far from faultless, will do future students much good, and can do none of them, if he has any brains of his own, much harm."

Most biographies after Froude's were shorter and less biased than Wilson's. Richard Garnett's *Life of Thomas Carlyle* (1887) is still one of the best short accounts. Garnett views Carlyle admiringly but not worshipfully as a literary artist whose portraiture may be compared with Rembrandt's and whose command of the language, like Shelley's, is supreme: "Shelley works his will with language gracefully, as one guides a spirited steed: Carlyle with convulsive effort, as one hammers a red-hot bar, but in both cases the end is achieved." John Nichol's *Thomas Carlyle* (1892) is based frankly on Froude and the obits, but translates Froude's affectionate picture of Carlyle's noble brooding nature into an uncertain indictment: "Carlyle was a great man, but a great man spoiled, that is, largely soured." Nichol does not know whether to praise or blame, so does both, accepting the fact of Carlyle's genius but condemning his "bigoted antagonism to all Utilitarian solutions," his dogmatism and petulance. For Hector Macpherson also (*Thomas Carlyle*, 1896), his idealism and opposition to progressive science, though they gave him a certain insight into the social diseases of his time, disqualified him as a healer.

Very different is J. M. Sloan's *The Carlyle Country, with a Study of Carlyle's Life* (1904), with its topographical approach to biography. All Carlyle's early haunts in Annandale, Nithsdale, and Galloway are described as the nurturing ground of his strong individualism, poetic vision, and romantic temperament. Sloan traces the history of the Carlyle clan, of the Burgher Seceders of Ecclefechan, and of the immediate Carlyle family through its successive moves from Ecclefechan to Mainhill to Scotsbrig, together with Carlyle's year at Repentance Tower, his marriage at Templand, and the couple's long sojourn at Craigenputtoch. Places associated with other distinguished Scots, Burns, Hogg, Irving, Ruskin, contribute to our understanding of Carlyle's love for the lowlands and his desire to be buried there instead of in Westminster Abbey. Edinburgh and London do not come into view. To his last days, Sloan shows, Carlyle drew strength from Dumfriesshire. R. S. Craig's *The Making of Carlyle, an Experiment in Biographical Explication* (1908) also explores Carlyle's early years, as determined chiefly by his parents and friends, his years at the university, and his marriage. But it is another attempt to correct Froude's "eloquent but uncomprehending biography" with its "Greek chorus wail over Carlyle's 'selfishness' and want of regard for one of Miss Welsh's status in society." Sloan endeavors to prove that Jane gained immensely by her marriage to Carlyle, and was no martyr but was rather "content so far as she ever could be content."

Osbert Burdett's *The Two Carlyles* (1930) does them much more justice. Froude's work is unreservedly praised; Jane was the unavoidably lonely wife of a genius who, though unhappy, would not have changed places with anyone. "Froude alone," says Burdett, "seems to have been equally attached to *both* the Carlyles." In addition to amplifying and confirming Froude, Burdett gives his own sensitive and sensible account of a usually misunderstood marital relationship based on his belief that "an angular and somewhat disordered soul [is] more interesting, more valuable, and more impressive, than the popular conception of a prophet, the romantic conception of an ideal husband." D. Lammond's *Carlyle* (1934) presents in some 130 pages little more than a summary of his life and career. Intellectual background and many important episodes are, perforce, scamped; Carlyle is viewed, finally, as a very difficult and wretched figure, disappointed in his hopes and frustrated by conflicting inner forces and by the conflict of these with the materialistic, changing conditions of the Victorian world.

The best single-volume biography is still Emery Neff's *Carlyle* (1932). Eminently fair, a product neither of the old Carlyle cult nor of the newer anti-Carlylean, it traces the development chiefly of his social and economic ideas, beginning with his early Calvinist training, his intellectual growth at the university, and the strong rebellion against eighteenth-century skepticism and nineteenth-century utilitarianism that led to his religious crisis. Describing the unstable state of the publishing market, Neff follows Carlyle's efforts to raise the standard of literary criticism in the journals and his gradual emergence as a social prophet whose remote Scottish background and assimilation of German thought enabled him to take an Olympian view of England's troubles. Each of the major works is examined as an outgrowth of Carlyle's thought and purposes and as it influenced the thought and actions of his contemporaries: *Sartor*, the proclamation of his victory over the negative revolt of Byronism; the *French Revolution*, a new kind of history; the *Latter-Day*

Pamphlets, a blast against liberalism. Though fully aware of Carlyle's artistry, Neff is critical of his haranguing style with its "exaggeration, over-emphasis, repetitiousness"—critical too of Carlyle's defense of the American South—yet, writing on the eve of the Second World War, Neff concludes with a strong defense of Carlyle's teachings and observes that civilized society now stands in as much need as the Victorians did of Carlyle's warnings against the consequences of democracy and *laissez-faire,* against unrestrained materialism and scientism.

Like Neff's work, Julian Symons' *Thomas Carlyle, the Life and Ideas of a Prophet* (1952) is a critical biography. Written a generation later, in a different social and political climate, it takes a darker view of its subject, although the portrait is generally sympathetic. Symons deplores what psychoanalytic critics have done to Carlyle, yet himself adopts a psychological approach: "The passionate force with which this prophet was to speak sprang not from the strength of his belief but from his psychological need to emulate his father, and his intellectual difficulty in doing so." Yet the book gives a perceptive account of the personal and intellectual influences which did mold his beliefs, and these are adjudged favorably as a remarkable congeries of social insights. Carlyle understood the "basis of force upon which all modern societies rest"; he knew that the industrial revolution "would involve the overturn of established society"; he saw that "liberties are obtained by one social class at the expense of another"; and, rejecting the Anglican church and its articles, he held fast to a formal belief in God. But these insights were perverted, Symons thinks, into a contempt for the people, a succumbing to the aristocracy, and "the vicarious sadistic lust for power of a disappointed man." Symons' failure to see the implications of Carlyle's spiritual and symbolic reading of society or to discern the function of Carlyle's grim humor in determining the meaning of his utterance results in a certain obliquity in Symons' conclusions. Neff's earlier work does not make this error.

Not a biography, but of immense biographical importance, is Hill Shine's *Carlyle's Early Reading, to 1834* (1953), a precise and nearly complete checklist of Carlyle's enormous reading during the Scottish period. Shine gives over 3,000 entries, with references to some 1,600 different works by nearly 1,000 authors, compiled from Carlyle's letters and notebooks, his published works, and other sources, with Carlyle's comments. The introductory essay outlines his intellectual development from his childhood orthodoxy to the period of his religious crisis and transcendental studies, to his shift in the 1830's to "realism" (Shine's term), that is, his practical concern with historical periodicity, antiabstract philosophy, social reform, redefinition of poetry as history, and rejection of German aesthetics. C. P. Finlayson, in "Thomas Carlyle's Borrowings from the Edinburgh University Library, 1819–1820" (*Bibliotheck*, 1961) has supplemented Shine's list.

There are numerous special biographical studies, of which we shall mention the following: two works on *Carlyle and the London Library*, one by Frederick Harrison (1906), the other by Simon N. Smith (1958); R. C Archibald's *Carlyle's First Love: Margaret Gordon, Lady Bannerman* (1910), an account of one of the originals of Blumine in *Sartor;* several accounts of another original of Blumine, Kitty Kirkpatrick, in G. Strachey's "Carlyle and the Rose Goddess" (*Nineteenth Century*, 1892), Lytton Strachey's "Carlyle" (*Portraits in Miniature*, 1928), and a chapter in C. R. Sanders' *The Strachey Family* (1953), "The Edward Stracheys, Carlyle, and Kitty Kirkpatrick," which throws light on Carlyle's pleasant obligation to Lytton Strachey's grandparents and on his ideas concerning British India and the problems of the British Empire; Oris Origo's *A Measure of Love* (1957), on Carlyle's relations with the Ashburtons; and Grace J. Calder's "Carlyle and Irving's London Circle" (*PMLA*, 1954) and "Erasmus A. Darwin, Friend of Thomas and Jane Carlyle" (*MLQ*, 1959).

Among biographies hostile to Carlyle the most cogent is Norwood Young's *Carlyle: His Rise and Fall* (1927). There are many telling blows in this book. Young assails Carlyle's part in the Governor Eyre case, his acceptance of the Squire forgeries, his lack of consideration for Jane, his handling of his sources for *Frederick the Great:* he is, in fact, so determined to put the worst complexion on all Carlyle's ways and works that he oversteps himself, as when, after denying that Carlyle's judgments affected political events, he asserts that the letter to *The Times* on the Franco-Prussian War (1870) "effectively smothered whatever hope there was" that England would aid France, or when he exonerates Edward Irving, but accuses Carlyle, of being intoxicated by success. Another polemic, less reasonably put, is *Quack, Quack* (1935), by Leonard Woolf, who attributes most of Carlyle's teachings to sadism.

Of the works which diagnose Carlyle medically, we need no more than mention G. M. Gould's *Biographic Clinics* (1903) and W. R. Bett's *The Infirmities of Genius* (1952). Among the psychoanalytic treatments to which he has been subjected, which cost him nothing, Jackson Towne's "Carlyle and Oedipus" (*Psychoanalytic Rev.*, 1935) is the strangest. The Oedipus complex is, of course, found, but it is also discovered that Froude's "prejudice against Carlyle" was

caused by jealousy: he was in love with Jane. A more elaborate
treatment is to be found in James L. Halliday's *Mr. Carlyle My
Patient* (1949). Surely no more inept work exists in the annals of
biography. It is a culling of Carlyle's more violent metaphorical
statements, taken literally, to prove that he was an anal type, with
paranoid traits, marked sadistic and masochistic tendencies, and
schizoid features. Example of procedure: [mis]quoting the following
from one of Carlyle's humorous letters to Robert Mitchell, "About
twenty plans have failed, I have about twenty more to try. [Yet] I
will make the doors of human society fly open before me, notwith-
standing my petards will not burst. I must mix them better, plant
them more judiciously; they shall burst and do execution too."
Halliday comments soberly, "As project after project failed he
wanted to blow people to pieces with bombs (petards)." The
psychoanalytical approach, with which we have no quarrel, may well
illuminate the author, but not the work if the critic starts with the
work. Thus it is taken more frequently by social scientists than by
literary critics, as in Herman Ausubel's *In Hard Times: Reformers
Among the Late Victorians* (1960).

   Much valuable biographical material about Carlyle lies in
Froude's edition of the *Letters and Memorials of Jane Welsh Carlyle*
(3 vols., 1883), in the volumes of her correspondence edited by
Leonard Huxley (1924) and Trudy Bliss (1950), and in such
biographies as Townsend Scudder's *Jane Welsh Carlyle* (1939) and
Necessary Evil: The Life of Jane Welsh Carlyle (1952) by Lawrence
and Elisabeth Hanson. One should also consult the correspondence
of those who knew him: Thackeray, George Eliot, Mill, Clough,
Browning, Ruskin, Forster, among many others.

IV. CRITICISM

1. GENERAL STUDIES

THOUGH THEY WERE relatively temperate, Carlyle's early works
   issued a challenge to the reader and tended to produce strong
agreement or disagreement. Almost from the beginning they attracted critical notice in the newspapers and periodicals. His *Life*

of Schiller (1823–24) was given favorable recognition in *The Times*, and reviews of his translation of *Wilhelm Meister* (1824), appearing in half a dozen journals, included De Quincey's excoriating one in the *London Magazine* (Sept. 1824), Lockhart's praise, in *Blackwood's* (June 1824) of the unknown translator, and Francis Jeffrey's commendation in his celebrated attack on Goethe in the *Edinburgh Review* (Aug. 1825). The less temperate *Sartor Resartus* (1833–34), alternately called a "heap of clotted nonsense" and a "Criticism upon the Spirit of the Age," had to wait a decade for full recognition, but the *French Revolution* and all the later works drew immediate, and widely varied, critical responses. Criticism of Carlyle generally, like the biographies, has been schizoid: some critics not able to make up their minds whether to praise or condemn his work; others praising or condemning it absolutely. The unfortunate consequence of Carlyle's pronouncements about work, might and right, and hero worship was their association first with imperialism, then with Prussianism, then with fascism. Three wars have exposed their dangerous implications and rendered his judgment in all matters suspect. The collapse of Carlyle's reputation in the twentieth century is one of the anomalies of modern literary history. Yet so complex was his thought, and so profound his influence among the Victorians, that it has been just as difficult for students of the Victorian period to leave him out of account. The consequence of this has been an increasing number of special, as it were, insulated, studies, which needed to make no final synthesis, of his early thought, his correspondence, his artistry, his influence.

Responsible criticism of Carlyle began with J. S. Mill's review of the *French Revolution* in the *London* and *Westminster Review* (1837), answering a recent attack on that work as "three long volumes of misplaced persiflage and flippant pseudo-philosophy." John Sterling's review of the *Miscellanies* (*London and Westminister Review*, 1839), Mazzini's "On the History of the French Revolution by Thomas Carlyle" (*Monthly Chronicle*, 1840) and "On the Genius and Tendency of the Writings of Thomas Carlyle" (*British and Foreign Review*, 1843; both reprinted in *Essays of Mazzini*, ed. William Clarke, 1887), the spirited essay on Carlyle in Richard Hengist Horne's *A New Spirit of the Age* (1844), written largely by Elizabeth Barrett, George Gilfillan's *A Gallery of Literary Portraits* (1845), Thoreau's "Thomas Carlyle and His Works" (*Graham's Magazine*, 1847), Emerson's review of *Past and Present* in *The Dial* (1843) and his *English Traits* (1856), and Taine's *L'Idéalisme anglais, étude sur Carlyle* (1864) — all reflect Carlyle's early impact as a literary, if not always a prophetic, genius.

The best critical studies of Carlyle have frequently been biographical, like the above-mentioned works by Neff and Symons. Louis Cazamian's *Carlyle* (1913; English trans. by E. K. Brown, 1932) is purely analytical; Cazamian attempts to define Carlyle's place in English literature as an idealist who thought he was destroying the disease of romanticism when he was in fact a carrier, and who, warring against utilitarianism, was himself "the supreme utilitarian." His was "the voice of inarticulate England," but his doctrine was bound up in the past and his writings appeal not to the mass but to the scholarly few. After admirable analyses of his moral and social ideas, Cazamian concludes on the extraordinary poetic imagination evident in his prose: "His vision of the world is that toward which the poets of the romantic generation had striven. . . . No poet has had in a higher degree, sublimity of imagination [or] has with greater power evoked the infinite, or the eternal silences which lie behind the transitory sights and sounds of life." Mary Agnes Hamilton's *Thomas Carlyle* (1926) is a study chiefly of his social teachings and in brief compass relates him to twentieth-century thought, arguing for his importance as a herald of the labor movement. Other general studies, mainly expository, are Bliss Perry's engaging *Thomas Carlyle: How to Know Him* (1915) and Augustus Ralli's *Guide to Carlyle* (2 vols., 1920). The latter provides summaries and commentary on all Carlyle's essays and books. Though a fervid admirer of these, Ralli dissents from Carlyle's doctrines of work and might is right which he says "were the children of pain," that is, products of the defeat of his early hopes and ideals by the science, democracy, and materialism of the Victorian world. The slender booklet *Thomas Carlyle* (1902) by G. K. Chesterton and J. E. H. Williams is a witty defense, justifying his theory of hero worship against misinterpreters, lauding his insight into great men and his cosmic humor, but rapping his impatience to achieve practical reforms quickly and his inability to understand other people's positions sympathetically. David Gascoyne's pamphlet *Thomas Carlyle* (1952) offers a comparable defense and a select bibliography for the student. In *Round by Repentance Tower* (1930) S. Sagar presents Carlyle sympathetically from the Catholic point of view. Sagar argues that Carlyle's vision was essentially a peasant's vision which was warped by Calvinism and then confused by German philosophy. When he tried Hero Worship, the "Half-way Institute," hoping to reconcile the opposing forces of the Christian church and democracy, he failed, and ended still a peasant, without a priest, having come close to being right, that is, a Catholic.

Numerous works attempt to define Carlyle's relation to the

romantic movement. Ashley Thorndike's *Literature in a Changing Age* (1925), about nineteenth-century literature's romantic inheritance as modified by the hostile environment of industrial democracy, is mostly about Carlyle, "who taught his age to look with imagination on its problems, and proposed remedies which were eventually adopted." His extreme language is laid to public neglect. For Charles Sarolea, in "The Tragedy of Thomas Carlyle" (*English Review*, 1931), it is "because Carlyle failed in all his endeavours . . . that his work is so interesting and instructive—more so than if he had succeeded." But Sarolea, though suggestive, writes uncritically, even superficially, and makes a number of unfounded generalizations. Holbrook Jackson's equally uncritical *Dreamers of Dreams* (1948) pictures Carlyle, along with Ruskin, Morris, Emerson, and others, whom he influenced, as a dreamer and idealist. Much better is J. W. Beach's treatment of him in *The Concept of Nature in Nineteenth Century English Poetry* (1936). Though not a poet, Carlyle is discussed as a major influence whose romantic conception of the divineness of nature "eased" the transition from a supernatural to a natural view of the world. Appealing to those who were "wearied by the search for truth and not prepared to make a clean break with the past," Carlyle is thus a transitional figure, related to both the romantics and the Victorians by the two periods of his nature philosophy, the early poetic transcendental (through *Sartor*), and the pragmatic, where nature means the order of the universe as manifested in history and human institutions. But he never lost the deep sense of wonder which Beach connects with the romantic tradition.

For George H. Mead, in *Movements of Thought in the Nineteenth Century* (1936, 1944), even more than for Cazamian, Carlyle's romanticism is rooted in the past. Mead holds that Carlyle, seeing clearly enough that society was still feudal, "wanted to preserve this feudal order." Mead sees only Carlyle's later conservative, not his lastingly radical, side, and overlooks his desire for a new order of society to be won through a new order of the spirit. In an essay on Carlyle in *Nineteenth Century Studies* (1949), Basil Willey points to his affinity with the religious side of romanticism with its emphasis on spiritual insights into reality, on love of the past, on imagination and faith, and like J. W. Beach regards his influence on many of his contemporaries as consoling and strengthening. His unorthodox faith saved Froude, Martineau, W. H. White, and others from Romanism on the one hand and from atheism on the other. In the opinion of Morse Peckham, in "Towards a Theory of Romanticism" (*PMLA*, 1951), Carlyle is not a true romantic.

Though he repudiated the conception of the cosmos as a static mechanism, he failed to arrive permanently at a "reintegration of his thought and art in terms of dynamic organicism." In *Sartor* he had achieved almost a radical romanticism but his "nostalgia for a static principle or static ground to the evolving universe was to prove his undoing. . . ." Peckham's recent retreat from the theory of romanticism presented in this essay has not, presumably, altered this theory of Carlyle. In any event it is echoed, with some variations, by Robert Langbaum in his *The Poetry of Experience* (1957). For Langbaum, Carlyle and his thinly disguised Teufelsdroeckh show how "the romantic quality of mind grows out of a total crisis of personality." The command of the Everlasting Yea, "Close thy *Byron,* open thy *Goethe*" (the Goethe of *Faust,* Part II), means repudiate that negative romanticism which is mere assertion of the will and turn to work and renunciation. But, says Langbaum, Carlyle forgot his own lesson, forgot that the point of *Faust* is the constantly developing man and that truth must not be allowed to harden into dogma. If Carlyle had not forgotten that truth *immer wird, nie ist* he might have continued to develop, and continued a romantic.

In his *Guide Through the Romantic Movement* Bernbaum assumes that Carlyle ceased to be a romantic after about 1841, when he began to glorify Machiavellian rulers and "became a false prophet." "But for that corruption," adds Bernbaum, "Romanticism was not responsible." Hoxie N. Fairchild, however, in his *Religious Trends in English Poetry* (Vol. IV, 1957), contends that corruption lies at the very heart of romanticism. Carlyle was "pure humanist" who made the romantic fusion of God and man, supernatural and natural, sacred and profane, and who, regarding "all religions as man-made symbols," exhibited that romantic spirit which attended the disintegration of Protestantism.

Gaylord LeRoy's *Perplexed Prophets* (1951) does not unperplex. Carlyle's "authoritarian nature" is once more explained psychoanalytically. LeRoy is critical of Halliday but essentially repeats his diagnosis, with help from Fromm's analysis of the authoritarian character as one of conflict between repressed instinctual drives and a tyrannical superego. This character somehow gave Carlyle his powerful influence, his clear-sighted social perceptions, then soured them into a reactionary philosophy and distrust of the common people. It is positively a relief, then, to find Carlyle called a Cyrenaic. In a brilliant essay, "Carlyle's Creative Disregard" (*MCR,* 1962), Paul West describes the quality in Carlyle's writings which shows him seeking intense experience, lusting for sensation, imaginatively exaggerating historical people and events to dazzle us, because he is lonely. This willful modification of people and events, his "creative disregard," West cites in order to distinguish Carlyle the protofascist from Carlyle the protosocialist. Torn "between what his nervous make-up required and what his human mind required," he wanted both order and justice. His heroes had to be truly high-minded. However impatient to get things done, he believed that "only right was might . . . [that] in the long run, might without right perishes." His Cyrenaic style which "to our own affluent idolatries" speaks plainly and sensibly "demonstrates what happens to a man who *is* a hundred years before his time, or half-a-dozen centuries too late."

C. R. Sanders explores another facet of Carlyle's romanticism in his excellent "The Byron Closed in *Sartor Resartus*" (*SIR*, 1964), in which he traces Carlyle's views on Byron from his and Jane's early enthusiasm to Carlyle's dramatic rejection in *Sartor*. Sanders shows this rejection to have been not sudden but gradual and incomplete, an admiration for Byron's struggles toward intellectual and spiritual maturity lingering to the end. Thus what looked like a turn "from Romantic individualism and self-centeredness to Victorian social-mindedness" was arrested by their common defiance of negation, their sense of drama in history, and their search for truth among shams, perhaps also by their Scottish blood. Yet to Carlyle, Byron was always a dandy and never reached maturity. "Not all of Byron was shut out; not all of Goethe was invited in."

2. CRITICISM OF INDIVIDUAL WORKS

Much criticism has been devoted to *Sartor Resartus* because it is the most original and influential of all Carlyle's works. It also represents the first fruition of his early struggles as a thinker and writer. Many a study therefore treats *Sartor* as the climax of his long literary apprenticeship. D. L. Maulsby's *The Growth of Sartor Resartus* (1899), S. B. Liljegren's "The Origin of Sartor Resartus" (*Palæstra*, 1925), and W. S. Johnson's *Thomas Carlyle: A Study of His Literary Apprenticeship, 1814–1831* (1911), are good examples. A remarkable work in Swedish, so far untranslated into English and therefore generally inaccessible, is Knut Hagberg's *Thomas Carlyle: Romantik och Puritanism i Sartor Resartus* (1925). Hagberg is concerned with the paradoxical existence of two opposite polarities in Carlyle: his Puritanism, which comes not only from his parents but from the Protestant revolt against Catholicism, and his romanticism which comes less from Germany than from his clan passion and the inborn tendency to mysticism of the Scottish Highlander (though he was a Lowlander!). Hagberg rightly stresses the limited extent of the German influence on Carlyle; he did not and could not understand Kant, or the Copernican revolution, and he accepted at the same time Schelling's thesis that nature is an immense organism with humanity a mere atom in the universe, and Fichte's that nature is an unreal appearance by means of which man realizes his destiny; and he espoused both an early sans-culottism and a later imperialism. These and other opposites Carlyle accepted, not because he was an eclectic, but because each thesis appealed to a profound part of his own nature—the Puritan and the Romantic— and *Sartor* is a unique expression of the union of those opposites in a work of art. More limited approaches to *Sartor* have been taken in Heinrich Kraeger's "Carlyles deutsche Studien und der 'Wotton Reinfred'" (*Anglia*, 1898), Otto von Lincke's *Über die Wortzusammensetzung in 'Sartor Resartus'* (1904), and A. C. Lorenz's *Diogenes Teufelsdroeckh und Thomas Carlyle* (1913). Studies of formative influence are A. O. Holmberg's mediocre *David Hume in Carlyle's "Sartor Resartus"* (1934), Susanne Howe's excellent chapter on Carlyle in her *Wilhelm Meister and His English Kinsmen* (1930), Berenice Cooper's "A Comparison of *Quintus Fixlein* and *Sartor Resartus*" (*TWA*, 1958), and Lore Metzger's "*Sartor Resartus*: A Victorian *Faust*" (*CL*, 1961). Metzger's article is a challenging, not invulnerable, attempt to prove that it was *Faust* that furnished Carlyle with "the pattern of genesis and regeneration" in Teufelsdroeckh, and that Teufelsdroeckh's character is compounded of the conflicting attributes of Faust and Mephistopheles. Without allowing for other influences, he argues that the duality in Teufelsdroeckh's nature is Fausto-Mephistophelian, then strips the incident of the Conversion on the *Rue de l'Enfer*, for which there is no direct parallel in *Faust*, of its autobiographical connections, in order to regard it exclusively as Teufelsdroeckh's effort to "resolve the conflict between his two souls." The article is illuminating nevertheless, and Metzger is quite right both in noting Carlyle's departures from Goethe's conception of nature and in showing how Carlyle broadened the pattern of conversion into "the palingenesia of society in which the Fausto-Mephistophelian polarity served the unending rhythm of annihilation and creation"—so long as it is understood that there are other analogues.

Not the pattern of conversion, but the particular account of Teufelsdroeckh's conversion in the second book of *Sartor* considered in relation to Carlyle's similar experience on Leith Walk in 1821 or 1822, is the subject of Carlisle Moore's "*Sartor Resartus* and the

Problem of Carlyle's 'Conversion' " (*PMLA*, 1955). Here it is argued that the *Sartor* account, though strongly autobiographical, is by no means literally so, that despite Carlyle's assertion of its literal truth, he dramatized and compressed into three short chapters an experience which took years to happen to himself. His rejection of the Everlasting No with its agonizing fears and doubts, which seems to have begun on Leith Walk, involved a struggle which did not end in victory even in 1825–26, the year of his marriage, for the spiritual and philosophical gains which make up the Everlasting Yea were not achieved altogether until 1830–31 while he was actually at work on *Sartor*. The persona of Teufelsdroeckh and the glowing narrative in *Sartor*, similar and yet dissimilar to his own character and experience, represent a triumph of Carlyle's artistry and creative imagination.

Several studies of the artistry in *Sartor* have appeared recently. Francis X. Roellinger, in "The Early Development of Carlyle's Style" (*PMLA*, 1957), contends that the style of *Sartor*, the first true Carlylese, was consciously developed to meet the requirements of Teufelsdroeckh. Alvan S. Ryan partially agrees, in "The Attitude toward the Reader in Carlyle's *Sartor Resartus*" (*VN*, 1963), but believes Roellinger neglected to distinguish between the styles of Teufelsdroeckh and the Editor. The Editor does not call the reader fool, and adopts a controlled tone of respect which recalls Carlyle's earlier review style. Three shorter pieces may be mentioned: D. P. Deneau's "Relation of Style and Device in *Sartor Resartus*" (*VN*, 1960), John Lindberg's "Artistic Unity of *Sartor Resartus*" (*VN*, 1960), and Richard A. Levine's "Carlyle as Poet: The Phoenix Image in 'Organic Filaments' " (*VN*, 1964).

The lack of a comprehensive critical book on *Sartor* is soon to be filled by the forthcoming publication of G. B. Tennyson's *SARTOR Called RESARTUS* by the Princeton University Press. This is an interesting and penetrating study of the genesis, the structure and style, and the meaning of the work, with important sections on its dynamic and intricate, but unified, structure, on *Sartor* considered as a novel, on Carlyle's imagery, on his use of fragments, and on many of the allusions. Tennyson has made an invaluable contribution to the study of Carlyle as both artist and thinker.

There is still no substantial book on the *French Revolution*. Oscar Browning's triumphant discovery that Carlyle had misrepresented the distance from Paris to Varennes by some thirty miles (*The Flight to Varennes and Other Historical Essays*, 1892) was effectively discountenanced by F. V. A. Aulard, whose "Carlyle historien de la révolution française" (introductory to the French translation, 1912) justified Carlyle's method and lauded his accuracy as a historian. There have been other attacks, by professional historians denying its right to be called a history, and other defenses, on both historical and literary grounds—little different, essentially, from the mixed reception it received when it first appeared (see R. T. Kerlen's "Contemporary Criticism of Carlyle's *French Revolution*," *SR*, 1912). We are not concerned here with Carlyle's qualifications as a historian, yet even in such studies as those by C. F. Harrold the question arises. In "Carlyle's General Method in *The French Revolution*" (*PMLA*, 1928) and "The Translated Passages in Carlyle's *French Revolution*" (*JEGP*, 1928), Harrold discusses the unique way in which Carlyle used his sources while at work. Though his aim was accuracy, even a painstaking accuracy, it was an accuracy to the event rather than to the source, to the spirit rather than to the literal wording. Obvious omissions or mistakes could be rectified; translated passages could be heightened for dramatic effect. The result, concludes Harrold, is both accurate and "literary" history, not objective, for all has been refracted through his mind and personality, yet impartial, as Aulard and Trevelyan maintain, for Carlyle took all sides in the fray. (See Trevelyan, *Life and Letters*, v, 391–410.)

A recent study is H. Ben-Israel's "Carlyle and the French Revolution" (*Historical Journal*, 1958). On the whole, this is a defense of Carlyle's work with a somewhat puzzling mixture of unreconciled praise and blame. Ben-Israel notes the strong romantic influence on Carlyle from Herder and Schiller, from Burke and Scott, and connects this with Carlyle's "subconscious method of writing history," that is, reading his sources until the authentic picture of events somehow "came," which sets aside rational judgment and procedure. Carlyle is first denied impartiality *except* as he avoided "a superstructure of systematic ideas" and narrow political judgments, then defended as an accurate historian against Oscar Browning, his *French Revolution* being preferred to Croker's as the "more significant history" because written by one who was of no party, either radical or conservative. Carlyle "did not give violence either moral or political sanction," and he "never lost the balance between material and ideal forces in the Revolution." Though Ben-Israel praises the vividness and sweep of Carlyle's work, he slights its literary qualities, calling the idea of "poetic history" Carlyle's "most extravagant idea about history." Alfred Cobban's "Carlyle's French Revolution" (*History*, 1963) is an admirably balanced statement of what Carlyle understood and misunderstood about that conflagration.

A comparison of *Past and Present*, Book II, and its source in Jocelin's *Chronicle* has provided the subject of many a graduate dissertation. That by Fritz Schneider, *Carlyles "Past and Present" und der "Chronica Jocelini de Brakelonda"* (1911) is not to be trusted. Grace Calder, however, in her *The Writing of Past and Present: A Study of Carlyle's Manuscripts* (1949), has given us a valuable and fascinating study of Carlyle's methods of composition and prose style. She corrects the erroneous notion that Carlyle wrote the work easily, and in five weeks; five months rather. After describing the first draft and the printer's copy, and establishing the borrowings from Jocelin's *Chronicle* which appear in each, Miss Calder subjects the two manuscripts to a detailed comparison, showing how Carlyle's revision resulted in a substantial improvement of the printer's copy in both organization and expression, and then elaborating the theory and practice of Carlyle's most effective stylistic devices. But these devices, abundantly illustrated from the manuscripts, and relating to diction, expansion, and syntactical and rhetorical patterns, on the one hand, are characteristic only of his style in *Past and Present*, and, on the other, only begin to characterize his practice as a skilled workman and creative artist whose unexplained genius "towers above and overshadows all possible demonstrations of his method."

Additional studies may be noted in John T. Fain's "Word Echoes in *Past and Present*" (*VN*, 1955), Frederic Harrison's introductory essay in his edition of *Past and Present* (1897), giving a Victorian Positivist's approving view, and an essay by Stanley T. Williams, "Carlyle's *Past and Present*: A Prophecy" (*SAQ*, 1922), in which the social and economic reforms advanced in the work are taken as accomplished.

Except for the storm of contemporary attacks which greeted them, the *Latter-Day Pamphlets* have been given little individual attention. James Hannay's pamphlet *Blackwood vs. Carlyle* (1850) was a vigorous counterattack and defense of Carlyle's ideas and style. There is an unpublished dissertation, E. A. Reiff's "Studies in Carlyle's 'Latter-Day Pamphlets'" (Iowa, 1937); for other work on the *Latter-Day Pamphlets* one turns to the relevant books by Cazamian, Neff, Symons, and to F. W. Roe's *The Social Philosophy of Carlyle and Ruskin* (1921). Two articles on the *Life of Sterling*, Anne K. Tuell's "Carlyle's Marginalia in Sterling's *Essays and Studies*" (*PMLA*, 1939), and William Blackburn's

"Carlyle and the Composition of *Sterling*" (*SP*, 1947), utilize Carlyle's marginalia on some of Sterling's manuscripts to illuminate Carlyle's composition of the biography.

On *Frederick the Great* there is a fair quantity of criticism, much of it German. M. Krummacher's *Englische Sprache und Stil in Carlyles "Frederick II"* (*Englische Studien*, 1888, 1889) is a representative study. A. Mämpel's considerably better *Thomas Carlyle als Künstler unter besonderer Berücksichtigung "Friedrich des Grossen"* contributes novel discussions of phantasy, of history as anecdote (showing influence of Novalis), of the dramatic aspects of Carlyle's historical narrative, and of Carlyle as a symbolist. R. A. E. Brooks, in the introduction to his edition of Carlyle's *Journey to Germany, Autumn, 1858* (1940), also examines Carlyle's practice as a historian in the accounts of twelve of Frederick's battles. Admitting some justice in Norwood Young's attack on the work, Brooks finds unjust the accusation that Carlyle failed to consult important sources which would have forced him to take a different view of the events, and concludes that Carlyle not only used all the available sources but used them critically to arrive at accounts of those battles which are more accurate and less biased than those in the sources. Fully aware of its defects, Brooks believes that *Frederick the Great*, though lacking "the flaming unity of *The French Revolution*, . . . more nearly reaches his own ideals" of what history should be. In his "B. W. Proctor and the Genesis of *Frederick the Great*" (*H.L.B.*, 1953), Brooks offers evidence that the first suggestion that Carlyle should write on Frederick came from Bulwer.

3. IDEAS AND ARTISTRY

The complex relation of Carlyle's thought to the German writers and thinkers whose works he read during the important 1820's when his ideas were maturing has preoccupied many scholars. Like William Taylor of Norwich, Scott, and Coleridge, he transmitted German literature and philosophy into England, but just how far he understood the philosophy, whether he drew his style from Jean Paul, the extent of his debt to Goethe, Schiller, Kant, Fichte, Novalis, and others are debatable matters, which have been most comprehensively treated by C. F. Harrold in his *Carlyle and German Thought, 1819–1834* (1934). Emphasizing both Carlyle's direct indebtedness to individual writers and his curious misunderstanding of some of their most important concepts, owing partly, perhaps, to Coleridge, Harrold shows that Carlyle drew his nature philosophy from Goethe's notion of the world as a vesture of the spirit and from certain doctrines of Kant, Fichte, and Schelling, loosely interpreted under the inspiration of Novalis; that Carlyle misread, perhaps willfully, Kant's distinction between Understanding and Reason, subordinating the Understanding to Reason as a "higher" faculty with mystical significance, virtually identical with Faith; and that he also misread Kant's idealism and denied space and time any reality whatever. Without neglecting the English background, Harrold has established the crowning importance of Carlyle's study of the German thinkers and his primary indebtedness to Goethe, Schiller, and Novalis for his Clothes Philosophy, his deep understanding of the symbolic nature of the world.

Hill Shine, in another important study, "Carlyle and the German Philosophy Problem During the Year 1826–1827" (*PMLA*, 1935), carefully measures the extent of Carlyle's reading of Kant, Fichte, and Novalis in 1826–27, "when he was trying hardest to understand the systems of German thought as systems," and traces the changes in his thought from aesthetic and humanistic concerns to transcendentalism, and through the Natural Supernaturalism shown him by Novalis to his later poetic realism. Shine concludes even more strongly than Wellek, Storrs, and Harrold that Carlyle was not a systematic philosopher himself and that his reading of the German philosophers was affected by a distaste for systematic philosophy which grew later into an aversion, but that he derived from it what he wanted most, a belief in "the permanent within the flux."

Other important studies are René Wellek's "Carlyle and German Romanticism" (*Xenia Pragensia*, 1929) and *Immanuel Kant in England: 1793–1838* (1931), V. Stockley's *German Influence as Known in England, 1750–1832* (1929), Margaret Storrs's *The Relation of Carlyle to Kant and Fichte* (1929), and A. Hildebrand's *Carlyle und Schiller* (1913). W. Witte, in his "Carlyle's Conversion" (*The Era of Goethe: Essays Presented to James Boyd*, 1959), argues piquantly that although Carlyle admitted his debt to Goethe, "Schiller had more to do with his 'conversion' than he knew, or than he cared to admit." Among studies of Carlyle and Goethe we mention: Jean Marie Carré's *Goethe en Angleterre* (1920), H. Plagens' *Carlyles Weg zu Goethe* (1938), A. Kippenberg's *Carlyles Weg zu Goethe* (1946), and W. M. Watt's "Carlyle on Muhammad" (*HJ*, 1955), tracing Carlyle's favorable opinion of Mohammed partly to Goethe's *West-Östlicher Divan*. Watt declares that Carlyle was "the first writer in either east or west to attempt to fathom the inner experience of the founder of Islam." Jurgen Kedenburg, in *Teleologisches Geschichtsbild und theokratische Staatsauffassung im*

Werke Thomas Carlyles (1960), investigates the Goethean side of Carlyle's conception of historical periodicity—alternating epochs of Belief and Unbelief—as a determinant of his theocratic ideal of government progressively achievable through heroes. Studies of Carlyle and Jean Paul have frequently related to prose style, for example, Henry Pape's *Jean Paul als Quelle von Thomas Carlyles Anschauungen und Stil* (1904), T. Geissendorfer's "Carlyle and Jean Paul Friedrich Richter" (*JEGP*, 1926), and J. W. Smeed's "Carlyles Jean Paul-Ubersetzungen" (*DVLG*, 1961). In his "Thomas Carlyle and Jean Paul Richter" (*CL*, 1964), Smeed argues convincingly for the "jeanpaulian" influences on the structural and thematic aspects of *Sartor*, though much the same ground was covered earlier by Wellek, Harrold, and others; but Smeed's inclination to find Carlyle's style inferior wherever it does not directly reflect the influence of Jean Paul's indicates a failure to understand Carlyle.

Since Carlyle is no longer regarded as a philosopher, we find studies rather of his philosophical and religious position and attitude. True, Leslie Paul in his series of BBC lectures published as *The English Philosophers* (1954) treats Carlyle along with Coleridge, Hamilton, and Stirling as a reviver of English philosophy after the stalemate of eighteenth-century skepticism, and J. H. Muirhead, in his *The Platonic Tradition in Anglo-Saxon Philosophy* (1931), devotes a chapter to "Carlyle's Transcendental Symbolism." But these assign him a historical importance in the lean context of nineteenth-century English philosophy rather than importance as an original or systematic philosopher. This does not mean that he has no philosophical position or that the steps by which he reached it are not important. Several scholars have been concerned with these questions. Hill Shine, in his *Carlyle's Fusion of Poetry, History, and Religion by 1834* (1934), follows a study of Carlyle's earlier struggles among the German philosophers with an examination of his effort to synthesize some of the ideas and opinions he had drawn from them, to reconcile his conflicting opinions, first of religion and poetry, then of poetry and history, finally of all three. He sought also to resolve the conflict between the principles of romantic tolerance and puritan intolerance. Gradually poetry became dissociated from fiction and allied with historical fact; then history and religion were both conceived as manifestations of the supernatural in the actual; but though poetry, history, and religion were now theoretically fused, he "took refuge" after Goethe's death in his doctrine of the unconscious, and relied more heavily on his Calvinist background. C. F. Harrold, in his "The Nature of Carlyle's

Calvinism" (*SP*, 1936), reaches the similar conclusion that Carlyle's thought was dominated by German Idealism till about 1834, thereafter by his underlying Calvinism which turned him away from philosophical toward social interests. Also from C. R. Sanders' *Coleridge and the Broad Church Movement* (1942) we learn that for Carlyle as for Coleridge philosophy and religion were linked, each tending toward the condition of the other, the priest becoming the philosopher who rejects orthodoxy but retains a silent respect for the Christian religion. C. F. Harrold, having examined the Calvinist, examined another important aspect of Carlyle's religion in "The Mystical Element in Carlyle" (*MP*, 1932) and "Carlyle and the Mystical Tradition" (*Cath W*, 1935). Carlyle is described as a mystical thinker rather than as a true mystic, who at moments "Caught the vision of the One" and "to the end wrote like a true mystic." Carlyle's "felt indubitable certainty of Experience" alludes to his mystical apprehension of the ineffable deity. His belief in the spiritual unity of all beings and his hunger for the infinite are evidence of his kinship with mystics and the mystical tradition. On the other hand, Harrold thinks that both the Calvinist and the mystical components of his faith were opposed by "his prideful and corrosive intellect" and that this clash is responsible for "the disharmony in his life and writings." Carlisle Moore, in "The Persistence of Carlyle's 'Everlasting Yea'" (*MP*, 1957), treating the tenets of the Everlasting Yea as articles of a positive religious faith, asks what happened to them during the years that followed their final formulation in 1830–31. Moore traces the course of his growing discouragement at the fiasco of the Chartist movement, the failure of the revolutions of 1848, and the death of Sir Robert Peel in 1850, to his latter-day bitterness at Englishmen who had not heeded his message even if they had heard it. Though he was unable to formulate a new message which was to have been called *Exodus from Houndsditch*, he never lost his faith in God, his transcendent view of the world, or his love and pity for suffering men.

As a literary critic Carlyle has been accorded a limited respect. Many of his ideas about literature derived from the German writers, or reflected the general romantic reaction against eighteenth-century rationalism and neoclassicism. Moreover, as F. W. Roe says, in his *Carlyle as a Critic of Literature* (1910), "It was more from necessity than from deliberate intention that [he] became for a period of years a critic of literature"; and, in Saintsbury's words, his "strictly critical inclinations, if not his strictly critical faculties, waned as he grew older." Saintsbury (*History of Literary Criticism*, 1906) holds him partly responsible, with Macaulay, for the poverty of criticism in the 1830's and 1840's. Roe's work presents Carlyle's critical opinions in their biographical and historical context, as influenced by English and German Romanticism and by the reviews. His part in the introduction of German literature into England, his brilliant revaluation of Burns, Boswell, and Scott, and his contributions to historical and comparative methods of criticism are discussed as evidence that at his best he was a "really great interpreter of men of letters and of literature." But Roe does not fail to note his hostility to fiction and poetry and his opposition to much of romanticism. For René Wellek (*A History of Modern Literary Criticism,* 1955), Carlyle reflects the influence of Coleridge's dialectical and symbolist view of poetry, though in prose, and illustrates the decadence of romantic criticism after the death of Hazlitt and Coleridge, though he was "the one impressive new figure." Noting that the terms "a Romantic," "a romanticist," and "Romanticism" were first used as critical terms by Carlyle, Wellek, like Saintsbury, regrets that he so soon "deserted criticism." Alba Warren (*English Poetic Theory, 1825–65,* 1950) regards Carlyle as a popularizer of the German theory of art as revelation. Carlyle sought to find in what sense poetry is true and unified, and by his insistence that artistic creation is unconscious, and therefore unanalyzable, is responsible for "the subversion of the creative act." His poetic, though it contains some truth, "is quite simply too transcendental. . . . He has the general romantic tendency to dissolve and blur distinctions into indefinable absolutes." A. Obertello, in *Carlyle's Critical Theories: Their Origin and Practice* (1948), while granting that Carlyle was a literary critic only to about 1832, after which he turned to social and political criticism, insists that his critical output was of inestimable value and importance. More than any of his contemporaries, says Obertello, he employed the biographical, historical, and comparative methods "with sympathy and penetration." He admits, however, that "Carlyle never was a pure critic of literature; his touchstone was morality rather than aesthetics." M. H. Abrams, in *The Mirror and the Lamp* (1953), treats Carlyle along with Mill and Keble, Victorians all, as really representing the extreme romantic, or expressivist, view of poetry. Regarding poetry as a revelation of genius, he subordinated it almost to the point of actually denying it. Yet his espousal of great art as the product of spontaneous and organic growth, not mechanical but dynamic, and symbolical, is significant.

Critics of Carlyle have found it difficult to classify his literary work. Not a poet proper, though with a poet's imagination, nor a novelist, though he dealt in fiction, an essayist but an extraliterary one—he seems rather to have been a historian, a social reformer, a prophet. Yet no one can deny his extraordinary literary power, his unique command of the language of description and portraiture, the poetic and dramatic effects of his prose. The one thing his contemporaries agreed on was his "literary genius," and critics continue to find fresh evidence of it. But his works are, in Coleridge's sense, imaginative, not imaginary, and their relation to the fiction of poetry and the novel is therefore central in any effort to define talent.

Carlisle Moore's "Thomas Carlyle and Fiction: 1822–34" (*Nineteenth Century Studies*, 1940) traces the changing course of Carlyle's ideas about fiction from his early admiration and his attempts to write short stories and a novel, through his growing respect, after 1828, for history and historical fact, to his outright condemnation of fiction in 1830 as "akin to lying." An examination of "Cruthers and Jonson" and his unfinished novel, *Wotton Reinfred*, indicates that he failed in these attempts because of his increasing absorption in transcendentalist ideas, and that it was not his failure, but these ideas plus his Calvinist conscience, that caused him later to repudiate fiction. Moreover, the repudiation was more theoretical than actual, and less complete than he thought, for he retained a lifelong fondness for certain works of fiction, and his own writings, like *Sartor* and the *French Revolution*, are distinguished by the use of fictional material and devices. Carlyle's rejection of fiction entailed the rejection also of much poetry, and this accounts for the advice he gave to Tennyson and Browning that they should turn to prose. Poetry, however, was only redefined. In another article by Moore, "Carlyle's 'Diamond Necklace' and Poetic History" (*PMLA*, 1943), Carlyle's effort to put into practice his newly-evolved theory that history when fused with poetry and religion is "the sole Poetry possible" is examined specifically in his experimentation in "The Diamond Necklace" with fictional, dramatic, and stylistic devices which enabled him to re-create both the immediate actuality and the eternal truths of past people and events. In this historical essay he served his artist's apprenticeship for the writing of the *French Revolution*. C. R. Sanders in his "Carlyle, Poetry, and the Music of Humanity" (*WHR*, 1962) suggests that what Carlyle objected to in the poetry of his day was not only its artificial cadence, tending to mere prettiness, but its lack of what he called "musical thought." A transcendental concept, this "sphere-music" demands that true poetry shall have a rhythm which is most appropriate to the thought, and that the thought, as in true prose also, shall be a lofty, even divine, truth given such expression that, without losing any of its heavenly quality, it becomes human. His doctrine of symbolism and his trenchant criticism of mechanical prettiness in poetry, Sanders says, influenced Browning, and perhaps through Browning influenced modern poets such as Hardy, Pound, Yeats, and Eliot. Finally, George Levine, in *"Sartor Resartus* and the Balance of Fiction" (*VS*, 1964), revives the question, initially raised by Moore, of why Carlyle so persistently used fictional devices, and traces the effect these had on the quality of his works. Stemming from his uncertainty "about means, about self, about audience," Carlyle's resort to fiction nevertheless produced in *Sartor* a fine balance between direct preaching and "openness to experience" which, Levine finds, was lost in the later works, and never regained, because of his increasing desperation. Carlyle could not sustain "the broad general mood which tended to make fiction the dominating form of the period." Unlike G. B. Tennyson, Levine sees *Sartor*, despite its stylistic brilliance, as static in structure, "a series of elaborate variations on a central position."

Efforts to derive Carlyle's style or the larger aspects of his craft from the Germans have given way to studies of his manifold originality. According to his mood, his materials, and his purpose, he had many different styles—his formal manner in the reviews, the informal calm of the *Life of Sterling*, and the varieties of Carlylese in the other major works. W. C. Brownell, in *The Genius of Style* (1924), prefers the style of *Sterling* as "altogether on a more elevated plane" than that of *Sartor:* "There is nothing restful," he says, "in tireless tumultuousness." Edwin Muir in an essay on "The Scottish Ballads" (*Contemporary Scottish Studies*, ed. C. M. Grieve, 1926) asserts that Carlyle's style came "bodily from the Scots pulpit" and was a hybrid of virtues of the English Bible and vices of the Scottish version of the Pslams of David.

More rewarding are studies which, like Vernon Lee's "Carlyle and the Present Tense" (*Contemporary Review*, 1904), recognize his unique imagination. Describing Dickens' use of the present tense as "melodramatic," Miss Lee states her preference for Carlyle's because, eliminating narrative, it makes his prose lyric; "no man's style was ever so organically personal as his, so intimately interwoven with individual habits of thought and feeling." Logan Pearsall Smith, too, in "The Rembrandt of English Prose" (*TLS*, 1934), discusses him not as a prophet or sham prophet, nor as a moralist, but as an artist who cared most for the "picturesque in man and nature" and "valued the good and evil of the world as a painter does his pigments." Though Carlyle's "master-obsession" was his relation to the mysterious universe, what delights *us* is his incomparable gift of expression. Equally valuable is C. R. Sanders' "The Victorian Rembrandt: Carlyle's Portraits of His Contemporaries" (*BJRL*, 1957) in which his descriptions of people are examined as evidence of his perennial love of human beings, his remarkably keen eye, and his extraordinary power of "suggesting what is indefinable in humanity." Like Grace Calder, Sanders recognizes in Carlyle's writing a magic "which defies analysis . . . he makes us suddenly aware that his subject belongs not to the earth merely but is a creature of infinitude, staring out at us from a strange, mysterious place where immensity and eternity meet."

An often overlooked side of Carlyle is his humor. Critics observe it, but briefly, and do not perceive its salutary presence in some of his most extravagant and otherwise offensive pronouncements, like that on Pig-Philosophy in "Jesuitism." The following are suggestive studies of this subject, which calls for larger investigation: W. S. Lilly, "The Humorist as Prophet" (*Four English Humorists of the Nineteenth Century*, 1895), T. W. Higginson, *Carlyle's Laugh and Other Surprises* (1909), and A. H. Upham, "Rabelaisianism in Carlyle" (*MLN*, 1918).

Another of Carlyle's talents, largely neglected since Otto Schmeding's *Über Wortbildung bei Carlyle* (1900), is taken up again by Harold Wentworth in "The Allegedly Dead Suffix-*dom* in Modern English" (*PMLA*, 1941), and by R. M. Estrich and Hans Sperber who, in *Three Keys to Language* (1952), discuss his numerous word coinages, not only as these influenced the language and other writers (more than half the coinages in -*dom* during the years 1800 to 1840 were the work of Carlyle) but also as a characteristic of his style which showed him creatively extending the language to express new ideas and special moods of ironic humor or of rebellion against contemporary and older purism: "clearly coinage was a necessity to his self-expression."

A new direction was given to the study of Carlyle's artistry by John Holloway's *The Victorian Sage* (1953). Holloway's purpose is to analyze the rhetorical devices by which the sage, who cannot prove his intangible truths, induces the reader to accept them almost unawares. Carlyle is the archetypal sage. The knowledge he teaches is not new but hidden; the universe which his insight reveals to the reader is spiritual and alive. His language, highly figurative and dramatic, is full of esoteric metaphors by which he controls meaning and conveys the sense of energy, or infinity, or the lurid, for example, the darkness imagery in *Cromwell;* and the dichotomy of language is used to conjure the clashing forces in man and the world.

Holloway's work should stimulate further studies of Carlyle's style and imagery, like that of R. L. Peters' "Some Illustrations of Carlyle's Symbolist Imagery" (*VN*, 1959).

Respecting Carlyle as a translator, C. T. Carr, in "Carlyle's Translations from German" (*MLR*, 1947), notes Carlyle's mild bowdlerizing and a few errors in *Wilhelm Meister's Apprenticeship*, a marked improvement in his translation of the *Travels*, and some formative influence of Jean Paul on his style in *German Romance*. There is another study by Olga Marx, *Carlyle's Translation of Wilhelm Meister* (1925), and of course Grace Calder's work on *Past and Present* (1949). Carlyle's theory and practice as a biographer have so far been dealt with only in general works like Waldo Dunn's *English Biography* (1913), and in two unpublished dissertations: Walter W. Waring's "Thomas Carlyle as a Biographer" (Cornell Univ., 1949) and Samuel C. Burchell's "Thomas Carlyle and the Art of Biography" (Yale Univ., 1951).

Carlyle's relation to the periodicals has received little individual attention. Two articles by M. H. Goldberg, "Jeffrey: Mutilator of Carlyle's 'Burns'" (*PMLA*, 1941) and "Carlyle, Pictet and Jeffrey" (*MLQ*, 1946), deal with his effort to have his work published, and published as he wrote it, in the *Edinburgh Review*. M. M. H. Thrall's *Rebellious Fraser's* (1934) thoroughly explains his connections with that periodical, and there are helpful references to Carlyle in L. A. Marchand's *The Athenaeum, A Mirror of Victorian Culture* (1941), M. M. Bevington's *The Saturday Review, 1855–1868* (1941), G. L. Nesbitt's *Benthamite Reviewing, The First Twelve Years of the Westminster Review* (1934), W. B. Thomas' *The Story of the Spectator, 1828–1928* (1928), E. M. Everett's *The Party of Humanity, The Fortnightly Review and Its Contributors, 1865–1874* (1939), Francis E. Mineka's *The Dissidence of Dissent: The Monthly Repository, 1806–1838* (1944), Josephine Bauer's *The London Magazine* (1953), and Diderik Roll-Hanson's *The Academy, 1869–1879* (1957).

In addition to the work done on the *French Revolution* and *Frederick the Great*, there are dozens of studies of Carlyle as a historian, ranging from the loyal praise of Trevelyan to the hostility of Norwood Young. G. P. Gooch, in *History and Historians in the Nineteenth Century* (1913), devotes a chapter to Carlyle and Froude, in which Carlyle is praised for his vivid style but chided for inaccuracies. The fullest study is Louise M. Young's *Carlyle and the Art of History* (1939), which incorporates most earlier work on the subject, and analyzes Carlyle's theory of history and historiography as it was formed by his English and German readings, then examines his application of these theories to the writing of the *French Revolution—Cromwell and Frederick* being dealt with more briefly. Attempting to free Carlyle's theory from sole dependence on his doctrine of hero worship, Mrs. Young makes stronger claims than C. F. Harrold did for his indebtedness to Herder, to Burke, and to the Saint-Simonians, but she makes little attempt to establish Carlyle's relation to other historians or to measure his broader influence. Hill Shine's *Carlyle and the Saint-Simonians, The Concept of Historical Periodicity* (1941) was written for the most part before the appearance of Mrs. Young's study. Treating the historical rather than the social aspects of the relation, Shine demonstrates that Carlyle's concept of periodicity—the alternation of organic and critical epochs—is derived from the writings of the Saint-Simonians, and follows this concept through *Sartor*, the *French Revolution*, *Past and Present*, and *Frederick*. René Wellek, replying to both Mrs. Young and Hill Shine in his "Carlyle and the Philosophy of History" (*PQ*, 1941), objects to their associating Carlyle with rationalistic schools instead of with the romantic, and contends that Carlyle derived from the Saint-Simonians only the formula for historical periodicity, the basic idea having come to him earlier through the "palingenesis" of Herder's *Ideen*. Ernst Cassirer too, following Wellek, in *The Myth of the State* (1946), says, "The attempts in recent literature to connect Carlyle with St. Simonism or to read into his work a sociological conception of history are futile." These attempts have continued, in D. B. Cofer's *Saint-Simonism in the Radicalism of Thomas Carlyle* (1931), Ella M. Murphy's "Carlyle and the Saint Simonians" (*SP*, 1936), F. A. Hayek's *The Counter-Revolution of Science* (1952), and R. K. P. Pankhurst's *The Saint-Simonians, Mill and Carlyle* (1957). In 1950 Hill Shine responded to Wellek in "Carlyle's Early Writings and Herder's *Ideen*: The Concept of History" (*Booker Memorial Studies*) with a rigorous examination of Carlyle's knowledge of the *Ideen*. Leaving unchanged his earlier position on Carlyle's derivation of periodicity from the Saint-Simonians, he finds that Carlyle drew from the *Ideen* four related historical concepts: organic nature as revelation, human history as revelation, the principle of change in both, and the survival in history of the morally worthiest. The last of these principles, the survival of the right rather than of the fittest, Shine regards as "the one that gives his thought . . . its greatest unity of meaning."

Since they are intimately related to all his other interests, Carlyle's social ideas have been discussed more often, perhaps, than any other aspect of his thinking. But there is no consensus. So indiscriminately have they been tied to recent political isms, that the twentieth-century critic has difficulty in understanding them in their nineteenth-century context. The best introduction is still Emery Neff's *Carlyle and Mill* (1926). Neff reveals the age through the conjunction of these two minds and personalities, which met on common ground until the issue of utilitarianism divided them and Carlyle stood nearly alone in his demand for an internal reform, a spiritual, not a Benthamic, radicalism. Edward Jenks's still valuable *Carlyle and Mill* (1888) is less a social study than a study of contrasting points of view. As a companion piece to Neff's work, F. W. Roe's *Social Philosophy of Carlyle and Ruskin* (1921) also contains a valuable analysis of the "Condition of England" against which Carlyle hurled his Question, of the social conditions which his sans-culottism was designed to alleviate, of his effort to halt the flood of laissez-faire democracy which he thought would lead either to anarchy or tyranny. His conception of force, says Roe, was inseparable from moral justice, even when he later grew embittered and seemed to espouse force for its own sake. There are two German dissertations, Heinrich Pahlev's "John Ruskin und Thomas Carlyle, mit besonderer Berücksichtigung des socialen Problems" (1925) and P. C. M. Schnell's "Die Kulturkritik bei Thomas Carylle und John Ruskin" (1953); and Raymond Williams' brilliant chapter in his *Culture and Society, 1780–1950* (1958), extracting the best of Carlyle's social thought from the early essay "Signs of the Times" (1829). Williams emphasizes the sense and balance of this essay and Carlyle's remarkably "direct response" to his age, which enabled him so accurately to discern its mechanical nature and its need for the spiritual. It was Carlyle's tragedy, says Williams, that his noble conception of spiritual reform should have been dragged down by the very society he sought to help. Alienated from his age, his proposed remedies unheeded, he lost that tolerance; and his call for leadership by the Aristocracy and Captains of Industry became, in "Shooting Niagara" (1867), "a contemptuous absolutism."

Carlyle's opposition to democracy has divided his critics into opposing armies of attack and defense. It is regrettable that so many have sought to blame him for the evils that came later, and have made no effort to see his ideas either *sub specie diei* or *sub specie aeternitatis*. On the other hand, his defenders, like D. A. Wilson, have been too much disposed to explain away all his faults. H. L. Stewart's "Alleged Prussianism of Thomas Carlyle" (*International Journal of Ethics*, 1918) and "Carlyle and His Critics" (*Nineteenth Century and After*, 1919) are clearly apologetic, and as Pieter Geyl remarks in *Debates with Historians* (1952), a "tone of extenuation and evasion" weakens the effectiveness of such Carlyle defenders as Willey, Trevelyan, Neff, and even Cazamian and Symons. Worse, perhaps, is the hostile and dogmatic tone of the attackers who sought a scapegoat for the war blame. Such are A. Kelly's *Carlyle and the War* (1915), Stuart P. Sherman's "Carlyle and Kaiser-Worship" (*The Nation*, 1918), E. Sellière's *L'Actualité de Carlyle: un précurseur du national-socialisme* (1939), Frank A. Lea's *Carlyle, Prophet of Today* (1943), and J. Salwyn Shapiro's "Thomas Carlyle, Prophet of Fascism" (*Journal of Modern History*, 1945). Apparently under the same fear, Edith Batho and Bonamy Dobrée, in *The Victorians and After* (1938), wrote that Carlyle would have wished to be Hitler in 1937, though maybe not in 1940, when, however, he would have "stood a strong chance of internment under 18B." In another class of works Carlyle's "fascism" is considered a subject for congratulation: G. Ricciardelli's *Benito Mussolini e Tommaso Carlyle* (1931), dealing with the mystic's prophetic ideas and how they inspired the happy union of the working class and the leaders of industry under Mussolini; Theodore Diemal's *Carlyle und der Nationalsozialismus* (1937); and P. Aldag's "Thomas Carlyle und die Juden" (*Hochschule und Ausland*, 1937), Aldag being a Nazi who welcomes Carlyle's presumed anti-Semitism as found in a little-known pamphlet, "The Jew—Our lawgiver" (1853), which was written, however, not by our Carlyle but by Thomas Carlyle, the advocate.

B. H. Lehman's *Carlyle's Theory of the Hero* (1928) is a friendly, historical study; a few years later H. J. C. Grierson in *Carlyle and Hitler* (1933), Sidney Hook in *The Hero in History* (1943), and Eric Bentley in *A Century of Hero-Worship* (1944) see in his demand for heroes a dangerous sign of uncontrolled subjectivism and egotism and an affinity with Nietzsche. For Bentley in 1944, it meant the menace of heroic vitalism, but a year later he admitted that "there is another Carlyle," the courageous questioner of his time, the radical from whose lifelong search for right leadership today's believers in democracy have much to learn. Unlike B. E. Lippincott in *Victorian Critics of Democracy* (1938), who wrote that Carlyle "would unquestionably have admired" Mussolini and Hitler, Ernst Cassirer asserts in *The Myth of the State* (1946) that "what Carlyle meant by 'heroism' or 'leadership' was by no means the same as what we find in our modern theories of fascism." Carlyle's heroes were sincere, did not lie, and had noble insight. Though the *Heroes* lectures contained a "dangerous explosive," Carlyle "ought never to be charged with being an advocate of contemporary National Socialist ideas and ideals." The trouble rose, says Cassirer, when hero worship lost its original meaning and was blended with race worship and both became part of the same political ideology. It needs to be observed that most of the attacks on Carlyle as a proto-Fascist are based on a radical misunderstanding of his conception of the hero, who was never a demagogue but always the servant and benefactor of the many, his rule not *by* but always *for* the people. In this connection one should consult Gerald M. Straka's "The Spirit of Carlyle in the Old South" (*Historian,* 1957), containing a letter of Carlyle's, dated 31 October 1851, expressing his disapproval of the condition of Negro slavery as "not at present a just [relationship] according to the Law of the Eternal," and requiring to be changed.

4. INFLUENCE

Carlyle's influence and reputation did not follow the same paths. After the 1840's his reputation shrank like a *peau de chagrin* with the successive publication of *Latter-Day Pamphlets, Frederick,* "Shooting Niagara," and the *Reminiscences,* while the influence of his early works continued unabated. Since his death the disparate claims that his work wrought great harm, that their effect was negligible, that they still speak to us today, have made all but impossible the task of measuring their actual influence, and no such study has been attempted. There are excellent beginnings, however, in the already mentioned volumes by Garnett, Neff, and Symons, and in special inquiries into his impact on individual writers and aspects of Victorian thought and literature. It is no longer possible to dismiss his ideas as H. D. Traill did at the end of the century, nor is it necessary to revive the Jekyll-Hyde image of Carlyle as found in J. F. Clark's "The Two Carlyles, or Carlyle Past and Present" (*Christian Examiner,* 1864) and G. M. Trevelyan's "The Two Carlyles" (*Littell's Living Age,* 1918). Two sides at least there were to Carlyle, but they are best regarded as P. E. More regards them in "The Spirit of Carlyle" (*Shelburne Essays,* 1st Ser., 1905) where, writing in the tradition of Froude and anticipating the work of Hagberg, he seeks to account for Carlyle's "great influence on the finest minds of his age," for "the genius of the man himself, the mystery of his brain, which no study . . . will explain," by the two conflicting yet complementary qualities of his nature, his almost Oriental sense of illusion, of spectral vision—life was "but a walking shadow"—and his egotism and aggravated self-consciousness which made him suffer from those shadows. Carlyle was too lonely, then, to found a school or have many disciples. The impact of his thought on the temper and conscience of his day is real, but indefinable. The best recent attempt to epitomize it is that of Raymond Williams in *Culture and Society* (1958). Ellen Moers, in *The Dandy: Brummel to Beerbohm* (1960), reminds us that the satirical attack on Bulwer in *Sartor* helped to drive Regency dandyism underground and usher in the Victorian countercult of sincerity, social responsibility, and hard work. Walter Houghton, in *The Victorian Frame of Mind* (1957), provides ample documentation to prove his claim that Carlyle was one of the four great Victorian prophets of moral earnestness. His influence on the Chartists, on labor, on the religious life of the times, is to be found in works by Roe, Neff, and Willey already mentioned. The Pre-Raphaelites seem to have been encouraged rather than influenced by him: see Henry Jervis' "Carlyle and 'the Germ'" (*TLS*, 1938). Quite early, Louis Cazamian, in *Le Roman Social en Angleterre* (1904), observed his antimaterialistic and political ideas reflected in the novels of Dickens, Disraeli, Mrs. Gaskell, and Kingsley; and more recently Russell A. Fraser has found his scorn of England's unheroic democratic society reflected in Thackeray and Trollope ("Shooting Niagara in the Novels of Thackeray and Trollope," *MLQ*, 1958). Kathleen Tillotson, in her admirable *Novels of the Eighteen-Forties* (1954), demonstrates not only that he exerted a dominant influence on the subject matter of the Victorian novel, but that his stringent criticism of novels in his *Essays* raised their quality: "After Carlyle, the rift between the 'prophetic' and the merely entertaining novel widens. . . . The 'novel proper' . . . was helped by Carlyle to a status in literature and life which it has hardly yet lost." Two unpublished dissertations may be mentioned here: Marjorie P. King's "The Influence of Carlyle's Biographical Criticism of Authors on British Periodicals of His Time" (Univ. of London, 1953), and George A. Knox's "Thomas Carlyle's Reputation in Nineteenth Century British Periodicals, 1850–1881" (Univ. of Oregon, 1949).

Frank Luther Mott, in "Carlyle's American Public" (*PQ*, 1935), dated Carlyle's influence in America from the appearance in 1836 of Emerson's edition of *Sartor*, when it became almost the sacred text of New England Transcendentalism. The publication of "The Nigger Question" in 1849 and of "Shooting Niagara" in 1867, however, seriously impaired his popularity in the North (though Whitman defended him) without making him more popular in the South. William S. Vance, in "Carlyle in America before *Sartor Resartus*" (*AL*, 1936), argued that he was known earlier than 1836 by his *Schiller*, *Wilhelm Meister*, and early essays. It was then pointed out by George Kummer ("Anonymity and Carlyle's Early

Reputation in America," *AL*, 1936), that the pre-*Sartor* publications of Carlyle in America were anonymous and that even Emerson was unable to associate Carlyle's name with his writings until 1832. In addition to several unpublished dissertations—W. S. Vance's "Carlyle and the American Transcendentalists" (Univ. of Chicago, 1944), H. E. Widger's "Thomas Carlyle in America: His Reputation and Influence" (Univ. of Illinois, 1945), B. L. Grenberg's "Thomas Carlyle and Herman Melville" (Univ. of North Carolina, 1963), and H. M. Fish's "The Influence of Thomas Carlyle on R. W. Emerson" (Univ. of Edinburgh, 1958)—there are numerous articles, of which we can mention only the following: Margaret Duckett's "Carlyle, 'Columbus,' and Joaquin Miller" (*PQ*, 1956), Joseph Slater's "George Ripley and Thomas Carlyle" (*PMLA*, 1952), Walter Blair's "The French Revolution and Huckleberry Finn" (*MP*, 1957), Suk-joo Kim's "A Comparative Study of Emerson and Carlyle" (*ELL*, 1962), J. J. Rubin's "Whitman and Carlyle: 1846" (*MLN*, 1938), G. Paine's "The Literary Relations of Whitman and Carlyle, with Especial Reference to their Contrasting Views on Democracy" (*SP*, 1939), and F. W. Smith's "Whitman's Poet-Prophet and Carlyle's Hero" (*PMLA*, 1940).

Although French scholars like Cazamian and V. G. Basch (*Carlyle, l'homme et l'œuvre*, 1938) have shown an interest in Carlyle, his reception and reputation in France have been in the last thirty-five years the concern almost exclusively of Alan C. Taylor, in three substantial works: *Carlyle, sa première fortune littéraire en France: 1825–65* (1929), *Carlyle et la pensée latine* (1937), and "Carlyle interprete de Dante" (*EA*, 1959).

Saburo Ota, in "Thomas Carlyle's Relation with Modern Japanese Literature" (*Se Lit*, 1961), discusses recent Japanese interest in Carlyle's Clothes Philosophy, and Kenneth W. Cameron, in "New Japanese Translations of Carlyle's Works" (*ESQ*, 1964), announces a new six-volume edition of Carlyle's works in Japanese, including *Sartor, Heroes, Past and Present*, and selections from the histories and letters.

Much of Carlyle's influence was personal, and his relationship to his closest friends often had little to do with intellectual influence. With Edward Irving, for example, who helped him so often, he exchanged love but not ideas. John Sterling, whom he also loved, he also influenced, as we learn from both his *Life of John Sterling* (1841) and Anne K. Tuell's *John Sterling: A Representative Victorian* (1941). As for Mill, who initially responded to Carlyle's force, we may take his word that "the good his writings did me, was not as philosophy to instruct, but as poetry to animate." We are not, however, to take Clough at his word when he told Emerson, "Carlyle has led us all out into the desert, and he has left us there," for, as Michael Timko demonstrates in "Arthur Hugh Clough: A Portrait Retouched" (*VN*, 1959), Clough "was able to find his own way out" of that desert and to achieve his own Everlasting Yea by turning Carlyle's doctrine of work to practical social ends. That Matthew Arnold owed a debt to Carlyle for his understanding of Goethe was pointed out by J. B. Orrick in his "Matthew Arnold and Goethe" (*PEGS*, 1928). In her stimulating essay, "Matthew Arnold and Carlyle" (*PBA*, 1956), Kathleen Tillotson cites numerous other debts to show that even after Arnold had repudiated Carlyle and rejected the gloomy part of his teaching denying man the right to happiness, he nevertheless continued to respond to the poet in Carlyle, and in his 1883 lecture on Emerson attempted to reconcile his earlier and later views of Carlyle's genius. D. J. DeLaura's "Arnold and Carlyle" (*PMLA*, 1964) is a more detailed study which reaches conclusions similar to Mrs. Tillotson's. There are some good studies of Carlyle and Browning: of Carlyle's presence in the "Parleying with Bernard de Mandeville" in W. C. DeVane's *Browning's Parleyings* (1927); of his influence on Browning's prose style in Donald Smalley's introduction to his edition of *Browning's Essay on Chatterton* (1948); of "Browning's 'Red Cotton Night-Cap Country' and Carlyle" (*VS*, 1964), by C. C. Watkins; and of "Carlyle, Browning, and the Nature of a Poet" (*EUQ*, 1960), by C. R. Sanders.

Many important aspects of Carlyle's influence have been only touched upon. Despite Roe's *The Social Philosophy of Carlyle and Ruskin* (1921), F. G. Townsend, in *Ruskin and the Landscape Feeling* (1951), says that the lack of a careful tracing of Carlyle's influence on Ruskin is "a remarkable omission of scholarship." C. R. Sanders in his "Carlyle and Tennyson" (PMLA, 1961) remarks that the full impact of Carlyle's mind on Tennyson's poetry needs to be investigated fully. The same is true of his relation to novelists like Dickens, Thackeray, George Eliot, and Meredith; to scientists like Tyndall, Huxley, and Macewen; to pioneers of the labor movement like Thomas Cooper, Keir Hardie, Patrick Geddes, Tom Mann, and Robert Blatchford; and to more recent writers like Yeats, Æ, Shaw, and D. H. Lawrence.

Among the many other works deserving mention we can list only the following: Mildred G. Christian, "Carlyle's Influence upon the Social Theory of Dickens. Part One: Their Personal Relationship," and "Part Two: Their Literary Relationship" (*Trollopian*, 1947); A. A. Adrian, "Dickens on American Slavery: A Carlylean Slant" (*PMLA*, 1952) ; Lawrence H. Houtchens, "Carlyle's Influence on Dickens" (Cornell Univ. dissertation, 1931) ; E. A. Hungerford, "Influence of Thomas Carlyle on the Social Novels of Disraeli, Dickens, and Kingsley" (Cornell Univ. dissertation, 1948) ; George J. Worth, "Three Carlyle Documents" [C. and James Hannay] (*PMLA*, 1956) ; William Irvine, "Carlyle and T. H. Huxley" (*Booker Memorial Studies*, 1950) ; Leonard Huxley, "Carlyle and Huxley: Early Influences" (*Cornhill*, 1932) ; John J. Gross, "Carlyle and the Social Novelists of the Forties" (Univ. of Oregon dissertation, 1942) ; Maria Meyer, *Carlyles Einfluss auf Kingsley* (Weimar, 1914) ; Alan L. Strout, "Writers on German Literature in *Blackwood's Magazine*" (*The Library*, 1954) ; R. C. Beatty, "Macaulay and Carlyle" (*PQ*, 1939) ; W. H. Rogers, "A Study in Contrasts: Carlyle and Macaulay as Book Reviewers" (*FSUS*, 1952) ; Michele Saponaro, "Una Donna tra Due Poeti" [C. and Mazzini] (*NA*, 1892) ; John W. Morris, "*Beauchamp's Career*: Meredith's Acknowledgment of His Debt to Carlyle" (*Studies in Honor of Hodges and Thaler*, ed. R. B. Davis, 1961) ; Willis D. Jacobs, "Carlyle and Mill" (*CEA*, 1959) ; H. Tristram, "Two Leaders: Newman and Carlyle" (*Cornhill*, 1928) ; J. B. Fletcher, "Newman and Carlyle: An Unrecognized Affinity" (*Atlantic Monthly*, 1905) ; E. D. Mackerness, "The Voice of Prophecy: Carlyle and Ruskin" (*Pelican Guide*, Vol. VI, 1958) ; C. H. Kegel, "Carlyle and Ruskin: An Influential Friendship" (*BYUS*, 1964) ; H. J. C. Grierson, "Scott and Carlyle" (*PBA*, 1928) ; James C. Malin, "Carlyle's Philosophy of Clothes and Swedenborg's (*SS*, 1961) ; Wendell S. Johnson, "Swinburne and Carlyle" (*ELN*, 1963) ; K. L. Knickerbocker, "The Sources of Swinburne's *Les Noyades*" (*PQ*, 1933) ; W. D. Templeman, "Tennyson's *Locksley Hall* and Thomas Carlyle" (*Booker Memorial Studies*, 1950) ; G. O. Marshall, Jr., "An Incident from Carlyle in Tennyson's Maud" (*N&Q*, Feb. 1959) ; D. T. Starnes, "The Influence of Carlyle on Tennyson" (*Texas Review*, 1921) ; W. B. Gragg, "Trollope and Carlyle" (*NCF*, 1958) ; Laura Fermi, *Thomas Carlyle* (1939).

One must be cautious, however, for the fair fields that lie open to the investigator of "influence" often turn into Fata Morganas. On the whole, the problem of problems in the study of Carlyle is how to define and assess his extraordinary poetic talent, that "spectral vision" of which P. E. More spoke, and his remarkable powers of expression. And this must be done without either ignoring his ideas or letting them take over, but rather by searching for that romantic fusion of thought and image in symbolic language which characterizes all his best work.

INDEX